WITHDRAWN

Illustrated Dictionary of World Religions

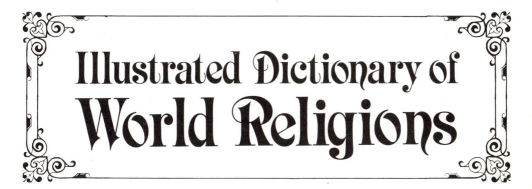

Illustrated Dictionary of
World Religions

Arthur A. Jones, M.A., B.D., Ph.D.

THE RELIGIOUS EDUCATION PRESS
A Division of Pergamon Press

The Religious Education Press
A Division of Pergamon Press
Hennock Road, Exeter EX2 8RP

Pergamon Press Ltd
Headington Hill Hall, Oxford OX3 0BW

Pergamon Press Inc.
Maxwell House, Fairview Park, Elmsford, New York 10523

Pergamon Press Canada Ltd
Suite 104, 150 Consumers Road, Willowdale, Ontario M2J 1P9

Pergamon Press (Australia) Pty Ltd
P.O. Box 544, Potts Point, N.S.W. 2011

Pergamon Press GmbH
Hammerweg 6, D-6242 Kronberg, Federal Republic of Germany

First published 1982

Acknowledgements
The author and publisher wish to thank the following individuals and organizations who kindly provided photographs
for use in this book:
Baptist Times: p. 29
Barnaby's Picture Library: pp. 147, 151 (Mihrab)
BBC Hulton Picture Library: pp. 17 (Anti-Semitism), 58, 69 (Dome of the Rock), 73, 126 (Jewish wedding), 145,
    221 (Shofar), 272
British Library: p. 139 (Magi)
Camera Press Ltd: pp. 89 (Ganges), 111, 125 (Kaaba), 151 (Devil's Pillar), 163
Esso Petroleum Co.: p. 155
Mansell Collection: pp. 49, 79 (Ethrog), 175 (Shwedagon Pagoda), 230, 231, 235, 278, 282
Mr L.W.T. Mercer: pp. 89 (Ganesha), 243, 257 (Buddha)
Ann & Bury Peerless: pp. 13, 50, 68, 69 (Dokhma), 92, 96, 105, 125 (Kali), 146, 160 (Nandi), 205
Popperfoto: pp. 18 (Apartheid), 20, 175 (Yasaka Pagoda), 248
Mr William Pridie: pp. 263, 269
Salvation Army: p. 207
Richard Shymansky Photography: p. 30
Trustees of the British Museum: pp. 7, 12, 17 (Anubis), 18 (Apocalypse), 26, 33, 37, 38, 40 (Bull roarer), 46, 57,
    67, 77, 84, 89 (Garuda), 90, 99, 102, 104, 110, 115, 126 (Karttikeya), 129, 132, 135, 139 (Maat), 153, 160
    (Guru Nanak), 171, 172, 191, 194, 195, 202, 219, 221 (Shiva), 225, 247, 249, 257 (Ushabti), 261, 270, 285
Victoria and Albert Museum (Crown Copyright): pp. 40 (Buddha), 71, 239

Printed in Great Britain by A. Wheaton & Co. Ltd, Exeter (TS)
ISBN 0 08-026441-7 (flexi)
ISBN 0 08-024176-X (hard)

FOREWORD

When the Open University decided to present a new course on 'Man's Religious Quest', it was considered that students would be helped by the provision of a glossary, which I was invited to compile. It was drawn up from terms used in the thirty-two units of the course, and during its preparation, a suggestion was made that a longer dictionary of terms drawn from world religions would be of interest and assistance to a much wider readership.

It is clear that for many reasons there is an increasing interest in the religions of mankind. The presence of children of many faiths has led to a reappraisal of the content of religious education, and new agreed syllabuses are recommending that children should be helped to understand something of the faith and practice of religions other than Christianity. Consequently, the study of world religions now has an important place in teacher training, and also in degree courses at many universities. Further, the desire for good community relations encourages us to learn as much as possible about one another's beliefs.

This dictionary has been compiled in the hope that it may assist this process of learning. Its definitions have been kept brief, in order to satisfy the needs of those who require basic information without a mass of detail. It is hoped that those who are interested in a particular religion will be able to use the Dictionary as a starting-point for further studies, and also to find comparable terms in other faiths.

The Open University readily gave permission for the Glossary to be used as the basis of a larger work, and for this permission I express my very great gratitude. My thanks are also offered to the members of the Course Team, who made valuable comments on definitions drawn from their units, and to others who have helped in a variety of ways.

I must express my very special thanks to a former colleague, Mr A. D. Woodfield, M.A., of Avery Hill College, who read through the definitions relating to Indian religions, and to Mr Peter Woodward, B.A., B.D., Chairman of the Shap Working Party on World Religions in Education, who has read through the complete typescript. Both offered most helpful and valuable comments and advice. I am grateful also to the Staff of the Library at King's College, London, for their ever-ready help in finding books and references. The Abbot of Nashdom has very graciously allowed me to use the Abbey Library, and I am grateful to him and to the Librarian, Dom Aidan Harker, who found me a peaceful corner in which to work and many books to study.

Finally, it is a great joy to express publicly my most grateful thanks to my family for their constant help; to my daughter for checking the typescript, and to my wife for much patience during its compilation and for undertaking most of the typing. The book is offered to her as a token of gratitude and affection.

Arthur A. Jones

 # ABBREVIATIONS

A	Arabic	d.	died	OT	Old Testament
b.	born	H	Hebrew	P	Pali
BCE	before Common Era	J	Japanese	Pn	Punjabi
C	Chinese	lit.	literally	S	Sanskrit
CE	Common Era	NT	New Testament		

Note The letters 'BCE' are retained for all dates before the Common Era. The letters 'CE' are omitted for all centuries in the Common Era, all years after 999 CE and earlier years if no confusion is likely.

Aaron

Elder brother of Moses (Exodus 6:20) who acted as spokesman at the meetings between Moses and Pharaoh. In the absence of Moses on Mt Sinai, Aaron yielded to the entreaties of the Israelites and made the Golden Calf. Later he was appointed High Priest, and the office was inherited by his descendants.

Ab

Fifth month of the Jewish year. The ninth of Ab is a fast commemorating the destruction of the Temple in Jerusalem in 586 BCE.

Abaddon (H)

Word meaning 'destruction' used in the Wisdom Literature of the Hebrew Bible to signify the region of the dead. In Revelation 9:11 it is the Hebrew name of the angel of the bottomless pit, whose Greek name is Apollyon.

Abba

Aramaic word meaning 'father' used three times in the NT in petition to God.

Abbasids

Dynasty of Islamic caliphs who ousted the Umayyad caliphate, transferred the capital from Damascus to Baghdad, and ruled from 750 to 1258.

Abbey

The proper use of this term is to describe a church or campus belonging to a community of monks under the rule of an abbot, such as the Benedictine order. It is now sometimes used of a church that is no longer occupied by a monastic community, such as Westminster Abbey in London.

Abbot

Title in the Western Church of the superior of a large religious house belonging to the Benedictines or the Canons Regular, usually for life. The corresponding head of a nunnery is an abbess.

Abd (A)

Term used by Muslims meaning 'slave' or 'servant', indicating the status of man as a doer of God's will.

Buckfast Abbey, Devon

Abel

According to Genesis 4:2, the second son of Adam and Eve. He was a shepherd, and was killed by his brother Cain, who cultivated the land. Cain was jealous because Abel's sacrifice of a lamb had been accepted by the Lord, whereas his own offering of grain was rejected. This story reflects the animosity between arable farmers and keepers of migrant herds in ancient times.

Abelard, Peter

(1079–1142) Christian philosopher and theologian. He lectured in Paris but was forced to flee because his love affair with Héloïse, niece of a canon of Notre Dame, offended the Church authorities. He put forward the Exemplarist theory of the Atonement, which states that the suffering Christ is our supreme example, but nothing more.

Abhidhamma Pitaka

Third section of the canon of scripture of the Theravada Buddhists. It is concerned with analysis of psychical and mental phenomena.

Abhidhammattha Sangaha

Textbook for Buddhist monks in Sri Lanka, in use from the 12th century. It is a digest of the subject-matter of the *Abhidhamma Pitaka*, and has been translated into English under the title *A Compendium of Philosophy*.

Cain and Abel offer their sacrifices to God

Abhinna (P)/Abhijna (S)

Buddhist term for superior spiritual faculties and powers. Modes of insight attained by the practice of dhyana.

Abhiseka

Buddhist term for consecration.

Abiku

Among the Yoruba, the spirit of a child who dies in the first week of life. It is regarded as fierce, and seeking to return to the wild.

Ablutions

1. *Christian* The washing of the chalice and the celebrant's fingers after Holy Communion or Mass. The full ritual prescribes one ablution of the chalice with wine, a second with water and wine, and a third ablution of the chalice and fingers with water only.

2. *Muslim* Personal cleansing before prayer. Muslims are required to wash hands and feet, ears, nose and mouth in a prescribed order, and fountains or taps are provided at mosques for this purpose.

Abracadabra

Word that has been widely used in magic to ward off plagues or evil spirits. It first appeared in Britain in 208 CE in the writings of a doctor attached to the court of the Roman emperor Severus. It was written in triangular form, dropping a letter from each line, and then recited. As the word shrank so, it was hoped, would the power of the evil spirit. An earlier comment in the writings of Basilides of Alexandria, *c.* 120 CE, appears to refer to this.

```
A B R A C A D A B R A
 A B R A C A D A B R
  A B R A C A D A B
   A B R A C A D A
    A B R A C A D
     A B R A C A
      A B R A C
       A B R A
        A B R
         A B
          A
```

Abraham

Israelite patriarch who left Ur of the Chaldees and settled in Canaan (Genesis 11). Because of his willingness, in obedience to the command of God, to prepare to sacrifice his son Isaac, God made a covenant with him, promising continual blessings upon him and upon his descendants for ever (Genesis 22). He is regarded by both Jews and Muslims as their ancestor. Muslims maintain that it was Abraham's older son Ishmael who was to be sacrificed (Qur'an 37:102). According to Muslim tradition Abraham, with the help of Ishmael, raised the Kaaba shrine in Mecca (Qur'an 2:125).

Absolute

In philosophy the independent, unconditioned, self-existent, existing without relation to other beings.

Absolution

In Christian theology the pronunciation of the forgiveness of sins through the love of God to those who have declared their penitence. It may be given during a liturgical service after a general confession or in private at a confessional, by a bishop or a priest.

Abstinence

1. Refusal to eat certain types of food, in accordance with the precepts of accepted dietary laws. Thus, for example, Jews and Muslims abstain from eating pork and Hindus from eating beef.
2. Penitential practice, common in some Christian religious orders, of not eating flesh (and sometimes fish or eggs) on Fridays and other days or periods of fasting such as Lent.

Abu, Mt

Mountain in Rajasthan, sometimes called the Olympus of India, where there are many Jain temples.

Abu Bakr

First Caliph, or successor of Muhammad. He ruled from 632 to 634 CE.

Abyss

Greek word meaning 'bottomless pit' used several times in the NT to describe the abode of demons or the place of the dead.

Academy

Grove or gymnasium near Athens where Plato and his successors taught.

Acarya (S)

Term meaning 'teacher'. Title of a Hindu spiritual director who teaches the *Vedas*, or a Buddhist instructor who teaches the Dhamma.

Achaemenid

Dynasty of Persian kings inaugurated by Cyrus I in 559 BCE which lasted until the invasion of Alexander the Great *c.* 330 BCE. This dynasty showed a more humane attitude to exiles such as the Jews, and allowed them to return home.

Acheron

River in southern Epirus in Greece which went underground and was thought to lead down to Hades.

Achilles

Hero of Homer's *Iliad*. He is depicted almost as the ideal Greek and was the bravest and most handsome. He embodied many virtues, being affectionate and loyal to his mother and friends, and honourable towards his foes; he was open-hearted and gentle at home, and always obedient to the will of the gods.

Acolyte

Highest of the four minor orders of the Latin Church, first mentioned in Rome in 251 CE. The other minor orders were porter, lector and exorcist. The acolyte's duties are to light the altar candles, carry processional candles and prepare the elements for the Eucharist.

Acropolis

Greek term indicating the highest point in the city, usually a fortified citadel. In Athens it was the site of the Parthenon.

Acts of the Apostles

Book in the NT, traditionally accepted as the work of St Luke, which tells the story of the Church from the Resurrection of Jesus and the martyrdom of Stephen to the start of the mission to the Gentiles and the missionary journeys of St Paul.

Adad

Storm god worshipped throughout ancient Mesopotamia and Asia Minor. He was also known as Hadad.

Adae

Ashanti word derived from a root meaning 'place of rest'; hence used for customs or rites associated with ancestor worship.

Adam and Eve

According to the account of the Creation in Genesis (1-3) and also the Qur'an (suras 2, 7), they were the first man and woman created by God and were placed in the Garden of Eden until they sinned and were driven out.

Adaran

Zoroastrian term for the second grade of holy fire, found in smaller or less important temples or agiari.

Adeste Fideles

Popular Christmas hymn, of anonymous authorship, probably written in the 17th century. The best known translation begins 'O come, all ye faithful, joyful and triumphant'.

Adha

See Id al-Adha

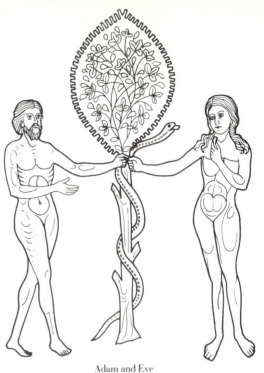

Adam and Eve

Adhan

Call to prayer made five times a day to Muslims from every mosque.

Adhikarana

Buddhist term for legal problems which form part of the rules of the Dhammakaya.

Adi Granth

Lit. 'first book'. Title applied to sacred writings of the Sikh religion, largely the work of the fifth Guru, Arjan, who incorporated poems of his predecessors with his own compositions. (See also *Guru Granth Sahib*)

Adonai (H)

Plural of 'majesty', meaning 'lord'. It is often used for the divine name in the Hebrew Bible, and in Jewish reading of the Scriptures it is read as a substitute for the unutterable name YHWH.

Adonis

Greek god of vegetation. The name may derive from the Semitic *adon* (lord). Adonis was loved by Aphrodite, but did not return her affection. Ultimately he was killed by a boar, and thereafter the pig was offered in sacrifice to him.

Adoptionism

Term used to indicate a type of heretical theology in the early Christian Church in which Christ is regarded as fully human and endowed with divine powers; thus he is not the true, but only the adoptive son of God.

Adoration

Act of worship. Since the Second Council of Nicaea in 787 CE, in the Christian Church this is offered to God alone, although owing to the doctrine of the Real Presence, adoration may be paid to the Blessed Sacrament. Relics and sacred objects may be offered veneration but not adoration.

Adosa (P)/**Advesa** (S)

Term used in Buddhist philosophical teaching to indicate the absence of hatred, an important element in the Buddha's teaching.

Advaita

Hindu term for non-duality; the fundamental unity of Brahman (ultimate reality) and Atman (human soul), expressed in the Upanishad formula *tat tvam asi*. It is derived from two words, *a* (not) and *dvaita* (duality).

Advent

Word derived from the root 'to come' which indicates the start of the Christian year. It marks the beginning of a period of penance, in contemplation of the mystery of Christ's incarnation.

Adventist

See Seventh Day Adventists

Advesa (S)

See Adosa

Advowson

Right of appointing a clergyman to a parish in the Church of England. This may belong to the bishop of the diocese or to the patron of the living, who presents his nominee to the bishop for installation.

Aegir

In Scandinavian mythology a giant who was regarded as the god of the sea.

Aelia Capitolina

Name given to Jerusalem after its restoration by the Roman emperor Aelia Hadrianus following its capture in 70 CE.

Aeneas

Trojan prince, hero of Virgil's *Aeneid*, which describes his travels after the fall of Troy. He is described by Virgil as *pius*, indicating his loving concern for his father and family, his honourable dealings with friend and foe, and his deep respect for the gods. At the end of his travels he landed in Italy, settled at Latium, and became the ancestor of the Romans.

Aesculapius

Greek god of the medical art, whose chief temple was at Epidaurus. The serpent was sacred to him because it was the symbol of renovation.

Aesir

Collective name for the great gods of Scandinavian mythology. The root meaning is probably 'wind'.

Aetherius Society

Founded in 1954 in London by Dr George King, who claims to be in telepathic rapport with a being from Venus named Aetherius. The Society believes that this world has been visited over the centuries by higher intelligences, including Krishna, Confucius and Buddha. Dr King claims that in this new Age of Aquarius he is guided by 'Master Aetherius' and 'Master Jesus' to undertake, with his followers, the concentration and storing of psychic energy to promote mankind's spiritual enlightenment. 8 July is observed as the holiest day of the year.

Affinity

Relationship created by marriage as distinct from a relationship by birth. Certain relationships of affinity are regarded as an impediment to marriage after the death of a partner. Lists of forbidden degrees of affinity are published in the Church of England *Book of Common Prayer* and the Roman Catholic *Codex Juris Canonici*.

Afikomen

Half of a matzah which is hidden for the children to search out during the Jewish Seder of the Passover.

Agama

1. Collection of scripture regarded as authoritative. The term is used in various traditions, e.g. Jainism, Tantrism, the Saiva Siddhanta and Mahayana Buddhism. These scriptures were originally written in Sanskrit.
2. Chinese translations of the sutras or sermons as collected by the Sarvastavadin school of Theravada Buddhism.

Agape

One of several Greek words translated 'love', it is used in the Greek NT when referring to the love of God and the love that Christians should show to one another. In the early Church it was used to describe a religious meal, the love feast, closely associated with the Eucharist. By the 2nd century, the term and the practice had gradually fallen into disuse, but it has been revived in the Liturgical Movement of the 20th century and in some places takes the form of a parish breakfast after Family Eucharist. It has also been revived as a rite for united services on the eve of Whit Sunday.

Aggadah (H)

Part of the Jewish oral law, dealing with biblical interpretations, theology and ethical matters.

Agha Khan

The imam, or leader, of the Nazari Ismaili Muslims. The title was first bestowed by the Shah of Persia in 1834, and the present holder of the title is the fourth.

Agiari

Gujurati word meaning 'house of fire', used to denote the ordinary Parsee/Zoroastrian temples which house the holy fire.

Agni

God of fire in Vedic literature. He is an important mediator between gods and men.

Agnostic

This term, derived from a Greek word meaning 'unknown', was coined by T. H. Huxley in 1869 to denote the philosophy that the existence of anything beyond the material world is unknown and cannot be known.

Agnus Dei

Formula beginning 'O Lamb of God' which is recited three times in the Western Eucharistic liturgy, after the Prayer of Consecration and before the Act of Communion.

Agrapha

Lit. 'unwritten'. Term applied to sayings of Jesus Christ which are not recorded in the four canonical Gospels, but have been found in other Christian manuscripts.

Ahankara

In the teaching of the Sikh religion, pride, regarded as one of the weaknesses that attack the human soul.

Ahara

Term used in Buddhist teaching. In a material sense it is nourishment. In a logical sense it is the condition for an object's existence.

Ahimsa

Doctrine of non-violence, harmlessness, respect for life. This is one of the elements of right thought in the Buddhist Eightfold Path. The rule forbidding the taking of life extends to the prohibition of killing animals for food. Mahatma Gandhi emphasized the importance of practising this doctrine in his endeavours to obtain independence for India.

Ahmadiyyah

Reform movement in Islam founded by Mirza Ghulam Ahmad (1839–1908), who announced himself as the expected Mahdi of Islam. This is a sect of Shiah Islam and is regarded by Sunnis as heretical and non-Islamic.

Ahriman

In Middle Persian Zoroastrian writings the name of the Evil One or the destructive spirit. He is named Angra Mainyu in the *Gathas*.

Ahu

Term used in the Zoroastrian religion for human reason.

Ahura Mazda

In the *Gathas of Zoroaster* the Wise Lord, the supreme creator. In Middle Persian writings he is named Ohrmazd.

Parsee symbol of Ahura Mazda

Aisle

Section or division of a church usually adjoining and parallel to the nave, and separated from it by pillars.

Ajami (A)

Word used by Muslims to indicate a 'foreigner', i.e. a person or thing that is non-Arabic. It is comparable to the Greek use of the term 'barbarian' to indicate anything or anyone not Greek.

Ajiva

Term used in Buddhist teaching for 'livelihood'. Right livelihood is the fifth step on the Eightfold Path as taught by the Buddha.

Akalis

Lit. 'immortals'. Body of militant ascetics among the Sikhs; they were the soldiers of Akal, the Timeless One (the true name of God), and were active in 1690.

Akasha

Term used in Buddhist teaching for space, or the spiritual essence of space. It is the primordial substance which has no cognizable attributes and is beyond description.

Akbar

Greatest of the Mughal emperors of India. Born in 1542, he became Emperor in 1555, took full control in 1560, and by conquering rebels and neighbouring states vastly extended his empire. Born a Muslim, he renounced his faith and founded a new 'divine faith' with tolerance for all sects. His rule was mild, generous and just. He died in 1605.

Emperor Akbar

Akeldama

Lit. 'field of blood'. Name given to the plot of land purchased with the thirty pieces of silver paid by the chief priests to Judas as a reward for betraying Jesus. According to Acts 1:19 Judas purchased it himself, but according to Matthew 27:7 it was purchased by the chief priests after Judas returned the money. According to tradition it was on the south side of the Hinnom Valley.

Akhand Path

The continuous reading of the *Adi Granth*, the Sikh holy book, which takes forty-eight hours.

Akiba

(50–135 CE)   Jewish rabbi who began systematizing the teaching of traditional law in the form of Mishnah repetition. He supported the revolt of Bar-Cochba, was taken prisoner by the Romans and burnt alive.

Akika (A)

Islamic sacrifice performed on the seventh day after the birth of a child.

Akodha (P)/**Akrodha** (S)

Term used in Buddhist teaching for the absence of anger. This is an important element in the way of life taught by the Buddha.

Akusala (P)

Term meaning 'unwholesome', or that which is evil and brings about a bad karma, and leads to a bad reincarnation. In Buddhism it indicates those volitions which are accompanied by greed, hate or delusion.

Al Afghani, Jamal al-Din

(1839–1897)   Muslim teacher who believed it was necessary to relate intellectual and scientific thought to the values of Islamic religion. He was associated with the Aligarh movement.

Al Ghazali

(1058–1111)   One of the greatest Muslim theologians. He turned from philosophy because he was distressed by its unbelief, and studied the mystics. His main influence in Islamic thought was his emphasis on the study of the Qur'an and the Hadith.

Ala

Ibo earth goddess. She is still the most important of all the deities as she is the spirit of the earth, the queen of the underworld, the ruler of the ancestors and the administrator of moral laws.

Aladura

Lit. 'owners of prayer'. Movement stressing prayer groups and spiritual healing which arose among the Yoruba in the Anglican Church of St Saviour in Ijebu-Ode, Nigeria in 1918.

Al-Ashari

(b. 872 CE)   Muslim teacher who rejected the Mutazilite doctrine of free will and established the orthodox tradition of Sunni theology.

Alb

Long white linen garment reaching from shoulders to ankles with tight sleeves and girded at the waist. It is derived from the Greek or Roman undertunic, and is worn by officiants at Mass or Eucharist.

Alban, St

First British Christian martyr. He was a Roman officer, converted by a priest whom he sheltered, and he died in the persecution under Diocletian *c.* 305 CE.

Albigenses

Heretical sect, also known as the Cathari, which arose in the 11th century, and took its name from Albi in the South of France. Following the failure of the Second Crusade, the Albigenses won many followers by the strict discipline of their lives and their attack on the wealth and power of the Church. They condemned the eating of meat, milk, eggs and other animal products, and rejected the sacraments of the Church. They were condemned by Church Councils in 1148, 1184 and 1215 because of their dualism. They believed that God had two sons, Satanel (evil) and Christ (good), but they did not believe that Christ had a real body, nor that he was crucified and raised from the dead.

Priest wearing an alb

8

Alchemy

This has two aspects. It signifies medieval chemistry, whose practitioners sought the philosophers' stone, which was believed to have the power of perfecting matter and transmuting lead into gold. It also signifies a mystical art in which the alchemist sought the spiritual transformation of his own nature. The theme of death and resurrection is frequently mentioned, and one of the rituals was the 'bath of rebirth'.

Alexander VI

(1451–1503)   Spanish prelate of the Borgia family, the nephew of Pope Calixtus III, who became Pope himself in 1492. A man of immoral life, he was a skilled diplomat and politician and a generous patron of the arts. He gave approval to the division of the New World between Spain and Portugal, and in Rome rebuilt the Castle of Sant'Angelo.

Alexander the Great

Son of Philip of Macedon, he became King of the Greeks (336–323 BCE) and conquered a great empire, extending to Egypt and India. According to some expositors, he appears in the Qur'an with the name Dhu'l Qarnaim, 'the two-horned'.

Ali

Nephew and son-in-law of Muhammad who claimed the caliphate on the death of Uthman in 656 CE. Ali was himself murdered five years later and the caliphate was reclaimed by the Umayyad clan, but the Shiite Muslims rejected this, and recognized the descendants of Ali, the Imams.

All Hallows' Eve

Also known as Hallowe'en, this was originally a festival of fire, and of the dead and the powers of darkness. It is celebrated on the night of 31 October, prior to the Christian festival of All Saints' Day on 1 November. It marks the transition from autumn to winter.

All Saints' Day

Christian festival observed on 1 November giving thanks for the witness of the lives and heroic deaths of all holy men and women who have suffered for their faith in Jesus Christ.

All Souls' Day

1. In some Christian churches prayers for the souls of the faithful departed are offered on 2 November, the day after All Saints' Day.
2. In some sections of Buddhism, a festival in August to help spirits who lack descendants. A large paper boat is burnt to help wandering spirits cross the Sea of Want.

Allah

Name, derived from the Arabic *al-ilah*, of the supreme being worshipped by the Muslims. He is the sole deity with no associates, and no images of him are permitted. The name of God in his essence and his attributes is rehearsed through the ninety-nine Most Beautiful Names, which are often recited with the aid of prayer beads.

Allegorical Interpretation

Supposition that biblical texts contain a meaning different from, and more significant than, the obvious literal meaning or interpretation. Books such as The Song of Solomon have frequently been examined from this point of view. The practice has been discouraged since the time of the Reformation.

Alleluia

Liturgical expression of praise derived from the Hebrew word 'Hallelujah', meaning 'Praise ye the Lord'. It occurs in Psalms 111–117 and Revelation, and in the Christian Church has become an expression of great joy.

Almoner

In the early Christian Church an officer responsible for dispensing alms. In England the Lord High Almoner, usually a bishop, assists the Sovereign at the distribution of alms on Maundy Thursday.

Almsgiving

Although the word 'alms' is not used in the Hebrew Bible, almsgiving was regarded as an expression of the compassion of God, and is in accordance with the concern of the Mosaic Law for the poor and with the social teachings of the prophets. In the NT Jesus approved of almsgiving but stressed the need for the right motive. In the early Christian community the first officers were elected to ensure a fair distribution of alms. In Islam almsgiving (zakat) is the third Pillar of Islam and is an obligation imposed on all the faithful.

Al-Nabi al-Ummi (A)

Lit. 'unlettered prophet'. Term used in Islam to describe Muhammad's role as the recipient of revelation without literary skill or theological learning.

Alobha (P)

Term used in Buddhist teaching for lack of desire; this is a very important element in the doctrine of the Buddha, because he saw desire as one of the root causes of suffering.

Alpha and Omega

First and last letters of the Greek alphabet. This term is applied to God in Revelation 1:8 and 21:6.

Al-Rahman/Al-Rahim

Lit: 'the merciful, the compassionate'. Two divine attributes named in the Bismillah which appears at the head of every surah in the Qur'an except surah 9.

Al-Rajim

Muslim name for Satan, the accursed one or 'the one who is stoned'. It is derived from a stone-throwing rite at Mina near Mecca which occurs towards the end of the Hajj.

Altar

1. *General*   Usually an elevated surface prepared for the offering of sacrifices to deities. Often the slaughtered animals were burned wholly or in part on the altar.

2. *Hindu*   Usually made of earth or clay to hold the sacred fire, into which butter or grain could be thrown at specified points in the ritual.

3. *Greek and Roman*   Set up in public places in honour of different deities and also in houses for the lares and penates. Offerings of fruit, flowers and libations were made at both.

4. *Christian*   In the early Church they were usually wooden tables in house churches, but by the 5th century they were more often stone, to accommodate the sacrifice of the Mass. During the Reformation many stone altars were smashed, and Protestant denominations now usually have a wooden communion table. Roman Catholic and Anglican churches retain an altar as the focal point of the church, for the celebration of the Eucharist.

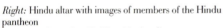

Right: Hindu altar with images of members of the Hindu pantheon
Below: Anglican altar (St Silas, Nunhead)

10

Alvars

Twelve poet saints of Tamil Vaisnavism who lived between the 7th and 10th centuries.

Am Ha-aretz (H)

Lit. 'people of the land'. Term applied to the peasants left in the Jerusalem area when Nebuchadrezzar took most of the citizens into captivity in Babylon in 586 BCE (2 Kings 24:14). In Ezra 9:1 and Nehemiah 10:31 they were the inhabitants of the land who did not observe the Mosaic Law, found by those Jews who returned from Babylon about 444 BCE. In rabbinic literature the term means 'vulgar crowd', 'ignorant persons' or 'traitors'.

Amanah (A)

Term in the Muslim religion to designate the trust of the earth given by God to man when he delegated to him authority over nature.

Amar Das

(1479–1574)   Third Sikh Guru, who instituted distinctive Sikh ceremonies, festivals and a place of pilgrimage. He was succeeded by his son-in-law Ram Das, and the remaining Gurus were all members of his family.

Amarapura

One of the three main communities of Buddhist monks in Sri Lanka.

Amaravati

In Hindu mythology the abode of the Immortals, the capital of the god Indra's heaven.

Amata (P)/**Amrta** (S)

Term used in Buddhism for immortality, or the absence of death. It can be used as an alternative term for nirvana.

Ambo

Raised platform in the earliest Christian churches from which the Scriptures were read. A later development was to have two, one for the Epistle and one for the Gospel. After the Reformation they were generally replaced by the pulpit, but the practice of having a pulpit and a lectern may be derived from the ambo.

Ambrose, St

Born at Trier in 339 CE, he practised as a lawyer and was appointed Governor of Aemilia–Liguria in 370. In 374 the Catholic laity of Milan demanded that he should be appointed their bishop, and to this end he was baptized, ordained and consecrated. He became famous as a preacher, converting Augustine in 386, and was a zealous upholder of Catholic orthodoxy and social morality and justice. He died in 397 and is honoured as one of the four Doctors of the Latin Church.

Amen (H)

Word meaning 'truly' or 'verily' used by Jews and Christians to express assent at the end of prayers, hymns and creeds.

Ameratat

In the teaching of the Zoroastrian religion, Immortality, one of the seven Amesha Spentas.

Amesha Spentas

Seven Bounteous Immortals who surround Ahura Mazda and, according to Zoroastrian teaching, are his characteristic attributes. They are: Holy Spirit, Good Thought, Right, Dominion, Piety, Welfare and Immortality.

Amice

Square of linen cloth with two tapes which is worn round the neck as part of the priest's Eucharistic vestments. It probably symbolizes the 'helmet of salvation', as it is first put over the head and tied. After the alb is put on the amice is folded back to form a collar.

Amida (J)

See Amitabha

Amidah (H)

Series of eighteen benedictions forming the central core of Jewish worship.

Amir Ali

(1849–1928)   Muslim writer and reformer in India. He founded the National Muhammadan Association in Calcutta in 1877, and in 1891 published *The Spirit of Islam* to demonstrate that Islam is a progressive civilizing force.

Amitayus

Amun (*c.* 900 BCE)

Amitabha (S)/**Amida** (J)
In Mahayana Buddhism the transcendent Buddha of Infinite Light, the personification of infinite mercy, wisdom, love and compassion.

Amitayus
In Mahayana Buddhism the transcendent Buddha of Infinite Life.

Amma
Supreme being or god among the Dogon tribe of Mali in West Africa.

Amoha
Term used in Buddhist teaching for wisdom or the lack of ignorant stupidity.

Amoraim (H)
Lit. 'speakers'. Title of Jewish teachers in the 3rd century who interpreted and harmonized the Mishnah and oral teachings; their work culminated in the Talmud.

Amos
Hebrew prophet who lived in Tekoa, south of Jerusalem, in the 8th century BCE. He was a shepherd called by God and journeyed north to Samaria and Bethel, where he delivered a series of fierce denunciations of the religious laxity and the moral and social depravity that he saw. His demands for righteousness and justice are contained in the book bearing his name in the Hebrew Bible; this is the earliest prophecy in book form in the Bible.

Amosu
Ashanti title of praise for God, meaning 'giver of rain'.

Amovwa
Ashanti title of praise for God, meaning 'giver of sunshine'.

Amphictyony
Association of tribes based on a common sanctuary. It has been suggested that the Israelite tribes were an amphictyony based on Shechem.

Ampulla
Latin term for a vessel containing liquid. Examples have been found in the catacombs in Rome, and it is thought that they may have been used for perfume or for oil to supply the lamps. A more modern use is to hold the sacramental oil blessed by a bishop for use in Unction.

Amritsar: Golden Temple

Amr (A)

Term used by Muslims to indicate the word of command given by God through which the world came into being.

Amrit

Sugared water used at the Sikh infancy ceremony of naming the child; more important, it is also used at the ceremony of initiation into the Khalsa, and of the initiation ceremony itself.

Amritdhari

Member of the Khalsa, or Sikh community, who has been through the initiation ceremony and has taken amrit.

Amritsar

Sacred city of the Sikhs in the Punjab, India, founded by the fourth Guru with help from the Emperor Akbar. Devout members of the faith make their pilgrimage to it in order to worship at the Golden Temple.

Amrta (S)

See Amata

Amulet

Charm worn to gain protection from misfortune, disease or illness, often inscribed with magical formulae.

Amun

God of air and wind in ancient Egypt. He was established at Thebes and in the Middle Kingdom was identified with Ra, as Amun-Ra.

Anabaptists

Lit. 're-baptizers'. Name applied to several groups of Protestant reformers, particularly in Germany and Switzerland in the 16th and 17th centuries. In their rejection of the Roman Catholic teaching on episcopal authority, the priesthood and the sacramental system they went beyond Luther and Calvin. They claimed that their teaching was based on Scripture and they insisted that all believers should be baptized as adults, even if they had already been baptized as infants. They refused to participate in war or in secular government, and they were fiercely persecuted as a danger to Church and State.

Anagarika (S)

Lit. 'homeless person'. Term used in Buddhist teaching for one who renounces home life and becomes a wanderer, but does not formally join a Sangha.

Analects

Short work of twenty chapters attributed to Confucius containing his basic moral, political and religious teaching. Also known as *Lun Yu'*, or *Selected Sayings.*

Analogy

Use of experience from human relationships and activities as a guide to the understanding of the divine nature, e.g. the parallel drawn by Jesus between a father's loving care for his son and God's care for his children (Matthew 7:11).

Anamnesis

Section of the liturgy of the Christian Eucharist commemorating the Passion, Resurrection and Ascension of Jesus Christ.

Anand (Pn)

Term used by the Sikh community to describe the bliss of marriage.

Ananda

1. Beloved disciple and cousin of the Buddha. He expounded the basic teaching of the Buddha, and later handed it down with faultless accuracy.

2. Sanskrit word meaning 'bliss'. According to the philosophy of the Vedanta it is one of the three attributes of the divine principle Brahman, together with sat and cit.

Ananse

Hero of West African folklore. He was a spider of great cunning who was able to deceive animals, men and sometimes God. In some of the tales Ananse himself appears as the Creator.

Anaphora

Central prayer of the Christian Eucharistic liturgy, containing the Consecration, the Anamnesis and the Communion.

Anasakti (S)

Hindu doctrine of selfless action; according to Mahatma Ghandhi this is the central teaching of the *Gita*, but not all Hindus agree with him.

Anathema

Originally something set up in a temple, or a votive offering; later something under a ban, or something cursed, for which the OT had the specific term 'herem'. Ecclesiastically, it is almost equivalent to excommunication, but it is wider, as it involves complete exclusion from the body of the faithful.

Anatta (P)/**Anatman** (S)

Lit. 'no self', or 'non ego'. This is the Buddhist doctrine that there is no permanent self, which is considered to be one of the characteristics (with anicca and dukkha) of all things.

Ancestor Worship

Belief in spirits, good and evil, and a desire to commemorate the dead have been widespread throughout history. Tombs in Ancient Egypt and throughout the Middle East and Mediterranean area have been found containing offerings to dead ancestors to make them well disposed to their descendants. The British anthropologist Herbert Spencer (1820–1903) wrote 'Ancestor worship is the root of every religion', but this is now regarded as doubtful, and scholars more frequently use the term 'the cult of the dead'.

Anchor

In the early Christian Church this was used as a symbol of hope and salvation, because of its cruciform shape and because of its purpose of giving security to ships.

Anchorite

Person who withdraws from the world to live a solitary life of prayer and meditation. In the early Christian Church the distinguishing feature of the anchorite was that he was enclosed by a bishop, and thereafter remained within his cell.

Andrew, St

Brother of Peter, but not one of the inner band of three among the disciples of Jesus Christ. According to tradition, he was martyred at Patras in 60 CE. Since about 750 CE he has been Patron Saint of Scotland.

Anga (S)

Lit. 'limb' or 'member'. Term used in Hinduism to describe works additional to the *Vedas*.

Angad

(1504–1552)   Second Sikh Guru. Guru Nanak chose him to be his successor in place of his own son.

Angel

Greek word for messenger used in the Bible and the Talmud for heavenly envoys sent from God.

Angelus

Devotion used in the Roman Catholic Church in the morning, at noon and in the evening; it consists of the Ave Maria, with versicles and a collect.

Anglican Communion

Church of England and other episcopal Churches, such as the Church of Australia and the Church of Canada, which are in full communion with the See of Canterbury. The bishops of the Anglican Communion meet every ten years at the Lambeth Conference.

Angra Mainyu

In the *Gathas of Zoroaster*, the evil, destructive spirit. In Middle Persian, he is named Ahriman.

Angya

Lit. 'pilgrimage on foot'. Now applied to one who makes a pilgrimage to a Zen monastery in order to be admitted as a novice. On arrival he may be kept waiting for several days before being allowed in to visit the Zen Master, as the pilgrimage and the waiting are regarded as a discipline which may lead to satori (enlightenment).

Anicca (P)**/Anitya** (S)

Buddhist doctrine of impermanence, which is held to be one of the three characteristics of all things.

Anima

Latin word meaning 'soul'. It is used by some writers to indicate the non-bodily aspect of man. In the psychological writings of C. G. Jung it is used of the feminine element within the psyche.

Animatism

Term introduced by R. R. Marett in 1899 to indicate a pre-animistic state in man's development, when it was believed that the world was 'animated' by impersonal forces; there was no clear distinction of spiritual beings, and magic and religion were indistinguishable.

Animism

Term used by E. Tylor in 1871 to denote 'the deep lying doctrine of spiritual beings'. These were often thought to inhabit natural objects such as trees and mountains. Tylor suggested that belief in spirits is the origin of religion.

Anitya (S)

See Anicca

Ankh

Egyptian sign of life, in the shape of a T or cross surmounted by a loop. It is sometimes called the crux ansata, or handled cross.

Anchor

Ankh, or crux ansata

Annaprasana

Hindu ceremony to mark the day when a baby takes its first solid food.

Annates

Payment of the first year's revenue from an ecclesiastical benefice which had to be made to the papacy. Payment to Rome from English benefices was forbidden by Henry VIII in the Annates Statute of 1534. The resulting funds were converted in 1704 into Queen Anne's Bounty for the benefit of poor parishes, and in 1948 were consolidated into the funds of the Church Commissioners.

Anne, St

According to tradition, the mother of the Virgin Mary. Although she is not mentioned in the Bible, devotion to her was widespread at an early date in the Church, but the cult was strongly attacked by the Reformers. Her feast-day is 26 July.

Anniversary of the Ascension of Baha'u'llah

Baha'u'llah died in exile in Bahji, near Akko in the Holy Land on 29 May 1892. His shrine is the holiest spot in the Baha'i world, and is a place of prayer and pilgrimage for all Baha'is.

Anniversary of the Declaration of the Bab

The Bab was the herald or forerunner of the Baha'i faith, and he declared his mission in Persia on 23 May 1844 to his first disciple, Mulla Husayn. This date is commemorated annually as a Baha'i holy day.

Anniversary of the Declaration of Baha'u'llah

See Ridvan

Annunciation of the Blessed Virgin Mary

Christian festival kept on 25 March to commemorate the visit of the Archangel Gabriel to the Virgin Mary to announce to her she had been chosen to be the mother of Jesus Christ.

Anointing

See Unction

Anrta

In the Hindu religion the concept of chaos as found in the Vedic scriptures.

Anselm, St

(1033–1109) Influential Christian theologian. Born in Lombardy, he entered a monastery at Bec in 1059, became Prior in 1063, and Archbishop of Canterbury in 1089, but was prevented by King Rufus from entering his diocese for some time. His book *Cur Deus Homo* (1098) had a great influence on medieval theology. It sets out a doctrine of the Atonement that the death of Christ was a satisfaction offered to the outraged majesty of God.

Anser (A)

Lit. 'helper'. Muhammad's allies or co-believers in Medina. They helped him and his followers after the Hijrah from Mecca.

Antaryamin

In the writings of the Hindu teacher Ramanuja this is the soul within the soul, or the inner controller.

Anthesteria

Spring festival in Athens dedicated to the god Dionysus; it was celebrated with offerings of wine and grain, and the sacred marriage between Dionysus and the wife of the Priest King; the ancestral spirits were believed to appear during this festival.

Anthony, St (of Egypt)

Born in 251 CE, in 285 he gave away his possessions and retired to the desert to lead a life of strict asceticism. His holiness and disciplined life attracted many disciples, and in 305 he agreed to organize a community of Christian hermits living under a common rule of life. This was probably the earliest monastic community, but the emphasis was on their solitariness within the community. St Anthony is said to have lived to a great age, dying in 356.

Anthropology

Study of man as a member of the animal kingdom. It is particularly concerned with man's origins and the development of society, and gives special attention to the life and environment of primitive tribes and their culture and religious ideas.

Anthropomorphism

Term derived from two Greek words meaning 'man' and 'form' used to describe the attribution of human form and characteristics to gods.

Anthroposophy

Religious–philosophical system based on the teachings of Rudolf Steiner (1861–1925). He was deeply influenced by the writings of Goethe and by Hindu philosophy. He taught that creation had its origin in living spirit, and that man as its highest development replaces God at the centre. Steiner developed an art of movement called 'eurythmy', and founded schools where children could be educated according to his ideas.

Anti-Christ

In the Bible this expression is used only in the Johannine epistles, where it signifies those who deny the Incarnation. It was frequently applied in the early days of the Church to particular persecutors such as Caligula or Nero, and later to the heretic Arius. Some Protestants at the time of the Reformation applied the term to the Pope.

Antinomianism

View that, for the Christian, grace has brought a freedom from the demands of the law, and that faith renders obedience to the law unnecessary. St Paul realized that this could lead to unbridled licence, and tried to show that the law and legalism are not identical, and that grace saves us from sin as well as from the demands of the law.

Antiphon

Sentences or psalms recited or sung alternately by two choirs, or two sections of a choir.

Anti-Semitism

Attitude and practice of prejudice against Jewish people. In the Middle Ages Jews were confined to ghettos and had no place in feudal society. In the 19th century there were organized massacres of Jews and pogroms in Russia. In the 20th century six million Jews were deliberately exterminated by the Nazis. More recently attempts have been made to discourage anti-Semitic activities. The World Council of Churches in 1948 and 1961 and Vatican Council II in 1966 condemned all manifestations of anti-Semitism.

Antyeshti

Funeral rites practised in village Hinduism.

Anu

Lit. 'heaven'. High god of Sumerian mythology. In the *Enuma Elish* he was the first of the gods to emerge from primeval chaos.

Anubis

Egyptian god of the dead, the son of Osiris and Nephthys. He is usually represented as a jackal or as a man with the head of a jackal.

Anti-Semitism: the notice reads 'I am a Jew but I will not grumble about the Nazis'

Anubis receiving the coffin of a dead man

Apartheid in action (South Africa)

Anunnaki

Term used in ancient Babylonian religion. Originally it meant 'gods of the underworld', but in later literature it was used interchangeably with 'Igigi' for 'great gods'.

Anussati (P)**/Anusmrti** (S)

Term used in Buddhist teaching for the recollection of certain truths as an aid to meditation. This relates especially to six particular subjects: the Buddha, the doctrine, the community, the heavenly sphere, morality and detachment.

Anyanwu

Ibo sun god who is also the god of good fortune.

Apartheid

Lit. 'apartness'. Form of racial segregation practised in the Republic of South Africa. The term was introduced by the National Party in 1948, and has been justified on biblical and theological grounds by the Dutch Reformed Church, but opposed by Christians of other denominations. It assumes the dominance of the white population, and places severe restrictions on the Bantu and coloured people.

Aphrodite

Greek goddess of love and beauty, whose name is derived from 'foam', indicating that she was born from the sea. She probably originated in Asia, crossed to Cyprus and thence to Corinth, her great centres. She surpassed all other goddesses in beauty.

Apocalyptic

Derived from a Greek word meaning 'revelation', it is applied to a type of literature that claims to reveal God's purposes, often concerning the end of the world. It is usually claimed as revelation from God to a seer or a prophet, and is found in the OT book Daniel, the NT book Revelation and in Zoroastrian works.

Apocrypha

Derived from a Greek word meaning 'hidden', it is often used to describe books included in the Septuagint but excluded from the Hebrew Bible, e.g. Ecclesiasticus. Some early Christian writings, e.g. the Gospel of Thomas, are sometimes described as apocryphal NT.

Apocalypse: this miniature (from an early 14th century French manuscript) illustrates Revelation 12:13–17

18

Apollinarianism

Early Christian heresy which takes its title from Apollinarius, Bishop of Laodicaea (310–390 CE). He taught that in Christ the human mind (nous) was replaced by the divine Logos, and that therefore the incarnate Christ was not fully man. Apollinarius thought that if Christ had had a human mind, which leads us into sin, he could not have been our Saviour. The doctrine was condemned at the Council of Constantinople in 381, and Apollinarius seceded from the Church.

Apollo

One of the great gods of the Greeks, although probably not Greek in origin. The son of Zeus and Leto, he is the god who punishes, but also the god who wards off evil, the god of prophecy and healing, and the god of music and song. He later became the sun god.

Apollyon

Greek name for the angel of the bottomless pit. (See Abaddon)

Apologist

Term applied to Christian writers of the first two centuries after Christ, such as Justin Martyr and Tertullian, who set out an 'apology', i.e. a reasoned argument for their faith.

Apostasy

In classical Greek this relates to political revolt or defection. In the Septuagint it always relates to rebellion against God, e.g. Joshua 22:22. In the Greek of the NT it relates to a deliberate turning away from God, or the forsaking of religious duties or customs, e.g. Acts 21:21. This is the usual meaning today.

Apostle

Derived from the Greek word meaning 'to send', and used as a title for the twelve disciples commissioned by Jesus Christ. The title was claimed by St Paul in virtue of his experience of the call of Christ on the road to Damascus.

Apostles' Creed

Statement of faith used in the Western Church. Its title is first found about 390 CE, but a legend soon sprang up that it was formulated by the Twelve Apostles. It was probably a baptismal confession, but it is now part of the Anglican daily services of Matins and Evensong.

Apostolic Fathers

Title given to those Fathers of the Christian Church in the age immediately following the NT period whose works are still available, e.g. Clement of Rome, Ignatius, Hermas, Papias, Polycarp and Tertullian.

Apostolic See

Title given to the Diocese of Rome because of its traditional association with the Apostles St Peter and St Paul.

Apostolic Succession

Doctrine that the authority conferred by Jesus Christ on the Apostles has been passed on to the bishops of the Church in an unbroken line of succession. In the Roman Catholic, Orthodox and Anglican Churches, the continuing episcopacy is believed to ensure, through its link with the Apostles, a valid sacerdotal ministry with authority to administer the Sacraments, but this is not accepted by the Reformed Churches.

Apothegmata

Term introduced into NT study by the German theologian R. Bultmann in 1921, in his development of the methods of Form Criticism. He broke the Gospel narratives down into Forms, and one of these he called Apothegmata, which has been translated as 'Pronouncement Stories'. These are stories telling of an event in the life of Jesus and ending with a pronouncement or a pithy summary.

Apotheosis

Pagan custom of deifying the emperor. In the Roman Empire this was the practice after his death until the reign of Domitian (81–96 CE), from which time emperors were sometimes deified during their lifetime.

Apotropaic

See Magic

Apple

Fruit that has appeared widely in religious mythology. In the Bible Eve tempted Adam with an apple.

In Greek mythology Hercules attained immortality by seizing the golden apples of the Hesperides, while Paris, choosing the most beautiful goddess, gave the golden apple of desire to Aphrodite. In Scandinavian myths the gods keep young by eating the golden apples of Idun, and in Welsh legends heroes go to Avalon, a paradise of apple-trees. It is probable that the apple symbolizes the sun, which is yellow at midday and red in the evening.

Apse

Semicircular eastern end to the chancel of a Christian church. This was universal in the early basilica-type churches; the altar stood on the chord of the apse, with seats for the bishop and presbyters behind it.

Apsu

In Mesopotamian mythology the underworld ocean on which the world was thought to float. In the *Enuma Elish*, Apsu is the husband of Tiamat.

Aquinas

See Thomas Aquinas

Arabic

Sacred language of Islam, as it is the language in which the Qur'an is written. Orthodox Muslims claim that their holy book cannot be translated into other languages, which can give only a general idea of the contents.

Arafat

Valley to the east of Mecca where all Muslim pilgrims stand for a long sermon which rehearses Abraham's exemplary resistance to evil. Here also they encamp to shout praises, chant texts and offer prayers.

Aramaic

Vernacular language of Palestine in the time of Christ. It is a Semitic language akin to Hebrew, which it had gradually ousted in popular use. Because of this the Hebrew scriptures were issued as Aramaic paraphrases, known as the Targums.

Aranyakas

Lit. 'belonging to the forests'. Hindu texts, attached to the *Brahmanas*, composed or studied in the forests of India.

Ararat

Mountainous area mentioned four times in the Bible, the best known being Genesis 8:4, which

Valley of Arafat during the Hajj, showing the pilgrims returning to the encampment after hearing the sermon at the hill of Arafat

recounts the grounding of Noah's Ark after the Flood. It almost certainly corresponds to Urartu, near Lake Van, which is mentioned in Assyrian inscriptions.

Arati

Practice observed among Hindus and Sikhs of waving a tray filled with flowers, fragrant incense and a light before the object of devotion.

Archbishop

In the early Christian Church a title given to the patriarchs of the principal sees. In modern times a title of a metropolitan bishop, or one who has jurisdiction over an ecclesiastical province.

Archdeacon

Anglican clergyman to whom the bishop has delegated administrative authority over the whole or part of the diocese. His duties include discipline and the care of ecclesiastical property.

Archimandrite

Title used in the Eastern Church. Originally it applied to heads of monasteries, the equivalent of abbots, but now it is applied to superiors of groups of monasteries and also to other important administrative officials.

Ardas

Formal prayer which is part of a Sikh devotional service.

Areopagus

Lit. 'Mars' hill'. Spur of land at the western end of the Acropolis in Athens where St Paul delivered an address on the true knowledge of God (Acts 17:22–31). It was also the title of a very ancient Athenian Council of great prestige which had special jurisdiction in matters of morals and religion.

Ares

Fierce Greek god of war, identified by the Romans with Mars; he was probably Thracian in origin.

Arhat/Arhant

Buddhist term for a worthy person. One who has travelled the Noble Eightfold Path, has reached the goal of earlier (Hinayana) Buddhism, and has attained nibbana.

Arianism

Term derived from the name of the philosopher Arius (250–336 CE). This was a Christian heresy stating that Christ was not eternal but was created by God, thus being an inferior deity. It was condemned at the Council of Nicaea in 325.

Aristotle

Greek philosopher born at Stagira in Macedonia in 384 BCE. He became a pupil of Plato in 367 BCE. In 342 BCE he was appointed by Philip of Macedon as tutor to his son, Alexander (the Great). In 335 BCE he returned to Athens and founded a school of philosophy in the Lyceum, where he used to walk about under a portico while lecturing. The school's name, the Peripatetics, may be derived either from the name of the portico (Peripatos) or directly from the Greek words *peri* (about) and *patein* (to walk).

Ariya (P)/Arya (S)

Classical epithet of reverence used in Buddhism and Hinduism, and applied to an ascetic on his path to nirvana.

Ariya-sacca

Term used in Buddhism meaning 'noble truth'; it refers particularly to the Four Noble Truths which form the basis of the Buddha's teaching.

Ariyatthangika-magga

Term used in Buddhism indicating the Noble Eightfold Path, which is the fourth of the Noble Truths.

Arjan

(1581–1606)   Fifth Sikh Guru, who built the Golden Temple at Amritsar.

Arjuna

Hindu epic hero, the third son of King Pandu and Kiriti, but also regarded as the god Indra's son. His dialogue with the god Krishna on the eve of battle forms the subject matter of the *Bhagavadgita*.

Ark

1. Vessel in which Noah and his family were saved from the Flood (Genesis 6–8).

2. Chest containing the Tablets of the Law which stood in the Holy of Holies in the Temple in Jerusalem (1 Kings 8).

3. The holy ark, a cabinet in a synagogue where the Scrolls of the Law are housed.

Armaiti

In Zoroastrian teaching, Devotion or Piety, one of the seven Amesha Spentas.

Arminianism

System of theology based on the teaching of the Dutch Reformed theologian Jacobus Arminius (1560–1609). He vigorously opposed the deterministic logic of Calvin, and taught that divine sovereignty is compatible with real free will in man, and that Jesus Christ died for all men, not only for the elect. This teaching was influential in England through the preaching of John Wesley.

Artaxerxes I

(465–424 BCE) King of Persia who subdued the Egyptians and made peace with the Greeks. In 444 BCE he allowed Nehemiah to return to Jerusalem to supervise the rebuilding of the Temple.

Artemis

Greek goddess of the chase and the hunt. The twin sister of Apollo, she is often his partner in legends. She was identified by the Romans with Diana.

Arthur, King

Heroic British figure of the 6th century. He married Guinevere and established the Knights of the Round Table, an order of chivalry the main aim of which was to search for the Holy Grail.

Arti

Hymn popular among Sikhs, attributed to Guru Nanak.

Arupa-dhatu

In Buddhist teaching the domain of the four highest meditative stages, prior to nibbana.

Arya (S)

See Ariya

Arya Samaj

Hindu reform movement founded in Bombay in 1875 by Dayananda Saraswati to work for the restoration of Aryan Vedic religion, and to reject all the later post-Vedic Hinduism.

Aryan

Term derived from a Sanskrit word *arya*, meaning 'noble', which was applied by the Vedic Indians to their own tradition and community.

Asalha Puja

Theravada Buddhist festival in July commemorating the first proclamation by Gautama the Buddha of the Four Noble Truths and Noble Eightfold Path.

Asana

Term used in Buddhist teaching for the position or bodily posture adopted for meditation, e.g. the lotus or padmasan.

Asase Ya

Lit. 'Earth Thursday'. Name of an earth goddess among the Ashanti of Ghana. Thursday is sacred to her. She is specially remembered at planting time, but has no temple or altar.

Asava (P))/**Asrava** (S)

Lit. 'defilement' or 'mental intoxication'. In Buddhist teaching there are four asavas, viz. kama (sensuality), bhava (lust for life), ditthi (false views) and avijja (ignorance). These prevent the contemplation of pure truth.

Asbab al-Nuzul (A)

Term meaning the occasions of the Descent, i.e. the situations in which Muhammad's inspired deliverances are to be understood. In literary terms this means the context, not the cause, of the Qur'an.

Ascension

According to Christian belief, the occasion marking the end of Christ's appearances on earth, following his incarnation, crucifixion and resurrection. The narrative in Luke 24 and Acts 1 tells of his ascension into heaven to assume full divine authority. Ascension Day is observed on the sixth Thursday, i.e. the fortieth day, after Easter.

Asceticism

Practice of abstinence or austerity for religious purposes. This is usually based on the belief that the desires of the flesh are a hindrance to holiness and the spiritual life. Asceticism has been commended in Hinduism, especially among those who have reached the status of sannyasin, and in Buddhism, especially by monks seeking enlightenment. In the Christian Church it is a practice common to members of religious orders.

Asclepius

Greek god of healing, the son of Apollo. In the *Iliad* he is called 'the blameless physician'.

Ash Wednesday

First day of Lent, the beginning of a period of penitence and fasting in the Christian Church. In some churches the palms of the previous year are burnt and the priest makes the sign of the cross with the ashes on the foreheads of the worshippers at the Eucharist.

Asha

In the teaching of Zoroaster, Right or Righteousness, one of the seven Amesha Spentas.

Asher

Eighth son of the Israelite patriarch Jacob, by Zilpah, Leah's handmaid. Also the tribe which occupied territory on the NW coast of Canaan, beyond Mt Carmel.

Ashkenazi

Description of the descendants of Jews who came from East and Central Europe. (Cf. Sephardi)

Ashoka

(273–232 BCE)   Emperor of India. Horrified by warfare, he embraced Buddhism, and summoned a council to regulate monastic order and lay piety.

Ashrama

1. Hindu centre of religious teaching and spiritual living.
2. Retreat house for meditation and self-discipline.
3. According to Hindu teaching, one of the four stages in life, viz. (1) a celibate student of the *Vedas*, (2) a householder, (3) a hermit or ascetic teacher, after his family has grown up, (4) a sannyasi (ascetic) at a holy place seeking liberation. This pattern of life applies primarily to Brahmans.

Ashur

Chief god of Assyria and the patron deity of the city of Ashur.

Asmodeus

Originally a Persian demon of great rage, he was imported into Jewish literature, and appears in the Book of Tobit as the evil spirit who upsets marriage. Acting on the advice of the Archangel Gabriel, Tobias drove away Asmodeus with the smoke of a burning fish.

Asperges

Ceremony in the Western Church of sprinkling holy water on the altar and on the congregation before the principal Sunday Mass.

Asrava (S)

See Asava

Assumption of the Blessed Virgin Mary

Dogma defined by Pope Pius XII in 1950. In the Roman Catholic Church this is a festival observed on 15 August. It celebrates the belief that on the completion of her earthly life Mary was assumed in body and soul into heavenly glory.

Assyria

Country in the upper Mesopotamian plain that was very important in the ancient world. Its great kings included Sargon I (c. 2350 BCE), Shalmaneser I (1274–1245 BCE) and Tiglath Pileser (745–727 BCE). Under Sargon II (722–705 BCE) Assyria destroyed Samaria, and took many Israelites into captivity. Assyrian domination was broken when the capital Nineveh fell to Babylonian attack in 612 BCE. The national god was Ashur; other popular deities were Ishtar, the goddess of war and love, Nebu, the god of wisdom, and Sin, the moon god.

Astarte

Principal goddess of the Phoenicians and the Canaanites; the goddess of fertility and the consort of Baal.

Astika

Orthodox Hindus who accept the Vedic revelation. They are usually classified under six headings or schools of thought.

Astral Body

Some writers on the occult have suggested that in the addition to a body of flesh and blood every person has an exact counterpart of finer material, an astral body. In this, one can stand outside oneself, or pass through material obstructions.

Astrology

Calculation of the movement of the heavenly bodies in the belief that their relative positions at the time of a person's birth influence his character and destiny.

Asuras

Lit. 'spiritual' or 'divine'. This term was originally used of the supreme gods of Hinduism. Later it was applied to demons and anti-gods of the Vedic hymns, against whom the Vedic gods struggled.

Atash Bahram

Term used in the Zoroastrian religion for the highest grade of sacred fire, the royal fire, found in only eight temples in India and two in Iran.

Athanasian Creed

Confession of faith used in Western Christendom, also known, from its opening words, as Quicunque Vult. It is phrased differently from the Apostles' and the Nicene Creed, and also embodies anathemas. It was probably written between 380 and 430 CE, but takes its name from Athanasius, Bishop of Alexandria, who argued strongly against Arianism at the Council of Nicaea in 325.

Atharva-veda

Last of the four collections of Vedic hymns, incorporating material as ancient as that in the other collections. Its concern is mostly domestic, within the realm of social relationships.

Atheism

Derived from the Greek words *a* (not) and *theos* (god). To the Greeks this meant complete scepticism or a dislike of traditional mythology. In modern use it generally implies a denial that there is any supreme being or deity.

Athene

Greek goddess, also known as Pallas Athene. The soldier daughter of Zeus, from whose head she sprang fully armed, she was the protectress of Athens, and also the goddess of agriculture and wisdom. She was identified by the Romans with Minerva.

Athens

Ancient capital of Attica and the centre of Greek culture. According to tradition it was founded by the hero Cecrops in 1550 BCE. The Persians caused great damage in 480 BCE, but Themistocles began the reconstruction, which was completed when Pericles commissioned the building of its crowning glory, the Parthenon, on the highest point of the Acropolis in 450 BCE. The schools of philosophy of Socrates, Plato and Aristotle added to the fame of the city, which continued to flourish in Roman times. Athens suffered severe damage at the hands of the Turks in 1456 and did not revert to the control of the Greeks until 1833.

Atman (S)**/Atta** (P)

Soul, self, or principle of life in Hindu thought. It sometimes applies to the individual soul, sometimes to the eternal soul, identical with Brahman, the ultimate reality. In Buddhist teaching the ego is illusory.

Athene (altar frieze)

Aton

Egyptian god who was not represented by an image, but was symbolized by the sun or the disc of the sun, depicted as a disc with rays in a fan shape each terminating in a hand. His worship was introduced into Egypt by Amenophis IV (Ikhnaton) about 1370 BCE as a monotheistic faith sweeping away the old gods, but on his death they were restored.

Atonement

Biblical term indicating reconciliation between God and man (at-one-ment), restoring a relationship that had been broken by sin. In the Hebrew Bible this is the purpose of the ritual of the Day of Atonement (Leviticus 16). The NT doctrine is that Jesus Christ, through his life and death and resurrection, is the saviour who brings about atonement.

Atta (P)

See Atman

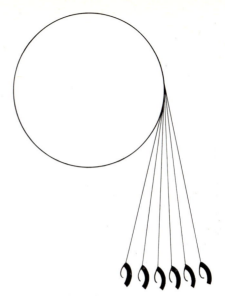

Symbol of Aton: the solar disc

Atum

First god of Heliopolis in ancient Egypt. His name may mean 'accomplished one'.

Augsburg Confession

Lutheran confession of faith drawn up in 1530, probably by Philip Melancthon. It is divided into two parts, the first containing the essential Lutheran doctrines in twenty-one articles, the second reviewing ecclesiastical abuses and offering remedies.

Augury

Divination based on the flight and behaviour of birds; a form of prophecy popular in the Roman Empire.

Augustine of Canterbury

Prior of St Andrew's monastery in Rome, he was sent by Pope Gregory the Great as a missionary to England, where he became the first Archbishop of Canterbury in 597 CE. He died in 605.

Augustine of Hippo

(354-430 CE) Theologian named as a Doctor of the Church. After studying philosophy, he was baptized into the Christian faith in 387, and from 396 until his death was Bishop of Hippo. He had to deal with three heresies, Manichaeism, Donatism and Pelagianism. His two books *Confessions* and *The City of God* had immense influence on subsequent theology.

Augustinian Canons

Communities of religious who seek to live a common life of poverty, celibacy and obedience, following the rule of St Augustine, but not in an enclosed monastery. The order received official approval in 1063, and they have a flexible rule which allows them to undertake parochial responsibilities. The main branch of the order today is known as the Canons Regular of the Lateran.

Augustus

(63 BCE–14 CE) C. Octavius, son of Atia and great-nephew of Julius Caesar. On the death of Julius, he joined the Republican party and was elected Consul. After a long struggle with Antony, he emerged victorious and was made Emperor in 27 BCE with the title Augustus. In 12 CE he assumed the office of Pontifex Maximus. During his lifetime, he was worshipped as a god in the provinces, and after his death he was deified in Rome and throughout the Empire.

Aumbry

Cupboard in the wall of a Church in which sacred vessels or books can be stored. In some Anglican churches it is used to keep the Reserved Sacrament, but this is not permitted in Roman Catholic churches.

Authorized Version

Version of the English Bible produced by fifty-four scholars appointed by James I in 1604. They worked in six companies, taking different sections of the Bible, and the complete work was published in 1611.

Avacara

Lit. 'sphere of existence'. According to Buddhist teaching there are three such spheres, kama, rupa and arupa.

Avalokiteshvara

Title used in Buddhism for one of the greatest Bodhisattvas. He is 'the Lord who is seen', or 'the Lord who lowers his gaze towards humanity in compassion and the wish to help'. This Bodhisattva is worshipped as the feminine Kwan Yin in China or as Kwannon in Japan.

Avalon

Celtic wonderland, like Elysium, where King Arthur is said to have been taken to recover from his wounds. The name may be derived from a word meaning 'apple'.

Avatar

Lit. 'descent'. This relates to the Hindu belief that the god Vishnu has been incarnated in ten or more avatars, of whom Rama and Krishna were the more important.

Avalokiteshvara (*c.* 12th century)

Ave Maria

Lit. 'Hail, Mary'. Roman Catholic devotion consisting of two verses from Luke (1:28, 42) and a prayer to the Virgin Mary. It is part of the Angelus and is repeated in the devotions of the Rosary.

Averroës

(1126–1198) Arabic philosopher, the name being a corruption of Ibn Roshd. He wrote on medicine, theology and law, but was chiefly renowned for his commentaries on Aristotle.

Avesta

Zoroastrian scriptures, of which only one-quarter is extant.

Avicenna

(980–1037) Arabic philosopher and court physician. He was influenced by Neo-Platonism, and believed that there was a hierarchy of emanations from the Godhead mediating between God and man. He distinguished between necessary and contingent being, holding that God is necessary and the universe contingent. He exercised considerable influence on early scholastic theology.

Avidya (S)**/Avijja** (P)

Lit. 'not knowing' or 'ignorance'. This is a term derived from two Sanskrit words, *a* (not) and *vidya* (knowing or wisdom), which describes the condition of individuals involved in the cycle of rebirth. In the Hindu Vedanta salvation comes through the displacement of avidya by true knowledge, the realization of the soul's identity with Brahman. In Buddhist thought avidya is the root of evil and the cause of desire.

Ayah (A)

Term for a verse in the Qur'an. It also indicates the 'sign quality' of events in nature and history in which perceptive men can read the divine power and mercy.

Azazel

In the Hebrew Bible a demon of the desert to whom the 'scapegoat' of the sin offering was despatched (Leviticus 16:1–28). In Enoch 6:8 he is a leader of fallen angels while in later Jewish and Muslim tradition he is the chief of demons.

Azrael

In Islamic theology one of the four Archangels, the angel of death.

Aztecs

Conquering people who entered the Valley of Mexico in the 12th century. They were sun-worshippers, built pyramids oriented to the sun, and offered the sun god human sacrifices. Their culture was very influential although they held power for only two centuries.

Ba

Egyptian word generally translated 'soul' but referring to the whole person after death.

Baal

Semitic word meaning 'lord' used by some communities as a name or title of God.

Ba'al Shem (H)

Lit. 'Master/Possessor of the Name'. Title given in popular Jewish literature, from the Middle Ages onwards, to one claiming to have secret knowledge of the Tetragrammaton and other holy names, and the ability to work miracles by the power of these names. It was later extended to writers of amulets and incantations, including the founder of modern Chasidim, Israel ben Eliezer.

Ba'al Shem Tob (H)

Lit. 'Master of the Good Name'. Title applied to Israel ben Eliezer (1700–1760), the founder of the Jewish sect of Chasidim. He lived a simple life of poverty but was rejected by the Talmudists because of a suspicion of pantheism in his teaching. He declared that the whole universe is a manifestation of the Divine Being who reveals himself in everything, even evil things. He believed that true worship is unification with God, and that the zaddik (holy man) can claim equal authority with the prophets.

Babalawo

Yoruba seer or Ifa priest.

Babar-vani

Four hymns of Guru Nanak, 'utterances concerning Babar', dealing with early events in Sikhism.

Babel, Tower of

According to Genesis 11:1–9, the men of the plain of Shinar decided to build a tower reaching to heaven, but God scattered them and confused their speech. The Tower of Babel, which may have been a reminiscence of a stepped ziggurat in Babylon, is thus a symbol of human pride and the confusion caused by language differences.

Babism

Religious movement in Persia founded by Sayid Ali Muhammad (1819–1850), who took the title 'Bab' (the gate). Now absorbed into the Baha'i faith.

Babylon

City on the River Euphrates (80 km south of modern Baghdad) which became the political and religious capital of Babylonia. Its greatest king was probably Nebuchadrezzar II, who in 586 BCE destroyed Jerusalem, plundering the Temple and taking many Jews into exile. Babylon itself fell when Cyrus I of Persia conquered it in 539 BCE. The name 'Babylon' is used in Revelation 16, 17 as the centre of evil and the focus of God's anger, but this is probably a hidden reference to Rome.

Bacchae

In Greek legend these were companions of Dionysus or Bacchus in his wanderings. In ancient Greek ritual celebrations they were priestesses of Dionysus who worked themselves into a frenzy with wine at the Dionysiac festivals.

Bacchus

See Dionysus

Badr, Battle of

    Two years after the Hijrah, Muhammad broke the tradition of months of truce and attacked the Quraish tribe because of their persistent hostility. Although few in number, Muhammad's followers won a great victory, but he was reminded that this came about through the power of Allah, not through his military skill. It is described in the Qur'an (8:1–19) as Yaum al-furqan: the day which demonstrated where right was.

Baghdad

    Capital city of Iraq. Situated on the River Tigris, it was founded in 762 CE by Caliph Almansur. It became an important centre of trade, with signs of splendour and luxury, in the reign of Haroun al Raschid, in the 9th century, and is the scene of tales in the *Arabian Nights*. It was one of the most important cities in the Muslim world but was devastated by Timur in 1401. Rebuilt, it became a place of contention between Persians and Turks. In 1917 it was captured by the British and in 1921 became the capital of the new Kingdom of Iraq under King Faisal I.

Baha'i Faith

    Religious movement arising within Persian Islam but regarded as completely independent. It was introduced by Baha'u'llah (1817–1892), whose advent was proclaimed by the Bab. Both the movement's spiritual and administrative centre and the golden-domed Shrine of the Bab are in Haifa. The Baha'i faith teaches the oneness of God, the essential unity of all religions, and the unity of mankind. It has no priesthood.

Baha'u'llah

    See Anniversary of the Ascension of Baha'u'llah, Baha'i Faith and Ridvan

Baiami

    In the belief of many Australian aboriginals, he is the 'all father', the creator of the world, of men and of animals, and the giver of laws and customs.

Baiga

    In Indian village Hinduism a village priest or the servant of a village deity.

Bairam

    Muslim festival. (See Id al-Adha)

Baisakhi

    Sikh festival celebrating the birth of the Khalsa in 1699, when Guru Gobind Singh baptized his first five disciples. This is a very joyous festival, now commonly known as Amrit as it is the occasion for initiation into the Sikh faith.

Bala

    Term used in Buddhism to describe faculties of a high degree, e.g. samadhi and panna.

Balagh (A)

    Term used by Muslims to describe the content of Muhammad's preaching, as distinct from the factors making for its acceptance.

Baldachino

    Canopy used to cover an altar. This can be simple and small or very ornate. The largest example is the baldachino on massive twisted columns created by Bernini over the high altar of St Peter's, Rome. The Reformers rejected this ornament, and it is now usually found only in Roman Catholic churches.

Balder

    Name meaning 'shining one'. Balder was the wisest and most beautiful of the Scandinavian gods, the son of Odin and Frigg. All plants and animals except the mistletoe swore not to harm him, and eventually he was killed by a sprig of mistletoe.

Banns of Marriage

    Public announcement in a Christian church of the intention of two persons to marry. The practice was approved at the Lateran Council of 1215. In England the Marriage Act of 1823 stipulates that the banns must be read by the parish priest on three successive Sundays prior to the marriage. The purpose is to give opportunity for inquiry if anyone raises a 'reason in law' why the persons named 'may not marry each other'.

Baodah

    Term used in the Zoroastrian religion for human perception.

Baha'i Shrine of the Bab on Mt Carmel, Haifa

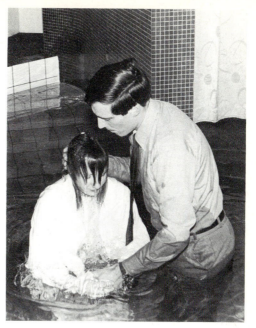

Baptism by total immersion

Baptism

Rite of initiation into a religious faith. Christian baptism has two symbolic meanings: (1) purificatory, the washing away of sins; (2) regenerative, the death of the penitent, seen in the immersion in water, followed by the rebirth of the initiate in the emergence from the water. In many churches the rite is now performed by the sprinkling of water, not by immersion. In the Graeco-Roman mystery religion of Cybele, baptism in bull's blood was regarded as efficacious for twenty years; if renewed, it was an eternal rebirth.

Baptistery

Building connected with or near to a Christian church in which the sacrament of baptism was administered. The earliest example is at Dura Europos, built about 250 CE. The practice of building separate baptisteries ceased c. 1000, as it became customary to administer the sacrament in the body of the church.

Baptists

Members of a world-wide Protestant Christian denomination which practises adult baptism by total immersion as a rite of entry into Church membership. They originated as a community of believers gathered together by John Smyth in Amsterdam in 1609, and the first Baptist chapel in London was opened by Thomas Helwys in 1612. Various groups of Baptists came together in 1891 to form the Baptist Union of Great Britain and Ireland. The first Baptist church in the United States was founded at Providence, Rhode Island in 1639 and the Baptists now form the largest Protestant denomination in America.

Barabbas

Thief and probably murderer who was freed by Pilate in response to public demand when Jesus was arrested. In accordance with the practice of freeing one prisoner at the Feast of the Passover, Pilate wished to free Jesus because he could find no fault in him, but he gave in to the crowd because he feared they might start a riot (Mark 15:6–15).

Barahi

In village Hinduism a ceremony which takes place on the twelfth day after the birth of a child to mark the end of the mother's ritual impurity.

Baraka (A)

Lit. 'blessing'. Term used in Islam to denote the wonderful power possessed by God, Muhammad and the saints to transmit blessings to the faithful.

Barat

Term used in village Hinduism to describe the party accompanying a Hindu bridegroom to his wedding.

Bar-Cochba

Jewish patriot who led the final revolt against the Romans from 132 to 135 CE. This ended with the destruction by the Roman forces of his fortress at Bethar near Jerusalem.

Bareshnum

Nine-day purification ceremony undertaken by Zoroastrians as an essential preliminary to the priestly religious ceremonies.

Bar-mitzvah

Lit. 'son of the commandment'. Ceremony in the synagogue to mark the attainment of religious maturity by a Jewish boy at the age of thirteen. He is then called up for the reading of the Law, and is required to put on the tephillin for morning prayer on the Sabbath following the ceremony. Thereafter he will wear the tephillin for daily prayers.

Barnabas

Jewish Christian from Cyprus who befriended Paul after the latter's vision on the road to Damascus (Acts 9:25). Barnabas introduced Paul to the Apostles and went with him on his first missionary journey, but they quarrelled and parted on account of John Mark, the nephew of Barnabas. Later they were reconciled, and Barnabas is regarded as the founder of the Church in Cyprus and its first bishop. Tradition says he was martyred at Salamis in 61 CE.

Bar-mitzvah boy

Barth, Karl

(1886–1976)   Protestant theologian who was also a courageous opponent of Nazism. His theology was firmly based on the Bible, affirming the supremacy and transcendence of God. He maintained that God's sole revelation is in Jesus Christ, and that the Word of God is his only means of communication with man.

Bartholomew, St

One of the twelve apostles of Jesus, mentioned in the synoptic Gospels and Acts. According to tradition, he visited India and suffered a martyr's death by being flayed alive. His feast-day is 24 August. He has been identified with Nathaniel by some scholars.

Baruch, Book of

Book in the Jewish Apocrypha which forms an appendix to Jeremiah. It contains an introduction, a confession, a sermon and canticles.

Barzakh

Term used in the Qur'an (23:106) for the barrier that marks the frontier of death and is crossed by the departed.

Basil, St

(330–379 CE)   One of the three Cappadocian Fathers of the early Church. He was appointed Bishop of Caesarea in 370 and was an influential theologian, writing on the Holy Spirit and other doctrines. His most lasting works were a liturgy, still used on occasion in the Eastern Church, and a monastic rule which still influences the life of monastic communities.

Basilica

Early form of building for Christian worship, modelled on the Roman building used as a law court. It usually had a nave, two aisles and a semicircular apse at the east end where the bishop presided facing the congregation. Today the title is given to certain privileged churches, four of which are in Rome.

Basilides

Gnostic teacher in Alexandria in the 2nd century who claimed to have a secret tradition from St Peter. He distinguished between the God of the Jews and the Supreme God who sent into the world his nous to dwell in Jesus, who thus suffered in appearance only.

Bast

Ancient Egyptian goddess portrayed as a woman with the head of a cat who was worshipped at Bubastis. She has sometimes been identified with Artemis or Diana.

Bath Qol

Lit. 'daughter of a voice'. Hebrew term used in rabbinic theology for a voice from heaven communicating a message from God. According to Midrash and Talmudic writings, it may be soft 'like the murmur of a dove' (Ber. 3a) or loud 'like the roar of a lion' (Rab.). It may be prophetic (Sanh. 102a) or a general admonition (Meg. 3a). Such a voice is referred to in the accounts of the baptism (Mark 1:11) and transfiguration of Jesus Christ (Mark 9:7).

Bayan (A)

Lit. 'disclosure'. One of the titles of the Qur'an (3:138), as the revelation which illumines and clarifies. Also the title of the Holy Book of the Bab, forerunner of Baha'u'llah.

Beads

See Prayer Beads

Beatific Vision

In the scholastic theology of the Catholic Church, this term refers to the intuitive knowledge of and union with God which constitutes the supreme joy of heaven and the ultimate goal of human existence.

Beatification

Act by which the Pope permits the veneration of a saintly Catholic in a particular church, diocese or country. Such a person receives the title 'Blessed'. Permission is given only after the most searching inquiries following the person's death, often after a period of many years.

Beatitudes

Series of nine sayings each beginning with the word 'Blessed' with which Jesus began the Sermon on the Mount (Matthew 5:3–12).

Becket

See Thomas à Becket

Bede, The Venerable

(673–735 CE) Sometimes known as the Father of English History, he was a devout monk and learned biblical scholar who spent most of his life in Northumbria. He was a prolific writer, but his most important work was his *Ecclesiastical History of the English Nation.*

Beelzebub

Originally this name was Baal-zebub, Lord of the Flies, referred to in the Hebrew Bible (2 Kings 1). In the NT Jesus was accused of healing people with his help. Beelzebub's reputation grew until he was regarded as stronger than Satan, and in Marlowe's play, Faust called him one of the five most powerful demons.

Beer Sheba

Southernmost town in ancient Israel, approximately 80 km south west of Jerusalem. It was the site of an important well, and the name is explained as the well of seven, viz. the seven lambs sacrificed to ratify a covenant between Abraham and Abimelech (Genesis 21:31). It is also associated with Isaac and Jacob, and is referred to critically in the prophecy of Amos (5:5; 8:14).

Begging Bowl

Receptacle carried by bhikkus of Theravada Buddhism on their daily round to receive gifts of food from their lay supporters.

Beguines and Beghards

The Beguines were sisterhoods and the Beghards were brotherhoods founded by Lambert le Begue, a revivalist preacher in the Netherlands in the 12th century. The Beguines lived a communal life but were permitted to have private property. The Beghards had a common life, a common purse and no private property. As an expression of their religious belief, they both undertook philanthropic activities and nursing of the sick. At times they were accused of heresy and condemned, but they survived until the French Revolution.

Behaviourism

School of psychology associated with J. B. Watson and B. F. Skinner which teaches that all aspects of human behaviour are shaped by particular combinations of rewarding or adversive stimuli; it emphasizes the importance of objective study of actual responses.

Bel

In the Babylonian religion the god of the earth, whose cult was centred at Nippur.

Belenos

In Celtic mythology the god of the sun; he was widely worshipped in Gaul and Britain.

Belial

Powerful demon in Jewish apocryphal writings. In the *Testament of the Twelve Patriarchs* he is the chief of devils, the prince of deceit. In the *War Document* of the Dead Sea Scrolls he is the leader of the forces of evil. The *Sybilline Oracles* predict that he will appear on earth, from Samaritan stock.

Bells

Bells have a close association with religion. They summon the faithful to worship, give warning of danger, toll for a funeral, rejoice for a wedding, and help to keep away evil spirits. In pagan thought the shell is regarded as female and the clapper as male, while bells for churches often have names, sometimes inscribed on the bell itself.

Beltane

Major festival of the Celtic year celebrated with sacred fires on the nights of 30 April/1 May and 31 October/1 November.

Benares

Town in India on the banks of the River Ganges which is one of the most sacred places of pilgrimage for Hindus. It has many temples, particularly to Shiva and Annapurna, and to die in Benares is regarded as a great happiness, as it is considered to be the gateway to heaven.

Tenor bell, Haslemere Parish Church

Benedicite

Song of praise put into the mouths of Shadrach, Meshach and Abednego as they stood in King Nebuchadrezzar's fiery furnace. It forms part of the *Song of the Three Holy Children*, which is included in the Septuagint text of the Book of Daniel. In the *Book of Common Prayer* it is an alternative to the Te Deum in the service of Matins.

Benedict, St

Known as the Patriarch of Western Monasticism, little can be said with certainty about his life. He was born in 480 CE and became a hermit about 500 CE. He attracted followers and in 530 CE founded a monastery at Monte Cassino, where he died in 550 CE. He composed a rule for the monastic life which is still the basis of monasticism today.

Benedictines

Members of a Christian monastic order founded by St Benedict of Nursia about 530 CE. This order has always put great emphasis on sacred learning, and has probably been the most influential of the monastic orders.

Benediction

Service which developed out of the Roman Catholic veneration of the Host. It is usually held in the afternoon or evening, and culminates with the blessing of the congregation with the Reserved Sacrament in the monstrance.

Benedictus

Words of thanksgiving uttered by Zachariah after the birth of his son (John the Baptist), recorded in

Luke 1:67–79; the title is the first word in the Latin version. The Benedictus is included in the Anglican service of Matins.

Benefice

According to the canon law of the Church, this is an ecclesiastical office with certain prescribed duties, such as an appointment as rector, vicar or parish priest. In return for the fulfilment of the duties specified revenues are made available.

Benefit of Clergy

Privilege of exemption from trial by a secular court on a charge of felony, granted to clergy, plus all who were tonsured, in the Middle Ages. The privilege was abolished in England in 1827.

Benjamin

Youngest son of the Israelite patriarch Jacob and his favourite wife Rachel. Also the tribe which claimed its descent from him, which occupied the region between Mt Ephraim and the hills of Judah.

Berakhot (H)

Lit. 'benedictions'. Title of the first Tractate of the Talmud, which contains nine chapters discussing the proper use of the Amidah, the Jewish Prayer of Eighteen Benedictions.

Berit (H)

Word meaning 'covenant' (q.v.).

Berit Milah (H)

Covenant of circumcision in Judaism.

Bernadette, St

Peasant girl (Bernadette Soubirous) from Lourdes in southern France who had a series of visions of the Virgin Mary in 1858. A spring whose water is believed to have miraculous powers of healing then appeared, and the site has become a major place of pilgrimage where the sick and disabled are taken for immersion in the water and services of prayer.

Bernard, St

(1090–1153) Cistercian monk who became Abbot of Clairvaux and established it as the chief house of his order. He taught that the work of salvation is accomplished by the love and grace of God co-operating with the freely willed activity of man.

Berossus

Priest of Marduk in Babylon in the 3rd century BCE who wrote a history of the Babylonians in Greek. It is known only from quotations by later historians such as Josephus and Eusebius.

Besant, Annie

(1847–1933) Leading member of the Theosophical Society. She broke away from the Church of England and joined the National Secular Society. In 1889 she came under the influence of Mme Blavatsky and went to India, where she supported a teacher named Krishnamurti.

Bestiaries

Medieval collections of stories about real or fabulous animals. The stories usually had a moral purpose and contained a great deal of symbolism.

Beth Din

Jewish court of three rabbis empowered to adjudicate on matters of Jewish law.

Bethel

Lit. 'house of God'. Important Israelite sanctuary where God appeared to Jacob in a dream (Genesis 28:10–22). On the division of the Kingdom, following the death of Solomon, Jeroboam I instituted the worship of the golden calf there (1 Kings 12:28).

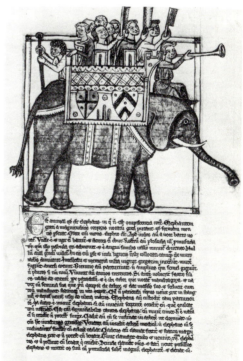

Page from a bestiary written in England (early 13th century)

Bethlehem: Church of the Nativity

Bhavacakra; Mahayana Buddhist wheel. The eight spokes symbolize the Eightfold Path; in the centre is yang/yin (from a Tibetan woodcut)

Bethlehem
Small town 8 km south of Jerusalem which was the birthplace of Jesus Christ (Luke 2:4).

Bhabhut
Ashes from a fire offering preserved by an Indian village Hindu worshipper.

Bhagat
Term used among Hindus and Sikhs for a devotee, one who practises bhakti.

Bhagavadgita
Lit. 'song of the blessed one'. (Some scholars prefer the translation 'song of the beloved' or 'song of the Lord'.) This is the most famous and popular Hindu scripture, being for many Hindus the centre of their love and devotion. It was probably composed in the 4th and 3rd centuries BCE, has eighteen chapters and seven hundred verses. It is part of the great epic the *Mahabharata*, and many devotional commentaries have been written to interpret it.

Bhagavat
Title conferred in Buddhism on one who is worthy of respect. It means 'blessed one'.

Bhagvan
Title or name used in Hinduism for the impersonal, supreme spirit: God.

Bhajan
Hindu hymn.

Bhakti
Lit. 'love' or 'devotion'. Attitude of loving adoration of God which develops into ardent worship, emphasized in the *Bhagavadgita*.

Bhakti-yoga
Way or discipline of bhakti, the Hindu practice of devotion described in the *Bhagavadgita*.

Bhavacakra
Term used in Buddhism for the symbol of the Wheel of Becoming mentioned by the Buddha in his Benares sermon.

Bhedabhedavada
Hindu doctrine of identity-in-difference as found in the *Brahmasutra* and expounded by Ramanuja. Brahman is seen as both identical with and different from Atman.

Bheru
Ferocious aspect of the Hindu god Shiva. His duty is the protection of wells, and his physical manifestation is a stone painted with lead oxide, often resembling the phallic representation of Shiva.

Bhikkhu (P)/**Bhikshu** (S)
Buddhist monk. Derived from a root meaning 'beggar', the name emphasizes the poverty of a member of the Sangha.

Bhima
The 'terrible' prince. According to Hindu mythology, he was the second of five Pandu princes, and was said to be the son of Vayu, god of the wind.

Bhopa
In Indian village Hinduism the title of a village priest, or servant of a local village deity.

Bhumi

Lit. 'ground'. Used metaphorically in Buddhism to indicate a stage on the way to illumination.

Bhut

Word used in Hindu mythology meaning 'ghost'.

Bhuvo

In Indian village Hinduism the title of a village priest, or servant of a local village deity.

Bible

Collection of scriptural writings sacred to the Jewish or Christian communities.

1. The Massoretic (Hebrew) text of the Jewish Bible contains thirty-nine books, divided into three sections: (*a*) the Law, containing the Pentateuch; (*b*) the Prophets, containing the Former Prophets (Joshua, Judges, Samuel and Kings) and the Latter Prophets (Isaiah, Jeremiah, Ezekiel and the twelve minor prophets); (*c*) the Writings, containing Chronicles, Ezra, Nehemiah, Job, Psalms, Proverbs and the Megilloth. This tripartite canon was referred to by Ben Sira in 180 BCE.

2. The Greek text of the New Testament contains twenty-seven books: four Gospels, Acts, thirteen epistles of St Paul, together with eight other epistles and Revelation. These, with the books of the Hebrew Bible (called by Christians the Old Testament), comprise the Christian scriptures, which were translated into English as the Authorized Version in 1611, the Revised Version in 1881, and numerous modern versions since.

3. The Latin text of the Bible, the Vulgate, regarded as authoritative by the Roman Catholic Church, contains an additional fifteen books, usually referred to as the Apocrypha, which are included in some other editions of the Bible.

Biel, Gabriel

(1420–1495)   One of the most influential of the Christian scholastic theologians. A member of the Brethren of the Common Life, he became Professor of Theology at Tübingen, where he expounded the Nominalism of William of Ockham. He also wrote a commentary on Peter Lombard and an exposition of the Mass.

Bifrost

Rainbow bridge across which the Norse gods of Askgard were thought to pass in order to stand under the World Tree and pass judgement.

Bilal

(581–641 CE) Abyssinian slave who became a disciple of Muhammad, went with him to Medina and was appointed the first muezzin. When the Muslims entered Mecca, Bilal called them to prayer from the roof of the Kaaba.

Bimah (H)

Desk or platform in a Jewish synagogue from which the Torah is read. Formerly it was at one end of the synagogue but it is now usually in the centre.

Bira

Term used by the Shona tribe of Africa referring to the ceremonies of ancestor worship.

Biradari

Term used in India for a local caste assembly or fraternity which enforces caste rules, settles disputes between fellow caste members, and before which heads of families have a right to speak.

Biretta

Hard square cap worn by clergy of the Western Church. Originally confined to higher graduates of universities, it became the customary head-dress of clergy in the 16th century. Priests wear a black biretta, bishops a purple and cardinals a red biretta.

Biretta

Birthday of Guru Nanak

Festival observed by Sikhs on 6 November, in honour of their founder and first Guru.

Birthday of the Prophet Muhammad

Festival of Mawlid, observed by most Muslims on the twelfth day of the fourth month of the Muslim calendar. It is a joyous festival, with narrations of the birth and life of the Prophet, and has been observed since the 10th century. Its observance is particularly encouraged by the Sufis, but is ignored by the Wahhabis.

35

Bishop

Highest of the three major orders in the Christian Church, the other two being deacon and priest. In Catholic theology, bishops are regarded as the successors of the Apostles and are usually consecrated by a metropolitan and two other bishops. In the Roman Catholic and Orthodox Churches and in the Anglican Communion only bishops can administer confirmation and confer holy orders. The insignia of a bishop are a mitre, crozier, pectoral cross and ring. Some Lutheran Churches, the Moravian and the Methodist Episcopal Church of America, retain the title for some senior ministers, but make no claim to Apostolic Succession.

Bismillah (A)

Phrase meaning 'in the name of God, the merciful, the compassionate' which prefaces every surah of the Qur'an except one (surah 9). It is the general Islamic invocation of God.

Black Friars

See Dominicans

Black Mass

Parody of the Mass celebrated in honour of the devil in satanic rituals.

Black Muslims

Movement among American Negro Muslims introduced by W. D. Fard in 1930. He was succeeded in 1934 by Elijah Muhammad, who claimed that he had been appointed Prophet by Allah. Black Muslims have been accused of racist teachings because they admit only Negroes to their services; this is regarded by many Muslims as a perversion of the faith of the Prophet.

Black Stone

One of the most sacred objects in the Muslim faith, this stone is set in the south-east corner of the Kaaba shrine in Mecca. According to tradition, it was delivered by the Archangel Gabriel into the safe keeping of Abraham and Ishmael (Qur'an 2:195).

Blasphemy

Speech or thought which expresses contempt for God or utters profanity. In England in the 16th and 17th centuries it was an offence against the law, but it is now regarded as a sin against religion or the faith.

Blavatsky, Mme Helena Petrovna

(1831–1891)   Co-founder of the Theosophical Society with Colonel Olcott. The Society did not bind itself to any particular religion but studied spiritualism and the occult. Her books include *The Secret Doctrine* and *Isis Unveiled.*

Blood

Because loss of blood can lead to loss of life, blood has often been considered not only as the 'river of life', but as life itself. Consequently, the central feature of most sacrifices is the gift of life in the form of blood, animal or human, to the deity. Covenants were sealed with blood, and the central point of the Christian Eucharist is the consecration of the wine with the words 'This is my blood of the New Covenant'. Because of the text 'The life of the flesh is in the blood' (Leviticus 17:11), Jews eat meat only after it has been prepared according to the rules of Kosher food and drained of its blood. Muslims are also forbidden to consume blood (Qur'an 2:173), while Jehovah's Witnesses forbid blood transfusions. There are many myths associated with the power of blood.

Boaz

See Jachin and Boaz

Bodh Gaya

Shrine and place of pilgrimage sacred to Buddhists because it is the place where the Buddha found enlightenment. It is also sacred to Vaishnavite Hindus, because for them the Buddha came to be identified as an incarnation of Vishnu.

Bodhi

Word used in Buddhist teaching to indicate enlightenment. The spiritual condition of a Buddha, a Bodhisattva or an Arhat.

Bodhi Day

Festival in Mahayana Buddhism to celebrate the enlightenment of Gautama Siddhartha when he became the Buddha. It is observed in December.

Bodhi Tree

See Bo-tree

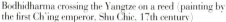

Bodhidharma crossing the Yangtze on a reed (painting by the first Ch'ing emperor, Shu Chic, 17th century)

Mask of a Bodhisattva (Japan)

Bodhidharma

According to tradition, the monk who brought Zen from India to China about 520 CE, having received the teaching by direct succession from the Buddha. He was the twenty-eighth patriarch in line from the Buddha, and the first patriarch of Zen in China.

Bodhisatta (P)/Bodhisattva (S)

Term used in Buddhism for one who has attained enlightenment (bodhi) but renounces entry into full nirvana in order to help other beings. It is also used for one on the way to enlightenment, a 'buddha to be'.

Bompu Zen

First of five types of Zen. 'Ordinary' Zen, i.e. ordinary meditation for the good of the mind.

Bon

Indigenous religion of Tibet. It is a crude form of nature worship which has affected Tibetan Buddhism, making it different from other forms.

Bonhoeffer, D.

(1906–1945) German pastor and theologian closely associated with the struggle of the German Confessional Church against the Nazi state. He was arrested in 1943, accused of plotting against Hitler's life, and executed in 1945. In his *Letters and Papers from Prison* he discussed the possibility of a non-religious interpretation of biblical concepts, and has been regarded as the originator of the programme later termed *Religionless Christianity*.

Boniface VIII

(1234–1303) Italian priest who became Pope in 1294 and tried unsuccessfully to reconcile the various states in Europe. In 1302, during a confrontation with Philip of France, he issued the famous Bull *Unam Sanctam*, in which he claimed absolute jurisdiction for the Pope over all men. Philip replied by taking him prisoner, and Boniface died a month later.

Boniface, St

(680–754 CE) Often known as the Apostle of Germany, Boniface was a Devonian. With the support of Pope Gregory II, he undertook missionary journeys in Germany, where he courageously felled the Oak of Thor at Geismar. In 743 he founded the Abbey of Fulmar, and in 747 became Archbishop of Mainz.

Bonze

Title given to a Buddhist monk in Japan. It is similar in meaning to 'bhikkhu'.

Bo-tree

Tree under which the Buddha was meditating when he found enlightenment. It is thought that it was probably the pipal or sacred fig. According to tradition, a shoot was taken from Bodh Gaya in the 3rd century BCE and planted in Sri Lanka, where it flourishes. Pilgrims collect its leaves.

Bourgeoisie

Term used by Karl Marx to designate the class of modern capitalists: owners of the means of production and employers of labour.

Boy Bishop

A medieval custom in England was to elect a boy to fulfil certain episcopal duties in church from St Nicholas's Day (6 December) until Holy Innocents' Day (28 December). The custom was abolished by Henry VIII.

Brahma (masc.)

Hindu creator god. First member of a triad with Vishnu and Shiva, which is sometimes depicted in sculpture as one figure with three faces. He is not mentioned in the Vedic scriptures, but appears in the *Mahabharata*.

Brahma Samaj

Reformed Hindu sect founded by Ram Mohan Roy in 1827.

Brahmacarin

In Hindu thought the first of four stages of life (ashramas): a student or celibate young person. This stage usually lasts twelve years.

Brahmacarya

Lit. 'holy living'. Hindu and Buddhist term for chastity, sexual abstinence or a life of discipline. This is one of the essential duties of a Buddhist monk.

Brahman (neut.)

Perhaps from a root meaning 'to grow', this term came to mean the holy power implicit in the whole universe, or the ultimate reality underlying the whole visible world, thus the absolute or God. Brahman is indescribable, has no attributes, and can only be spoken of as 'not this; not that'.

Brahman/Brahmin

Priestly class, or first of the four classes in India. Their life is divided into four stages (ashramas). They are 'twice born', and at their initiation ceremony they are invested with sacred white threads, worn at all times from the left shoulder.

Brahmanas

Hindu texts which take the form of commentaries on or expositions of the Vedic hymns.

Brahmanda

Egg of Brahma. This is the Hindu name for the universe, which has twenty-one zones. There are six heavenly zones and then the earth; below these are seven regions of the nether world, Patala, where Nagas and mythical creatures dwell. Lower still are the seven zones of Naraka, hell or purgatory, each zone increasing in misery.

Brahmasutra

Collection of aphorisms about Brahman attributed to Badarayana which, with the *Upanishads*, forms the basis of Vedanta philosophy.

Brahma-vihara

Term used in Buddhism for four spiritual abodes or divine states of mind: metta (love), karuna (compassion), mudita (sympathetic joy) and upeksa (serenity).

Bran

Early Welsh deity, the son of Llyr.

Bread

Sometimes called the staff of life. The breaking of bread as a corporate act symbolizes friendship or brotherhood. Jesus Christ called himself the bread of life (John 6:35), and at the Last Supper he broke bread with his disciples (Mark 14:22). This

Brahma

is recalled in the Christian service of Holy Communion, in which bread (his body) is consecrated with wine (his blood) and distributed to the worshippers.

Brethren

Protestant sect which first appeared in Plymouth in 1830, under the leadership of B. W. Newton. They object to national Churches and also to other dissenting Churches, as they do not acknowledge any form of Church government, nor any office of ministry. They practise adult baptism, and their main service is usually a form of breaking of bread, to which all believers are welcome. In 1845 a split occurred, some Brethren under the leadership of John Darby demanding a definition of principles and a limitation of membership. The Darbyites have developed into the Strict or Exclusive Brethren, who reject any contact with other Christian bodies or membership of trade unions or professional bodies, and do not allow non-members to attend their services.

Brethren of the Common Life

Association founded in the Netherlands in the 14th century to foster Christian life and devotion among laymen who remained in their ordinary vocations. They put great emphasis on teaching, and their schools won a high reputation, including among their pupils Thomas à Kempis and Pope Hadrian VI.

Breviary

Prayer book containing the services of the Roman Catholic Church for every day of the year, as distinct from a missal, which contains the prayers and readings for the Mass.

Bridegroom

Second of the seven grades of Mithraic initiation. Protected by Venus.

Brigid

Celtic goddess of rivers and waters.

Brigid of Kildare, St

Early saint of the Irish Church.

Brindaban

See Vrindaban

Brownists

Followers of Robert Browne (1550–1663) who formed independent congregations in Norwich and elsewhere. Owing to persecution many of them migrated to the Netherlands, and they are regarded as the founders of the Congregational Church.

Brunner, Emil

(1889–1965) Swiss Protestant theologian who became Professor of Dogmatics at Zurich. Differing from Karl Barth, he taught that there is a certain knowledge of God available from the orders of creation, of which the family is an important example. He strongly supported inter-denominational and inter-faith dialogue, and one of his most important works was *The Mediator*.

Bruno, St

(1032–1101) Founder of the Carthusian order. He was educated in Cologne and became a canon there about 1057. In 1080 he laid plans for the Order. In 1090 he was summoned to Rome by Pope Urban II, who needed his counsel, and although he obeyed, he was allowed to found the monastery of La Torre, where he lived and died.

Buber, Martin

(1878–1965) Jewish Chasidic theologian. He was a native of Vienna and played an important part in the Zionist movement. His most influential book, which affected the thinking of many theologians, was *I and Thou*. In it he examines the relationship between man and things, which he terms the 'I–It' relationship; from this he sharply distinguishes the relationship between man and man and between man and God, which he terms the 'I–Thou' relationship.

Bucer, Martin

(1491–1551) Leading figure in the Protestant Reformation in Strasbourg. He was ordained priest within the Dominican order, but left to join Luther and was an active preacher throughout Alsace. His theological views moved closer to the teaching of Zwingli, and in 1549 he came to England, where he was made Regius Professor of Divinity at Cambridge and helped Archbishop Cranmer in the preparation of the *Book of Common Prayer*.

Buddha (Tibet, 14th century)

Bull roarer

Buddha

Title meaning the 'enlightened one' assumed by Gautama Siddhartha after his enlightenment *c.* 531 BCE. Mahayana Buddhism recognizes more than one buddha, but not more than one alive at the same time.

Buddha-dhamma

Term used in Theravada Buddhism to indicate the content of the teaching of the Buddha.

Buddha-sasana

Term used in Theravada Buddhism to indicate the discipline taught by the Buddha.

Buk

Name used by the Nuer tribe for a female spirit, mother of Deng.

Bull

1. Among many peoples this animal has been a symbol of virility and strength and power. In Egypt, Amen-Ra was called the Bull of Heliopolis. In Sumeria, Enlil was a bull god, and in the Hindu *Rig-Veda*, some hymns are devoted to bull gods. In Crete there was the myth of the fierce minotaur, half man, half bull, that was slain by Theseus, and also the semi-religious practice of bull jumping. In Rome Mithraism gave a central place to the bull in its ritual.

2. Papal edict sent to the Churches of the Roman Catholic Communion containing a decree, order or decision which the faithful are expected to accept. The name comes from the Latin word *bulla* (seal), since a lead seal was formerly affixed to the document.

Bull Roarer

Long thin blade to which a cord is fastened. When whirled in the air, it produces a deep sound which is interpreted by the aborigines of Australia as the voice of a supernatural being.

Bulla

Amulet in the shape of a phallus often worn by adolescent boys in classical Rome.

Bultmann, Rudolf

(1884–1977)   German Protestant theologian, Professor of NT studies at Marburg, who emphasized a system of study entitled 'Demythologization'. He believed that the Gospels are based on a mythical concept of the universe, and that all elements of myth must be eliminated before the significance of the Gospels can be discovered.

Bundahishn

Zoroastrian religious document containing an account of the creation and structure of the world.

Bunka-no-hi-culture Day

Japanese national holiday to emphasize the importance of promoting reading and all forms of culture.

Bunyan, John

(1628–1688)   Author of *The Pilgrim's Progress*. Little is known of his early life except that he was born in Bedfordshire and became a brazier or tinker. Later he became an Independent preacher and was imprisoned by the Royalists, during which time he began his writing.

Burial

The disposal of a body after death is nearly always attended by ritual and ceremony. Burial in the ground, usually in an area specially reserved for this, has been the most widespread custom, though in some areas and periods caves have been used. For a modern Christian burial the corpse is normally placed in a coffin, and a committal service is read by a priest or a minister as the coffin is lowered into the ground.

Burka (A)

Veil or covering worn by some Muslim women to prevent men, other than their husbands, from seeing them. This custom is not so widely practised now as Muslim women in urban areas tend to adopt Western fashions.

Burse

Case made of two squares of stiffened material (about 23 cm square) in one of the Christian liturgical colours. It holds the corporal (a white linen cloth on which the bread for Holy Communion is placed) and is laid on top of the chalice when the priest carries the Eucharistic vessels from the sacristy to the altar.

Bushido (J)

Lit. 'military knightly habits'. Word used to describe the training and ethics of the feudal Samurai warriors of Japan.

Buto

Ancient snake goddess of the Egyptian Delta. Represented by a uraeus, she was associated with Horus and Osiris and was regarded as the guardian of Lower Egypt.

Byzantium

Ancient Greek city which the Emperor Constantine made his capital city in 330 CE, changing its name to Constantinople. At the council held there in 381 the bishop of the city was given pre-eminence immediately after the Pope, and in 451 he was granted the title 'Patriarch'. The city

Muslim woman covered by a burka

contained the magnificent Church of St Sophia, one of the largest in the world. Constantinople remained the capital of the Eastern Empire until 1453, when it was captured by the Turks, who converted St Sophia into a mosque. The city was renamed Istanbul in 1923.

Cabala

See Kabbalah

Caedmon

First English Christian poet (d. 680 CE). He was a tenant on the Abbey land at Whitby and claimed to have had a vision which inspired him to the praise of God. Instructed by the monks, he wrote hymns and verse paraphrases of the Scriptures in Anglo-Saxon.

Caiaphas

Jewish high priest, son-in-law of the previous high priest, Annas. He conducted the first trial of Jesus (Matthew 26:57) and demanded that Pilate should issue the death sentence. He was appointed in 18 CE and deposed in 37 CE.

Cain

Eldest son of Adam and Eve, described in Genesis 4:8 as the first murderer. When his brother Abel's sacrificial offering of a lamb was accepted by the Lord and his own offering of grain was rejected, Cain was jealous and angry, and killed his brother. This story probably reflects the early animosity between arable farmers and nomadic keepers of flocks and herds.

Caitanya

Hindu Vaisnavite reformer who lived in Bengal from 1485 to 1533. He was famous for his devotion to Krishna, and was regarded by his followers as an avatar of Vishnu.

Cak

Term used by the Nuer tribe of Africa for 'creation', the material world known to the senses.

Caliph

Title derived from the Arabic word *kalifa* (successor) and used to indicate the chief defender of the Islamic faith. Sunni Muslims regard Abu Bakr as the first Caliph in Medina, but Shiah Muslims reject the first three and start with Ali. The Abbasid caliphate founded Baghdad in 750 CE and remained there until 1258, when they transferred to Cairo. In 1517 the Turks forcibly removed the Caliph to Istanbul, where the caliphate remained until it was abolished by the Turkish National Assembly in 1924.

Calvary

Place where Jesus was crucified. The name derives from the Latin *calvaria* (skull; in Hebrew, *golgotha*), possibly because skulls of executed criminals were to be found there, or because the site is skull-shaped. The name is mentioned only in the Authorized Version of Luke 23:23, and the exact site is unknown. An ancient tradition locates it where the Church of the Holy Sepulchre now stands.

Calvin, John

(1509–1564)   French reformer and theologian. He studied theology and law in France, but persecution caused him to flee to Basle in Switzerland. In 1536 he accepted an invitation to be preacher and professor of theology in Geneva, where he remained for the rest of his life, apart from three years in Strasbourg. His book *The Institutes of the Christian Religion* has been one of the most influential theological works in the Reformed Churches.

Calvinism

School of Protestant theology based on the teaching of John Calvin and particularly stressing predestination, election, original sin and total depravity. This is the theological outlook accepted among Baptists, Presbyterians and the Reformed Churches of France, Holland and Switzerland.

Campanile

Church bell-tower, especially one that is a separate, detached building. This originated in Italy, and the earliest examples, from the 6th century, are in Ravenna. The best known is probably the Leaning Tower of Pisa.

Cana

Village near the Sea of Galilee where Jesus performed his first miracle of changing water into wine (John 2:1–11).

Canaan

Land, later known as Palestine, to which Abraham migrated from Ur of the Chaldees, and which the Israelites occupied after the Exodus from Egypt, settling in twelve tribal divisions.

Candlemas

Festival observed in the Christian Church on 2 February. The name derives from the practice of blessing the supply of candles to be used in church during the year, and distributing lighted candles to the congregation. This recalls an alternative name for the festival in the Anglican Calendar, the Presentation of Christ in the Temple, which commemorates Christ as the true light of the world. In the Roman Catholic calendar the festival is known as the Purification of the Blessed Virgin Mary.

Candles

Candles are very commonly used in religious services as a symbol of light. In Anglican and Roman Catholic churches they are placed on the altar during liturgical services, and often candles are lit at shrines to symbolize prayers or votive offerings. The Jewish Sabbath is inaugurated by the lighting of candles at the beginning of a service in the home, and is ended by the extinction of the Havdalah candle in a goblet of wine.

Canon

1. Priest who is a member of the chapter of a cathedral or collegiate church. In the Church of England, the residentiary canons at a chapter meeting elect the Crown's nominee to the bishopric.
2. The Canon of the Mass is the consecratory prayer in the Roman Catholic Mass containing the words of Institution. It follows the Preface and Sanctus, and in the Latin text begins with the words 'Te igitur'. The Canon consists of a number of short prayers recited without pause.
3. Musical composition in which the different parts take up the same theme successively in strict imitation.

John Calvin

Campanile: the Leaning Tower of Pisa

Canon Law

Corpus of ecclesiastical laws concerning faith and morals issued by councils or synods of the Catholic Church. The Corpus Juris Canonici approved by Pope Gregory IX in 1227 remained in force in the Roman Catholic Church until 1917, when it was replaced by the Codex Juris Canonici. The canon law of the Church of England was approved by Parliament in 1603, and was amended in certain details in 1947.

Canon of Scripture

List of books recognized by a religious community as authoritative and to be used in public worship. The Jewish community accepts the tripartite Canon of Law, Prophets and Writings. The Christian Church accepts this plus the twenty-seven books of the NT. Buddhist communities accept the *Tripitaka*, Hindus distinguish between sruti (revealed, e.g. the *Upanishads*) and smriti (remembered, e.g. the *Bhagavadgita*). Muslims recognize the Qur'an, and Sikhs the *Guru Granth Sahib* as authoritative.

Canonization

Solemn act in the Roman Catholic Church by which the Pope decrees that a holy man or woman should be included in the list or canon of the saints. The examination of the propriety of canonizing a particular person is often a long process during the course of which he or she may first be venerated and called 'Venerable', then beatified and called 'Blessed', and finally canonized and called 'Saint'.

Canopy

1. The huppah, a covering on four posts, held over a Jewish bride and bridegroom during the wedding ceremony.
2. Awning carried over the Blessed Sacrament in processions on Corpus Christi Day and similar occasions.

Cantate Domino

Title of Psalm 98, being its first words in the Latin version. In the Anglican *Book of Common Prayer* it is printed as an alternative to the Magnificat in the order for Evensong.

Canterbury

The Diocese of Canterbury dates from the arrival of Augustine in 597 CE, and the Cathedral is the mother church of the Anglican Communion. The Archbishop of Canterbury is the Primate of All England.

Canterbury Tales

Collection of stories written by the English poet Geoffrey Chaucer (1340–1400). The *Prologue* is a long poem introducing the members of the pilgrimage from Southwark to Canterbury. After this, different characters tell stories to entertain the company during their journeying. They reveal a great deal about society, religion and the Church in the 14th century.

Canticles

Songs or prayers derived from biblical writings, other than the Psalms, which are sung at various liturgical church services. Examples are the Benedicite, Magnificat and Nunc Dimittis.

Cappadocian Fathers

Three teachers of Christian theology in the 4th century: Basil the Great, Gregory of Nazianzus and Gregory of Nyssa. They were the chief exponents of Christian orthodoxy, and they successfully opposed the Arian heresy at the Council of Constantinople in 381 CE.

Capuchins

Offshoot of the Franciscan order founded about 1550 by Matteo di Bassi. It places strong emphasis on poverty and austerity, and has been active in preaching and missionary work, especially among the poor.

Cardinal

Term first used of any priest attached to a church, then limited to priests in charge of churches in Rome, and now used of the most important bishops of the Roman Catholic Church, who form the College of Cardinals. They are the Pope's counsellors and reside in Rome unless they are the presiding bishop of the Roman Catholic Church in another country. They are given the title 'Eminence', and when there is a vacancy in the Apostolic See, they meet in secret conclave to elect a new Pope.

Cargo Cults

Religious manifestations that have occurred in the Pacific islands of Melanesia. The main feature is the rise or arrival of a prophetic type of leader who promises the early coming of a saviour, usually on a ship or plane loaded with consumer goods such as radios, furniture or canned food. When the promised day passes, the prophet usually sets another date, explaining that he has made a miscalculation.

Carmel

High ridge in Israel, overlooking the modern port of Haifa, where Elijah overthrew the prophets of Baal, after offering sacrifice to the God of Israel (1 Kings 18). A Christian church was built there about 500 CE, and in 1154 it became the home of the Order of Our Lady of Carmel (Carmelites).

Carmelites

Christian monastic order founded in Palestine in 1154 by St Berthold. It emphasizes poverty, solitude and asceticism, and abstinence from meat. Because of their white mantles they were known as the White Friars. The women's order was founded in 1452 to foster the contemplative life. The order has produced some great mystics, including St Teresa and St John of the Cross.

Carol

Song of joy, originally accompanied by a dance. The word is now generally used of popular hymns or religious songs sung at Christmastide.

Carthusians

Strictly contemplative order of Christian monks founded in 1084 by St Bruno. The monks are vowed to renunciation of the world, and to living in silence and separately in their own lodgings, meeting only for the Offices and Mass. Their mother house is at La Grande Chartreuse, near Grenoble.

Cassock

Long robe worn by clergy. A black cassock is the official dress of Roman Catholic priests in church and in their parishes. Bishops wear purple cassocks, cardinals red, and the Pope white.

Caste

Castes are division or groups within Indian society. They are not the same as the four classes or varnas, but arose as a result of the mutual contact of many tribal and other groups with endogamous or caste-exclusive traditions. Throughout India there are many hundreds of castes and subcastes.

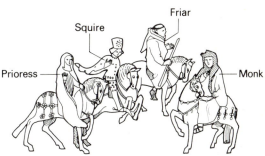

Four of the pilgrims who appear in *Canterbury Tales*

Castor and Pollux

Brothers known as the Dioscuri, the sons of Zeus, or the heavenly twins. Many legends were told about them, some with conflicting details. The commonest is that they were the sons of Zeus and Leda, born from the same egg. Castor, skilled with horses, was mortal; Pollux, a skilled boxer, was immortal. When Castor died in battle, Pollux asked Zeus to allow him to share his fate, and Zeus rewarded them both by placing them among the stars as Gemini.

Casuistry

Ability to bring general moral principles to bear upon particular cases. In Catholic moral theology, this is linked with the practice of the confessional, where the priest has to decide, for example, if the sin confessed is mortal or venial, and the circumstances aggravating or extenuating.

Priest wearing a cassock

Cat

Cats have always roused strong emotions and have long-standing religious associations. In Egypt the cat goddess was Bast or Bubastis, and in Rome, Diana was sometimes portrayed in cat form because they were both linked with the moon. The cat fell from grace because it became associated with witches as their familiar, and in some countries the black cat is regarded as the embodiment of Satan, who landed in a blackberry bush after being thrown out of heaven, though in other countries it is a symbol of good luck.

Catacombs

Burial places used by the early Christian Church. They were situated outside the city (notably at Rome), and consisted of underground labyrinths of galleries with niches hollowed out of the soft rock in which corpses were sealed. They were also used secretly for worship.

Catafalque

Small platform or stage covered with a pall for the coffin or effigy of a deceased person during the funeral service, usually a Requiem Mass.

Catechesis

Instruction given to Christian catechumens in the early Church in preparation for baptism. It is also used to describe books containing such instructions.

Catechism

Originally used of oral instruction in preparation for baptism, this term is now used of elementary introductions to the faith, often in the form of question and answer. There are examples in the Anglican *Book of Common Prayer* and the *Larger Catechism* of the Presbyterian Church.

Catechumen

Person undergoing training or instruction in preparation for baptism in the Christian Church. In the Apostolic Church catechumens were allowed to join the congregation at the beginning of the service, but went out before the Canon of the Eucharist began.

Cathars

Religious sect in N. Italy and S. France in the 12th and 13th centuries, also known as the Albigensians. Their central rite was baptism with the Spirit; their teaching was a form of dualism and they won hundreds of converts. To combat them, the Catholic Church set up the Inquisition and caused many to be tortured and brutally put to death.

Egyptian mummy of a cat

Cathedral

Church which contains the throne *(cathedra)* of the bishop of the diocese, hence the mother church of the diocese.

Catherine, St

(1347–1380) Christian nun. Born in Siena, from an early age she demonstrated a fanatical religious zeal and experienced heavenly visions and voices. Popes sought her advice, and she was canonized in 1461, eighty-one years after her death.

Catholic

Derived from a Greek root meaning 'universal', this word was used in Christian literature by St Ignatius of Antioch. Before the Reformation it was applied to the universal Church and its doctrine. Since the Reformation it has usually been applied to the Roman Catholic Church and faith as distinct from Protestantism. The Vincentian Canon, drawn up by Vincent of Lerins *c.* 450 CE, defined Catholic belief as 'what has been believed everywhere, always and by everybody'.

Caunri

Most important day in Hindu marriage ritual, when the bride and bridegroom walk seven times round the sacred fire, blessed by the priest.

Cautes/Cautopates

Terms used in Mithraism for torch-bearers portrayed in reliefs. Cautes holds an upturned torch;

Cautopates holds a downturned torch. They symbolize the rising and setting sun, or birth and death.

Cecilia, St

Patron saint of music. She was a Roman matron of saintly character, who was martyred early in the 3rd century. Her relics were discovered in the catacombs by Pope Paschal I (820 CE) and transferred to the church in Rome which bears her name. Her feast-day is 22 November.

Celibacy

In religious terms this is the acceptance of the unmarried state as a vocation to preserve ritual purity. It has always been highly regarded by the Roman Catholic Church, and at the Council of Trent was made compulsory for clergy.

Celsus

Pagan philosopher whose attack on Christianity *True Discourse* (180 CE) is known only from quotations in a reply *Contra Celsum* written by Origen. Celsus praised Christian moral standards, but objected to the doctrines of the Incarnation and Crucifixion and the claims of the Church to be the channel of salvation.

Celtic Church

Church which existed in the British Isles before the mission from Rome led by Augustine in 596 CE. Little is known of its strength or its leaders, as the Saxon invasions of the 5th century destroyed churches and records. At the Synod of Whitby in 664 English Christians made their submission to Rome, but the Celtic tradition lingered on in the North and in Wales and Ireland.

Censer

See Thurible

Cerberus

Dog which guarded the entrance to Hades. Early poets, such as Hesiod, described him as having fifty or more heads, but later writers described him as having three heads and the tail of a serpent.

Ceres

Roman spiritual power of growth in corn, identified with the Greek goddess Demeter.

Cetana

Term used in Buddhist teaching for volition, one of the factors of consciousness.

Chaba

Title used by the Ila tribe of Africa for God, meaning 'giver'.

Chac

Rain and vegetation god of the Maya of Central America. He was probably their most popular deity.

Chalcedon, Council of

Fourth Ecumenical Council of the Christian Church (451 CE), which issued an important definition. This reaffirmed the title 'Theotokos' (Mother of God) for the Virgin Mary, and affirmed concerning Jesus Christ the existence of one person in two natures which are united unconfusedly, unchangeably, indivisibly and inseparably.

Chalice

Cup or goblet, customarily of silver, used in the Christian Church to contain the wine consecrated in the Eucharist.

Ch'an (C)

See Zen

Chalice

Chancel

Term now used of the area of a church to the east of the nave. Originally it was restricted to the sanctuary, but was extended to include the choir. In medieval times the chancel was often separated from the nave by a screen, as the sanctuary is today in Orthodox churches.

Chandogya Upanishad

One of the earliest upanishads, part of the *Sama-veda*, named after the priests who chanted texts. It begins by recommending meditation on the sacred syllable 'Om' and its object is to explain the various meanings which the syllable may assume in the mind of a devotee until the highest meaning is reached, viz. Brahman, the intelligent cause of the universe.

Chantry

Benefice used to pay a priest to say Masses for the soul of the chantry founder, or the chapel in which the Mass was said. These were numerous in the 14th and 15th centuries and chantry priests were often local schoolmasters. In 1547 all chantries were suppressed and their endowments were applied to public funds, some being used to found grammar schools.

Chanukkah (H)

Feast of Dedication celebrated by Jews on 25 Kislev, commemorating the achievement of Judas Maccabaeus in defeating Antiochus V Epiphanes and rededicating the Temple in 165 BCE. It is also known as the Feast of Lights, from the use of a candelabrum with eight branches and an additional light from which the others are lit on the eight days of the Feast, recalling the miraculous provision of oil in the Temple for eight days on the first occasion of its celebration.

Chapel

Originally a structure in which the kings of France housed the cape *(capella)* of St Martin. The word was later applied to any shrine containing relics, and then by extension to small places of worship attached to schools or colleges. In England it is often used of Nonconformist places of worship to distinguish them from parish churches.

Chapter

Originally a section of a monastic rule read daily in a monastery. It was then extended to mean the members of a religious house meeting for instruction and discussion. It is now also used for the corporate body responsible for the organization of a cathedral, under a dean or provost.

Charismatic

Term indicating a person or object possessing spiritual gifts or the power to inspire followers with devotion and enthusiasm. It is often applied to a religious leader or to one who claims to have received religious insight or inspiration, and to have the gift of healing or speaking in tongues.

Charity

In Christian teaching, love of one's fellow men, the greatest of the three theological virtues (faith, hope and charity). It was specially commended by St Paul in 1 Corinthians 13. It is a vital element in the life of the Jewish community, and in the form of almsgiving is one of the Five Pillars of Islam. Charitable provision for the needs of monks is a duty imposed upon the faithful laity in Buddhism.

Charlemagne

(742–814 CE) First Holy Roman Emperor. As King of the Franks he subdued Lombardy, Saxony and parts of Spain, and on Christmas Day 800 he was crowned Emperor by Pope Leo III.

Charoset (H)

Mixture of chopped fruits and wine made into a chutney used in the Jewish Seder of the Passover. It symbolizes the mortar used by the Israelites in Egypt when they had to make bricks for their masters.

Charterhouse

Religious house belonging to the Carthusian order. A charterhouse was established in London in 1371, and on the site a community was gradually built up including a chapel, almshouse and school.

Chasidim (H)

1. Movement in the 2nd century BCE opposed to the Hellenizing of Jewish life and practice. The Essenes and the Pharisees were offshoots of the Chasidim.

2. Jewish movement which arose in the mid-eighteenth century, led by Israel ben Eliezer (1700–1760), and stressed the power of simple, joyful piety rather than the intellectual requirements of Talmudic learning. It has strong mystic inclinations and its members have a distinct hair-style, dress and worship.

Chasuble

Derived from the Latin *casula* (cottage), it is used for the outermost vestment worn by a priest at the celebration of the Christian Eucharist. The modern shape is almost circular with a hole in the centre for the head. The material is usually linen or damask in one of the liturgical colours, according to the season of the church year.

Chanukkah: lighting the candles (New York)

Priest wearing a chasuble

Chatavan

Hindu rite observed six months after the birth of a child, often linked with the name-giving ceremony.

Chathi

Hindu ceremony observed on the sixth day after the birth of a child, to mark the beginning of the mother's return from a state of ritual impurity.

Chazenut (H)

Cantorial art which includes the correct chanting of the scripture in a Jewish synagogue.

Chela

Indian village practitioner who seeks to overcome the effects of sorcery by exorcism and the use of mantras. In some areas he is called an ojha.

Chemosh

God of the Moabite tribe on the east bank of the Jordan (Numbers 21:29).

Cherubim

Plural of 'cherub'. In the OT these are depicted as celestial beings. They guarded the Tree of Life (Genesis 3:24) and the Ark of the Covenant (Exodus 25:18), and figures of cherubim were placed in Solomon's Temple (1 Kings 6:26).

Chih

Term meaning 'wisdom', reflected in the sense of right and wrong. It is one of the cardinal virtues recognized by Confucianism.

Children of God

Group founded in California by David Berg in 1968 as an offshoot of the 'Jesus Revolution'. The movement spread rapidly in America and now has 'colonies' in sixty countries. It is organized in strictly communal style and members on joining give up all possessions, in accordance with the instructions of Jesus, and take a new biblical name. They believe that Jesus was the Son of God, a committed revolutionary, and that we are living in the last days when capitalism and communism will destroy each other, making way for godly socialism.

Chilenga

Title used by the Ila tribe of Africa for God, meaning 'Creator'.

Chiliasm

See Millenarianism

Chinese New Year

Family festival observed on the first day of the first month of the lunar calendar. Celebrations with presents, parties and fireworks continue for fifteen days.

Chinvat Bridge

In Zoroastrian teaching the Bridge of the Separator across which the souls of the dead are led after judgement. It leads the righteous to heaven but the wicked into the abyss of hell. It is sometimes described as a knife-edge bridge off which the wicked fall.

Chowri being waved over the *Guru Granth Sahib* in the Golden Temple, Amritsar

Choir

1. Body of singers trained to lead the worship in Christian churches. In the early Church the music was plainsong or a Gregorian Chant. The use of harmony came in the 15th century, and in the 18th century the music used in cathedrals and large churches was often so complex that professional choirs were needed. Choirs were often placed in a gallery at the west end.

2. Part of a church containing the seats of the clergy, between the altar and the nave. In most Anglican cathedrals and parish churches the body of singers also has stalls there and it is almost coterminous with the chancel.

Chowri

Whisk made of yak's hair, a sign of respect and dignity, waved continuously over the *Guru Granth Sahib*, the Sikh holy book, during the course of a service.

Chrism

Sacramental use of consecrated oil practised in the Roman Catholic and Orthodox Churches in baptism, confirmation and ordination. In the Church of England it is found in the coronation service, and is now frequently practised in the anointing of the sick.

Christadelphians

Religious body founded by John Thomas in 1848. They believe that they have revived the practices of the Church of the 1st century, so have no paid ministry. Their distinguishing doctrine is that at the second coming of Christ, God will raise up all who have loved him and allow them to dwell for ever in this world. The rest of mankind will perish absolutely.

Christening

See Baptism

Christian Aid Week

Week in May sponsored by the British Council of Churches. Special services are held, and fund-raising efforts promoted to support charitable causes in various parts of the world.

Christian Science

Movement founded by the publication of *Science and Health*, by Mary Baker Eddy, in 1875. It emphasizes the goodness of God and the absoluteness of the Spirit. The material world is considered to be an illusion, and man is healed of sickness by learning that there is nothing to heal. The Christian doctrine of the Trinity is rejected, but each man should endeavour to realize his own divine sonship. There is no ordained ministry, but the movement recognizes a number of full-time practitioners, services being conducted by Readers. The movement is officially entitled the Church of Christ Scientist, controlled from the mother church in Boston, Massachusetts, and it publishes an international daily paper of considerable influence: *The Christian Science Monitor*.

Christian Socialism

Movement aiming at social reform promoted by members of the Church of England in the 19th century to counteract the influence of Utilitarian doctrines. Among the leaders were F. D. Maurice and Charles Kingsley, who hoped to improve the conditions of the workmen of England. They organized evening classes and working-men's colleges, but they were disappointed by the poor response, and the movement faded out in the preoccupation of the country with the Crimean war, but it had an influence on the formation of trade unions.

Christianity

Religion of the followers of Jesus Christ. The name 'Christian' was first used at Antioch about 40 CE (Acts 11:26) and the designation 'Christianity' was current in Rome during the Neronic persecution of 64. At that time it was regarded as a quasi-political movement. It is now applied to the faith of all Churches or denominations which acknowledge Jesus Christ as Son of God, Lord and Saviour.

Christmas

Christian festival celebrating the birth of Jesus Christ. The date, 25 December, appears to have links with the Yule feast of the Norsemen and the Roman festival of Saturnalia. The Christmas tree is said to have been introduced into England by Prince Albert in 1841 from his native Germany, where it was used in a number of winter celebrations.

Christology

Section of Christian theology which deals with the significance of Christ for the Church. It is concerned with his birth, person, nature and claims or standing as man and as God, Messiah, Son of Man, Son of God and Saviour.

Christopher, St

The name means 'one who bore Christ' and he may be a legendary figure, though according to tradition he was martyred in Asia Minor in the 3rd century. He was one of the best-known saints of the Middle Ages because it was a common custom to have a mural opposite the entrance door showing him as a big, strong man carrying the Christ Child. He is the patron saint of travellers.

Chronicles, Books of

Two books in the Hebrew Bible, traditionally ascribed to Ezra. After an introduction concerning the twelve tribes of Israel, they concentrate on a history of the Kingdom of Judah from the reign of David to its destruction by Nebuchadrezzar. It is an ecclesiastical history, mainly interested in the House of David and the Temple.

Chung Yung

Title of one of the books of Confucius, meaning *Doctrine of the Mean.* It is a philosophical work considering the relationship of human nature to the moral order of the universe.

Church

Term used to describe the whole community of Christians throughout the world, or various communities of Christians organized in different ways according to their interpretations of the instructions of Jesus Christ to his disciples. The term is also used to refer to the buildings in which Christians carry out their worship.

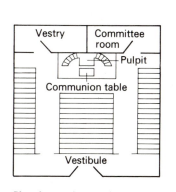

Plan of a typical Nonconformist church

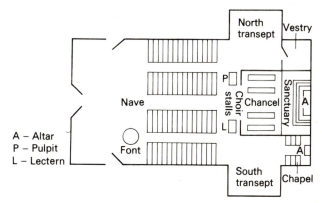

Plan of a typical Anglican parish church

Church Army

Anglican evangelical organization founded in 1882 by Prebendary Wilson Carlile, on the model of the Salvation Army. In addition to evangelical work it undertakes social and moral welfare work.

Church of England

See Anglican Communion

Church of Jesus Christ of the Latter Day Saints

Sect founded in 1830 by Joseph Smith in the United States. They accept the Bible and the Book of Mormon, which Smith claimed was revealed to him on gold plates by an angel. They set up a community at Salt Lake City in Utah, where they were dubbed Mormons, the name by which they are generally known. At first they were subject to harsh persecution because they practised polygamy. This practice has ceased and they are now a highly respected community which has spread throughout the world because of their great missionary zeal.

Church of South India

Church numbering about one million members which was inaugurated on 27 September 1947 by the union of three groups of Christians: (1) four dioceses of the Anglican Church of India, Burma and Ceylon; (2) the South India Province of the Methodist Church; (3) the South India United Church. It is based doctrinally on the Lambeth Quadrilateral of 1888 and, though not fully Episcopal, it claims to preserve Congregational, Presbyterian and Episcopal elements. It has limited intercommunion with the Church of England.

Churching of Women

Form of thanksgiving by women after childbirth. The custom is probably based on the ancient Jewish rite of Purification (Leviticus 12:6), but the present Church of England and Roman Catholic forms of service are based on the Sarum rite.

Ciborium

Vessel, like a chalice with a lid, used to hold the bread or wafers consecrated in the Christian Eucharist.

Circumcision

Religious rite (called Berit Milah) in Judaism of cutting the foreskin of boys on the eighth day after birth, performed by a qualified mohel. It is also practised by most Muslims and by some Christians, though it is not prescribed in the Qur'an or in the NT. It is also a practice in traditional African religion.

Cistercians

Order of White Monks, founded at Citeaux in 1098 by Robert de Molesme. By the end of the 13th century there were about seven hundred Cistercian houses in Western Europe. Their order emphasized secluded communal intercession and adoration. Their houses were plain, unadorned and in secluded areas, and their life was planned on a strict form of the Benedictine rule.

Cit

Hindu term for consciousness, one of three essential properties of the eternal self, with ananda and sat.

Cittamatra

Term used in Hinduism to denote the aspect of nirvana as spirit or mind or nothing-but-thought.

Clement of Alexandria

(150–215 CE) Christian theologian who was equally at home in biblical and classical studies. He was the first to welcome Greek philosophy as an ally rather than an enemy of Christianity, believing that the Logos taught Hebrew prophets and Greek philosophers before being incarnate in Christ. His orthodoxy was questioned because he did not condemn Gnosticism but said that the Christian is the true Gnostic.

Codex

Manuscript in volume form as distinct from the earlier form of a scroll. Modern translations of the Bible depend to a great extent on the *Codex Vaticanus* in the Vatican Library and the *Codex Sinaiticus* in the British Museum. Both are written in Greek and probably date from the 4th century.

Col

Nuer spirit associated with rain and lightning.

Coliseum

Great amphitheatre in Rome begun by Vespasian in 72 CE and completed by Titus in 80 CE. It could hold over 50 000 spectators and was used for gladiator contests and wild-beast fights. Many Christians were mauled to death by animals in the arena.

Collect

Short prayer usually containing an invocation, a petition and an ascription of glory to God. The Roman Catholic Missal and the Anglican Prayer Book contain different collects for every Sunday and Saint's Day in the Christian year.

College

1. Community of priests in classical Rome responsible for religious formulae and observances.
2. Community of students living under a master and tutors and forming a constituent part of a university.
3. Order of Roman Catholic cardinals, responsible for electing a new Pope.

Colossians, Epistle to the

One of St Paul's letters in the NT. It was written to combat false teaching that had infiltrated into the Church. St Paul offers positive teaching, emphasizing the greatness and glory of Christ, who is the Head of the Church.

Colosseum

See Coliseum

Colours

Symbolic meanings are associated with colours in many communities. In Christianity the liturgical colours are green, the colour of nature, for Trinity, purple, the colour of penitence, for Advent and Lent, white, the colour of purity, for Easter and Christmas, and red, the colour of blood, for Saints' Days. Black, associated with darkness, is the colour for mourning and funerals. White is the colour for weddings and baptisms. Blue is the colour for festivals of the Virgin Mary, possibly because she is regarded as the Queen of Heaven. Buddhist monks wear robes of saffron-yellow, the colour of the sun, to symbolize light or enlightenment. Hindus and Sikhs wear red for weddings and white for funerals.

Comforter

Title of the Holy Ghost in John 14–16 in the Authorized and Revised Versions. The Greek word is *paraclete*, of which the more usual translation is 'advocate' or 'helper'.

Commendam

Granting of revenues of an ecclesiastical benefice to an individual temporarily, during a vacancy. This practice was abolished in England by an Act of Parliament in 1836.

Communion

The order for administering the Holy Communion in the Church of England was drawn up by Archbishop Cranmer, and in the first Prayer Book of 1549 it was entitled 'The Supper of the Lord and the Holy Communion, commonly called the Mass'. It contained a General Confession, Absolution, Prayer of Humble Access, Consecration, and Words of Administration. A distinctive feature of the Anglican Communion service is that the laity receive both bread and wine. (See also Eucharist, Holy Communion, Lord's Supper and Mass)

Communion of Saints

Ninth article of belief in the Apostles' Creed. The general interpretation takes it to mean the communion of each Christian with Christ and through him with all other Christians in heaven or earth. Others restrict the meaning to the fellowship of Christians on earth. It has also been suggested that 'saints' should be understood as a neuter, 'holy things', meaning the sharing of Christians in the Sacraments.

Communism

Political theory that all property should be vested in the community, each individual receiving according to his needs and working according to his capacity; in the teaching of Karl Marx it is a revolutionary movement seeking to establish the dictatorship of the proletariat.

Compline

Last of the canonical offices of the Western Church, said before retiring for the night. Some scholars think it was compiled by St Basil, but it is more likely that it was the work of St Benedict, who included it in his rule.

Compostella

City in N.W. Spain whose full name is Santiago de Compostella, because it is considered to be the burial place of St James the Apostle. The shrine of St James has been for centuries one of the most popular centres for Christian pilgrimage, and because pilgrims often picked up scallop shells from the beach nearby, the scallop became a badge or symbol worn by pilgrims in the Middle Ages.

Conclave

Locked apartment in which the Roman Catholic College of Cardinals is confined during their deliberations to elect a new Pope. This practice was adopted in 1271 and has been followed ever since.

Concupiscence

Term used in moral theology for an inordinate desire for temporal ends which has its seat in the senses. Its more general meaning is an immoderate desire to satisfy the sexual, physical appetites.

Confession

1. Acknowledgement of one's sins or guilt, made as a member of a congregation or privately to a priest in order to receive counsel, penance or absolution.

2. Profession of faith or a declaration of religious belief, e.g. the Augsburg Confession or the Westminster Confession.

Confirmation

Rite of admission into full communicant membership of the Christian Church, usually involving the laying on of hands by a bishop. It is believed to be the means of bestowing the Holy Spirit on the baptized and strengthening them for the profession and practice of their faith. In Roman Catholic theology it is described as one of the seven sacraments.

Confucius

Latinized form of K'ung Fu'tzu, Grand Master Kung, who was the greatest sage of China (551–479 BCE). His teachings are contained in the *Analects*, a book of twenty chapters, entitled *Lun Yu*, dealing mostly with filial piety and right conduct. He is said to have had three thousand pupils.

Confucius

Congé d'élire

Lit. 'permission to elect'. According to the Act of Supremacy 1559, when an English bishopric falls vacant the Sovereign issues a congé d'élire to the dean and chapter of the diocese, together with the name of a nominee. In the Middle Ages, failure to elect the royal nominee would have rendered them liable to the penalties of praemunire, but the penalty today is uncertain, as the situation has never arisen.

Consecration

Word used in several senses in the Christian Church:

1. The blessing of the bread and wine in the Prayer of Consecration in the Eucharist.

2. The raising of priests to the office of bishop by the laying on of hands of other bishops.

3. The blessing of a church or an altar or other church furnishings or vessels for divine service, usually performed by a bishop.

Consensus Tigurinus

Formula of faith agreed in 1549 by John Calvin, representing the French-speaking Swiss, and Henry Bullinger, representing the German-speaking Swiss followers of Zwingli. It was mostly concerned with the doctrine of the Eucharist.

Constance, Council of

Council (1413–1417) which brought to an end the Great Schism in the Roman Catholic Church. Two popes, John XXIII and Benedict XIII, were deposed and Gregory XII resigned, leaving the way clear for the Council to elect Odo Colonna, who took the name Martin V. This

Council also condemned the heresies of Wycliffe and Huss, and handed over the latter for execution.

Constantine

(247–337 CE) Roman Emperor who, after his victory at the Milvian Bridge in 312, declared Christianity a tolerated religion. In 325 he summoned the Council of Nicaea, which settled the Arian controversy within the Church.

Constantinople

See Byzantium

Consubstantiation

Doctrine of the Eucharist associated with Luther which holds that after consecration the substances of the body and blood of Christ and of the bread and wine coexist in union with each other.

Contemplation

Term used to describe non-discursive mental prayer; it is usually considered a more advanced form of spiritual exercise than meditation.

Convent

Building in which a religious community lives. Originally it applied to either male or female communities, but now it is usually restricted to houses of nuns.

Conversion

Although the word has been little used by Christian theologians, past or present, Catholic or Protestant, it stands for an important principle with two aspects. Within a religion such as Christianity it may mean the process of repentance, change and regeneration by which a person turns to God, which may be sudden and immediate or a slow gradual experience. Between religions it means a process of rejecting one and accepting another.

The Christian Church has a long history of missions seeking to convert people of other faiths, and at various times Islam has campaigned to win new followers. Judaism, Hinduism and Buddhism do not encourage conversion to the same extent.

Cope

Semicircular cloak worn at solemn ecclesiastical services in the Christian Church. In the Anglican Church this was authorized in the 1549 Prayer Book, forbidden by the 1552 Prayer Book, and permitted by the 1662 Prayer Book. It is now extensively used on festal and special occasions.

Copernicus, Nicolaus

(1473–1543) Astronomer and theologian. In a book written in 1530, *On the Revolutions of the Celestial Orbs*, he put forward the hypothesis that the sun is the centre of the universe, that the

Priest wearing a cope

planets revolve around it and that the earth revolves on its own axis. This was contrary to the teaching of the Catholic Church and his book was banned.

Corban

Semitic term with several meanings:
1. Word in the Hebrew Bible for any kind of sacrifice including a vow offering or something devoted to God.
2. Sacred treasury in which gifts for the Temple or for the poor were kept.
3. Word used in vows to indicate that what was consecrated to God could not be appropriated by another person.
4. In Islam, a sacrifice which is part of the Hajj (pilgrimage to Mecca).
5. In Islam, a prayer in the Friday service at a mosque.

Corinthians, Epistles to the

In the NT there are two epistles with this heading, but most scholars think that St Paul wrote four letters in the course of his ministry to the Corinthians. The first letter deals with divisions, immoralities and problems of a Christian Church in a heathen city, and culminates in a wonderful hymn of love (1 Corinthians 13). The second letter deals with further practical problems, the efforts of Titus to bring peace to the community, a collection for the poor in Jerusalem, and the possibility of a visit by St Paul himself.

Corn

This cereal has been cultivated for more than 7000 years, and because it is a basic human need it has been frequently associated with a protective deity, usually female, such as Demeter (Greek) and Ceres (Roman). In some parts of the world ploughing is associated with religious rites, and harvesting corn has universally been associated with rituals of thanksgiving and celebration of the power of life. In the form of bread, it plays a vital part in the Seder of the Jewish Passover and in the ritual of the Christian Eucharist.

Corporal

In the usage of the Western Church, this is a square piece of linen on which the bread and wine are placed to be consecrated at the Eucharist.

Corpus Christi

Lit. 'body of Christ'. This is a festival of the Roman Catholic Church, celebrated on the Thursday after Trinity Sunday, to emphasize the belief that Christ is substantially present in the consecrated Host, as taught in the doctrine of Transubstantiation. The festival is not included in the feast-days of the Anglican Church.

Cosmogony

Theory of the origin of the world. It may be speculative, scientific or theological, but is not necessarily linked with a belief in creation by God.

Cosmological Argument

Argument for the existence of God based on the existence of the world. It depends on the principle of causality, and maintains that no satisfactory explanation of experience can be given without assuming the existence of a self-sufficient primary cause.

Council

Within the Christian Church, an assembly of bishops for the maintenance of discipline and the promulgation of doctrine. Notable examples are the Council of Nicaea (325 CE), the Council of Chalcedon (451) and the Second Vatican Council (1962–1965).

Counter Reformation

General term for the reform movement within the Catholic Church at approximately the same time as the Protestant Reformation of Luther and Calvin. New, reformed religious orders such as the Capuchins, Theatines and Barnabites were founded in the early 16th century, and the Society of Jesus received papal recognition in 1540. Pope Paul III inaugurated the Council of Trent in 1545 and it remained in session until 1563, issuing decrees that reshaped the life of the Church.

Courier of the Sun

Sixth of the seven grades of Mithraic initiation; protected by the sun.

Coven

Gathering of witches. Traditionally a coven consists of thirteen witches, i.e. a leader representing the Devil with twelve followers, probably a black-magic imitation of the Last Supper.

Covenant

1. Agreement between men, or between men and God.
2. Promise made by God to grant certain blessings if the recipient keeps specified laws. The OT records a covenant *(berit)* with Noah, with Abraham, and with Israel at Sinai. The NT looks to a new covenant made through Christ with the Church.

Covenanters

Name given to Scottish Protestants who in 1638 signed a National Covenant protesting against the attempt by Charles I to introduce the English Prayer Book into Scotland. The English Parliament in 1643 made a Solemn League and Covenant with the Scots and even undertook to introduce Presbyterianism into England. After the death of Cromwell and the accession of Charles II, the Covenant was denounced by the English Parliament in 1662 and the dissenting ministers were persecuted under drastic penal laws. Many were executed or killed in raids by the army. Those who survived formed a sect which eventually joined the Free Church.

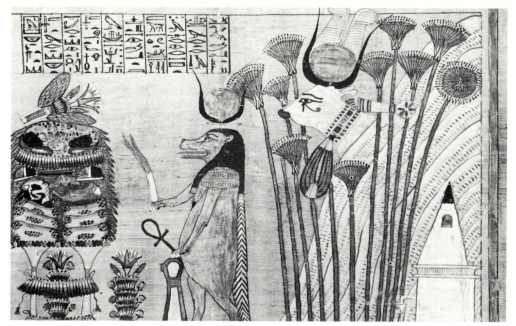

Egyptian goddess Hathor, in the form of a cow, with a god representing the Nile

Cow

For centuries this animal has been regarded as a symbol of fertility and life. In Egypt Hathor, the mother of the sun god, was depicted as a cow, as also was Nut, the sky goddess. In India and in Hinduism the cow is protected as a sacred animal, because it is the symbol of divine bounty in the earth, and all products of the cow must be treated with great care.

Cowl

Garment with a hood worn by most monastic orders. The hood is usually part of a cloak, but some orders wear a cowl which is a detachable hood.

Cowper Temple Clause

Important item in the history of religious education in England. When the Education Act of 1870 was under discussion, controversy raged among the Church of England, the Free Churches and teachers involved in religious education concerning the content and denominational bias of the subject in schools. The Cowper Temple Clause (clause 14 in the 1870 Act) enacts that in state schools 'no religious catechism or religious formulary which is distinctive of any particular denomination shall be taught'.

Coyolxauhqui

Lit. 'golden bells'. In Aztec mythology a name of the moon, who is portrayed with golden bells on her cheeks.

Cranmer, Thomas

(1489–1556)   Anglican divine who helped Henry VIII to obtain a divorce from Catherine of Aragon and was appointed Archbishop of Canterbury in 1532. He became an influential adviser of Edward VI, and was largely responsible for drawing up the Prayer Books of 1549 and 1552. He was burnt at the stake in the reign of Mary for denying the doctrine of Transubstantiation.

Creation Myths

Term applied to various versions of the account of the creation of the world. An ancient Egyptian myth tells of an act of creation by the male and female deities Shu and Tefnut, who had themselves been produced by Atum. A Sumerian myth tells how Enki created mankind out of clay models. The most famous creation myths are probably the Mesopotamian *Enuma Elish* and the Hebrew account in Genesis. The *Enuma Elish* tells how Marduk became leader of the gods, slew the goddess Tiamat and created the earth out of her body. The Genesis account tells how God brought order out of chaos and then created the earth, vegetation, animals and finally man.

Creed

Formal statement of religious belief. The earliest Christian creeds were short baptismal formulae, but early in the life of the Church the Apostles' Creed emerged, probably in Rome. The Nicene Creed was adopted at the Council of Nicaea in 325 CE and the Athanasian Creed was probably drawn up in the 5th century.

Cremation

Practice of disposing of the bodies of the dead by burning. This was carried out in classical Greece and Rome but fell into disuse in the Christian era. It was reintroduced into England in 1872 with the founding of the Cremation Society. It was decreed in a trial in 1884 that the cremation of a dead body did not constitute an offence, and in 1902 the Cremation Act gave official sanction to cremation. It is a regular practice in Hindu and Buddhist communities.

Crescent

Shape of the waxing moon, thus a symbol of increasing power. It was adopted as the badge of the Ottoman Turks, and has become the emblem of Islam.

Crib

Representation of the manger in which Mary placed Jesus (Luke 2:7). A crib, with figures of the Holy Family and shepherds, is often placed in churches on Christmas Eve and remains until the octave of the Epiphany (13 January). The first crib is said to have been introduced into the church at Greccio in 1223 by St Francis of Assisi.

Croesus

Last king of Lydia (560–546 BCE). Warned by an oracle that if he went into battle he would destroy a great empire, he promptly attacked Cyrus, King of Persia, and was utterly defeated.

Cromwell, Oliver

(1599–1658)   Soldier and politician, he became the leader of the Puritans. Elected M.P. for Cambridge in 1640, he immediately asserted the religious and political views of the Puritans. He regarded the Civil War of 1642 as a religious struggle, and saw that the Puritan cause could triumph only with the removal of the King, Charles I, who was executed in 1649. In 1653 Cromwell was installed as Lord Protector, and he did his best to reform the law, improve morals, and to further education throughout the land.

Cromwell, Thomas

(1485–1540)   Adviser to Henry VIII. He became an M.P. in 1523, and after the downfall of Wolsey was appointed Vicar General and ecclesiastical adviser to the King. In this capacity he instituted the Dissolution of the Monasteries, and was granted several of their estates. After he had arranged the marriage between Henry VIII and Anne of Cleves, which greatly annoyed the King, he was charged with treason and beheaded.

Crescent and star: the emblem of Islam

Thomas Cromwell (studio of Holbein)

Cross

Upright stake, usually with a cross-beam, used extensively by the Romans for the execution of criminals. Since the crucifixion of Jesus Christ, the cross has become a Christian symbol of the shame and humiliation that he suffered for mankind, and also of the glory and love of God which is revealed through his vicarious suffering on the cross. Prior to the Christian era, the equal-armed cross (sometimes surrounded by a circle) was a common symbol of the sun, while the crux ansata, a T-shaped cross with a handle on the top, was the Egyptian ankh, the symbol of life.

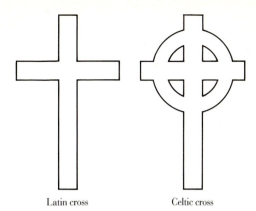

Latin cross   Celtic cross

Crown

Circular ornament, usually of gold, placed on the head to indicate supreme importance. This practice is now limited almost entirely to the remaining monarchs of the world. At one time the Pope wore a special tiarra known as the Triple Crown, but this has been discontinued. At weddings in the Orthodox Church crowns are held over the heads of the bride and bridegroom.

Crozier

Crook-shaped staff of office carried by bishops and abbots. Its origin may be traced to the rods used by Roman lictors and augurs, or to the shepherd's crook, symbolizing the bishop's office as chief pastor in his diocese, and remembering the title of Jesus as the Good Shepherd.

Crucifixion

Form of execution by fastening to a cross practised by the Assyrians and Carthaginians, and later adopted by the Romans when dealing with slaves and insurgents. It was abolished by Constantine. (See Cross for the Christian symbolism)

Crusades

Military endeavours by Christian nations of the West from the end of the 11th century till the 13th century to conquer Palestine and free Jerusalem from the Turks. Eight crusades are usually listed. The first started in 1096, and after many battles Jerusalem was captured in 1099. The third, in which Richard I of England took part, began in 1187 when Saladin captured Jerusalem and ended in 1192 with a truce between Saladin and Richard, giving Christian pilgrims free access to Jerusalem. The seventh (1249) and the eighth (1270) were led by Louis IX of France (St Louis), but had little effect other than an extension of the truce.

Crozier

Cuius Regio Eius Religio

Principle embodied in the Augsburg Agreement of 1555 which states that whoever has ruling power in a region has the right to decide the religion of that region. This was intended to give authority to those princes who had changed from the Catholic faith to Lutheranism. The principle was threatened by Emperor Ferdinand II in 1618, and this caused the Thirty Years War. At the end of the war, the Peace of Westphalia (1648) reaffirmed the principle, and extended it to Calvinist states.

Cult

System of religious worship. Devotion to a person or an object.

Cuong

Nuer term for righteousness or right conduct.

Cupid

Roman name of Eros, the god of love, the son of Aphrodite and Zeus. He is usually represented as a handsome boy, full of tricks, the constant companion of his mother.

Curail

In Hindu thought a female ghost.

Curate

The proper meaning of this title is a clergyman who has the cure of a parish, i.e. has the charge of it as rector or vicar. It is now more generally used to denote an assistant priest or one who looks after a parish during a vacancy.

Curia

Papal court and officers through whom the Roman Catholic Church is governed. It includes the various official congregations, tribunals and curial offices.

Cybele

Nature goddess of the Ancient Near East. She was worshipped with her son (or lover) Attis in rites involving great noise and frenzy led by eunuch priests. In Imperial Rome the cult was considered scandalous and was suppressed.

Cynics

In Greek, 'dogs'. Nickname given to the followers of Diogenes (400–325 BCE), who rejected morality and tried to live on nothing. Some were depraved beggars, but others were more noble characters.

Cyprian of Carthage

Pagan rhetorician who was converted to Christianity in 246 CE, and because of his great learning and the purity of his life, was elected Bishop of Carthage in 248. He lived during the fierce persecutions of the Emperor Decius and he was concerned at the ease with which lapsed Christians were received back into the Church; he demanded suitable penance and delay. In 258 Cyprian himself was arrested and after imprisonment was martyred.

Cyril of Alexandria

Cyril became Patriarch of Alexandria in 412 CE and is regarded as one of the strongest advocates of Trinitarian theology. At the Council of Ephesus in 431, he was instrumental in securing the condemnation of Nestorianism, which declared that there were two separate persons in the incarnate Christ. He insisted on the importance of the title 'Theotokos', applied to the Virgin Mary.

Cyrus I

Founder of the Persian Empire. In 559 BCE, he became King of Anshan; in 550 BCE, King of Media; in 547 BCE, King of Persia; in 538, he defeated Babylon and claimed the title 'King of all Lands'. He was killed in battle in 529 BCE. He showed a more humane attitude to conquered people, and allowed those Jews who so wished to return to Jerusalem from Babylon.

Dabistan

Mystical Parsee text which had some popularity in the 18th century until its claim to antiquity was shown to be spurious.

Dadgah

Zoroastrian term for the third grade of holy fire, which may be kept in the home or a temple.

Daena

Zoroastrian term for that part of man which is judged after death.

Daevas

Term used in Zoroastrian theology for evil spirits.

Dagda

The Great Father or the Good God of the Celts. Probably in origin he was a fertility god, but he is often depicted as a brave warrior.

Dagon

Ancient Mesopotamian god who was particularly worshipped by the Philistines and is mentioned in connection with them in the OT. The name may be derived from *dag* (fish) or from *dagan* (corn).

Dahej

Dowry paid by a Hindu bride's father to the groom's father; this is an important element in the marriage ritual.

Daijo Zen

Fourth of the five types of Zen: Great Vehicle (Mahayana) Zen. Meditation for the purpose of seeing into one's own nature.

Dakshina

Fee paid to an Indian purohit (family priest) for the performance of a religious ceremony.

Dalai Lama

Head of Tibetan Buddhism (now a refugee in India). Leader of the Yellow Hat Monks, he is regarded as the reincarnation of the Bodhisattva Chenresi (Avalokiteshvara).

Dalmatic

Vestment reaching to the knees worn over the alb by deacons at High Mass. It has two broad strips of material, coloured according to the ecclesiastical season, running from front to back over the shoulders. In England, a dalmatic is also worn by the Sovereign at the coronation service.

Damascus

Capital city of modern Syria. It appears to have been founded in the 2nd millennium BCE and was an important centre of trade in the time of Abraham. It was favourably situated near two rivers, the Abana and Pharpar, and was a communications centre, linking caravan routes in all directions. It is frequently mentioned in the Bible, perhaps most dramatically as the scene of the conversion to Christianity of Paul of Tarsus.

Priest wearing a dalmatic

Dan

1. Fifth son of the Israelite patriarch Jacob and first son of Bilhah, Rachel's maid.
2. Smallest of the twelve tribes of Israel. They first settled on the coastal plain, but were driven out and forced to migrate to the northern hill country.
3. Northernmost city of Canaan. Formerly Laish, it was renamed when the Danites conquered it on moving into the area.

Dana

Term used in Buddhism and Hinduism for the virtue of giving alms to the poor and needy, and particularly in Buddhism to the bhikkus. In Buddhism it is one of three acts of merit, the others being moral conduct and meditation.

Daniel

Chief character in a book in the Hebrew Bible of the same name. Faithful to his Jewish beliefs in the face of persecution, he became the chief adviser to King Darius.

Danu

Mother goddess of Celtic religion who presided over gods and men. She was associated with the hills and the earth, and the harvests were regarded as her gift.

Dar al-Harb (A)

Lit. 'house of war'. Term used by Muslims for those areas of mankind as yet unsubdued by Islam.

Dar al-Islam (A)

Lit. 'house of Islam'. Term used by Muslims for the geographical realm and true domain of Islamic faith and practice.

Darbar Sahib

The Golden Temple in Amritsar, the chief centre of Sikh pilgrimage.

Darbyites

See Brethren

Darius I

(542 BCE–486 BCE) Member of the Achaemenid dynasty, the fourth king of Persia. During his reign the Hebrew prophets Haggai and Zechariah were allowed to resume the work of rebuilding the Temple in Jerusalem.

Darsania

Priests of Hindu devatas in Indian villages who claim to have darsan (insight or vision) as a result of a direct communication from the deity.

Darshana

Term used to indicate one of the six orthodox systems of Hindu philosophy. The root meaning of the word is 'view of the nature of things'.

Darwin, Charles

(1809–1882) English scientist who was appointed naturalist to the surveying voyage of H.M.S. Beagle (1831–1836). Darwin collected vast quantities of specimens and spent many years analysing the results. In 1859 he published *The Origin of Species*, which caused a revolution in biological science and expounded the theory of evolution. He followed this with *The Descent of Man* in 1871, and both books were bitterly attacked by many leading churchmen, as they appeared to undermine the teaching of Genesis on the creation of man by God.

Dasam Granth

Lit. 'book of the tenth'. Collection of Sikh hymns, attributed to Guru Gobind Singh, the tenth Guru.

Darius I (from the Darius Vase, Naples)

62

Dashara/Dussehra

Conclusion of the autumn festival of the Hindu goddess Durga. It is also observed as the festival celebrating the victory of the Lord Rama over King Ravana of Lanka.

Dastur

Title of a high priest of the Parsees.

David, King

King of Israel who captured Jerusalem and introduced the Ark of the Lord into the city. He first appears as a shepherd boy who won acclaim by defeating the Philistine giant Goliath. He was anointed by Samuel, and came to the throne after the death of Saul in battle. Many of the Psalms are attributed to him, and Jewish Messianic hopes were centred on his family and descendants.

David, St

Patron saint of Wales. He died about 600 CE, but little is known of his life. He seems to have come from a noble family and is reputed to have founded at least twelve monasteries. His feast-day, 1 March, was authorized *c.* 1120.

Day of Atonement

See Yom Kippur

Day of Judgement

See Last Judgement

Dayaka

Term used in Buddhism for a lay supporter of the bhikkus who provides food, robes and medicine.

De Profundis

First words of the Latin version of Psalm 130, meaning 'out of the deep'. It is one of fifteen Psalms used for the Gradual, and is traditionally recited in a Requiem Mass.

Deacon

In the NT deacons were church officers, probably administrative, certainly with a less important role than a bishop. In the Roman Catholic and Anglican Churches today, the diaconate is the first step in the hierarchy. A deacon is not authorized to celebrate the Mass or Eucharist, but a man must be made a deacon before he can be ordained a priest or consecrated as a bishop.

Deaconess

In the early Christian Church, a title given to women who were officially appointed for duties such as caring for the sick, instructing women catechumens, and assisting with the baptism of women. In the 19th century the office was revived in the Church of England and the Free Churches. Women are dedicated to lifelong service in the Church, usually by the laying on of hands by a bishop or by a senior minister.

Dead Sea Scrolls

Collection of Hebrew manuscripts discovered in caves at Qumran, near the Dead Sea, from 1947 onwards. They contain biblical texts, including a

A portion of the Dead Sea Scrolls

complete scroll of Isaiah, commentaries on biblical books, and many documents relating to the life and organization of a community generally thought to have been Essenes.

Dean

The dean of a cathedral is the head of the chapter and is responsible for the services and the supervision of the fabric. In rank he is next to the bishop. A rural dean assists the bishop in the administration of part of an archdeaconry.

Deborah

One of the six Judges of Israel whose activities are related in the Book of Judges. The only female Judge, she exhorted Barak to lead an army recruited from most of the Israelite tribes and overthrow Jabin, King of Canaan. Her name means 'bee', which was a symbol of royal power among the Egyptians while among the Greeks it was a title reserved for specially honoured women.

Decalogue

The Ten Commandments, given by God to Moses on Mt Sinai. The biblical account is in Exodus 19–20 and Deuteronomy 5.

Decretal

Papal letter, on a particular topic, which has the force of law within the Roman Catholic Church. The first decretal on record was sent by Pope Siricius in 385 CE to the Bishop of Tarragona.

Dedication

The setting apart of a building to be used as a church: this is usually done in a solemn service conducted by a bishop, but if the building is intended for temporary use, it may be dedicated by a priest.

Deism

Belief in the existence of God but not in revealed religion or in a personal providence. This was widespread in England in the 17th and 18th centuries.

Delos

Smallest of the islands of the Cyclades, reputed to be the birthplace of Apollo and Artemis. The island was held in great reverence because of the Temple of Apollo, which was the centre of his worship and also the site of a famous oracle. It is now without permanent residents.

Delphi

Small town on the slopes of Mount Parnassus which housed the most famous oracular shrine in ancient Greece, sacred to Apollo.

Demeter

Corn goddess of the Greeks and the protectress of agriculture. Her daughter Persephone was carried to the underworld by Hades (Pluto), but because Demeter in anger caused a drought on earth, Zeus forced Hades to allow Persephone to spend two-thirds of the year with her mother. Demeter was identified by the Romans with Ceres.

Demiurge

English transliteration of a Greek word meaning 'craftsman' which was applied to the Divine Being by Plato in the *Timaeus*. It was used by Gnostic writers to indicate a deity responsible for creating the material universe, whom they considered inferior to the Supreme Being.

Demonology

Study of men's beliefs about evil spirits or forces. There are few references in the Hebrew Bible to demons or devils, but by NT times belief in them was common among Christians, Jews and pagans. There are many stories in the Gospels of Jesus casting out demons, and the exorcism of evil spirits has played an important part in the life of the Christian Church.

Deng

Chief of the Nuer spirits, the son of the god Kwoth.

Dengyo

(767–822 CE)   Monk who founded the Tendai sect of Buddhism, which grew very rapidly, at one time having three thousand temples.

Denis, St

Apostle to the Gauls who set out from Rome in the 3rd century, made many converts and became the first bishop of Paris. He was martyred there on the orders of the Roman governor, whom he had defied.

Denkhart

Religious work which contains a compendium of Zoroastrian lore.

Deri

Small domed Hindu shrine, usually made of plastered brick and not much more than 1 m high, found in many Indian villages.

Dervish

Member of a religious fraternity within Islam. It is a Persian term meaning 'mendicant', the Arabic equivalent being *fakir*. They practise special devotions of a mystical nature, akin to the Sufis. The Whirling Dervishes were founded in the 13th century by Jalal al-Din Rumi and remained a separate community. As their name implies, they practise whirling dances which become more and more rapid and exhausting in the hope of inducing ecstatic experiences.

Whirling Dervishes (17th century Persian manuscript)

Desatir
Mystical text read by Parsees which was popular until its claim to antiquity was seen to be spurious.

Descartes, R.
(1596–1650)   Philosopher and scientist who has been described as the founder of modern philosophy. He based his philosophical reasoning on mathematical principles and began from the affirmation 'Cogito ergo sum' (I think therefore I am). He went on to declare that the first distinct idea outside the self is God, and this is his main argument for the existence of God and the veracity of his own ideas. His critics accused him of arguing in a circle.

Determinism
System of philosophy which maintains that the entire universe and all human activity are subject to the law of cause and effect, and that free will is an illusion.

Deucalion
In Greek mythology the son of Prometheus. He figures in the Greek story of the Flood, according to which he was saved in an ark which he had built.

Deutero-Isaiah
Title usually given to chapters 40–66 of Isaiah, to separate them chronologically from chapters 1–39. It is generally accepted that most of the material in Isaiah 1–39 comes from Isaiah of Jerusalem (*c.* 700 BCE), but Deutero-Isaiah has a different outlook and is thought to have been written in the later years of the Babylonian Exile (550–538 BCE). Some scholars have further separated chapters 56–66 as Trito-Isaiah, but this is not universally accepted.

Deuteronomy
Fifth book in the Bible, containing addresses by Moses and the Book of the Covenant; it is part of the Torah.

Deva
In Buddhist and Hindu teaching, superhuman, spiritual beings; the shining ones.

Devata
In Hindu worship, a minor divinity, a demigod or a godling.

Devekut (H)

Lit. 'cleaving'. Practice of devotion by which the barriers to spiritual communion between man and God are removed. Jewish commentators explain it as meaning the imitation of God's attributes of mercy and kindness.

Devil

Many religions have personified the power of evil in order to avoid the suggestion that God causes evil. In the Bible there are references to various agents of evil, called in Leviticus 17 the 'sa'ir' and in Deuteronomy 32 the 'shed'. In Job, Satan is a servant of God rather than a devil. In the NT the usual title is 'demon'; the leader of the demons is called Beelzebub in Mark 3 and Satan in Luke 11.

Dhamma (P)/**Dharam** (Pn)/**Dharma** (S)

Word with a variety of meanings, e.g. 'right', 'virtue', 'law', 'object of thought', 'truth', 'justice', 'doctrine'. A popular Buddhist affirmation is 'I take refuge in the Dhamma', here understood as the Buddha's teaching. In Hindu writings it means 'righteousness' or 'right conduct', 'duty' or 'way of life'. In the Sikh community it stands for 'religious duty', which is expressed in the code of the Khalsa. In Abhidharma Buddhism dharmas are those elements which are analytically ultimate.

Dhammacakka Day

Day of the turning of the Wheel of the Law. Theravada Buddhist full-moon festival of the first proclamation of the truth by the Buddha to five ascetics in Benares.

Dhammakaya

Term used in Buddhism for one of the Three Bodies of the Buddha. This is the Buddha as the personification of truth or absolute reality. The term is also used to refer to the Body of the Law.

Dhammapada

Important book in the Buddhist Pali canon consisting of four hundred and twenty-three verses of sayings of the Buddha, arranged in twenty-six chapters.

Dharam (Pn)

See Dhamma

Dharam Khand

In the teaching of the Sikh Guru Nanak this is the first of five stages or steps towards man's liberation. This is the stage of religious duty, the recognition of God's law and providence.

Dharamsala

Indian building used as a charitable religious hospice, or temporary accommodation for travellers, especially pilgrims; a place of worship.

Dharana

Beginning of Buddhist meditation, which consists of fixing the thoughts on a single object, which can be external or a thought within.

Dharma (S)

See Dhamma

Dharma Shastra

Term used in Hinduism for treatises on ethics.

Dharma Sutras

Term used in Hinduism for manuals of ethics.

Dharmavinaya

In early Buddhism, the doctrine or discipline which provided the basis for the community's religious life.

Dharmic Complex

Term used for a mode of Hindu religious motivation: the quest to acquire merit and to be reborn well. The avoidance of sin and the acquisition of merit is accomplished by adhering to one's dharma.

Dhatu

In early Indian religion the six psychological elements of existence; six sense objects, i.e. the five sense organs plus manas.

Dhikr (A)

Muslim practice of the recollection of God by mention of his names, reciprocally to God's reminder to men, which is in the Qur'an.

Dhimmi (A)

Non-Muslim subject under Islamic rule in one of the tolerated minorities. He is subject to special taxes in lieu of zakat.

Dhyana (S)

Word meaning 'meditation' or 'reflection'. The sixth chapter of the *Bhagavadgita* is entitled *Dhyana-Yoga*, and sets out a discipline of meditation. In Buddhism it is a more advanced form of meditation involving intense or ecstatic concentration in which the self is eliminated and samadhi, or perfect contemplation, is experienced. The term 'Zen' is said to be derived from 'dhyana'.

Diana

Roman goddess of the wildwood, identified with the Greek goddess Artemis. Diana of Ephesus was a distinct goddess of Asiatic origin, probably the great mother goddess of fertility, as she is represented with many breasts.

Diana

Diaspora

Dispersion of the Jewish people throughout the world, often referred to by the Hebrew word *galut*. It applies particularly to the scattering of the Jews after the fall of Jerusalem in 70 CE.

Diatessaron

Edition of the four Gospels in a continuous narrative compiled by Tatian in 150 CE. It had a wide circulation in Syriac-speaking churches until the 5th century, when it was replaced by the four separate Gospels.

Didache

Very early Christian manual of morals and religious practice, possibly dating from the 1st century. It has sixteen chapters; the first six describe the Way of Life and the Way of Death, the following nine deal with topics such as baptism, the Eucharist, prayer and fasting, and the last chapter is a prophecy of the second coming of Christ.

Dies Irae

Opening words of one of the greatest and best known of the Latin hymns of the Middle Ages, written, according to tradition, by a 13th century Franciscan, Thomas da Celano. Originally intended for private devotion, the meaning of the words, 'Day of wrath', has made it particularly suitable for use in a Requiem Mass, or Masses on All Souls' Day.

Dietary Laws

Rules which govern the categories of food which may or may not be eaten by different communities. In the Hebrew Bible, Leviticus 11 sets out a long list of animals which may not be eaten by the Jewish community. In the Qur'an, surah 5 notes animals which may not be eaten by Muslims. In Hinduism, the sanctity of the cow means that it is unlawful for Hindus to eat any product of the cow or bull.

Digambaras

Lit. 'space-clad', i.e. clothed only with air. One of the two main divisions of Jain ascetics; these were the more conservative, and among their acts of self-mortification they practised nudity and castigation. The other division was termed the Svetambaras.

Digha Nikaya

One of the five nikayas, or collections of suttas, making up the *Sutta Pitaka* of the Buddhist canon of scripture.

Diksha

Term used in Hinduism for the initiation given to one seeking to become a sannyasi, and for ritual consecration by a priest before a worshipper is allowed to offer a sacrifice.

Din (A)

Muslim term for religion in general and religious duties in particular; it incorporates the five basic obligations of the Muslim. The term also means 'divine judgement'.

Divali: blessing the year's accounts

Diocese

Territorial administrative unit within the Christian Church. It is governed by a bishop, sometimes with the help of suffragan bishops, and is divided into parishes, which are in the care of priests. The parishes are grouped into rural deaneries and archdeaconries to assist the administration of the diocese.

Diocletian

(245–313 CE) Roman emperor. Of humble origin, he became a soldier and was declared Emperor by the army in 284. He reorganized the Empire, dividing it into four areas and delegating much authority to his three fellow tetrarchs. During most of his reign Christians enjoyed peaceful toleration, but in 303 he sanctioned widespread persecution with the destruction of churches and the burning of Christian books. This continued sporadically until the accession of Constantine as Emperor in 312.

Diogenes

(412–323 BCE) Philosopher of the Cynic school. He lived on the coarsest food, walked barefoot, wore ragged clothes and slept in a storage vessel. His aim was to show that to gain virtue one must renounce physical pleasure and the conventions of society.

Dionysus

Greek god of nature and wine, worshipped in ecstatic, sometimes orgiastic rites. He was also called Bacchus.

Disciple

General term for a pupil, learner or follower, particularly applied to followers of religious leaders such as Jesus Christ or the Buddha.

Divali

Festival of Lights at the end of the Hindu year and the beginning of the new year, when lamps are ceremonially lit and presents exchanged. It is associated with Lakshmi, the goddess of wealth and consort of Vishnu. Houses are cleaned and decorated and brightly lit ready for her to visit them. For Sikhs its significance is that it recalls the day of the release of the sixth Guru, Hargobind, from Gwalior Fort.

Divination

Interpretation of the past or insight into the future, or the attempt to discover the future by magic or supernatural means.

Divine Light Mission

Movement set up in Hardwar, India in 1957 by Sri Hans Ji Maharaj, who claimed to be the Satguru (perfect master or true teacher) who could initiate followers into 'The Knowledge'. On his death in 1966 he was succeeded as Satguru by his son Guru Maharaj Ji, then only eight years old. Maharaj Ji visited London and then America in 1971, attracting large crowds and setting up a Palace of Peace and many communities. The mission claims that Maharaj Ji is the Messiah of God incarnate, and it teaches 'The Knowledge' through a system of four different techniques of meditation.

68

Diviner

One who attempts to predict or control the future by inspiration, intuition or magic.

Diwan

Lit. 'royal court'. Term used by Sikhs for an act of public or corporate worship.

Do (J)

See Tao

Docetism

Teaching found in the early Christian Church which considered that the humanity and the sufferings of the earthly Jesus Christ were apparent rather than real.

Doctor of the Church

Title of honour originally conferred upon four outstanding Christian theologians: Ambrose, Augustine, Gregory the Great and Jerome. In the Middle Ages the list was extended to more than twenty theologians.

Doctrine

See Dogma

Dog

One of the animals worshipped in ancient Egypt. The god Anubis, who guided the souls of the dead to the underworld, was depicted as dog-headed. This is probably associated with their reverence for Sirius, the dog-star, which is the brightest in the sky and is used for navigation. Judaism and Islam abhor the dog as an unclean scavenger. In Hindu mythology the four-eyed Dogs of Yama guard the gates of hell, a task performed in Greek mythology by Cerberus, a dog-headed monster.

Dogen

(1200–1254)   Founder of the Soto division of the Zen sect of Japanese Buddhism.

Dogma

Tenet or principle of belief which is stated by the Christian Church to be true and acceptance of which is obligatory. This is to be distinguished from doctrine, which is taught as true but acceptance of which is not considered to be a matter of obligation.

Dokhma

Tower of Silence in which Zoroastrians expose the bodies of the dead to vultures.

Dokusan

Term used in Zen Buddhism for a formal, private interview with the Master.

Dome of the Rock

Muslim mosque in Jerusalem, also known as the Mosque of Omar, which is built on the site where the Jewish Temple stood. The rock is the place from which Muhammad is said to have ascended to heaven, and also the place where Abraham prepared to sacrifice Isaac. The dome itself symbolizes the heavens.

Dokhma

Interior of the Dome of the Rock. The sacred rock is visible in the foreground

Dominicans

Roman Catholic monastic order founded by St Dominic at Toulouse in 1212. At first they were a mendicant order, and because of their long black cloaks were known as the Black Friars. In 1425 they obtained permission to receive donations and ceased to be mendicant. Many famous scholars, including St Thomas Aquinas, have belonged to this order, which was put in charge of the Inquisition and the censorship of books.

Donatism

Schism within the Christian Church which appeared in N. Africa in 311 CE. The appointment of Caecilian as Bishop was rejected on the grounds that his consecrator had been a traditor during the Diocletian persecution. The Numidian bishops consecrated Donatus, from whom the schism takes its name. The Roman Church condemned their action, but there was considerable support for the rigorist position, and the separated African Church continued until the invasions of the Saracens in the 7th century.

Dosa

Term used in Buddhism for fault, hatred, anger, or ill will. It is one of the fires which must be allowed to die out before nirvana can be attained. (See also Moha and Raga)

Double Predestination

Augustine taught that man's vocation depends on an eternal decree of God, and that some men, but not all, are predestined to salvation. The first extension of this doctrine into double predestination appears to have been made by a 9th century Benedictine monk, Gottschalk, who taught that some are predestined to blessedness and others to damnation. He was condemned at the Synod of Quiercy in 849 CE. The doctrine of double predestination was propounded again by John Calvin, who taught that only the elect are saved by Christ's atoning death, while the reprobate are condemned by God's eternal decree. This became the official teaching of the Calvinist Churches at the Synod of Dort in 1619.

Dove

Bird which has been venerated by many different communities. It was apparently associated in Greek mythology with Aphrodite, while according to Virgil two doves guided Aeneas to the Golden Bough. The dove as a symbol of peace derives from the story of Noah (Genesis 8), in which the dove brings an olive-branch back to the Ark. The dove as a symbol of the Holy Spirit derives from the account of Christ's baptism (Matthew 3; Mark 1), when a dove appeared to him as he rose from the water.

Doxology

Form of words ascribing praise and glory to God. Examples are the short Gloria Patri, the longer Gloria in Excelsis and the hymn by T. Ken beginning 'Praise God, from whom all blessings flow'.

Dragon

Composite mythical beast which figures prominently in ancient mythology and religious legends, and also in medieval folklore, representing the forces of evil and terror. Revelation speaks of a war fought by Michael and his angels against the dragon at the end of the world. The patron saint of England, St George, is often depicted in the act of slaying a powerful dragon.

Dreams

Dreams are mysterious experiences and have consistently been interpreted as divine messages. Egyptian papyri and inscriptions from the 2nd millenium BCE speak of messages from the god Re in dreams. The *Epic of Gilgamesh* records a warning of a flood given in a dream by the gods. The Hebrew Bible records many messages given by God in dreams, e.g. to Jacob and to Joseph. In ancient Greek and Roman society dreams were regarded as an important means of communication from the gods, and it was a common practice to sleep at a sanctuary in the hope of receiving a message. Dreams also figure in the NT, e.g. those of the Wise Men, Peter and Paul. Modern psychotherapy, particularly the systems of Freud and Jung, places great importance on the analysis of dreams.

Druids

These were the members of the priesthood of pre-Roman Celtic religion in Britain and Gaul, and are mentioned by several Greek and Roman writers from the 2nd century BCE to the 4th century CE. The name possibly derives from that of the oak-tree, which was regarded as sacred and was usually found in their sanctuaries. They also regarded mistletoe as sacred, because it was white and rare, and cut it only on the sixth day of the moon. Little is known of their beliefs but astrology probably played an important part, and in the modern revival of the Order of the Druids, the most important ceremony takes place at the dawn of the summer solstice at such places as Stonehenge and Glastonbury Tor.

Druj
In the teaching of Zoroaster this is falsehood, wickedness or disorder, the opposite of asha.

Druzes
Communities in the Lebanon and Syria whose religion originated in Islam. Their particular belief is a recognition of the divine in humanity. The name is derived from that of their founder, Darazi.

Du'a (A)
Lit. 'blessing'. Term used by Muslims for different forms of prayer, with particular reference to the first surah of the Qur'an. This surah is the basis of all formal prayer, or salat, one of the Five Pillars of Islam.

Dualism
Belief in the existence of two principles, good and evil, in the universe.

Dukkha (P)/Duhkka (S)
Central feature of Hindu and Buddhist thought; in the latter it is the first of the Four Noble Truths. (1) Pain or suffering. (2) That which results from change. (3) The realization that all things are just aggregates of changing elements.

Duns Scotus
(1264–1308)   Medieval Franciscan philosopher. He gave first place in his teaching to love and the will and maintained that natural law depends on the will of God. He was a strong defender of the doctrine of the Immaculate Conception, and believed that the Incarnation would have taken place even if there had not been a Fall. The word 'dunce' derives from his name, which was used as a term of derision by humanists criticizing the scholastic theologians.

Dunstan, St
(909–988 CE)   Benedictine monk at Glastonbury who became Archbishop of Canterbury. He assisted King Edgar of Mercia in a thorough reform of Church and State and established many monastic houses throughout the land.

Durga
Hindu goddess, one of the names of Devi, the wife of Shiva, regarded as the personification of his active energy.

Durga Puja
Hindu autumn festival of Sri Durga, the divine mother, consort of Shiva, celebrated in October with family reunions and social gatherings.

Duryodhana
Leader of the Kaurava army in the Battle of Kivinkshetra described in the Hindu epic poem the *Mahabharata*. He is called 'evil minded' and he was killed by his adversary Bhima when it appeared that his army was winning.

Durga slaying the buffalo Mahishasura (Mysore, early 13th century)

Dussehra
Hindu festival, also called Vijaya-Dashami. It celebrates the victory of Lord Rama over King Ravana of Lanka. It also marks the conclusion of the celebration of Durga and bids her farewell.

Dvaita
Doctrine of dualism in relation to God as opposed to selves and the universe, taught by Madhava and held by many Hindus.

Dvija
Hindu term for one who is 'twice-born', applied to the three upper classes or varnas.

Dyaus-Pitar
In the Vedic literature the sky god, who is the father of the gods. In Greek mythology he is Zeus, and in Roman mythology, Jupiter.

Ea

High god in Babylonian mythology who shared the dominion of the universe with Anu and Enlil, his particular sphere being the sweet-water ocean. He is the king of wisdom, and the god of artists and craftsmen.

Eagle

Because of its great size, its powerful flight and its ability to outsoar all other birds, the eagle has been a popular emblem of royalty and divinity. In ancient Egypt Horus, the son of Isis and Osiris, was symbolized by a falcon (a member of the same family) and in the 3rd millennium BCE a double-headed eagle was the symbol of Ningursu of Lagash. The standard of the Roman legions was referred to as the eagle, and in Christian iconography the eagle is the symbol of St John. In more recent times it was the symbol of the Holy Roman Empire, and was retained by Austria after the Empire fell; it is now the symbol of the United States of America.

Earth Mother

In the history of man there has always been a connection between the earth and a mother goddess. Figurines of clay or stone in pregnant form with large breasts have been found in shrines dating from 4000 BCE onwards. In Egypt the goddess Isis was the earth mother. In Greece the name Demeter means either 'corn mother' or 'earth mother', and she demonstrated her power by spoiling the harvest when her daughter was taken to the underworld by Pluto. The Romans transferred her powers to the vegetation goddess Ceres. In African tribes the earth mother is known by a variety of names, e.g. Ala, Asase, Ya, Li and Obasi.

Easter Day

Most joyful festival of the Christian Church, celebrating the resurrection of Jesus Christ from the dead. Its importance is emphasized by the long penitential period of Lent and the solemn liturgy of Holy Week, followed by the joyful and triumphant anthems of Easter Day. The traditional Easter greeting is 'The Lord is risen', with the response 'He is risen indeed'.

Eastern Orthodox Church

Section of the Christian Church that is dominant in Eastern Europe. Its full title is the Holy Oriental Orthodox Apostolic Church. From the founding of Constantinople as the capital of the Eastern Empire in 330 CE, rivalry developed between its bishop and the Bishop of Rome. In 867 Pope Nicholas I and Patriarch Photius excommunicated each other, but the breach was healed. Then in 1054 Pope Leo IX and Patriarch Michael Cerularius excommunicated each other, and that situation remains despite several attempts at reconciliation. The Orthodox Church accepts seven sacraments, but recognizes no visible vicar of Christ on earth, and rejects the filioque clause in the Creeds, i.e. the doctrine that the Holy Spirit proceeds from the Son as well as the Father. It permits the marriage of parish priests but bishops are celibate, chosen from monastic orders.

Ebionites

Lit. 'poor men'. Sect of Jewish Christians which flourished in the territory east of the Jordan in the first centuries of the Church. They practised communal living of a strictly ascetic type, rejecting worldly possessions. Doctrinally, they considered Jesus to be the human son of Joseph and Mary, inspired by the Holy Spirit at his baptism. They insisted on the keeping of the Mosaic Law and used only the Gospel of St Matthew.

Ecclesiastes

Title of a book in the Hebrew Bible, the author of which calls himself Qoheleth, i.e. 'the preacher'. The theme of the book is the search for a key to the meaning of life.

Ecclesiasticus

Jewish apocryphal book of the type known as Wisdom Literature. In the Septuagint it is entitled 'The Wisdom of Jesus, the Son of Sirach'. It was probably written in the 2nd century BCE and contains fifty-one chapters, dealing with the doctrine of God, wisdom, the law and moral conduct.

Eckhart, Meister

(1260–1327) German Christian mystic whose teaching has survived through his sermons. He emphasized that God is mind or intellect rather than being, and he was condemned as a heretic in 1326 for teaching that there is a divine spark in every human being.

Eclipse

An eclipse of the sun, and to a lesser extent of the moon, was an occasion of alarm and fear in the early history of man, because it appeared to interrupt the regular cycle of day and night. Priests were called on to perform various rites and the ending of the eclipse proclaimed their success. Even today, although the exact time can be calculated, it is an awe-inspiring experience and often leads to prophecies of doom.

Ecstasy

Lit. 'being outside the body'. Abnormal condition in which the mind or spirit experiences a state of rapture. Many saints have claimed this in the course of their growth in the mystic life. Some sects have practised various rituals designed to induce ecstatic experiences.

Ecumenical Movement

Movement within the Christian Churches aiming at fuller mutual understanding and co-operation, with the possibility of unity of the Church. Its starting-point is reckoned to be the Edinburgh Missionary Conference in 1910, and its major achievement so far, the establishment of the World Council of Churches.

Eddas

Lit. 'grandmothers'. Two collections of Icelandic literature: one in verse, comprising epic tales of the Scandinavian gods, and one in prose, containing a synopsis of northern mythology.

Eddy, Mary Baker

(1821–1910) American who founded the Church of Christ Scientist (Christian Science). She was born in New Hampshire and after consistent ill health became a patient of Dr P. P. Quimby in 1862. He practised mental healing and wrote about a Christ Science of Healing, and Mary Baker Eddy seems to have used many of his ideas in her book *Science and Health* (1875). She rapidly won followers and established a church in Boston, for which she wrote a *Manual of Discipline*. Since then the movement has spread to most countries of the world.

Greek Orthodox priests

Mary Baker Eddy

Eden

In the Hebrew Bible the Garden of Eden is the site of paradise, where Adam and Eve were created (Genesis 2:8–17). In Isaiah 51:3 and Ezekiel 28:13 it is mentioned as an area of fertility and abundant trees. The name is probably connected with the Babylonian *edinu* (plain). It is also found in the Qur'an (surah 9), referring to paradise, but some translators render it as 'garden of perpetual abode'.

Edinburgh Conference

The World Missionary Conference of 1910 in Edinburgh set up the International Council, and is regarded as the forerunner of the Ecumenical Movement. The World Conference on Faith and Order of 1937 in Edinburgh approved a proposal which led to the formation of the World Council of Churches in 1948.

Edomites

In biblical times this was the tribe that occupied territory to the south-east of the Dead Sea. They were considered to be descendants of Esau, but were constantly in conflict with Israel.

Edward VI

(1537–1553)   Son of Henry VIII and Jane Seymour, he became King in 1547. Under the guidance of the Protector Somerset and Archbishop Cranmer, he authorized the publication of the *Book of Homilies*, in 1547, and two editions of the *Book of Common Prayer*, in 1549 and 1552. He took a great interest in education and founded many grammar schools, some of which still exist, bearing his name.

Egg

The egg has from man's earliest days been a symbol of life. Ancient Egyptian writings contain a description of the birth of the sun god Re from an egg. In Hindu mythology the golden world egg Hiranygarbha hatches out Brahma, who creates the universe. A Chinese legend says that P'an Ku, the first man, appeared from the cosmic egg. In Egyptian and Greek architectural decoration the egg (the symbol of life) often alternates with the dart (the symbol of death). In the Christian Church the giving of Easter eggs to symbolize the resurrection of Christ is a practice which goes back to at least the 6th century.

Egungun

Lit. 'skeleton'. Secret cult among the Yoruba tribe of West Africa whose members perform dances to remember or placate the dead, and to purge the town from pollution by the dead.

Egypt

One of the great nations of the ancient world, with a history and list of kings going back several thousands of years. The King, or Pharaoh, was worshipped as the incarnation of Horus, the sky god, and the sun god Atum was the supreme deity. For many centuries Egypt was an important factor in the balance of power in the Mediterranean area. After the conquest of Egypt by Alexander the Great in 332 BCE, the country was usually under the domination of a foreign power, but the Islamic conquest in 641 CE heralded a new era, and since that time the country has been predominantly Muslim, though there is a strong Coptic Christian Church.

Ehud

Second of the Israelite Judges whose achievements are recorded in the Book of Judges. Ehud delivered Israel from the oppression of Eglon, King of Moab.

Eidetic Vision

Term used in phenomenology to indicate a human capacity for seeing a phenomenon as it is, for grasping the essentials of a situation.

Eight

1. Because of its shape, with crossing lines, eight stands for a new beginning. In Jewish tradition a male baby is named on the eighth day; in many Christian churches the font is octagonal; Genesis 8 recounts the survival of Noah and his family (eight persons) during the Flood and their fresh start in life; in his ethical teaching the Buddha enunciated the Eightfold Path to the new life.

2. Eight is also the first cubic number, and the cube is the symbol of the earth. Eight is thus the number of the materialist, ambitious for power. The expression 'to have one over the eight' means to get drunk or lose power through over-indulgence.

Eightfold Path

Scheme of moral and spiritual training, formulated in the Buddha's fourth Noble Truth, which is intended to lead to deliverance from suffering. It is set out in a threefold plan: (1) intellect – right understanding and thought; (2) moral – right speech, action and livelihood; (3) meditative – right effort, mindfulness and contemplation.

Eisai

(1141–1215) Buddhist master who introduced the Rinzai sect of Zen into Japan.

El Shaddai

Title applied to God in the Hebrew Bible narrative of Exodus 6:3. It is translated as 'God Almighty' in the English versions, and indicates that the Lord who had made promises to the Patriarchs had power to fulfil them in his dealings with Moses.

Elder

Church officer in Presbyterian and Baptist Churches. Their duties are usually administrative, but some are permitted to conduct services, preach and assist the pastor.

Election

1. Jewish belief, based on statements in the Hebrew Bible, that the Jews were selected by God for a special divine purpose.
2. Doctrine in Christian theology, particularly associated with Augustine and Calvin, which states that at the beginning of creation God elected some of mankind to eternal life, passing over the remainder or condemning them to eternal damnation.

Eleusis

Site in ancient Greece where mysteries, i.e. secret rituals, were celebrated in honour of Demeter. In origin they were probably agricultural ceremonies, but they developed into large-scale festivals lasting many days, with processions from Athens and the initiation of devotees into various degrees of the mysteries.

Eleven

This is the number of revelation, of going beyond the human to a higher plane. The reason is probably that eleven disciples remained faithful to Jesus Christ and received the blessing of the Holy Spirit. At the same time it is one short of twelve, the number of perfection, and it has been suggested that many team games have eleven players to symbolize that which is imperfect, striving to reach the goal of perfection.

Elijah

The most important prophet in Israel in the 9th century BCE. He fought against the introduction of Baal worship by King Ahab and Queen Jezebel, and is particularly remembered for a dramatic incident on Mt Carmel (1 Kings 18) when he challenged the Baal priests and demonstrated that the Lord alone was the true god to be worshipped by Israel. As Moses symbolizes the Law so Elijah symbolizes the Prophets, and in these roles they were seen with Jesus at his transfiguration (Matthew 17:3). At the end of his ministry Elijah was translated to heaven in a whirlwind and chariot of fire, and Jewish eschatology has expected his return to herald the coming of the Messiah. In readiness for his return a glass of wine is poured for him during the Seder of the Passover and the door is left open for him to enter.

Elim Pentecostalists

Groups of Pentecostalists who came under the influence of the Welsh evangelist George Jeffreys and amalgamated in 1915 to form the Elim Foursquare Gospel Alliance. In addition to belief in divine healing and speaking with tongues (common to all Pentecostalists) the Elim groups put more emphasis on Bible-based evangelistic campaigns. They also have a more centralized government.

Elisha

Hebrew prophet of the 9th century BCE who became the successor of Elijah (1 Kings 19). He was the leader of a group known as Sons of the Prophets, and although there is a greater element of miracle or magic in the stories about Elisha, he did not have the individuality or strength of character of Elijah.

Elixir of Life

Medieval alchemists believed that the philosophers' stone had universal curative powers. Paracelsus (1493–1541) claimed to have a secret panacea that gave the vital energy which would make his patients immune to any illness. However the true aim of the elixir of life was not only to cure human ills, but to confer the gift of immortality.

Elizabeth I

(1533–1603)   Daughter of Henry VIII and Anne Boleyn, she became Queen of England in 1558. She tried to find a compromise between the extremes of Catholicism and Calvinism, and she reissued the Prayer Book in 1559, making changes with this in mind. In 1570 she was excommunicated by the Pope; in reply Convocation approved the Thirty-nine Articles in 1571, and the Mass was proscribed. The defeat of the Spanish Armada in 1588 gave a new impetus to nationalism and strengthened the position of the Anglican Church.

Elm

According to Teutonic mythology the first woman, Embla, was created from an elm-tree by the gods Odin, Hoenir and Loki, who gave the tree breath, soul and warmth.

Elohim (H)

Plural form usually translated in English Bibles as the singular 'God', because in Jewish thought there is only one supreme, true god who possesses all powers. In the Middle Ages magicians, believing that the real name of God contained his essence, inscribed 'Elohim' on their magic circles to infuse divine power and ward off evil influences.

Elysium

Sometimes called the Elysian Fields, in Greek and Roman thought the regions inhabited by the blessed after death.

Ember Days

Groups of three days observed in the Christian Church as days of fasting and abstinence. Originally associated with seed-time, harvest and vintage, they are now associated with the ordination of clergy and follow Ash Wednesday, Whit Sunday and Holy Cross Day (14 September).

Emin

The Emin (meaning 'the faithful') is an esoteric group founded by a student of the occult with the pseudonym Leo. The aim of the group is to introduce its members, through joint study, to a wide range of subjects such as astrology, tarot, herbalism and healing. The aim is not the accumulation of knowledge but the development of each person in accordance with 'natural principles and fundamental laws'.

Emperor Worship

From the earliest years of Egyptian history, the Pharaoh was regarded as divine and was offered worship as the incarnation of God. In ancient Persia great kings received obeisance, and the Greeks gave divine honours to several heroes. In 331 BCE Alexander the Great was declared divine by the priests in Egypt and worshipped as a god, the son of Jupiter-Ammon. In the early Roman Empire the Emperor was not worshipped independently in his lifetime, but his name was coupled with Roma, and he was deified after death. The Emperor Aurelian founded a new state cult in 274 CE in which the Emperor was equated with the sun as lord of the Roman Empire. This was short-lived as the conversion of the Emperor Constantine to Christianity in 312 CE brought emperor worship in the Roman Empire to an end.

Empiricism

Philosophical theory which states that sense experience is the source of all knowledge. It maintains that the mind is at first a clean slate on which all the characters are inscribed by experience. This teaching is particularly associated with the writers Locke and Hume.

Encyclical

Circular letter sent to the Christian Churches in a specified area. In the Roman Catholic Church it applies only to a letter sent by the Pope. In the Church of England it applies to a letter sent on behalf of all the bishops at the conclusion of the Lambeth Conference.

Endogamy

Limitation of marriage to members of one group, community or tribe.

Enlightenment

Experience of enlightenment, or satori, is the goal of Zen Buddhism. It may come through the use of koan or mondo and may be sudden, brief or lasting. It is a state of consciousness in which a man passes beyond the present world to absolute peace. In Judaism this was the title given to a rationalist movement of the 18th and 19th centuries.

Enlil

High god of Babylonian mythology who shared the dominion of the universe with Anu and Ea. He was the 'king of the lands', the king of the gods, and the hurricane was his weapon.

Enuma Elish

Babylonian creation epic. These are the first two words, meaning 'When the heavens above', of the first of seven tablets, probably written about 1750 BCE. They not only give an account of the Creation but show how Marduk became the supreme god of Babylon.

Epa

Yoruba cult society whose members perform dances wearing large masks, sometimes 1⅓ m high, for the general well-being of the community.

Ephesians, Epistle to the

One of the epistles in the NT attributed to St Paul. Some scholars have questioned its authorship, but it contains a wonderful description of the eternal purpose of God in Christ, to be worked out in his Church, described as the Body of Christ.

Ephod

Garment, mentioned in the Bible, worn by the priests of Israel. The ordinary ephod, made of linen, is distinguished from the ephod worn by the High Priest, which was made of costly material and decorated with gold, purple and scarlet. It draped from the shoulders to the waist.

Epa mask

Ephraim

Second son of the Israelite patriarch Joseph. He inherited half of his father's patrimony from Jacob. The tribe bearing his name occupied territory in the central highlands of Canaan.

Epic of Creation

This title usually refers specifically to the Babylonian account of the Creation, the *Enuma Elish*. This is inscribed on seven clay tablets, each with about one hundred and fifty lines, relating the story of the Creation, the birth of the gods, the victory of Marduk over Tiamat and his rise to supremacy. The date of this Epic is probably *c.* 1750 BCE.

Epiclesis

Term which originally meant 'invocation by name'. Now generally used for the petition in the Orthodox Eucharist invoking God to send the Holy Spirit upon the bread and wine in order that they may become the body and blood of Christ.

Epictetus

(55–135 CE) Stoic philosopher who was a freedman of Nero. He did not leave any written works, but one of his disciples collected his discourses into a short manual, the *Enchiridion*.

Epicurus

Greek philosopher born in Samos in 342 BCE; he moved to Athens in 306 BCE and established his own school, the Epicureans. He taught that the highest good is happiness, by which he meant peace of mind resulting from the cultivation of all the virtues, not sensual enjoyment. He died in 270 BCE.

Epiphany

Lit. 'manifestation'. Christian festival held on 6 January to commemorate the manifestation of Christ to the gentiles, represented by the three Wise Men.

Episcopacy

System of church government by bishops, found in the Roman Catholic, Orthodox and Anglican Churches.

Epistemology

Branch of philosophical study which examines the nature and validity of knowledge.

Epoche

Term used in phenomenology to indicate suspension of judgement.

Erasmus

(1466–1536)   One of the greatest scholars of the Renaissance period. He was known throughout Europe and was offered professorships by several universities. He produced a much praised edition of the Greek NT and edited Latin texts. He wrote a *Handbook for the Christian Soldier* and *Praise of Folly*, a satire on the corruption of the Church. He was not happy with the excesses of some of the Reformers, and in his last years was in conflict with Luther. He was criticized by some Reformers and some Catholic leaders because of his humanist leanings.

Erastianism

Teaching of Erastus (1524–1583) that in a state which professes one religion the civil authorities have the right and duty to exercise jurisdiction in all matters, civil and ecclesiastical, and to punish all offenders.

Eros

Greek god of love, identified by the Romans with Cupid. He was the son and companion of Aphrodite, and is portrayed as a beautiful but wanton boy, with golden wings and a golden bow and arrows.

Eschatology

Lit. 'doctrine of last things'. The belief that there will be an end to the world, probably in judgement; it is more a concern for the destiny of mankind than an interest in scientific speculation.

Esdras, Books of

Latin and Greek form of Ezra. In the Vulgate there are four books of Esdras, but in the Septuagint only two. In English translations, 1 Esdras of the Vulgate is entitled Ezra, 2 Esdras is Nehemiah, and 3 and 4 Esdras are in the Apocrypha as 1 and 2 Esdras.

Eshu

Yoruba god of mischief who sows seeds of jealousy and evil.

Essenes

Jewish mystics and devotees of the Torah from the 2nd century BCE to the 2nd century CE. They often separated themselves in communities, as at Qumran near the Dead Sea. Entrance to the order was by a novitiate and a strict period of probation.

Esther

Heroine of a book in the Hebrew Bible of the same name. She became the wife of King Ahasuerus, and was able to save the lives of many Jews threatened by the plots of Haman, the King's chief officer. The Book of Esther is read in the evening of the Jewish Feast of Purim, and the congregation is encouraged to applaud when her name is mentioned but to boo at the name of Haman.

Eternal Life

Term used in St John's Gospel which is almost synonymous with 'kingdom of God' in the Synoptics. It indicates the special quality of life enjoyed by those who commit themselves to Jesus Christ as Lord, and has nothing to do with chronology.

Ethics

Branch of philosophical study concerned with morals, human conduct and character, and concepts of right and wrong. Different systems of ethics have been associated with Greek philosophers such as Plato, Aristotle and Epicurus, with Utilitarian philosophers such as Hobbes and Mill, and scientists such as Spencer. Religions have propagated their own systems of ethics which adherents are expected to follow.

Ethrog

Citron fruit. One of the four species of plant carried in the synagogue service on the Feast of Tabernacles.

Etruscans

Inhabitants of Etruria, probably of Pelasgian origin, though this is uncertain. They were highly civilized and were governed by an aristocracy. They became subject to Rome after defeat in 283 BCE, and received the Roman franchise in 91 BCE.

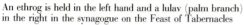

An ethrog is held in the left hand and a lulav (palm branch) in the right in the synagogue on the Feast of Tabernacles

Euripedes

Eucharist

Lit. 'thanksgiving'. One of several terms used for the central liturgical act of the Christian Church, which originates from the Last Supper of Christ with his disciples. Other terms used are Mass or Holy Communion.

Eumenides

Lit. 'well-meaning goddesses' or 'soothed goddesses'. This is a euphemism for the fearful, avenging deities who dwelt on Tartarus, dreaded by gods and men. They were called the Furies by the Romans.

Euripides

(455–406 BCE) Greek tragic poet. He was a friend of Socrates, who admired him because he portrayed men as they are, and brought the ancient heroes and heroines down to the standard of ordinary men and women.

Eurythmy

See Anthroposophy

Eusebius

(260–340 CE) Bishop of Caesarea and the Father of Church History. He was present at the Council of Nicaea in 325, where he presented a compromise creed that was rejected. He was not a great theologian, but his *Ecclesiastical History* in ten books presents an invaluable account of the Church from the Apostolic Age to his own day.

Eve

According to Genesis, the name of the first woman, formed from one of Adam's ribs. The name means 'mother of all living'. By falling for the temptation of the serpent and persuading Adam to eat the forbidden fruit, she brought punishment on them both, and is held responsible for the entry of sin into the world.

Evensong

Customary name for the service of Evening Prayer in the Anglican Prayer Book. It is based on a conflation of Vespers and Compline.

Evil

Throughout human history men have been conscious of a struggle between good and evil. The latter is often depicted as a struggle against the will of God. One school of thought, including Zoroastrianism, sees two centres of power: good and evil, or light and dark. Others see one supreme, good centre of power, with many forces of evil constantly in rebellion or on the attack. Some see the struggle as everlasting, others prophesy the ultimate triumph of good.

Evolution

Biological theory associated with the names of Charles Darwin and T. H. Huxley. Darwin's book *The Origin of Species* (1859) and Huxley's book *Evolution in Biology* (1878) caused an uproar in church circles because the suggestion that the human race belongs to the order of Primates and has evolved by selection appeared to deny the biblical teaching that man is the creation of God. Theologians and biologists are now agreed that the theory of evolution as a method is compatible with belief in the overall design of God's creation.

Ex Cathedra

Lit. 'from the chair' or 'from the throne'. At the Vatican Council of 1870 the Roman Catholic Church affirmed that when the Bishop of Rome makes a pronouncement as the successor of St Peter, i.e. *ex cathedra*, his words on faith and morals have the infallible character of apostolic doctrine.

Ex Nihilo

Lit. 'out of nothing'. An essential feature of the Christian doctrine of the Creation is that everything comes from God, that nothing had prior existence, and that God has created everything from the beginning.

Ex Opere Operato

Term used in connection with Roman Catholic sacramental theology asserting that the sacrament itself is an instrument of God, and that provided the conditions of its institution are fulfilled, grace is conferred. This expresses a belief in an objective mode of operation, independent of the subjective attitude of the priest or the worshippers.

Exclusive Brethren

This movement broke away from the Plymouth or Open Brethren under the leadership of John Darby in 1845. They believe they have recovered the truth about the Church as set out in Scripture: that it should be separate from the world and that true believers should have no fellowship with other communities because of their false doctrines. They have a strict moral code, and refuse to belong to trade unions or professional bodies or associations.

Excommunication

Judgement or verdict of an ecclesiastical court which excludes the guilty person from participating in the liturgy or sacraments of the Christian Church. Such persons can not be buried in consecrated ground. The Talmud lists forty-four offences which are punishable by excommunication from the Jewish community. This penalty can be imposed only by a rabbinic court.

Exegesis

Theological discipline concerned with the explanation of biblical texts. Many schools of thought have emphasized different methods. In the early Church the Fathers of Alexandria favoured the allegorical method, whereas the School of Antioch searched for the literal sense. The period of the Reformation showed the difference between the Catholic exegesis according to church doctrine and Protestant exegesis according to guidance of the Holy Spirit. Modern exegesis takes account of linguistics, textual studies, and the comparative study of religion.

Existentialism

The modern use of this term dates from the philosophy of S. Kierkegaard (1813–1855), a Danish religious thinker. Negatively, he criticized schools of philosophy that concentrate on universal essences while ignoring individual existence. Positively, he sought to recover the real personal being. This has been developed by atheist philosophers such as Heidegger and Sartre through pessimism, and by the Christian philosopher Gabriel Marcel through hope. The philosophy was condemned by Pope Pius XII in *Humani Generis* (1950).

Exodus

1. Second book in the Bible. It contains the record of the escape of the Israelites from Egypt, the beginning of the wilderness wanderings and the giving of the Law by God on Mt Sinai; it is part of the Torah.
2. Historically, the term is primarily applied to the occasion when Moses led the Israelites from slavery in Egypt to freedom, and this is commemorated annually in the Passover Festival.

Exogamy

Custom which compels a man to marry outside his own tribe.

Exorcism

Driving out of demons or evil spirits from the body of a possessed person or from a place by the invocation of the superior power of a deity.

Expiation

The general meaning of this term in Christian theology is that Jesus Christ, by his sacrifice on the Cross, paid the penalty, or made amends for the sin of mankind. This is based on NT texts where Christ is described by a Greek word usually translated 'propitiation'.

80

Exsurge Domine

Title of a papal bull issued by Leo X in June 1520 in condemnation of Martin Luther and his teachings. It contains forty-one propositions dealing with various items of the Catholic faith which Luther had challenged. It marks a turning-point in the Reformation, as Luther burned the bull in December 1520, and thus formally broke with the papacy.

Extra Sensory Perception (ESP)

Term indicating the reception of information by a person through means other than the senses. It is the area of study known as parapsychology, often identified by the Greek letter psi. The three commonest types of ESP are clairvoyance, precognition and telepathy.

Eye

In symbolism the eye stands for intelligence and spirituality, but also for terror. It enables us not only to see, but to affect what we see. It is sometimes connected with the sun, as the all-seeing eye that watches the world and is the source of light. On the other hand there are many legends showing dread of the evil eye. Some people were thought to be cursed with this and unable to control it, while others could use its powers at will. The peacock's tail terrifies some people because of its many 'eyes', put there, according to Greek mythology, by Hera to spy on her husband Zeus.

Ezekiel

One of the major prophets of the Hebrew Bible. His message is concerned with the Jews in exile in Babylonia in 586 BCE. It is not certain whether he lived in Jerusalem or Babylon or both. The closing chapters envisage the reunion of the tribes of Israel and Judah, the rebuilding of the Temple, and the restoration of sacrificial worship. His prophecy is remarkable for its apocalyptic imagery.

Ezra

1. Hebrew scribe who was allowed to return to Jerusalem by Artaxerxes to revive the life of the city and enforce the strict observance of the Jewish Law. He held a public reading of the Law, and insisted that all non-Jewish wives should be divorced. There is a difference of opinion among scholars about the date of his journey, viz. whether it was 458 or 398 BCE.

2. Book in the Hebrew Bible relating the events of Ezra's journey and reforming activities.

Faith
1. Term almost synonymous with 'religion' or 'system of religious belief', e.g. the Christian faith or the Muslim faith.
2. Commitment or response to what is believed and accepted as divine truth. Christian theologians describe it as the first of the theological virtues, the other two being hope and charity (love).

Fakir
Lit. 'poor man'. Title used in Islam for religious ascetics who give up home life and lead a mendicant existence, sometimes as solitaries, sometimes in communities.

Falah (A)
In Islamic teaching well-being and prosperity; the true good of life to which Muslims are summoned in the call to prayer.

Falashas
Inhabitants of Amhara in Ethiopia who claim descent from Jewish immigrants during the reign of Jeroboam. They practise circumcision and keep the Jewish feasts but do not use Hebrew.

Falasifa
Muslims who tried to combine their faith with Hellenistic philosophy. Their leading scholars were Avicenna and Averroës; they stressed the eternity of the world and the exaltation of philosophy over prophecy, but denied the resurrection of the body.

Fall
Term used to describe the disobedience of Adam and Eve, recorded in Genesis 3:1 ff. and in the Qur'an 2:36. This is regarded by some schools of thought as the origin of sin which set the human race under the judgement of God.

Familia
Total household in ancient Rome, including members of the family, servants and slaves.

Fana
Term used in Sufi Islam for the passing away of the self, either permanently or momentarily.

Fard (A)
Duty or obligation whose performance will be rewarded while its omission will receive punishment. Islamic law distinguishes between a fard binding on everyone and a fard binding on only a group or community.

Farvardian
Zoroastrian festival for remembering the dead at Towers of Silence in Bombay and other Parsee centres.

Fasad (A)
In Islamic teaching the corruption or disorder which men cause on earth.

Fasting
Discipline of the body's natural appetites, which has a long history in all religions. It is found in the early Greek Eleusinian mysteries and in the Jewish fast on the Day of Atonement. Hindu and Buddhist teachers are under an obligation to fast regularly. Islam observes the month of Ramadan as a fast, and in the Christian Church the forty days of Lent are a period of fasting. (See also Festivals, Feasts and Fasts)

Fate

Derived from the Latin *fatum* (spoken decree). The Greeks called the goddess of fate Nemesis, and she had three assistants: Clotho, the spinner of destiny, Lachesis, the weaver of the web of chance, and Atropos, who cut the thread. In Scandinavian tradition these appear as the three Norns. The Islamic teaching of kismet and the Christian doctrine of predestination come very near the idea of an unchangeable fate or destiny. The Islamic expression 'Imshallah' and the Christian expression 'D.V.' *(Deo volente)*, both meaning 'God willing', reflect this. In Buddhism and Hinduism the doctrine of karma suggests that, by a universal law, a man's deeds determine his fate in a future life.

Father

1. Name or title of God used in the OT, e.g. Isaiah 64:8, Malachi 2:10, and in the NT, e.g. John 10:15, Romans 8:15.
2. Title given to the theologians of the early Christian Church who by their writings and in councils defined the faith and promulgated the Creeds.
3. Highest of seven grades of Mithraic initiation, protected by Saturn.

Fatihah (A)

Lit: 'opener'. Title of the first surah of the Qur'an, which not only opens the book but, according to the teaching of some Muslims, contains the basic thought of the whole of the Qur'an.

Fatima

1. Daughter (605–633 CE) of Muhammad and Khadija. She married Ali, the Prophet's cousin, and bore two sons, Hasan and Husain. On the death of Muhammad, Fatima quarrelled with the Caliph Abu Bakr, and her husband and sons became the founders and leaders of the Shiah Muslims, some of whom accord Fatima almost divine veneration.
2. Small town in Portugal that has become a shrine and place of pilgrimage since May 1917, when three children claimed to have had a series of visions of Our Lady of the Rosary. Her message was the practice of penance, the recitation of the Rosary, and devotion to the Immaculate Heart of Mary. Over the spot there is now the Basilica and Shrine of Our Lady of Fatima.

Fatwa

Legal opinion given by a Muslim mufti by which the Shari'ah is applied to cases or issues so that its authority and precedents may be upheld.

Feasts

See Festivals, Feasts and Fasts

Fertile Crescent

Fertile arc of land from the Persian Gulf through the alluvial plain of the Tigris and Euphrates Rivers, curving round through Syria and Israel, skirting the northern edge of the Arabian desert and continuing south to Egypt and the Nile. This was the cradle of several ancient civilizations, including Sumer and Akkad, the Hittites and the Babylonians.

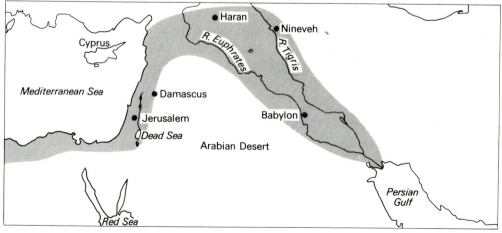

Fertile Crescent

Fertility Cults

Religious rites intended to promote the growth of crops and the strength of the tribe. It is clear that, before man understood biological processes, he was impressed by the cyclical character of fertility, and that he believed that the cycle was controlled by supernatural powers or gods. It was therefore necessary to keep the goodwill of the gods by offerings and thanksgivings, usually in the spring and at harvest. Fertility cults took many forms: sometimes sacrifices of animals or human beings, when blood would be sprinkled over the fields; sometimes libations, gifts of grain, oil or wine; sometimes a sacred marriage, when the act of intercourse was expected to persuade the gods to give fertility to the fields.

Festivals, Feasts and Fasts

All religions have times of rejoicing and of repentance. Feasts of rejoicing may be associated with historic events such as Christmas and Easter and the Sikh Feast of Baisakhi, or with the cycle of nature as in the Jewish Feast of Tabernacles, or with a particular belief as in the Hindu Feast of Dushera. Penitential fasts provide an opportunity for the contemplation of man's sins and needs. Examples are Lent in Christianity, Ramadan in Islam and the ten days of penitence leading to the Day of Atonement in Judaism.

Fetial

Priestly official in ancient Rome responsible for the religious aspects of dealings with other states.

Fetishism

Worship of an inanimate object by primitive tribes because of its supposed magic powers or because it is thought to be inhabited by a spirit. The word is derived from the Portuguese *feitico*, which early Portuguese explorers applied to images and magical charms they found among African tribes.

Fig

First plant mentioned in the Bible, as Adam and Eve are said to have used its leaves for clothing. Legend suggests that Judas Iscariot hanged himself on a fig-tree. It was venerated by the Romans

Fetish stool with human and animal skulls   Agni, the Vedic god of fire

84

because the cradle of Romulus and Remus became lodged in the roots of a fig-tree. Buddha attained enlightenment while meditating under a bo-tree, a species of fig-tree.

Filioque

Latin word meaning 'and from the son'. It was inserted in the Nicene Creed by the Western Church at the Council of Toledo in 589 CE, after the words 'the Holy Ghost, . . . , Who proceedeth from the Father'. This formula, known at the Double Procession, has never been accepted by the Eastern Orthodox Church.

Fiqh (A)

Jurisprudence; the legal order of Islam as exercised in the courts and expounded by the several schools of law.

Fir

As evergreens, the fir and pine have often been symbols of fertility, constancy and immortality. The fir was sacred to Cybele, the mother of the gods, and was also connected with Attis and Osiris. In modern times it has played and still plays an important part in Christmas celebrations.

Fire

For man fire is an enemy and a friend. It is thus the agent of sacrifice, and also of purification and renewal. God appeared to Moses in a burning bush (Exodus 3); Elijah was carried to heaven in a chariot of fire (2 Kings 2), and the Holy Spirit came upon the Apostles in tongues as of fire (Acts 2). In Hinduism Agni is the god of fire, and fire is sacred to Zoroastrians and Parsees. Jains believe that fire is alive and refuse to extinguish it. Ordeal by fire has been a widespread practice, and many festivals terminate in bonfires to symbolize the end of a year or the destruction of the past.

Firmament

Lit. 'made solid'. Word used in Genesis 1:6 and Ezekiel 1:26 to refer to the dome of heaven. This reflects an early Semitic belief that heaven was a solid vault dividing the upper, celestial waters from the lower, terrestrial waters.

First Fruits

Jewish festival of thanksgiving details of which are set out in Exodus 23. First fruits of the harvest, in the form of two loaves, were presented at the Temple on the Feast of Weeks, Shavuoth, celebrated fifty days after the Passover. This is now chiefly associated with Israel's spiritual harvest, the revelation at Sinai and the giving of the Ten Commandments. In modern Israel the first fruits often take the form of gifts for the Jewish National Fund.

Fish

One of the earliest symbols used in Christian art, because the letters of the Greek word for fish, *ichthus*, were taken as an acrostic giving 'Iesous Christos Theou Uios Soter', meaning 'Jesus Christ, God's Son, Saviour'. Today it is the badge of a Christian organization which helps the disabled and needy.

Fitnah (A)

Originally trial or persecution borne by believers because they accepted the message of Muhammad; later used to describe sedition or conspiracy against the Islamic state.

Fitrah (A)

Natural constitution of man, as divinely designed and so fitted to the ultimate religion of Islam (Qur'an 30:30).

Five

Number of special significance. Writers in the ancient world identified four elements plus the life-giving spirit, thus five represented the animate world of nature. Ancient Chinese philosophy spoke of five agents or basic elements of the universe: wood, fire, earth, metal and water. Their interaction gave rise to the myriad things of the universe, engendered by Yang and Yin. Man has five senses. In the Bible there are five books of Moses, the Pentateuch, and the Gospel of St Matthew has five sections to match this. It is also recorded that Christ suffered five wounds on the Cross.

Five K's

Symbols worn by initiated Sikhs who have entered the brotherhood (Khalsa): (1) kesh (uncut hair and beard); (2) khanga (steel comb); (3) kaccha (short pants); (4) kara (steel bangle); (5) kirpan (short sword).

Five Pillars of Wisdom

Five duties incumbent on all Muslims: (1) profession of faith and confession of the unity of God (shahadah); (2) prayer (salat); (3) almsgiving (zakat); (4) fasting (saum); (5) pilgrimage to Mecca (hajj).

Flagellation

In the ancient world whipping was thought to stimulate the circulation and thus be good for health. Self-flagellation has sometimes been practised by religious communities as a form of penance. In the 13th and 14th centuries flagellants roused hysteria in many parts of Europe by arranging processions in which men and women whipped one another while making public confession of their sins.

Flamen

Title given to priests in ancient Rome, derived from a root meaning 'burnt offerings', with obvious reference to their religious duties.

Flood

An account of a devastating flood in the early days of human history occurs in the literature of many races. In Genesis 6–9 there is the story of Noah, who was saved from the Flood in an ark that he had built. The Babylonian *Epic of Gilgamesh* tells how Utnapishtim was warned by Ea of an impending flood and advised to build an ark in which he and his family would saved. Other similar stories come from Mesopotamia, concerning Xisuthros, from Sumeria, concerning Ziusudra, and from Greece, concerning Deucalion.

Font (St Marychurch, Devon)

Font

Receptacle for water used in the baptism of infants; it is usually near the door of the church, to show that baptism is the symbolic ceremony for admission to the Church. Fonts are often octagonal, because eight is the numerical symbol of a new beginning.

Forty

This has been a significant number from very ancient times. It was sacred to the Babylonian god Ea, and at Babylon and Nineveh was the number of offerings to be made to the gods on festivals. With seven, it is the most frequently mentioned number in the Bible. The Flood rains lasted forty days; Moses was on Mt Sinai and Jesus in the wilderness for forty days, and the Israelites journeyed for forty years in the wilderness after the Exodus. It is possible that sometimes 'forty days' was used to indicate a long but unspecified period.

Four

Traditionally four is the number of the earth, because the ancient world recognized four elements, and because the earth is bounded by the four cardinal points of the compass. Christianity has the four Gospels and Buddhism has the Four Noble Truths. Yet four is often regarded as the most unlucky number, because it is tied to the earth with all its troubles.

Four Noble Truths

Set of principles through which the Buddha gained enlightenment: (1) the Truth concerning the nature of suffering; (2) the Truth concerning the cause of suffering; (3) the Truth concerning the cessation of suffering; (4) the Truth concerning the Eightfold Path, which leads to the cessation of suffering.

Four Sacred Events

Festivals commemorating events in the history of the Buddha: (1) his birth; (2) his enlightenment; (3) his first sermon; (4) his death.

Foursquare Gospel

See Elim Pentecostalists

Francis of Assisi

(1182–1226) Founder of the Franciscan order. Born into a prosperous family, he heard a call from God to renounce wealth and luxury, and in 1208 he gathered together a group of friends, who lived in poverty according to a simple rule, and rapidly attracted other followers. Francis was not happy as an organizer, but preferred to undertake preaching tours, demonstrating with great humility his devotion to God, his compassion for humanity and his love of nature.

Franciscans

Christian order of friars founded by St Francis of Assisi and granted recognition in 1210. They are dedicated to absolute poverty and the renunciation of worldly pleasure, and to preaching the Gospel and caring for the sick and needy. Their spirit is one of joyous praise of God's creation.

Frankincense

See Incense

Fravashi/Fravahr

Term used in the Zoroastrian religion for man's heavenly self or guardian spirit.

Freemasonry

Brotherhood which has its origins in the 12th century, when English stone masons formed a religious fraternity which later concerned itself with the education and morals of its members. This was abolished by Edward VI in 1547, but was re-established in the 18th century, when lodges were rapidly formed throughout Europe. In the Latin countries the lodges were openly hostile to the Church, and the Roman Catholic Church has several times condemned Freemasonry, most recently in 1884. In England and Germany Freemasonry expects of its members an undogmatic belief in God, but it is chiefly concerned with social and philanthropic activity. It is impossible to analyse the teachings of Freemasonry as they are closely guarded secrets which initiates swear not to reveal.

Frey

Norse deity, the god of sunshine and fertility. He was popular in Iceland, Norway and Sweden and his chief temple was at Uppsala.

Freya

Norse deity, the sister of Frey and the wife of Odin. She was originally concerned with fertility, and became the goddess of love and the patroness of singers. The pig was regarded as sacred to her, but she was portrayed as riding in a chariot drawn by cats.

Friar

Member of one of the mendicant orders, e.g. the Franciscans, Dominicans or Carmelites.

Friday

In the Christian Church Friday has been kept as a weekly commemoration of the Passion of Christ. Many Christians observe it as a day of fasting or abstinence from meat. In Islam Friday is the day of the week commemorating the creation of Adam. It is the day when sermons are preached in the mosques, when the communal nature of prayer is stressed.

Frigg

Norse deity, the wife of Odin and the goddess of love; she is probably to be identified with Freya. She was the mother of Balder, and asked all plants to protect him. Unfortunately she forgot the mistletoe, and Loki caused him to be killed with an arrow made from that plant.

Fulfilling Father

From the Latin *pater patratus*, a Roman official charged with the declaration of war and the concluding of treaties.

Fundamentalism

Term denoting the views of extreme Protestant bodies which teach the literal infallibility of the Bible, and a rigid adherence to doctrines such as the Virgin Birth, Substitutionary Atonement and the Second Coming.

Furies

Roman name for the Greek Eumenides, avenging goddesses who dwelt on Tartarus, dreaded by gods and men.

Furqan (A)

Lit. 'revelation', or 'the distinguisher' or 'the criterion'. Title applied by Muslims to the Qur'an, but also used in the Qur'an of other scriptures.

Gabars

Remaining Zoroastrians of Persia, as distinct from the Parsees of India. The name may be derived from the Arabic word *kafir* (infidel). There are now very few Gabars left.

Gabriel (H)

Lit. 'strong man of God' or 'God's mighty man'. Name of one of the four archangels, with Michael, Raphael and Uriel. He is mentioned in the Book of Daniel as the interpreter of two of Daniel's visions, and in the Gospel of St Luke as the messenger of God who announced the forthcoming births of John the Baptist and Jesus. According to Muslim tradition he dictated the Qur'an to Muhammad.

Gad

Seventh son of Jacob, the Patriarch of Israel, and Zilpah, the handmaid of Leah. The Israelite tribe named after him occupied territory to the east of the Jordan.

Gah

Term used in the Zoroastrian religion for the five religious divisions of the day.

Galatians, Epistle to the

One of the earliest of St Paul's letters in the NT. It was written to converts who were being urged to retain Jewish practices such as circumcision and food laws as a prerequisite for admission to the Christian Church. The Epistle argues that the Christian is not bound by the Jewish law.

Galilee

Area of Palestine which was the scene of the boyhood and early ministry of Jesus. Some of his disciples were fishermen on the Sea of Galilee.

Gallican Rite

1. Liturgical forms used in Gaul before Charlemagne imposed the Roman rite.
2. Non-Roman rites of the early Western Church.
3. Neo-Gallican liturgies of the 17th and 18th centuries.

Galut (H)

Term for the Dispersion of the Jews. (See Diaspora)

Games

In ancient Greece, athletic competitions held periodically as solemn festivals in honour of a god (usually Zeus), providing a period of truce. The Olympic games were held every four years. In Rome there were various contests, religious in origin but secularized. The gladiatorial 'games' originated in Etruscan funeral rites.

Gandharva

In the *Rig-Veda* he was a heavenly being who guarded the sacred drink soma, knew the heavenly secrets, and had power over women. In later literature there are many gandharvas who dwell in Indra's heaven and are musicians to the gods.

Gandhi, N. K.

(1869–1941)   Hindu reformer who stressed the doctrine of selfless action or soul force, and developed a non-violent protest movement in his struggle to free India from British rule. He is often called Mahatma Gandhi, or just the Mahatma (great soul).

Ganesh Chaturthi
Hindu festival of Ganesha, the elephant-headed god of wisdom and good fortune. It is celebrated in the autumn and clay models of elephants are taken out in procession.

Ganesha
Hindu elephant-headed god, the son of Shiva and Parvati. According to Hindu mythology Shiva cut off his son's head in anger, and then, as Ganesha's mother was very upset, replaced it with the head of the first creature he met, which happened to be an elephant. Ganesha is popular as the god of wisdom and good fortune, and it is a common practice to offer worship to Ganesha before proceeding to the worship of another god, or before any major enterprise, in order to ensure good fortune in the subsequent enterprise.

Ganges, River
River sacred to Hindus. It rises in the Himalayas and flows more than 2400 km, discharging into the Bay of Bengal. Hindus consider it a duty to bathe in the River Ganges or at least wash in water from it, and it is regarded as a great blessing to die in the holy city Benares, on the banks of the Ganges.

Ganjitsu
Most important holiday–festival in Japan, celebrating the beginning of the new year. It is comparable to the celebration of Christmas in the Western world.

Garant
Practice in Indian village Hinduism of burying certain personal possessions at a crossroads in order to transfer sickness or affliction from one family to another.

Gargoyle
In Gothic architecture projecting spouts for disposing of rainwater from roof gutters were often carved in grotesque forms such as monstrous animals or demons. Sometimes, as at Notre Dame in Paris, gargoyles were added for decoration, or to frighten off evil spirits.

Garuda
In Hindu mythology the bird on which the god Vishnu rides. It is half man and half vulture, and is the king of the birds. Garuda stole nectar (amrita) from the gods for his mother. Indra fought him and recovered the nectar but had his thunderbolt smashed in doing so.

Gatha
Hymn or set of verses composed by Buddhist monks in a state of spiritual insight.

Gathas
Oldest section of the Zoroastrian scriptures, the *Avesta*. There are seventeen gathas or hymns, which contain the teaching of Zoroaster and form part of the Yasna.

Garuda (11th–12th century)

Shrine dedicated to Ganesha (Singapore)

Hindus bathing in the Ganges

Gautama

Clan name of Siddhartha, son of the ruler of the Sakya tribe in Nepal. He probably lived from 563 to 483 BCE, and on his enlightenment was known as the Buddha. Many miraculous legends surround his birth. He left home when twenty-nine, seeking an answer to the problem of suffering; he found no help in asceticism, but achieved enlightenment through meditation. He assembled Sanghas, communities of monks, teaching the Four Noble Truths and following the Eightfold Path.

Gayatri

Most sacred verse in the *Rig-Veda* (ref. 3, 62, 10), named from its metre. It is called the Mother of the *Vedas*, and is repeated by Brahmins on rising, at noon and before sleeping.

Gayomart

In Zoroastrian mythology the primal man created by Ahura Mazda in the sixth stage of the Creation.

Ge

In Greek mythology she was the first being who sprang from chaos, after which she gave birth to Uranus and Pontus. She was the earth mother, known to the Romans as Tellus.

Geb

Ancient Egyptian god regarded as the earth. He was the son of Shu and Tefnut, and the brother and husband of Nut, the sky goddess, by whom he was the father of Isis, Osiris and Set.

Gedo Zen

Second of the five types of Zen. Lit. 'outside way', i.e. Zen practices outside the Buddhist framework.

Gehenna

In Jewish apocryphal literature a place of burning or torment, the equivalent of hell. The word is derived from Ge Hinnom, the Valley of Hinnom outside Jerusalem, where continual fires burned the city's rubbish.

Gelede

Yoruba cult in which masked dancers perform rites as a protection against harm from witchcraft.

Gemara

Aramaic word meaning 'completion', designating comment on and discussion of the Mishnah. The Mishnah and the Gemara make up the Talmud.

Gematria

In the Jewish Kabbalah, a method of interpreting the words of Scripture by calculating the numerical value of the Hebrew letters and finding other words or phrases of equal value.

Gelede mask

Gemini

Lit. 'twins'. The reference is to Castor and Pollux, the twin sons of Leda and Zeus. Gemini is the third sign of the zodiac, covering the period 22 May to 21 June. In the constellation Gemini, the two brightest stars are Castor, a double star, and Pollux, a little less than first magnitude.

Genesis

First book in the Bible, containing accounts of the Creation, the Fall, the Flood, the Tower of Babel and the Patriarchs of Israel; part of the Torah.

Geneva Bible

English translation of the Bible published in 1560. It was the first edition to introduce verse numbers, and was widely popular until the introduction of the King James Bible, which was published complete in 1611.

Genius

Roman spirit of male fertility within the family. In earliest times it was regarded as the continuing, living power of ancestors; later it was regarded as a guardian angel.

Genizah

Room attached to a synagogue where disused scrolls and other old manuscript books are stored. In the genizah of an ancient synagogue in Cairo portions of manuscript from the 9th century were discovered. They contained a previously unknown text, and have been published as *Fragments of a Zadokite Work*.

Gentile
This was originally a term for 'nations', but in the Bible it came to have the meaning 'non-Israelite', and it now means 'non-Jewish'.

Genuflexion
Kneeling briefly on the right knee with the body erect. Act of reverence performed by some Christians before the Blessed Sacrament.

Geonim
Two Jewish academies in the Babylonian cities of Sura and Pumbeditha, which flourished from the 8th to the 13th century. They expounded the Talmud and compiled legal codes to apply the Talmud in civil and religious matters.

St George (by Donatello)

George, St
Christian martyr and patron saint of England. Little is known of him, but there is probably a reference to him in Eusebius. The story of his slaying the dragon is first found in 12th century literature. His standard is a red cross on a white ground, and his feast-day is 23 April, the day of his martyrdom under Diocletian in 303 CE.

Get
Jewish bill of divorce. This is granted under conditions and regulations set out in the Mishnaic order, Nahsim. These are based on the Torah (Deuteronomy 24:1–4), and the issuing of the get secures for the wife freedom to remarry.

Gethsemane
Garden near the Mount of Olives where Jesus went to pray after the Last Supper, and where he was arrested (Mark 14:32–52).

Getig
Term used in Zoroastrianism to indicate the manifest world.

Ghaib, al
Muslim term for the unseen, the realm of divine mystery.

Gharat
Party accompanying a village Hindu bride as she goes out to meet the bridegroom prior to the wedding ceremony.

Ghat
Flight of steps leading to a river landing-place (usually on the Ganges). Burning ghats are places for Hindu cremation, the most famous being in the holy city of Benares.

Ghee
Type of clarified butter used by Hindus for sacrificial rites and for cremation.

Ghetto
Term for a part of a town in which certain people, usually Jews, are compelled to live. The word is derived from the Italian *borghetto* (little town). The first ghetto was established in Rome in the time of Pope Paul IV.

Ghibellines
See Guelphs and Ghibellines

Ghost
Spirit or manifestation of a dead person appearing to the living. Belief in ghosts has, in many societies, been linked with belief in personal survival after death. Virgil describes in the *Aeneid* the visit of Aeneas to the underworld, where he saw the ghosts of many heroes. Ghosts are generally thought to be the spirits of ancestors returning to their home, or troubled spirits returning to the place of their distress. Many fears, superstitions and legends have gathered round the subject, but no satisfactory scientific explanation has been advanced.

Gideon
Fourth of the Israelite Judges whose achievements are recorded in the Book of Judges. He delivered Israel from oppression by the Midianites, and was invited to be king, but he refused, saying, 'The Lord shall rule over you' (Judges 8:23).

Gilgamesh
Hero of an Akkadian epic and King of Erech. Part of the epic concerns his longing for everlasting life, and how he found and lost the flower which would have granted him immortality.

Gilgamesh, Epic of

Long Babylonian epic poem known from eleven tablets of the 7th century BCE discovered at Nineveh in 1872. The poem contains an account of a flood from which Utnapishtim and his family were saved in an ark which he built in response to a warning from the god Ea. It also relates the search by Gilgamesh for everlasting life.

Gita

See *Bhagavadgita*

Glebe

Land devoted to the maintenance of the incumbent of a parish. It can be cultivated by the parson or by a tenant to whom he leases it.

Gloria in Excelsis

First words in Latin of the hymn 'Glory be to God on high', which is part of the liturgy of the Mass and the Eucharist. In the Mass it is sung after the Kyries, but in the Anglican Prayer Book of 1662 it was placed at the end of the service, immediately before the Blessing. In the present liturgical revision in the Anglican Church it can be inserted in either place. The original setting of the words is found in St Luke's account of the birth of Jesus, where they are sung by the choir of angels to the shepherds (Luke 2:14).

Glossolalia

Speaking with tongues; ecstatic utterances under the inspiration of a powerful religious experience. The gift came to the disciples of Jesus on the day of Pentecost, when they were filled with the Holy Spirit (Acts 2:4). It has been practised intermittently in the Church through the centuries, and is now regarded by Pentecostalists as a necessary expression of the spirit granted to those who have been born again.

Gnosticism

Derived from the Greek word for knowledge, this is a term applied to systems of belief which claim to impart special knowledge of God, of his relation to the world and men, and of redemption only to the enlightened, who go through special initiation ceremonies. Different schools which developed under leaders such as Marcion, Valentinus and Ptolemaeus were strongly opposed by the early Church because they minimized the place of faith in the path to salvation.

Goat

Frequently associated in mythology with Pan or with the Devil. In the scapegoat ritual (Leviticus 16), one goat was sacrificed while the other was driven out into the wilderness for Azazel, after being symbolically laden with the people's sins.

Gobind Singh

Tenth Sikh Guru who in 1699 initiated the new community or Khalsa. He baptized five followers, giving them the name Singh, and presenting to them the five symbolic emblems which are still the typical signs of a Sikh. His birthday, in January, is kept by Sikhs as a festival.

God

The derivation of the English word is uncertain, but it indicates the supreme being, creator and ruler of the universe. The word is used with varying shades of meaning in different religions. Judaism, Christianity and Islam are strictly mono-theistic, whereas Hinduism recognizes many forms of God in the shape of different gods and goddesses with a variety of functions.

Godparents

Sponsors at a Christian baptism. They undertake responsibility for the spiritual welfare of the newly baptized, and in the case of a child, for its Christian upbringing and usually its care in the event of the death of its parents.

Guru Gobind Singh

Gog and Magog

In Ezekiel (38–39) Gog is described as a terrible ruler from the north. In Revelation 20:8 Gog and Magog stand for all the enemies of the Kingdom of God. In the Qur'an (18:98) they appear with Dhu'l Qarnaim (Alexander the Great). In British legend they were the last survivors of a race of giants overcome by Brutus.

Golden Bough

Bough which grew in the tree at Nemi, guarded by the priest of Diana, the King of the Wood. Anyone who could slay the priest and pluck the golden bough from the tree could claim the right of accession to the priestly office. According to Virgil (*Aeneid*, book 6). Aeneas had to pluck the golden bough from the shrine of Diana before he was allowed to visit the underworld. Sir James Frazer published a massive study of magic and religion with the title *The Golden Bough* in 1890.

Golden Calf

1. Cult object set up during the wilderness wanderings by Aaron, in response to the demands of the Israelites, when Moses was long delayed on Mt Sinai (Exodus 32).
2. Two cult objects set up by Jeroboam I, one at Bethel, the other at Dan, when he led the revolt against Judah and inaugurated a separate Kingdom of Israel (1 Kings 12:28–30).

Golden Rose

Ornament in the form of a rose made of gold with inset jewels which is blessed by the Pope on the fourth Sunday in Lent and presented to a distinguished person or community for special services rendered. The origin of the custom is unknown, but in 1049 Pope Leo IX described it as an ancient practice. Among the notable recipients have been Henry VIII of England, Isabella II of Spain, Napoleon III of France and the city of Basle.

Golden Rule

The words of Jesus 'Whatsoever you wish that men would do to you, do so to them' (Matthew 7:12). The same principle, though in negative form, is found in Tobit 4:15, Philo-Hypothetica 7:6, Confucius, *Analects* xv:23, Aristotle, *Nicomachean Ethics* ix:4, Seneca, *Epistles* 47:11, and Rabbi Hillel, *Shabb* 31a.

Golden Temple, Amritsar

Chief centre of Sikh pilgrimage. It was built by the fifth Guru, Arjan, beside the Pool of Immortality. It is also known as the Hari Mandir (the Temple of God) or the Darbar Sahib (the Lord's Court).

Good Friday

The most solemn day in the Christian year, commemorating the crucifixion of Jesus Christ. It is kept as a day of fasting, and churches are stripped of ornaments. Many churches hold a three-hour service from noon to 3 p.m. meditating upon the Crucifixion.

Gopis

Cowmaidens among whom Krishna lived when he took refuge at Vrindaban from the threats of the evil Kamsa. The stories of his many love affairs with the Gopis are regarded by Hindus as parables illustrating the love between God and human souls. Radha was Krishna's favourite, becoming his consort, and their tender love is the theme of many devotional songs. Vrindaban, the home of the Gopis, is a favourite Hindu place of pilgrimage.

Gorgon

In Greek mythology one of three sisters whose heads were covered with snakes instead of hair. The gaze of one of the three, Medusa, turned to stone anyone who beheld her. Perseus succeeded in cutting off Medusa's head by looking only at her reflection in a mirror, or his shield, while she slept.

Gospel

The Greek word for 'gospel' means 'good news', and the Christian gospel is the good news that God has fulfilled his ancient promises, and that through Jesus Christ a way of salvation has been opened for all. 'Gospels' applies particularly to the four gospels of Matthew, Mark, Luke and John, which record the good news.

Got

Term used by Sikhs for an exogamous caste grouping within the larger caste group known as the zat.

Gotra (S)

Lit. 'cow shed'. Term used in Hinduism for an enclosure, a family, a section, or a clan within the caste system.

Goy

Yiddish slang term for a gentile or non-Jewish person.

Grace

In Christian theology, the favour and mercy of God freely shown to men in the incarnate life and atoning death of his son, Jesus Christ. Grace opens the way to forgiveness of sins and the justification of the sinner. Catholic and Orthodox theology stress the part played by the Sacraments as 'efficacious signs' of grace, and conceive grace as an intrinsic transformation of man by a new godlike quality. Protestant theology teaches that grace comes as a gift from God alone.

Gradual

Lit. 'step'. Antiphon, usually from the Psalms, or a hymn, sung in the Christian Eucharist between the Epistle and the Gospel. Its name is derived from the ancient practice of singing it on the altar steps.

Grail

Usually interpreted as the chalice used by Jesus at the Last Supper, the Grail became the subject of many legends. The most famous was the quest for the Holy Grail by King Arthur's Knights of the Round Table.

Grail Foundation

Community founded by Oskar Bernhardt (1875–1941), who wrote a book entitled *In the Light of Truth* and took the name Abd-ru-shin, related to a former incarnation as an Arab prince. In 1928 he set up a community at Vomperberg, Austria, where he wrote his *Grail Message.* The community grew until the Second World War, when the Nazis commandeered the Centre. In 1945 it was returned, and the community flourished and spread to other countries. It claims to be based absolutely on Christ's teaching, and organizes lectures on Bernhardt's religious philosophy, and a variety of topics including diet and spiritual healing.

Gram-devata

Tutelary deities or godlings in Indian village Hinduism. These have strictly limited, local jurisdiction.

Granth

Word used in the Sikh religion for the accepted scriptures, particularly the *Guru Granth Sahib.*

Great Vehicle

English translation of 'Mahayana', the larger section of Buddhism. It is the northern school of Buddhism found in Tibet, Mongolia, China, Korea and Japan, and regarded by the Theravadins as a corruption of original Buddhism. Mahayana Buddhists put a greater emphasis on compassion, and regard the Buddha as a superhuman being.

Greek

Language in which the books of the NT were written. This form of Greek, known as Koine, must be distinguished from classical Greek, as it is simpler and more concise. It is also different from modern Greek.

Green

As the colour of vegetation, green is symbolic of life, and is prominent in spring festivals. Liturgically, it is the colour for vestments used in the Christian Eucharist from Trinity Sunday to Advent.

Gregger

Rattle used at the Purim service in a Jewish synagogue whenever the name of Haman is mentioned during the reading of the Book of Esther.

Gregorian Calendar

The calendar as reformed by Pope Gregory XIII in 1582; it was slow to win acceptance but is now in use in most Christian countries.

Gregorian Chant

Method of chanting the Psalms introduced by Pope Gregory I about 600 CE. He considered that the existing system, introduced by Ambrose of Milan, which used only four scales, was too limited. Gregory doubled the number of scales and changed the position of some of the semitones, using the term 'modes' for his new system. Choirs thus had access to a greater variety of chants and were given greater rhythmic freedom.

Gregory I

(540–604 CE)   Benedictine monk. His austere and saintly life and his renunciation of great wealth in order to build monasteries revealed him to be a born leader, and he was elected Pope in 590. He was named as the last Doctor of the Church, and is reckoned to be the founder of the medieval papacy. He reorganized the estates of the Church throughout Italy, and in 597 sent Augustine to undertake a mission in England with forty of his monks. He was a prolific theological writer, and introduced the Gregorian Chant, which gave choirs greater flexibility in singing the liturgy. He is generally known as Gregory the Great.

Gregory VII

(1021–1085)   Hildebrand, a native of Tuscany who became Pope in 1073. He set about a reform of the Church and aimed at a moral revival. He was opposed by several monarchs, but in 1077 the Emperor submitted to him and did penance. Gregory gained spiritual freedom for the Church and loosened its involvement in the feudal organization of Europe.

Grhastha

In Hindu thought the second of the four stages of life, i.e. being a householder and bringing up a family. Sikhism uses the term, believing that salvation can be achieved in the context of everyday life, or in the vocation of being a householder.

Grotius, Hugo

(1583–1645)   Dutch theologian and jurist. After holding important government offices he was accused of being too friendly with enemy countries and imprisoned in 1618. He escaped, but thereafter constantly had to change his residence. He wrote several books on theology, but his greatest work was a legal treatise *De Jure Belli ac Pacis*, which has earned for him the title 'Father of International Law'.

Guelphs and Ghibellines

During the period 1300–1500 the papacy was weak because of the 'Babylonish Captivity' in Avignon (1309–1377) followed by the Great Schism (1378–1415). At the same time the Holy Roman Empire was also experiencing internal strife, and throughout the period the Guelphs were the supporters of the Pope while the Ghibillines were the supporters of the Empire.

Guk

Nuer word for 'leather bag'. It is also used for 'prophet', as he is regarded as the receptacle of the spirit.

Gun

Term used in Sikhism for an attribute, quality or virtue. In man it is a gift from God which man does not possess in himself.

Gunas

Three forces or qualities through the interplay of which, according to Hindu thought, the universe evolved. These are sattva (goodness or brightness), rajas (passion or energy) and tamas (dullness or darkness).

Gurbani

Total expression of the word of God, which Sikhs believe comes to them through the *Guru Granth Sahib*.

Gurdjieff Society

George I. Gurdjieff (1870–1949), born in America, did much to introduce Eastern mystical thinking to the West. For forty years he travelled widely, searching out occult teachings and secret disciplines. In 1914 he settled in Moscow to write, but was driven out by the Russian Revolution, and in 1922 founded a society of his followers at Fontainebleau. He called his teaching 'the fourth way', the first three being the way of the fakir (physical discipline), the monk (emotional discipline) and the yogi (intellectual discipline). Gurdjieff aimed at stimulating the whole person and releasing inner energy, and his methods involved hard physical labour, sacred dances and advanced philosophical study. The Society does not aim to be a popular movement but welcomes those who wish to investigate the latent possibilities in man.

Gurdwara (Pn)

Sikh temple or a building for corporate worship.

Gurmukh

Term used by Sikhs to indicate a person who hears the Guru's word and endeavours to obey it.

Guru

Holy man or spiritual instructor in Indian religions, particularly Hinduism and Sikhism. In the Sikh community there were ten gurus, from Guru Nanak (1469–1539) to Gobind Singh (1666–1708). After the death of Gobind Singh the title was conferred on the sacred book, and the *Guru Granth Sahib* is now the only guru acknowledged by Sikhs.

Guru Granth Sahib

Holy book of the Sikh religion, containing the *Adi Granth* and other writings. It was put into its present form by the tenth Guru, Gobind Singh

Gurdwara Rikab Gant, Delhi

(1666–1708), who was the last human guru. Since his death the *Guru Granth Sahib* has been the only guru recognized by the Sikhs, and its presence is necessary for Sikh worship and Sikh weddings.

Gwan Buthni

Master of ceremonies at a Nuer sacrifice.

Gwan Kwoth

Nuer prophet; lit. 'possessor of the spirit'.

Gyan Khand

In the teaching of the Sikh Guru Nanak, the second of five stages or steps towards man's liberation. This is the attainment of knowledge, or the apprehension of the hidden qualities of creation.

Gyani

Religious teacher attached to a Sikh gurdwara or place of worship.

Guru Granth Sahib as centre of a Sikh wedding ceremony (Punjab)

Habakkuk

One of the prophetic books of the Hebrew Bible. Little is known of the prophet himself, but his work seems to date from the close of the 7th century BCE, as he mentions the invasion of Judah by Babylon in 606 BCE.

Habiru

Migrant tribesmen in the ancient Middle East, also known as Apiru. They are frequently mentioned in the Tell el Amarna Tablets addressed to Pharaoh Ikhnaton (1370–1353 BCE), because they were attacking Egyptian border towns.

Hadad

See Adad

Hades

Originally the god of the underworld, identified by the Romans with Pluto, who seized Persephone and forced her to spend three months each year in the underworld. Later the word was used for the underworld itself, the abode of the shades.

Hadith

Traditions of Islam which preserve many sayings of the Prophet Muhammad and stories about him. The Hadith is second in authority only to the Qur'an, and is most important Islamic source material, being parallel to the tradition from the standpoint of directives and law known as Sunna.

Hafiz

Muslim who has learnt the Qur'an by heart.

Haftarah (H)

Passage from the Prophets read in a synagogue on the Sabbath as a supplement to the Torah.

Hagar

Maidservant of Sarah by whom Abraham had a son, Ishmael (Genesis 16). When Isaac was born to Sarah, Hagar and Ishmael were driven from the encampment, and their sufferings are recalled in the annual Islamic Hajj to Mecca.

Haggadah (H)

Prayer book used by Jews at the Seder ritual on the eve of the Passover.

Haggai

One of the prophetic books of the Hebrew Bible. Haggai returned from exile in Babylon to Jerusalem in 537 BCE, and tried to stir up enthusiasm for the rebuilding of the Temple. This was accomplished in 520 BCE.

Hagiography

Study and writing of the lives of saints, involving the examination of primary sources, and the assessment of their importance in relation to their historical background.

Haiku/Haikai

Japanese verse forms of seventeen syllables. One of the many art forms influenced by Zen. The seventeen syllables are divided into three lines, the first usually having five syllables, the second seven and the third five. The purpose of the verses is not instruction but the deep enjoyment that will bring intuition or perception.

Hair

In many parts of the world, over a very long period, there has existed a belief that strength, vitality and magic power reside in the hair. In many folk tales the cutting of hair is followed by disaster. An example is the biblical story of Samson (Judges 16), who was bound by a Nazirite vow not to cut his hair but was beguiled by Delilah into revealing the secret of his vow and thus his strength. She cut his hair while he slept, and when he woke his strength was gone and he was captured and blinded. Members of the Sikh Khalsa, men and women, never cut their hair, nor do the men shave. Members of the Hare Krishna movement shave their heads but leave a topknot by which they hope Krishna will lift them to heaven. In some African tribes where the hair is kept short cutting must be done when the moon is waning, and the cut ends of hair must be buried in order to prevent an enemy from gaining possession of them and causing evil to the owner.

Hajj (A)

Muslim pilgrimage to Mecca and its environs in the sacred month; this is the Fifth Pillar of the Islamic religion. The details and order of the pilgrimage are governed by very strict regulations. The pilgrims in their special robes visit the Great Mosque, then process seven times round the Kaaba and try to touch the Black Stone. After this they visit the shrine of Abraham, and run to Safa and Marwa, remembering Hagar's search for water. The following day there is a sermon at the Mosque delivered by an imam. The next day the pilgrims journey 21 km on foot or by camel to the hill of Arafat and stand from midday until dusk listening to exhortations. That night they sleep under the stars, and the next morning go to Mina for the stoning of the Devil. Each pilgrim throws seven pebbles into a great heap. Then comes Id-al-Adha, the sacrifice of a sheep, and they go back to the Great Mosque to wash in water from the Well of Zamzam.

Halakhah (H)

Legal system of Judaism.

Hallah (H)

1. Form of bread. In the Hebrew Bible it is a special loaf set aside as part of the grain sacrifice (Exodus 29:2, 23; Leviticus 7:13). It is now popularly used for special loaves baked for eating on the Sabbath.

2. Tractate in the order Zera'im setting out the laws governing the offerings of grain, bread, fruit and tithes.

Decorative cloth used to cover the hallah (loaves)

Hallel (H)

Word meaning 'praise'; the title given to Psalms 113–118, which are used in the Jewish liturgy for New Moon, Passover, Pentecost, Tabernacles and Chanukkah.

Hallelujah (H)

Liturgical word meaning 'Praise ye the Lord'. It is found in many Psalms, and has been taken into Christian worship, often in the Greek form, Alleluia.

Hallowe'en

See All Hallows' Eve

Halo

Nimbus, usually a circle of light, behind the head or the whole body, used by artists to represent the effulgence of light around a holy figure.

Hammistagan

In Zoroastrian teaching a place midway between heaven and hell, for those whose good and evil deeds are equal.

Hammurabi

(1792–1750 BCE) King of Babylon renowned as a lawgiver and administrator. The Law Code of Hammurabi, containing two hundred and eighty-two laws inscribed on a stele 2.5 m high, was discovered in 1902 in Susa. Many of the laws are similar to those in the Mosaic code, and they throw much light on conditions in the ancient Near East.

Hana Matsuri

Japanese flower festival held in honour of the birthday of the Buddha.

Hanif (A)

Seeker after true religion, a description applied to Abraham in the Qur'an; a God-fearer before the coming of Islam.

Hanukkah

See Chanukkah

Hanuman

Monkey chief and god in Hindu mythology; the son of the wind, Pavana, he was able to fly through the air. He is prominent in the *Ramayana*, which tells how he built a bridge from India to Sri Lanka by which Rama crossed to rescue Sita from the demon king Ravana.

Haoma

Plant sacred to Zoroastrians. In its natural state it gives physical strength; when ritually pressed and consecrated, it gives heightened spiritual powers. It represents the heavenly priest and son of God. (See also Soma)

Hara

1. High central mountain, the abode of Mithra in the ancient Iranian account of the cosmos.
2. Lit. 'stomach' or 'abdomen'. In Zen teaching this is the source of psychosomatic power.

Hara-kiri

Lit. 'slitting the belly'. Form of suicide permitted in Japan to certain criminals, as a more honourable death than execution. It is sometimes resorted to by persons who wish to avoid a situation of dishonour.

Harappa

Site of an ancient city in northern India. It is in the Indus valley and was a centre of Indian culture *c.* 2500–1500 BCE. Excavations have revealed a citadel, brick houses, and stone figures which may be a mother goddess and a male deity. Seals with symbols such as the swastika have been discovered but inscriptions have not yet been deciphered.

Hanuman

Hare Krishna

First words of a chant or mantra used by a movement known as Krishna Consciousness, founded in 1965 by Swami Prabhupada. It is the basis of the movement's devotional activity, and the full wording, which is constantly repeated, is 'Hare Krishna, Hare Krishna, Krishna, Krishna, Hare, Hare'.

Harem (A)

Lit. 'prohibited' or 'banned'. Word used in Islamic countries to signify the women's apartments in a household, forbidden to any man except the husband.

Hargobind, Guru

(1595–1644)   Sixth Guru of the Sikh religion, he was responsible for building the shrine of Akal Takht by the Golden Temple at Amritsar.

Harijans

Lit. 'sons of Hari'. Term applied by Gandhi to Hindu untouchables to show his concern for them, as it means 'sons of God'.

Haroset

See Charoset

Haruspicy

Divination through the observation and interpretation of the entrails of an animal previously sacrificed.

Hasidim

See Chasidim

Haskalah (H)

Jewish word meaning 'enlightenment' often applied to a movement of the 18th century led by Moses Mendelssohn, which resulted in a new emphasis on education and a resurgence of the study of Hebrew and the Jewish scriptures in a modern context.

Hatha Yoga

Practice of physical yoga or bodily gymnastics.

Hathor

Ancient Egyptian goddess depicted as the heavenly cow held up from below by Shu, the air god. She was later identified with Isis.

Haumai

In Sikh teaching a quality of self-centredness or egoism in man; it is the catalyst of violence, doubt and sorrow, and must be eliminated before there is hope of salvation.

Haurvatat

In Zoroastrian teaching Wholeness or Welfare, one of the seven Amesha Spentas.

Havan

See Hom

Havdalah (H)

Service in a Jewish house at the end of the Sabbath when a special candle of plaited wax is extinguished in wine, and a spice box is passed round to savour the sweet scent of the holy day that is ending, and to prolong its fragrance into the coming week.

Hawk

Bird sacred to Horus in Egypt and to Apollo in Greece. In symbolism it is frequently connected with the sun.

Hawthorn

Usual emblem of May Day festivals. According to Christian legend it was used for the crown of thorns at the crucifixion of Jesus Christ.

Hazel

Traditionally the plant used to provide sceptres for kings, staves for Christian pilgrims and wands for magicians. Jewish tradition describes the rod of Moses as hazel, and it is still used by water-diviners as the rod for dowsing.

Hearth

In pre-Christian times the hearth was not only the centre of the home, but often also the altar of the domestic gods, e.g. the Greek goddess Hestia and the Roman penates.

Havdalah candle and spice box

Heaven

In the Bible this is a term used for the habitation of God and his angels, and also for the ultimate destiny of the righteous. References usually indicate a state of joy where the faithful Christian, assured of forgiveness of his sins, enjoys the eternal blessing of God. In the Qur'an (13:35; 47:12) this is described as paradise.

Hebrew

Semitic language in which the Jewish scriptures are written and in which the synagogue services are conducted. Classical Hebrew had been replaced by Aramaic in general use by the 1st century BCE, and modern Hebrew is a further development.

Hebrews, Epistle to the

One of the books in the NT. The author is not named, but tradition has assigned it to either Paul or Barnabas; more recently Apollos has been suggested. It appears to be addressed to Jewish Christians, and it expounds the work of Christ in his office as High Priest.

Hecate

Minor goddess of the Greek pantheon; she was connected with the underworld, and was mistress of ghosts, spectres and all things uncanny.

Hector

Trojan hero of Homer's *Iliad*. He was the bulwark of the city's defence, and the bravest of its warriors. Even when defeat was certain he offered fierce resistance, and after he was killed by Achilles and dragged round the city, his body was returned for honourable burial. He was the personification of loyalty, honour and all manly virtues.

Heder

Common name for the old-fashioned elementary school for the teaching of Judaism. It was usually a private institution, held in the house of the teacher.

Hedonism

Ethical doctrine which maintains that the proper end of moral effort is pleasure.

Hegira

See Hijrah

Heimdall

Deity in Scandinavian mythology who keeps watch on the bridge Bifrost, which connects the domain of the gods with that of men.

Hekdesh (H)

Term used in the Jewish community originally signifying property consecrated to the needs of the Temple in Jerusalem. After the destruction of the Temple, rabbis ruled that property could no longer be consecrated, but it could be dedicated to help the poor. In Israel today the term applies to the endowment of property, approved by a religious court and administered according to religious law, for the relief of poverty or for the advancement of education.

Helen of Troy

According to Greek legend, the daughter of the god Zeus and the mortal Leda. She became the wife of Menelaus of Lacedaemon, was abducted by Paris, son of King Priam, and carried away to Troy. She was considered to be the most beautiful woman of her time, and her abduction gave rise to the Trojan War, described by Homer in the *Iliad*. After the death of Paris and the destruction of Troy she was reconciled with Menelaus. In Marlowe's play *Dr Faustus*, her beauty so overwhelmed Faustus that he exclaimed, 'Was this the face that launched a thousand ships?'

Helena, St

(255–330 CE) Mother of the Emperor Constantine. According to tradition she discovered the cross on which Jesus Christ had been crucified, and over the place of crucifixion built the Church of the Holy Sepulchre in Jerusalem. She also founded basilicas in Bethlehem and on the Mount of Olives.

Helicon

Celebrated range of mountains in Boeotia, Greece, sacred to Apollo and the Muses.

Heliopolis

Lit. 'city of the sun'. There were two places so named.
1. Centre of Egyptian sun worship in Lower Egypt, called On in the Bible.
2. City in Syria, also known as Baalbeck, an important centre of the worship of Baal, one of whose symbols was the sun.

Hell

In the Bible one of the abodes of the dead, also called Hades or Sheol or the Pit. Hell is primarily a state of eternal punishment for sin. In the Qur'an (11:17) it is the place reserved for unbelievers.

Henotheism

Belief in one god considered worthy of worship, while acknowledging that other gods may exist.

Henry VIII

(1491–1547) Son of Henry VII, he was King of England from 1509. He was deeply interested in theology, and was given the title 'Defender of the Faith' by Pope Leo X in 1521. In 1533 he was excommunicated by Pope Clement VII for divorcing his wife Catherine. In 1535 Parliament declared him to be Supreme Head of the Church; he seems to have wished to retain most of the doctrines of the Church while promoting the independence of the Church of England from Rome.

Liver map used in hepatoscopy (clay, S. Babylonia, *c.* 1700 BCE)

Hepatoscopy

Art of foretelling the future by examining the structure of the liver of a sacrificed animal. It was practised in Babylon, and many liver 'maps' are to be seen in museums.

Hephaestus

Greek god of fire and the patron of blacksmiths. He was identified by the Romans with Vulcan.

Hera

Greek goddess, the consort of Zeus, whose name means 'mistress'. She was identified by the Romans with Juno, and was the goddess of marriage and of women.

Heracles

Greek form of the name Hercules, the most celebrated of the heroes of antiquity. The son of Zeus and the mortal Aecmene, he performed many courageous deeds, and on his death he was granted immortality and was worshipped as god and hero.

Herem (H)

In the Hebrew Bible this word indicates a person or thing which was separated from common use, either because it was an abomination to God (Exodus 22:20) or because it was consecrated to him (Leviticus 27:28). It is often translated 'ban' or 'devoted thing'. Sometimes an enemy was declared 'herem', to be wiped out (Deuteronomy 7:1–5). Later jurists reinterpreted it to mean an ordinance to preserve the purity of Israel's faith rather than destroy other people (cf. Zechariah 14:11). In post-Talmudic law 'herem' meant the excommunication of a Jew from all contact with the Jewish community, in punishment of a serious crime.

Heresy

Religious belief or practice contrary to the orthodox or generally accepted doctrine of the faith. Heresies have sometimes been suppressed with fierce persecution.

Herm

Pillar with a phallus and often a head of Hermes, to whom it is sacred.

Hermas

One of the Apostolic Fathers of the Christian Church, and author of a book entitled *The Shepherd*, written in response to visions. This book is in three parts: five Visions, twelve Mandates, and ten Similitudes. The Mandates contain teaching on Christian behaviour and virtues, while the Similitudes contain teaching on Christian principles such as penance and the forgiveness of sins.

Hermeneutics

Science and art of interpretation, especially of ancient writings. In Christian theology it seeks to

102

establish the way by which the reader arrives at the true meaning of the words of the Bible. It is the attempt to understand the gospel in terms of the existential situation of today.

Hermes
Messenger of the Greek gods, and hence the protector of travellers and traders. He was identified by the Romans with Mercury.

Hermetic Literature
Collection of Greek and Latin writings representing a religious philosophy of the Hellenistic period, and bringing together Platonic and Stoic teachings. The writings were at one time attributed to Hermes Trismegistus.

Hermit
Person who, for religious reasons, retires into a solitary life. The first Christian hermits mentioned lived in the 3rd century in Egypt. The practice has been more popular in the East than in the West, and today there are probably more Hindu hermits than Christian. The four stages of a Hindu Brahmin's life culminate in a period of forest-dwelling hermit-style existence.

Hermod
In Scandinavian mythology a son of Odin and the brother of Balder. When Balder was killed, Hermod went down to the world of death and jumped over the gates of hell in an endeavour to bring his brother back to the upper world.

Hero
In Greek mythology a figure of the past, the founder of a city, or ancestor of a clan, worshipped as a kind of demigod.

Herod the Great
(70 BCE–4 CE) Second son of Antipater the Idumaean. He received the Kingdom of Judaea from Antony and Octavian in 40 BCE, and ruled with ability and brutality. He rebuilt the Temple in Jerusalem on a magnificent scale, but was hated by his subjects. In the last year of his reign Jesus Christ was born, following which Herod ordered the massacre of the young children in Bethlehem.

Herzl, Theodore
(1860–1904) Father of political Zionism and the founder of the World Zionist Organisation. His book *The Jewish State*, published in 1895, became the textbook of the Zionist movement, and the first Zionist Congress was held in 1897. He envisaged not only a home for Jews in Palestine, but a political Jewish state.

Hesiod
Greek poet of the 8th century BCE whose work *Theogony* gives an account of the origin of the world, and the legends concerning the birth of the gods.

Hestia
Greek numen of the hearth. Vowed to a perpetual virginity, she became the goddess of domestic life. She was identified by the Romans with Vesta.

Hesychasm
Doctrine and practice of the Hesychasts, a school of quietists which arose among the monks of Mt Athos in the 14th century.

Hetu
Term used in Buddhism for a cause or antecedent condition.

Heuristic
Derived from the Greek verb 'to find', this word is applied to systems that assist the discovery of truth. In education it applies to methods in which the pupil discovers things for himself.

Hexagram
Six-pointed figure made by superimposing one equilateral triangle pointing upwards on one pointing downwards. This was a symbol of fire and of water, and was regarded in the Middle Ages as a powerful protection against evil. The Star of David, the emblem of Israel, is the best-known hexagram in contemporary use, being found in every synagogue. The origin and reason for its connection with David are unknown, but it has been found on Jewish amulets of the 12th century.

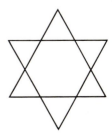

Egyptian hieroglyphs

Hexameron

Account of the creation of the universe in six days. The fullest version of this appears in Genesis 1.

Hexapla

Comparative version of OT texts compiled by Origen *c.* 240 CE. He set out the OT in six columns: the first in Hebrew, the second containing the Hebrew text transliterated into Greek characters, followed by four columns giving different translations including the Septuagint.

Hierarchy

Priesthood or other community organized in successive grades. The Orthodox, Roman Catholic and Anglican Churches have a threefold order consisting of bishops, priests and deacons.

Hieroglyph

Lit. 'priestly writing'. Usually applied to the system of picture-writing employed by priests in the tombs, temples and monuments of ancient Egypt. The key to the translation of hieroglyphs came with the discovery of the Rosetta Stone.

Hierophant

Priest of a mystery cult; an interpreter of esoteric doctrines.

Hierophany

Act of manifestation of the sacred in which something sacred reveals itself to us. (A term introduced by Mircea Eliade in *The Sacred and the Profane.*)

Hifz al Qur'an

Term used in Islam for keeping the words of the Qur'an in the heart, or memorizing them as the due participation of an Islamic believer.

High God

Omniscient and omnipotent creator god, usually living in or associated with the sky. The term 'high god' appears to have been used first by Andrew Lang in 1898 with the same meaning as 'sky god' or 'supreme god'. The high god, though supreme and all powerful, was not the only god, but had lesser deities serving him, or sometimes opposing him. Such gods are found in the ancient world, examples being Anu, the Akkadian god of heaven, Ea, the Babylonian creator god, the Greek Zeus and the Roman Jupiter. The Yoruba god Olodumare is an example from African religions.

High Priest

According to the biblical account, Aaron, the brother of Moses, was appointed the first Israelite High Priest (Exodus 28). Doubts have been cast on this by some critics, but recent research accepts the probability of the antiquity of this office. The High Priest was vested with a special breastplate and mitre, and he alone was allowed to enter the Holy of Holies in the Tabernacle or the Temple. The office appears to have been hereditary until the time of Antiochus V Epiphanes, who sold it to the highest bidder, but after the victories of Judas Maccabaeus the office was claimed by one of his descendants, Aristobulus (104 BCE); since the destruction of Jerusalem in 70 CE the office has ceased to exist, but in Christian theology Jesus Christ is described as 'our great high priest' (Hebrews 4:14).

Hijrah (A)

Word meaning 'migration'. It is particularly applied in Islam to an event in 622 CE when Muhammad and about a hundred of his followers migrated from Mecca to Medina, about 300 km away, and established a community there. The date marks the beginning of the Islamic calendar.

Hillel

Jewish teacher of the 1st century BCE and a leader of the Pharisees, reputed to be a descendant of David. He taught patience, moderation and a love of peace.

Hinayana

Buddhist term meaning 'lesser vehicle' used by Mahayana Buddhists to indicate the doctrine of the Elders or Buddhists of Sri Lanka and S.E. Asia. It is the monk's way of salvation, sometimes understood as the conservative interpretation of Buddhism.

Hinnom, Valley of

Valley to the south of Jerusalem which joins the Kedron Valley. In early times it was a place of human sacrifice, and was described by Jeremiah as a 'Valley of Slaughter' (7:31–2). According to Kimchi (c. 1200) rubbish was continually burned there. This gave rise to the use of its Hebrew name, Gehinnom, as a place of punishment for sinners (2 Esdras 7:36) or torment after the Last Judgement (Matthew 10:28).

Hiranygarbha (S)

Golden egg or womb which, according to the *Rig-Veda*, evolved in the beginning and then established heaven and earth. In the Laws of Manu, Hiranygarbha is described as the seed of the self-existent, which became a golden egg in which the self-existent was born as Brahma.

Hiri

Buddhist term for moral shame, in the sense of being ashamed to do wrong.

Hisab

Term used in Islam for the vindication of the message of Muhammad, as distinct from its simple preaching.

Hittites

People whose empire occupied Syria, the Lebanon and the Euphrates River area and was founded about 1800 BCE. It reached its climax in 1350 BCE, and collapsed about 1200 BCE. There are similarities between their laws and the laws of the Hebrew Pentateuch, but there were differences of religious outlook, e.g. the Hittite king and queen acted as priest and priestess in their rituals, which were based on the agricultural year. The Hittite capital at Boghaz Koi has been extensively excavated.

Hola Mohalla

Sikh spring festival derived from the Hindu festival of Holi, but designed to strengthen their sense of community.

Holi

In Hinduism the spring festival of Krishna, commemorating his games with the Gopis. It is celebrated for five days with bonfires, street dancing and processions with images of Krishna and his consort Radha, during which people throw red powder and coloured water over one another in a spirit of fun and rejoicing.

Maharaja playing Holi

Holiness Movement

The teaching of the Holiness Movement is that after conversion a person who has experienced the saving power of God can obtain through the Holy Spirit a second blessing and be entirely sanctified. This seems to have developed from the teaching of Count Zinzendorff (1700–1760), leader of the Moravian Brethren, whose ideas were made known in England by John Wesley. 'Holiness' has been preached by some Methodists and by the Salvation Army, but the only separate sect to make it a central tenet is the Pentecostal Church of the Nazarene. This was founded in 1907, and in 1919 it dropped the word 'Pentecostal' from its title, because it did not believe that the gift of tongues necessarily followed the experience of holiness.

Holocaust

In the Hebrew Bible this word is applied to the sacrifice, otherwise termed the 'whole burnt offering' (Genesis 22:3; Amos 5:22). Since the Second World War it has been particularly applied to the extermination by the Nazis of six million Jews between 1939 and 1945.

Holy

Originally something set aside from secular use, and dedicated to the service or use of the deity. This could apply to persons such as priests, objects such as altars or places such as shrines.

Holy Communion

Title usually applied to the central sacramental service of the Church of England. It was used by Cranmer in the first *Book of Common Prayer* of 1549, and appears in all subsequent revisions. It was used in the Proposed Prayer Book of 1928 and in the experimental series of services issued since then. The service is based on the Sarum rite with Confession and Absolution, a Prayer of Humble Access, Consecration and Administration, but the title draws attention to the fact that it is a communion of the people, who receive both the bread and the wine. (See also Communion, Eucharist, Lord's Supper and Mass)

Holy of Holies

The phrase means the 'most holy place' and it is applied to the inner sanctuary of the Tabernacle erected by the Israelites in the wilderness (Exodus 37), or of the Temple in Jerusalem (1 Kings 6:19). Only the High Priest was permitted to enter the Holy of Holies, where the Ark of the Covenant was set up.

Holy Innocents

Term used in the Christian Church for those children in Bethlehem, aged two or under, who were massacred at the order of Herod the Great, in an attempt to kill the infant Jesus. They are remembered on 28 December.

Holy Roman Empire

The Europe of the West which came into being at the coronation of Charlemagne on Christmas Day 800 CE. It was brought to an end by Napoleon in 1806.

Holy Saturday

In the Christian Church the day before Easter, when in many churches the paschal candle is lit at an evening service to symbolize the coming of the light of the Resurrection, after the darkness of Christ's crucifixion and burial.

Holy Shroud

Linen cloth, preserved in Turin Cathedral since 1578, which bears the imprint of a human body with the wounds suffered by Christ upon the Cross. It is venerated by many Christians as being the shroud wrapped round Christ when his body was prepared for burial.

Holy Spirit

Third person of the Christian Trinity. Following the ascension of Christ, the Holy Spirit, the Paraclete, came upon the disciples at the Feast of Pentecost. Through the Holy Spirit, God the Father continues his redemptive work made manifest in Jesus Christ. The Church has experienced great difficulty in formulating its belief concerning the status and activity of the Holy Spirit, but the most widely accepted formula is 'Three persons in one god', or 'Three in one and one in three'. In Zoroastrianism Holy Spirit is one of the seven Amesha Spentas. It is the only one which man cannot share with God, as through it God bestows the gift of immortality.

Holy Week

The seven days from Palm Sunday to Easter Eve (or Holy Saturday), kept by the Christian Church as a time of meditation on the suffering and crucifixion of Christ.

106

Hom/Havan

Term used in village Hinduism for a form of worship involving a fire offering.

Homer

Greek poet of the 8th century BCE whose poems *Iliad* and *Odyssey*, based on the war between the Greeks and the Trojans, and the subsequent journeys of Odysseus, give vivid pictures of the gods in action, and the interrelation of divine and human activity.

Homiletics

Art of preaching. This could be considered a branch of pastoral theology, as it studies methods of delivering sermons or homilies in a manner that enables the congregation to gain spiritual benefit and an understanding of the gospel message.

Homoousios

Term which means 'being of the same substance as the Father'. It was used at the Council of Nicaea in 325 CE and was inserted in the Nicene Creed to express the unity of Christ with God. The term was put forward in opposition to the Arians, who regarded Christ as a creature of God, and to the semi-Arians, who preferred the word 'homoiousios', i.e. of similar substance to the Father.

Honen

Influential teacher of Buddhism in Japan (1133–1212) who popularized Amidism. He was founder of the Jodo sect.

Hope

Second of the theological virtues mentioned by St Paul in 1 Corinthians 13:13, together with faith and charity (love). It may be defined as a desire and search for future good, and is thus confined to this world, as it has no place in heaven or in hell. St Peter wrote 'we have been born anew to a living hope through the resurrection of Jesus Christ from the dead' (1 Peter 1:3).

Horns

Worn as a head-dress, often on a helmet, horns symbolize strength, probably through association with the bull, and also fertility, probably through association with the shape of the crescent moon, sacred to Diana and Venus.

Horus

Son of Isis and Osiris, the Egyptian god of the sun, worshipped in the form of a hawk. He was the chief god of ancient Egypt, with whom the Pharaoh identified himself during his lifetime.

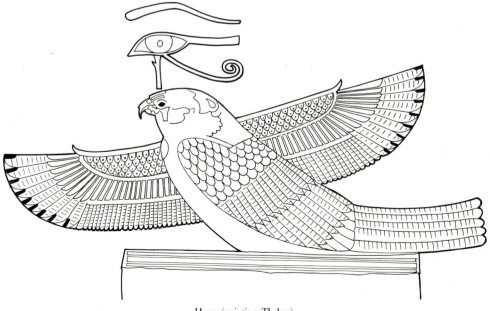

Horus (painting, Thebes)

Hosanna

Greek form of a Hebrew petition meaning 'Save, we beseech thee'.

Hosea

Israelite prophet of the 8th century BCE whose message is included in the Hebrew Bible. He used the experience of his own marriage to convince the Israelites of the grace of God, and the need for a loving relationship with him.

Hospitallers

Order of knights founded early in the Crusades to provide protection and hospitality for pilgrims and crusaders. In the 12th century the Order spread to Europe. Its centre was at Rhodes in 1310 following the fall of Acre, and in Malta from 1530. After the Order surrendered Malta to Napoleon in 1798, it fell into disrepute.

Hosso

Most influential form of Buddhist religion in the Nara period (8th century) in Japan. It was a religion for the spiritual elite only, and was replaced by the more universalist Tendai sect.

Host

Title given to the consecrated bread in the Christian Eucharist. The word, which is derived from the Latin *hostia* (sacrificial victim), emphasizes the Roman Catholic doctrine that Christ is present in person in the substance of the bread, after the Words of Consecration have been said, offering a bloodless sacrifice.

Hours, Canonical

Times of daily prayer set out in the Breviary and used particularly in Christian monasteries. The seven Hours recognized in the Western Church are Matins and Lauds, Prime, Terce, Sext, None, Vespers and Compline.

Hsin

Word used by Confucius meaning 'good faith' or 'trustworthiness', one of the five cardinal virtues recognized by Confucian teaching.

Huaca

Term for a sacred shrine among the Incas. These vary in form and may be a pile of stones, a pyramid or a temple.

Hubris

Greek term for insolent pride in man resulting in an offence to God.

Huda (A)

Term meaning 'guidance'. It is one of the titles given to the Qur'an.

Huguenots

French Protestants of the 16th and 17th centuries who were persecuted by the authorities as heretics. In 1598 they were given civil rights by the Edict of Nantes, but this was revoked by Louis XIV in 1685. Their rights were not restored until after the French Revolution.

Hui Neng

(638–713 CE)   Sixth Patriarch of Zen in China. He was the founder of the Southern School.

Huitzilopochtli

National god of the Aztecs; lit. 'humming-bird on the left'. His symbol was the sun, and the sun rising in the south (the left) was represented by a humming-bird.

Hukam

In Sikh thought the term for God's will, the cause of the creation of the world.

Hukm (A)

Judgement or decision which arises from the power and wisdom of God. It is one of the titles of the Qur'an (13:37).

Humanism

1. *Renaissance*   Study of the humanities, especially the classics of Greek and Roman writers, e.g. Plato, Aristotle and Cicero.

2. *Ethical*   Attitude of mind which rejects creeds, and seeks the right and the good in individual life and in society without reference to faith in God. The ideal is the 'open society', founded on justice, tolerance and intellectual humility.

3. *Scientific*   Any one of the range of beliefs which look to science as the only source of knowledge about the world or of solutions to human problems.

Humble Access, Prayer of

Prayer in the Anglican and Methodist orders of Holy Communion which immediately precedes the Prayer of Consecration.

Hun Pic Tok

War god of the Maya, named after the eight thousand spears brandished by his warriors.

Huppah (H)

Canopy on four posts beneath which a Jewish bride and bridegroom stand for the marriage ceremony. There is a tradition that trees are planted on the birth of a son (cedar) or a daughter (pine) so that when they marry the trees can be cut down to provide the wood for the huppah posts. (See also illustration of Jewish wedding on p. 126)

Husain

Second son of Ali, the son-in-law of Muhammad. When his brother Hasan was murdered in 680 CE, Husain, as the grandson of Muhammad, attempted to seize the caliphate, but his plans went astray and he and his followers were wiped out in the massacre of Karbala on the tenth day of Muharram. This tragedy is remembered annually by Shiah Muslims as the Passion of Husain.

Huss, John

(1369–1415)   Bohemian reformer. While rector of Prague University and a popular preacher, he began translating the works of Wycliffe and preaching his doctrines. He was excommunicated by Pope John XXIII in 1412, and appealed to the Council of Constance. Despite a guarantee of safe conduct from the Emperor, he was condemned and burnt as a heretic in 1415.

Hutterites

Extreme Protestant group, a branch of the Anabaptists, founded in Moravia about 1520 by Jacob Hutter. They survive today in Canada and the United States. They live in communities, usually farming, and have all things in common. They are presided over by a minister, have a very strict moral discipline, and as far as possible, avoid contact with affairs outside the community.

Hyksos

The word probably means 'rulers of foreign countries' or 'desert warriors', and it is applied to a mixed group of tribes who invaded Egypt and overthrew the rulers c. 1710 BCE. The Egyptian historian Manetho (3rd century BCE) depicted the horror and brutality of the invasion. The Hyksos dominated Egypt in the 15th, 16th and 17th Dynasties, but in 1570 BCE in a revolt led by Ahmose I, founder of the 18th Dynasty, they were driven out. This was at one time identified with the Exodus of the Israelites, but the two events are now considered to be quite separate.

Hymns

Sacred poetry set to music and sung in public worship. Hymns are used in many different religious traditions.

Hystaspes, Oracle of

Oracle which was widely circulated in the Roman Empire, and was known to the early Church. It was considered to be of Zoroastrian origin, and as it foretold the fall of the Roman Empire and the end of the world, it was banned as seditious.

I Ching

Chinese Book of Changes, one of the most influential of the Confucian classics.

Ibeji

In Yorubaland a pair of wooden figures bought by the mother of twins; they are regarded as the spiritual selves of the twins, and if one twin dies, the image becomes a substitute.

Ichthus

See Fish

Icon

Painting or mosaic of Jesus Christ or one of the saints used in the Orthodox Church as an aid to the devotion of worshippers.

Iconography

Drawing pictures or making images of divine beings as aids to worship. Examples exist from every period of human history, from the cave paintings of the Stone Age, through Renaissance art, e.g. the *Last Supper* by Leonardo da Vinci, to the present time, e.g. the tapestry in Coventry Cathedral designed by Graham Sutherland.

Iconostasis

Screen in Byzantine churches which separates the sanctuary from the nave. It is pierced by three doors, the central or royal door leading to the altar.

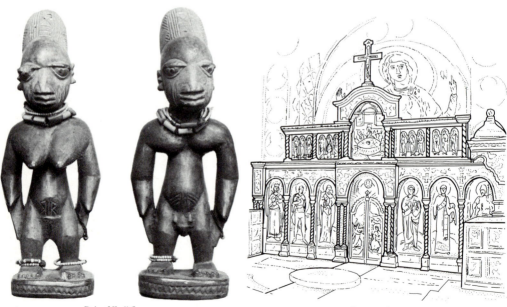

Pair of Ibeji figures   Iconostasis

110

Id al-Adha (A)

Feast of Sacrifice. Festival and sacrifice observed throughout the Muslim world on the day when pilgrims offer their sacrifice in the Valley of Mina, near the end of the pilgrimage to Mecca. It is also known as Bairam.

Iddhi (P)/**Siddhi** (S)

In Buddhist thought powers of the mind not yet developed in the average man. It can also mean the acquisition of psychic power by ascetic practice and meditation.

Idea of the Holy

Book written in 1917 by Rudolf Otto (1869–1937) which has had a great effect on subsequent theological writing. Otto believed that religion is a non-rational response to the holy or the numinous, which he described as a 'mysterium tremendum et fascinans' (a mystery which both terrifies and attracts). He believed that his theories applied equally to the religion of the OT and the NT and to the mysticism of the East.

Idealism

Philosophical theory which maintains that material objects are only ideas in a mind, and that the subjective or ideal existence is the only true being. Idealist philosophers have claimed Plato as the founder of the system, but the principal Idealists in modern times have been Schelling, Hegel and Berkeley.

Ideology

1. System of beliefs shared by a group of people, providing a rationale for their way of life.
2. System of shared beliefs considered as forming social bonds and as being sustained by social factors rather than considerations of the truth or falsity of the beliefs.
3. According to Karl Marx the ruling ideas of an epoch; the ideal expression of the dominant material relationships.

Id-l-Fitr (A)

Muslim festival marking the end of Ramadan. It is marked by joyous celebrations, services, special foods and gifts, giving grateful thanks after a month of fasting.

Idol

Derogatory word indicating an image or cult object which is thought to debase the worship of those who offer devotion to it. In the Hebrew Bible the Golden Calf, Pillars and the Asherah are described as idols.

Ifa

Great oracle of the Yoruba associated with the god Ifa or Orunmila. Ifa is also associated with healing, possibly because many oracular inquiries are concerned with illness and health.

Igigi

Term used in ancient Babylonian religion. Originally it meant 'gods of the world above', but in later literature it was used interchangeably with 'Anunnaki' for 'great gods'.

Ignatius, St

(35–107 CE)   Bishop of Antioch. Origen described him as the second Bishop, the successor of St Peter. Little is known of his life, except that he was taken to Rome under military escort and on the way he wrote a number of letters to the Churches in Ephesus, Magnesia and Rome, begging them not to try to save him, as he did not wish to be robbed of the crown of martyrdom.

Ignatius Loyola

See Loyola

Iho

Lit: 'elevated one'. The supreme deity of the Maori religion.

Ihram (A)

Term used in Islam for the state of ritual purity required of one taking part in the annual pilgrimage to Mecca. It begins with the niyyah, or intention, and is signified by the white garb draped over the left shoulder, leaving the right shoulder bare, that all pilgrims wear. While wearing this garb all merchandizing, sexual activity and unworthy behaviour are forbidden.

Muslim pilgrims wearing traditional white garb (Mecca)

Ijaz (A)

Term used in Islam for the state or quality of matchless eloquence attaching to the Qur'an as revelation whereby it constitutes a literary miracle.

Ijma (A)

Consensus, or converging of approval in Islam; the means whereby the Muslim community in Sunni Islam identifies loyal development in Islamic law and usage.

Ijtihad (A)

Individual initiative of experts or pioneers by which new situations in Islam are faced and new responses to them are developed.

Ik Omkar

Sikh affirmation meaning 'God is one' with which the *Guru Granth Sahib* opens.

Ikebana

Japanese term for flower arrangements that have symbolic meaning in Zen Buddhism.

Ikhlas (A)

Surah 112 of the Qur'an is entitled at-Tauhid (the unity), and it sets out the unity of God: 'He is Allah, the One . . . there is none comparable to Him.' Ikhlas is the sincere religion of Islam based on the divine unity set out in this surah, which has been called the essence of the Qur'an.

Ikhnaton

Name adopted by the Egyptian Pharaoh Amenophis IV of the 14th century BCE when he rejected the worship of the god Amun. He instituted the monotheistic worship of Aton, whose symbol was the sun's disc with rays terminating in hands.

Ile-Ife

Holy city and ancestral home of the Yoruba. According to Yoruba myth the creation of the world took place there, and it became the cradle of mankind, the original home of all things.

Iliad

Long Greek poem in twenty-four books by the poet Homer dealing with the last year of the siege of Troy and its eventual capture by the Greeks. It tells of the activities of two heroes, the Trojan Hector and the Greek Achilles, and of the interventions of various gods and goddesses during the fighting.

Illuyankas

Coiled, fiery dragon in Hittite mythology who was attacked by the god of thunder. The dragon was identified with the sea, the coils representing the waves.

Ilm

Term used in medieval Islam to indicate competence in religious lore, but now widened to include all forms of knowledge.

Ilm-I Kshnoom

Modern movement among Parsees, with mystical elements, founded by B. N. Shroff (1857–1927) which aims at the achievement of spiritual purity.

Image

Material representation in animal, human or mixed form used for cultic purposes. Images are widely used in Hinduism, but are strictly forbidden in Judaism and Islam.

Imam

In Islam a person who leads public worship in a mosque or elsewhere; this is not a priestly office and the imam has no authority. The Shiah Muslims gave the title 'Imam' to their leaders, descendants of the Prophet Muhammad through his daughter Fatima.

Iman (A)

Term used in Islam for faith, or the activity of belief, as the correlative to din.

Imitation of Christ

Manual of spiritual devotion attributed to Thomas à Kempis (1380–1471), a member of the Brethren of the Common Life, a lay devotional order in the Netherlands.

Immaculate Conception

This doctrine, which was formally defined in 1854 by the papal bull *Ineffabilis Deus*, states that 'the Virgin Mary in the first moment of her conception . . . was preserved immune from every stain of original guilt'. This had been a popular Catholic belief for many centuries, and the bull permitted its celebration, its feast-day being 8 December. The doctrine has not been accepted by the Orthodox, Anglican or Protestant Churches.

Immanence

Doctrine of the omnipresence of God in the world. In the Christian faith it is balanced by the parallel doctrine of divine transcendence.

Immanuel (H)

Word meaning 'God with us'. It is used in two verses in Isaiah (7:14; 8:8), the first of which appears to refer to the child whose birth Isaiah had foretold. In Matthew 1:23 the word and Isaiah's prophecy are applied to the birth of Jesus.

Immortality

Doctrine that the soul of man survives the death of the body. Many Greek philosophers (e.g. Plato in *Timaeus*) taught a natural immortality of the soul, which at death escapes from the prison of the body to begin a new form of existence. Christian theology accepts a conditional immortality dependent on the resurrection of Christ, believing that by faith in Christ the believer is saved from the death of sin to experience the fulness of eternal life. Jewish belief is grounded in God, and immortality is the homecoming of the soul of man to the development of the divine relationship with God.

Imprimatur

Certification granted by a Roman Catholic bishop giving his authority or permission for a book to be published. This is given after the diocesan censor has issued a document *Nihil Obstat* which states that the theological or moral treatise to which it is appended contains nothing offensive to Roman Catholic teaching.

Imshallah (A)

Word meaning 'if God wills'. It is widely used by Muslims as an expression of pious hope, similar to the Christian D.V. (*Deo volente*).

Incantation

Repetition of rhythmical phrases, often to music, in order to influence supernatural forces. It is often associated with magical practices.

Incarnation

In Christian theology the doctrine that the eternal word of God, the second person of the Trinity, became flesh as Jesus. The NT emphasizes that he lived a full human life, subject to man's limitations such as tiredness and hunger, but that his deity was not reduced or diminished. St Paul says, 'In him dwells all the fulness of the Godhead bodily' (Colossians 2:9). In Hinduism avatars are considered to be successive appearances or incarnations of different deities, particularly Vishnu, whose nine incarnations in varied form lead up to the tenth, Kalkin, who is yet to come. Some Hindus accept Christ as an incarnation of God. In Buddhism the Dalai Lama of Tibet is held to be a new incarnation of previous Bodhisattvas.

Incense

Gum or spice which produces sweet, aromatic smoke when burned. This is used in the worship of many religions throughout the world. It is variously interpreted as a sweet offering to the deity, or as a symbol of the prayers of the worshippers, or as a purification cloud to scare away demons and evil spirits.

Incubation

Practice in ancient Greece of sleeping in a sacred place in order to receive enlightenment or instruction through dreams.

Incubus

Demon or evil spirit who was thought to descend upon sleeping women, either to cause nightmares or for sexual intercourse.

Index

Short for Index Librorum Prohibitorum, a list of books which the Roman Catholic Church instructs its members not to read. It was first published at the Council of Trent in 1557, and has been periodically revised. Since 1917 it has been under the control of the Holy Office.

Indra

Most powerful of the Vedic gods. A sky and storm god, he fought the dragon Vritra and overcame drought. Later he declined in importance and was replaced by Shiva or Vishnu.

Indulgence

Doctrine held in the Roman Catholic Church that temporal punishment in purgatory may be shortened by undertaking acts of merit or by drawing upon the treasury of merit accumulated by Christ and the saints. The selling of a special indulgence to finance the rebuilding of St Peter's, Rome, provoked Luther's protest which led to the Reformation.

Indus, River
Chief river of N.W. India and Pakistan. It rises in the Himalayas and flows for 3300 km to the Indian Ocean at Karachi. In the Valley of the Indus, the remains of an advanced civilization dating back to before the 3rd millenium BCE have been excavated, notably at Harappa and Mohenjo-Daro. Temples have been found with cult objects apparently representing a mother goddess and a male seated in a yogic position.

Infallibility
At the Vatican Council of 1870 the Roman Catholic Church declared that the definitions of the Pope made *ex cathedra* on matters of faith and morals were to be considered infallible.

Initiation
Ceremony of admittance into adulthood or membership of a society. Often this is accompanied by tests involving pain or endurance to make sure the person is worthy, or by solemn religious rites such as Confirmation, Bar-mitzvah, the Amrit ceremony, or investiture with the sacred thread in Hindu and Parsee practice.

Inquisition
Special ecclesiastical institution for suppressing heresy. In 1252 Pope Innocent IV authorized the use of torture in the questioning of suspected heretics. The Inquisition in Spain, directed against Jews and Moorish converts, was instituted in the 15th century. The chief inquisitors were the Dominicans and Franciscans.

Inspiration
In Christian thought this is usually applied to the Scriptures. It can imply that God breathed into the minds of writers, giving them the power to put divine truths into words, or that God breathes into the words so that they become the vehicle of truth to the reader. The term 'verbal inspiration' is used by Fundamentalists to indicate a literal or scriptural inerrancy.

Institutes of the Christian Religion
Major theological work of John Calvin. The first edition was published in 1536 and had a prefatory letter to Francis I of France. It was frequently revised until the last edition of 1559–1560, which is in four parts dealing with (1) God the Creator, (2) God the Redeemer, (3) the Holy Spirit and (4) the means of grace and the Church. It has been termed the textbook of reformed theology.

Interdict
Punishment within the Roman Catholic Church excluding the faithful from participation in spiritual activities. An interdict can be personal, imposed by a diocesan bishop, local, applying to a particular church or place, or general, applying to a wide area or district. Local and general interdicts can be imposed only by the Pope.

Inti
Tribal god of the ruling dynasty of the Incas. He was the sun god and the god of fertility.

Intichiuma
Australian aboriginal ritual of the Aranda tribe for increasing the families of men and animals.

Intinction
Practice of dipping the Eucharistic bread or wafer into the wine. It is sometimes used in the Anglican Church as a convenient way of giving Communion to the sick or the disabled.

Introit
Opening act of worship in the Mass in the Western Church, consisting of a Psalm and the Gloria Patri.

Invention of the True Cross
According to Christian legend, the three crosses on which Jesus and the two thieves were crucified were discovered by St Helena, the mother of Constantine, about 300 CE, and the true cross was identified by a miracle. It is commemorated on two feast-days, 3 May and 14 September.

Iona
Small island in the Inner Hebrides where St Columba founded a monastery in 563 CE. It became the centre of Celtic Christianity from which missionaries travelled to many parts. The Iona Community,

whose centre is on the island, was founded by the Rev. George Macleod in 1958 for fellowship in prayer and for the expression of Christian theology in social service.

Irenaeus

(130–200 CE)   Reckoned to be the first great Catholic theologian, he became Bishop of Lyons in 178. He wrote an important book attacking all forms of Gnosticism, by putting forward a positive doctrine of Christianity. He developed the theory of the recapitulation or the summary of human evolution in the humanity of Jesus Christ, and he insisted on the unity of the Father and the Son.

Isa

Name applied to Jesus in the Qur'an and used of him by Muslims.

Isaac

Son born to the Israelite patriarch Abraham and his wife Sarah when both were long past the normal age of parenthood. At the call of God Abraham prepared to sacrifice Isaac, but at the last moment divine intervention provided a ram for the sacrifice, and promised rich blessings to Abraham's descendants because of his faithful obedience. The Bible traces Jewish descent from Abraham through Isaac, whereas the Qur'an traces Arabic descent through Ishmael, the older son of Abraham and Sarah's maid, Hagar.

Isabella I

(1451–1504)   Daughter of John II, King of Castile, and wife of Ferdinand, King of Aragon, known as Isabella the Catholic. She was devoted to the Christian faith and with Cardinal Ximenes' help she so strengthened the Church in Spain that it was able to resist the Reformation. Isabella and Ferdinand encouraged Columbus in his voyages of discovery, and recaptured Granada from the Moors, making Spain one of the strongest Catholic countries in Europe.

Isaiah

Major prophet of the Hebrew Bible who lived in Jerusalem, c. 760–680 BCE. He prophesied in the reigns of Jotham, Ahaz and Hezekiah, and seems to have been a member of the royal family. He assured Hezekiah that the Lord would not allow the holy city Jerusalem to be overthrown by the Assyrians. Chapters 40–66 of the Book of Isaiah were probably written by a later author, or authors. (See also Deutero-Isaiah)

Ishmael

Son of Abraham and Hagar (Genesis 16:15), he is described in the Qur'an (19:55) as a prophet, and is considered the father of the Arabs. According to the Qur'an (2:119–125), he helped Abraham build the Kaaba, and placed the Black Stone in it. Muslim teaching maintains that Ishmael, not Isaac, was prepared for sacrifice by Abraham.

Ishtar

Babylonian astral deity, the goddess of the morning and evening star, the wife of Anu. In Sumerian mythology she successfully sought for Tammuz in the underworld after his death and brought him back to life. She has been identified with the West Semitic goddess Astarte, and with the Roman goddess Venus.

Ishvara (S)

Term meaning 'lord', 'master', 'king', 'god' or 'object of meditative devotion'. It is most commonly applied to Shiva as the supreme being or the creator lord, but in the *Bhagavadgita* it is applied to Krishna, as the lord of beingś.

Isis

Egyptian goddess of the earth and then of the moon, the wife of Osiris and the mother of Horus. With great patience and piety she searched for and reassembled the scattered limbs of Osiris after he had been murdered and dismembered by his brother Set.

Isis seated with Horus on her knee

115

Islam

Religious teaching, faith, obedience and practice, and the widespread community which has arisen from the message of the one God, Allah, preached by the Prophet Muhammad. The message was given to the Prophet in a series of revelations, and is enshrined in the Qur'an. Without a capital, 'islam' indicates the quality of submission or surrender to the divine word inculcated in Islam. (See also Muslim)

Islamic New Year

The Muslim calendar begins with the Hijra, or migration of the Prophet Muhammad from Mecca to Medina in 622 CE, where he and his friends organized themselves into a religious community. It is customary on New Year's Day to remember this by the reading of stories about the Prophet and by the exchange of gifts with relatives and friends.

Isles of the Blest

In ancient Greek thought the dwelling-place of the dead who have lived good lives.

Ismailis

Branch of the Shiah Muslims sometimes called the Seveners, because they believe the seventh Imam was the last and greatest. They have been regarded as fanatics and esoterics because they have absorbed non-Islamic teaching on emanations and spiritual intermediaries.

Isnad

Attestation of a tradition about Muhammad going back for its truth to his companions, through a chain of intermediaries.

Israel

Name given to the patriarch Jacob after the episode of wrestling with a stranger (Genesis 32:28). The traditional meaning of the name is 'God strives', but a more likely meaning is 'God persists'. The name was later applied to the tribes descended from ten of his sons which united with the tribes of Judah to form the Kingdom of David. The Kingdom broke up on the death of Solomon, and the ten northern tribes became the Kingdom of Israel. In 722 BCE these tribes were taken into captivity by the Assyrians, but the name survived as the title of a religious community. Since 1948 Israel has been a state occupying much of the land formerly known as Palestine.

Isra'wal Miraj

According to the Muslim Hadith this was a night journey of the Prophet Muhammad, guided by Gabriel, from Mecca to Jerusalem and then to heaven.

Issachar

Ninth son of the Israelite patriarch Jacob, by Leah, one of his wives. Also the name of the Israelite tribe descended from him, which occupied territory south of the Sea of Galilee.

Ite, Missa Est

Original formula of dismissal in the Latin Mass of the Roman Catholic Church, from which the word 'Mass' was itself derived. It means 'Depart, it is finished'.

Itmi'nan (A)

Term used in Islam for inner tranquillity, or a settled state of spirit and heart following faith and prayer.

Ittihad (A)

Technical term used by Islamic Sufi mystics to describe the union of the creature with the Creator.

Itzamna

Sky god of the ancient Mayas.

Izanagi and Izanami

The sky father and earth mother of primitive Japanese myths.

Jachin and Boaz

    Names of the two decorated bronze pillars that stood at the entrance to Solomon's Temple. They may have been fire pillars symbolizing the divine presence, or possibly symbols of the Tree of Life and the Tree of Knowledge in the Garden of Eden.

Jacob

    Second son of Isaac and Rebekah, he supplanted his brother Esau and bought his birthright. Jacob's twelve sons were the eponymous ancestors of the tribes of Israel (a name later given to Jacob) except Levi, who was granted the priesthood, and Joseph, whose two sons succeeded him.

Jagannatha (S)

    Word meaning 'world lord' used in Hinduism as a title for Vishnu and Krishna.

Jagat

    Word used in the Hindu religion to indicate the cosmos of moving beings, or that which can be felt, heard or smelt.

Jahiliyyah (A)

    State of ignorance or unruliness which preceded the rise of Islam in Arabia and the light of the Qur'an.

Jahweh

    See Yahweh

Jainism

    Ancient faith which is an offshoot of Hinduism. Its doctrines were first taught by Mahavira (died 468 BCE) but its adherents claim that the faith had been in existence from a much earlier date. The name is derived from the word *jina* (conqueror), a title given to twenty-four saviours, of whom Mahavira was the last. It does not recognize a supreme deity, though there are denizens of the cosmos. Its main emphases are: (1) non-violence, or ahimsa, i.e. the taking of life and the eating of meat are forbidden; (2) monastic asceticism, i.e. laymen cannot attain nirvana.

Jajmani

    Word used in village Hinduism derived from the Vedic term for a patron who employed a priest to perform a sacrifice for the benefit of the community. It is now commonly used to describe the relationship that exists between members of the specialist dependent castes and members of the dominant castes.

Jamadut

    Term used in Sikhism for the angels of death.

Jamapuri

    Term used in Sikhism for the city of the dead.

James

    1. Name of two of the disciples of Jesus: the son of Zebedee and the son of Alphaeus.
    2. Title of an epistle in the NT. It is difficult to establish the authorship, but an early tradition suggested James, the brother of Jesus. Luther called it an 'epistle of straw', because of its emphasis on works as well as on faith.

Jamshedi Naorozi

Zoroastrian New Year's Day as celebrated in Iran.

Janam Ashtami

Hindu nativity festival in August celebrating the birth of the Lord Krishna.

Janam Sakhi

Lit. 'birth evidences'. Term used in Sikhism for hagiographic narratives, or collections of stories about Guru Nanak.

Janeu

Sacred thread with which Hindu boys in the twice-born castes are invested on the day of their initiation.

Jansenism

Movement within 17th and 18th century Catholicism based on the teaching of C. O. Jansen (1585–1638), who sought to maintain the theology of Augustine, and attack the Jesuits. It has two major themes: (1) that without special grace from God the performance of his commandments is impossible to men; (2) that the operation of grace is irresistible. Pascal supported the movement but it was condemned in the papal bull *Unigenitus* of 1713. In 1723 Dutch Jansenists withdrew from obedience to Rome, and formed the Old Catholics.

Janus

Old Roman deity of opening and closing, represented with two faces looking different ways, to whom the month of January was dedicated. His temple in the Roman Forum had two doors, shut in time of peace, open during war.

Japa

Repetition of the name of God, practised by Hindus as a devotional exercise.

Japji

1. Long hymn with which the *Guru Granth Sahib*, the Sikh holy book, opens.
2. Word meaning 'remembrance' applied to Sikh morning and evening prayers.

Jara-phunka

Form of exorcism practised by a mantravidh in Indian village Hinduism; he combats the evil spirit with the aid of a mantra.

Head of Janus

Jataka

Lit. 'birth stories'. Collection of five hundred and fifty mythological stories of former lives of the Buddha.

Jati

Lit. 'birth'. Alternative term for the Hindu caste system. It is also a term for family, lineage or rank.

Jehovah

Modern form of the Hebrew divine name which arose through a misunderstanding. The Hebrew name, the tetragrammaton YHWH, is never uttered, but the title Adonai (Lord) is substituted. In the text, the vowels of Adonai are printed beneath the consonants of YHWH, and the name Jehovah results from a conflation of the two.

Jehovah's Witnesses

Christian sect founded in 1870 by Charles Russell of Pittsburgh with the title 'Zion's Watch Tower Tract Society'. Reconstituted by Judge Rutherford in 1916, the society took its present title in 1931. Its main theme is the imminent return of Christ's kingdom. Christ is said to have returned secretly in 1914, but the date of his reappearing and the establishment of the New World is not known.

Jen

Term used by Confucius meaning 'benevolence', which shows itself in the feeling of sympathy for others. It is one of the five cardinal virtues recognized by Confucianism.

Jerusalem: Dome of the Rock

Jephthah
One of the six Judges of Israel whose achievements are recorded in the Book of Judges. He delivered Israel from the Ammonites, but in response to a vow he had to sacrifice his daughter.

Jeremiah
One of the major prophets in the Hebrew Bible. He was hated and distrusted by many of his contemporaries because he prophesied the overthrow of Jerusalem. When this happened in 586 BCE, he fled to Egypt.

Jericho
One of the oldest cities in the world, about 15 km north-east of the junction of the Jordan and the Dead Sea. Archaeologists have excavated strata going back to 7000 BCE. It was the first city impeding the Israelites' entry into the Promised Land, and Joshua 6 tells how the walls collapsed after a week-long siege culminating in a march seven times round the city.

Jeroboam
1. Ephraimite, the son of Nebat, who led a revolt of ten tribes against King Rehoboam, son of King Solomon, and founded the separate Kingdom of Israel, about 930 BCE. The Bible is very critical of Jeroboam I because he set up shrines at Dan and Bethel each containing golden calves in opposition to the Jerusalem Temple.
2. Jeroboam II (793–753 BCE) was one of Israel's most illustrious kings. He made Samaria an extremely powerful fortress and restored Israel's boundaries almost to their original positions.

Jerome, St
(342–420 CE)   Biblical scholar. After serving as a priest in many places, he settled in 386 at a monastery in Bethlehem, and devoted the rest of his life to study. His greatest achievement was the translation of the Bible, including the Apocrypha, into Latin, which, as the Vulgate, became the accepted text of the Roman Catholic Church. One of the four Doctors of the Latin Church.

Jerusalem
1. City captured and extended by David, King of Israel, and where his son Solomon built the Temple; the capital of modern Israel, thus sacred to the Jewish people.
2. City where Jesus Christ was crucified, and where the Church of the Holy Sepulchre stands, thus sacred to the Christian community.
3. City which contains the Dome of the Rock, the Mosque of Omar, thus sacred to Islam.

Jesuit
Member of the Society of Jesus, which was founded by Ignatius Loyola, a Spanish knight converted after serious war injuries. Papal approval for the new order was granted in 1540. The order has a centralized and disciplined organization, with stress on missionary and educational activity. Members take the three monastic vows, to which the solemnly professed add a vow of absolute obedience to the Pope.

119

Jesus Christ

Name and title by which the Christian Church declares its faith that the Saviour is the Son of Man, born to Mary, and also the son of God, the incarnate Word, one with God the Father.

Jesus Liberation Front

Movement which arose from street evangelism in Hampstead, London in 1971. Young people began to meet together and started an intensive campaign with posters, tracts, tapes and millions of Jesus stickers. As a result, vast numbers joined the movement. Services are free and unstructured with a great deal of music. Leaders are given various titles, e.g. Apostles, Elders, Prophets, Pastors, Teachers. Witnessing for Christ is important, and the movement emphasizes that it wishes to stimulate the life of the Church not compete with it.

Jew

This term may be considered from three different aspects:

1. *Racial*   One who is born into a family descended from one of the tribes of Judah.

2. *National*   A citizen of the state of Israel.

3. *Religious*   One who practises the religion of Judaism. An exact and precise definition of the word 'Jew' has not been agreed, but is constantly being discussed as many borderline cases have to be considered.

Jezebel

Wife of King Ahab who introduced the worship of Baal, together with hundreds of priests and prophets, into Israel (*c.* 880 BCE). She was confronted by the prophet Elijah, who triumphed over the priests and anointed Jehu, who ultimately brought about her downfall and death. The name Jezebel became a term for a woman of extreme wickedness.

Jhana

Term used in Buddhism for a state of serene contemplation attained by meditation.

Jiania (Pn)

Term used by Sikhs for the soul of man.

Jihad

Lit. 'striving' or 'holy war'. This refers to the duty imposed by the Qur'an on every Muslim to fight against polytheists (8:39) or Christians and Jews (9:29) in order to propagate the faith. A true jihad must be carefully defined and led by an imam or Muslim head of state. According to Sufi teaching, which many modern Sunni Muslims accept, the true jihad is against sin in oneself.

Jina

Term used in the Jain religion for twenty-four great teachers or 'conquerors of life and death'. The first is said to have lived millions of years ago, and the last was Mahavira (599–527 BCE).

Jinn

Demons or spirits, frequently mentioned in the Qur'an, e.g. 15:27 and 11:24. Muhammad was sent to preach to them and some repented of their infidelity.

Jiriki

Lit. 'self' or 'own power'. Term used in the Pure Land sect of Buddhism, in contradistinction to 'tariki', to indicate the way of salvation by self-power or self-effort.

Jiva

Term for the life principle or the soul found in some Hindu religious writings.

Jizyah

Tax payable by non-Muslim subjects under Islamic rule.

Jnana (S)

Hindu term for knowledge or wisdom which comes from direct insight into the nature of ultimate reality; this is one way to salvation.

Joachim of Flora

(1132–1202)   Cistercian monk who devoted himself to writing theological works of an apocalyptic nature. His central doctrine was a Trinitarian interpretation of history, i.e. the Age of the Father, with mankind under the Law, the Age of the Son, with mankind under grace, and the Age of the Spirit, which he believed would see the rise of many new religious orders.

Joan of Arc

(1412–1431)   Also known as the Maid of Orleans. As a young girl she experienced visions, and heard voices urging her to save France. She persuaded Charles VII to allow her to lead the troops, and in 1429 she raised the Siege of Orleans, then accompanied the King to his coronation. In 1430 she was captured and handed over to the English, who burnt her as a witch and heretic in 1431.

Joan, Pope

The legend of Pope Joan is that in 1100 a woman in male disguise was elected Pope after a distinguished scholastic career. After two years she gave birth to a child during a procession at the Lateran and died immediately afterwards. The first reference to the legend appeared in the 13th century, but no evidence has ever been found to substantiate it.

Job

Central figure in a book of the same name in the Hebrew Bible. He was a righteous man who suffered grievously, and questioned God to discover the cause.

Jodo

Japanese sect of Pure Land Buddhism which proclaims the Buddha of Infinite Light and Great Compassion. It was founded by Honen about 1175.

Joel

Prophet whose message is contained in a book of the OT. Little is known of his background or dates, but there is emphasis on the outpouring of the Spirit, and the coming judgement of the enemies of God.

John

1. One of the disciples of Jesus; the brother of James and the son of Zebedee.

2. Author of the fourth Gospel. The identity of the writer is one of the greatest problems of NT scholarship. John the Apostle has been suggested, or a 'Johannine school', or a follower of John the Baptist, amongst others. This Gospel has a different pattern and structure from the synoptic Gospels, as it contains longer discourses of a more theological nature. It shows Jesus Christ as the incarnate Word, the Son of God.

3. Author of three NT epistles. The second epistle is from John the Elder, and the others are almost certainly from the same pen. Little is known of John the Elder, except that he was probably writing from Asia Minor.

4. Author of Revelation. This book is ascribed to St John the Divine, whom some scholars identify with John the Apostle. The Greek of St John's Gospel is different from that of Revelation, and it seems likely that the authors were different. St John the Divine was a visionary, and the book contains a series of visions culminating in the Last Judgement and the coming of a new heaven and a new earth.

John the Baptist

Son of Elizabeth and Zechariah in their old age, he was the cousin of Jesus and grew to manhood in the wilderness of Judaea. His preaching heralded the ministry of Jesus, who received the blessing of the Holy Spirit when John baptized him. John was imprisoned by Herod, and beheaded because of the anger of Herodias, whom he had denounced.

John of the Cross, St

(1542–1591) Spanish Christian writer on mysticism. His book *The Ascent of Mount Carmel* is a commentary on his poem *The Dark Night of the Soul*. His teaching is sometimes described as 'absorption mysticism'.

Jonah

Central character of a book of the same name in the Hebrew Bible. Jonah was told by God to go to Nineveh, but took ship in the opposite direction. During a storm he was thrown overboard and swallowed by a great fish. When he was disgorged he obeyed God and preached to the citizens of Nineveh (non-Jews), who repented and were forgiven.

John the Baptist baptizing Jesus (18th century Ethiopian manuscript)

Joriki

Psychosomatic power which followers of Zen believe develops as a result of following Zen practices. The ability to respond effectively to the environment with an undivided mind.

Joseph

1. Eleventh son of the Israelite patriarch Jacob, and the first son of his favourite wife Rachel. Special favours shown by Joseph's father roused the envy of his brothers, and he was sold into slavery in Egypt. Eventually he rose to be chief officer to Pharaoh, and was able to save his family in time of famine. His patrimony was divided between his two sons, who became the ancestors of the tribes of Ephraim and Manasseh.

2. Husband of Mary, the Mother of Jesus.

Josephus

Jewish historian at the end of the 1st century who wrote two important books: *Jewish Antiquities* and *A History of the Jewish People.*

Joshua

Israelite hero who took command of the people on the death of Moses, and led them to their settlement in the Promised Land. His achievements are related in the biblical book bearing his name.

Josiah, King

One of the great kings of Judah, he ruled from 639 to 609 BCE. He instituted a religious reformation in Judah, including the restoration of the Temple. During the building work the High Priest discovered the 'book of the law' in the Temple, and Josiah led his people in an act of penitence and a celebration of the Passover. He was killed by Egyptian troops at the Battle of Megiddo.

Joya No Kane

Festival in Hindu and Shinto temples when one hundred and eight peals of bells are rung to mark the removal of evil in preparation for the New Year.

Jubilate

First word of the Latin version of Psalm 100. In the Anglican *Book of Common Prayer* this is printed as an alternative to the Benedictus at Morning Prayer.

Jubilee

1. In the Jewish Law (Leviticus 25) a year occurring once every fifty years when slaves regained their freedom, and property that had been sold was returned to its original owners.

2. In the Roman Catholic Church a Holy Year declared by the Pope when he opens the Holy Door of St Peter's, Rome and grants a special Indulgence. This was instituted by Pope Boniface in 1300, and has been observed at varying intervals since then.

Jubilees, Book of

Apocryphal Jewish work, sometimes known as 'The Little Genesis', probably written in the 1st or 2nd century BCE, by an author of rigorist outlook. It reinterprets the biblical creation narrative and other events in terms of years, weeks of years and jubilees.

Judah

Fourth son of the Israelite patriarch Jacob and his wife Leah. The tribe which claimed him as its ancestor overran the coastal plain and settled in the south of Canaan. They survived the captivity of the tribes of Israel by the Assyrians in 722 BCE, but were defeated and taken into exile by the Babylonians in 586 BCE.

Judaism

Faith and practice of the Jewish people. It is customary to date its beginning at the time of the Babylonian Exile in 586 BCE, when the experience of living in a foreign land caused the Jews to re-examine their faith and their practices (without a temple). Fuller development of the faith took place between 70 CE, when Jerusalem was destroyed and the Jews were dispersed, and c. 500 CE, by which time the Talmud had been compiled.

Judas Iscariot

Disciple who betrayed Jesus for a reward of thirty pieces of silver, and afterwards committed suicide. The High Priest used the money which Judas threw back at him to purchase a burial ground, Akeldama, the field of blood (Matthew 27:5–8).

Judas Maccabaeus

See Maccabees

Juddin

Zoroastrian term for an unbeliever.

Jude

Title of a short epistle in the NT. The author is described as the brother of James, and the epistle seeks to expose false teachers and teaching.

Judgement Day

See Last Judgement

Judges, Book of

Seventh book in the Hebrew Bible; it follows chronologically the Pentateuch and Joshua, mentioning the twelve charismatic leaders, or Judges, six by name only, and six in detail.

Judith

Heroine in a book of the same name in the Jewish Apocrypha. She was a beautiful widow and when the Babylonians besieged Bethulia she visited their camp. There she charmed the general Holofernes with her beauty, and when he fell asleep she beheaded him. The Babylonians then withdrew, and she returned to the city in triumph.

Julian of Norwich

(1342–1413)   English mystic. She claimed to have ecstatic visions and wrote an account of them in *The Sixteen Revelations of Divine Love.*

Julius II

(1443–1513)   Giuliano della Rovere, a Catholic priest from Savona. He was created a cardinal by his uncle, Pope Sixtus IV, in 1471, and held many high offices. On the election of the Borgia Pope Alexander VI in 1492 he fled to France, but in 1503 was himself elected Pope. He personally led the papal troops into battle, and formed the Holy League in order to defeat France. He was a great patron of the arts, and used the genius of Michelangelo, Raphael and Bramante to beautify the Vatican.

Jum'a (A)

Lit. 'assembly'. Name of Friday and the Friday midday prayer, which is obligatory for Muslims. Friday congregational prayer at a mosque includes two prostrations and a sermon.

Juno

Roman power of fertility in women, identified with the Greek goddess Hera.

Jupiter

Roman sky god, one with the Greek god Zeus; he was worshipped on Capitol Hill. The name appears to be a contraction of the Indian divine name Dyaus-Pitar.

Justification

Christian term for the event by which the sinner passes from a state of condemnation to being declared just or righteous. In traditional Christian doctrine, man is regarded as originally sinful and in wrong relation to God, but unable to put himself right. Protestant theology emphasizes that justification is achieved by faith alone. Catholic theology teaches that justification is achieved by faith reinforced by the grace that is mediated through the Sacraments.

Justin Martyr

(100–165 CE)   Christian apologist. He was trained as a philosopher, but was converted to Christianity in 130. His first apology was written to the Emperor Antoninus Pius in 155 and his second to the Roman Senate in 161. Shortly afterwards he was denounced as a Christian, and on refusing to sacrifice to Roman gods, was beheaded.

Justinian

(483–565 CE)   Celebrated lawgiver who became Emperor of Constantinople in 527 and was called 'the Great'. He appointed a commission of jurists, and they ultimately produced four vast works, viz. the *Institutions, Digesta, Codex* and *Novellae.* These were gathered together under the general title *Corpus Juris Civilis,* and they form the Roman Law as received in Europe.

Justus

Priest who came to Britain with Pope Gregory's second group of missionaries in 601 CE. He was made the first Bishop of Rochester in 604, and Archbishop of Canterbury in 624.

Ka

Term used in ancient Egyptian religion for a spirit or divine power. At first it was associated only with the Pharaoh, but in later times a ka was said to be born with everyone.

Kaaba (A)

Word meaning 'cube' used for the sacred shrine in Mecca (12 m long, 11 m wide and 15 m high) set in the courtyard of the Mosque, towards which all Muslims turn in prayer. It is covered by a black cloth, renewed annually, into which the confession of faith is woven. In the east corner is set the Black Stone. Tradition says it was built by Abraham and Ishmael, and pilgrims on the Hajj endeavour to touch it as they walk round it seven times.

Kabbalah/Cabala

Lit. 'that which is handed down'. This term covers Jewish esoteric lore, and is the general term for Jewish mysticism.

Kabir

(1440–1518)   Leading exponent of bhakti who was a tanner by trade. He possibly influenced Guru Nanak. Some of his hymns are included in the *Guru Granth Sahib*, the Sikh holy book.

Kabod (H)

Word meaning 'glory', regarded as an attribute of God.

Kaccha

Symbolic undergarments, breeches, worn by members of the Sikh Khalsa, as one of the five symbols of their faith.

Kaddish

Prayer of sanctification frequently used as part of Jewish mourning ceremonies.

Kafir (A)

Word originally meaning 'concealing' or 'ungrateful' which later developed to mean 'unbelief' or 'infidel'. It is now used in Islam of all who do not follow that faith.

Kalam (A)

Lit. 'speech'. Science of Islamic theology, or the setting forth of the divine attributes according to Islamic revelation.

Kali

Lit. 'black'. The dark, fierce consort of Shiva, depicted with garlands of skulls. She is also the goddess who has overcome fear, and can give peace, health and children to her devotees.

Kalimah (A)

Title given to the shahadah (confession) made by Muslims: 'There is no god but God: Muhammad is the apostle of God.'

Kalkin

Tenth avatar of Vishnu, who is yet to come, at the end of this dark age, to destroy evil and restore goodness.

124

Kalpas

According to Hindu thought, these are alternating ages of activity and repose, each one forty-two thousand million years in duration, through which the universe evolved.

Kam

In Sikh teaching lust, one of the five weaknesses which attack the human soul.

Kama

Buddhist term for lust, pleasure or desire, regarded as an obstacle to spiritual progress. It is personalized in Hinduism as the god of love, and is sometimes identified with the Buddhist mara (evil).

Kama-dhatu

Buddhist term for the plane of material desire or passion.

Kami

Word used in the Shinto religion and in Japanese mythology to indicate gods or superior and sacred beings: some are noble, some base; some are strong, some weak; some are good, some bad.

Kamma (P)

See Karma

Kammanta

Buddhist term for action. Right action is the fourth step in the Eightfold Path.

Kandy

Town in Sri Lanka noted for its temples, particularly the Buddhist Temple of the Tooth, which treasures a sacred relic of the Buddha.

Kangha

Symbolic wooden comb worn by members of the Sikh Khalsa as one of the five symbols of their faith.

Kant, Immanuel

(1724–1804)   German philosopher. His two books *The Critique of Pure Reason* (1787) and *The Critique of Practical Reason* (1788) mark a turning-point in philosophical method. He held that knowledge is the result of a synthesis between an intellectual act and what is presented to the mind from outside. In his study of religion and morals he rejected the three traditional proofs of God's existence, but introduced the concept of the categorical imperative.

Kapilavastu

Birthplace of the Buddha.

Kapital, Das

Major work of Karl Marx, written in 1867, setting out his teaching on Communism.

Kaaba

Kali

Kara

Steel bangle worn by members of the Sikh Khalsa as one of the five symbols of their faith.

Karaites

Jewish group in the 8th century, founded by Anan ben David, which renounced the Talmud and took its stand exclusively on the Scriptures.

Karam Khand

In the teaching of the Sikh Guru Nanak, the fourth of the five stages or steps towards man's liberation. This is the stage of grace.

Sikh symbol of sword (khanda) and bracelet (kara)

Karbala

City 96 km south-west of Baghdad sacred to the Shiah Muslims, because in 680 CE Husain and his followers were massacred there; this event is commemorated annually in the Passion of Husain.

Karma (S)/**Kamma** (P)

Lit. 'deeds' or 'doing'. Term found in Hindu and Buddhist thought with several shades of meaning, e.g. the moral character, good or bad, of an action; the deeds which determine one's destiny in a future reincarnation; the causal law according to which good actions procure good rebirths and bad actions bad rebirths; retribution; the force which determines the whole destiny of man and the fruit, effect or result of former action. One can improve one's karma by meditation and religious practices.

Karma Marga

In Hindu teaching the path of action leading to salvation.

Karmayoga

Discipline of action, or spiritual exercise through work, taught in the *Bhagavadgita*.

Karna Chedan

Hindu religious ceremony for the piercing of girls' ears, at the age of five.

Karttikeya

Hindu god of war, often portrayed with six heads, riding on a peacock.

Karuna

Lit. 'compassion'. One of the two pillars of Mahayana Buddhism, the other being prajna (wisdom). The term is also used for the second Brahman vihara, identifying oneself with the suffering of others.

Karttikeya

Jewish wedding. The ketubah is being read to the bridal couple, who are standing under the huppah

Kasb (A)

Lit. 'acquisition'. Teaching of a leading Islamic theologian, Al-Asha'ri, purporting to reconcile divine disposition with human responsibility in the formula: 'God wills it *in* the will of the doer, who thus acquires the deed.'

Kashrut (H)

Jewish dietary laws. (See also Kosher)

Katha

Reading of Hindu scriptures by a Brahman priest, sponsored by a worshipper.

Katonda

Name of the high god worshipped by the Ganda tribe of Uganda.

Kattandiya

Leaders of Buddhist ritual in Sri Lanka villages.

Kaur (Pn)

Word meaning 'princess'. Name given to female initiates of the Sikh Khalsa.

Kauravas

The Hindu epic poem, the *Mahabharata*, is based on a battle between two sections of the Kuru tribe. The Kauravas are cast as the villains, while the Pandavas, led by five brave brothers, are the heroes who are supported by Krishna.

Kavvanah (H)

Lit. 'directed attention'. Term used in Jewish rabbinic literature to denote a state of mental concentration and devotion at prayer.

Kaya

According to Buddhist thought the material component of man, the body. The term can also be used to refer to the 'body of the law'.

Kedushah (H)

Lit. 'sanctification'. Title given to Jewish prayers which are restricted to communal worship.

Kehillah (H)

Community of Jews organized round a synagogue, which serves as a place of prayer, instruction and judgement.

Keisaku

Flat-ended stick used by a Zen master to keep his students mentally alert during meditation.

Kells, Book of

Beautifully ornamented copy of the Gospels written in the 8th century at the Monastery of Kells. It is considered to be the finest example of Irish manuscript writing in existence.

Kendo (J)

Lit. 'way of the sword'. The art of swordsmanship, which involves religious symbolism.

Kenosis

Christian doctrine that the divine Logos, by his incarnation, divested himself of his divine attributes of omniscience and omnipotence. It is based on the Greek verb in Philippians 2:7, which can be translated 'he emptied himself'.

Kerygma

Term used in Christian theology for the preaching or element of proclamation in the early Church, as distinct from didache, or teaching.

Kesh

The long, uncut hair of members of the Sikh Khalsa, tied in a special knot, as one of the five symbols of their faith.

Keshdharis

Lit. 'those who keep their hair uncut'. Term applied to members of the Sikh community, the Khalsa, who have been through the initiation ceremony and have taken amrit (symbolic sugared water).

Ketubah (H)

Marriage document received by a Jewish bride setting out the duties which the bridegroom undertakes to perform on her behalf.

Keys, Power of the

Term symbolizing the authority of Christ over his Church and over death and Hades (Revelation

1:18). In Matthew 16:19 it is used to signify the authority given to Peter as leader of the Apostles. The Roman Catholic Church claims that this authority has passed to the Popes as successors of Peter, giving them authority over the Church on earth.

Khadija

Wealthy widow who employed Muhammad as a camel-driver. They married, and when Muhammad began to have experiences of revelation, Khadija recognized his call to be a prophet; she encouraged him and loyally supported him throughout her life, and bore him a son (who died) and a daughter.

Khalifah

See Caliph

Khalsa

The Sikh brotherhood, founded by Guru Gobind Singh in 1699, to which men and women are admitted at an initiation ceremony involving the use of amrit (symbolic sugared water).

Khanda

Symbolic double-edged sword, representing power and divinity, used in the Sikh Amrit ceremony.

Khandha (P)/Skandha (S)

Buddhist term for the five aggregates that make up human nature, or what is erroneously thought to be the self. These are rupa (material form), vedana (sensation), sanna (perception), sankhara (volition) and vinnana (consciousness).

Kharijites

Minority sect in Islam, also known as the Seceders. They rejected both Sunni and Shiah teaching, and maintained that the community had the right to elect its own head and the duty to depose him if he were found guilty of sin.

Khordad Sal

Parsee festival, held on 1 September, marking the birthday of the prophet Zarathustra.

Khota

Term used in village Hinduism for the anger of an Indian village deity, regarded by the villagers as a cause of suffering in their midst.

Khutbah (A)

Term used in Islam for the sermon preached on a Friday in a mosque.

Kibbutz (H)

In Israel a voluntary collective community, mainly agricultural, in which there is no private wealth, the community being responsible for the needs of the members and their families. Starting from a single group at Deganyah in 1909, more than two hundred communities have now been established, with nearly one hundred thousand members.

Kiddush (H)

Prayer of sanctification recited at the beginning of the Jewish Sabbath, and on other holy days.

Kingdom of God

The Kingdom of God is central to the teaching of the NT though many theologians prefer the translation 'Kingly rule'. John the Baptist (Matthew 3:2) and Jesus (Matthew 4:17) both began their ministries by proclaiming that the Kingdom was at hand. Some parables, e.g. the Tares and the Ten Virgins, suggest that it is in the future, perhaps at the return of Christ. Others suggest that it is here (Matthew 12:28) or 'within you' (Luke 17:21). The NT demonstrates a close relationship between the Kingdom and the Church, e.g. Peter is the rock on which the Church is built and also has the keys of the Kingdom, but the two are not identical.

Kings, Books of

Two books in the Hebrew Bible which record the history of Israel and Judah from the reign of Solomon to the destruction of Jerusalem in 586 BCE by the Babylonians.

Kinhin

Term used in Zen Buddhism for 'walking' meditation as distinct from sesshin, which is intense meditation.

Kirk

Scottish word equivalent to 'church'. It is embodied in the term kirk-session, which is the lowest court in the Church of Scotland, consisting of the minister and the elders of a local congregation.

Kirpan

Short knife carried by members of the Sikh community, the Khalsa, as a symbol of active resistance to evil. It is one of the Five K's, symbols of the Sikh community.

Kirtan

Devotional songs used by Sikhs in the public worship held in gurdwaras.

Kismet

Turkish word for destiny or fate. It is used in some Islamic countries as a term for predestination.

Kiswa (A)

Lit. 'robe'. Term used in Islam for the black brocade curtain which covers the whole Kaaba shrine at Mecca. It is renewed every year, and pieces of the old one are sold as relics.

Kitab (A)

Lit. 'book'. Term applied primarily to the Qur'an, but also used of the scriptures given to earlier prophets such as Moses, David and Jesus.

Knox, John

(1513–1572)   Scottish reformer. A forthright and fiery preacher, he was in constant trouble with the authorities. In 1551 he became Chaplain to Edward VI and helped to draft the Second Prayer Book, but on the accession of Mary he fled to the continent and became English chaplain in Geneva in 1556. Back in Scotland in 1559 he became leader of the Reforming party, and drew up the *Scottish Confession*, the first *Book of Discipline* and a *Treatise on Predestination*.

Koan

Lit. 'problem' or 'riddle'. Term used in Zen Buddhism for a word or phrase of nonsensical language which cannot be solved by the intellect.

Kohen (H)

Title given to priests in the Jewish Temple. The priesthood ceased when the Temple was destroyed, but the title survives in the surname Cohen, and members of this family, claiming descent from the priestly class, have certain privileges in the synagogue.

Kojiki (J)

Records of Ancient Matters, the oldest Japanese book, almost a sacred scripture in Shintoism.

Kol Nidrei (H)

Lit. 'all vows'. Jewish prayer chanted in the evening liturgy of the Day of Atonement. Very moving musical settings have been written for this by Jewish composers.

Koran

See Qur'an

Kosher (H)

Term applied to those categories of food which Jews are permitted by their faith to eat, and also to the preparation of such food in accordance with their dietary laws.

Krishna

One of the most popular Hindu gods, an avatar or incarnation of Vishnu. There are many legends of his life and death, but in the *Bhagavadgita* he is the supreme deity, and the divine instructor of Arjuna. The love of Krishna for Radha is the subject of many religious poems, and is a symbol of divine–human love.

Krishna among the Gopis (cowmaidens)

Krishna Consciousness

Branch of Hinduism that owes much of its inspiration to the teaching of Caitanya (b.1485) and is based on the practice of Bhakti Yoga. It was introduced to the West by His Divine Grace, Swami Prabhupada in 1965. It has attracted vast numbers of followers in America, but few elsewhere. Its basic book is the *Bhagavadgita*, and its basic practice is the constant chanting of the Hare Krishna mantra. It has four rules: no eating of animal foodstuffs, no intoxicants, no illicit sex, no gambling. A distinctive feature of adherents is their shaven head with a long topknot by which they hope Krishna will deliver them from this world.

Krodh

In Sikh teaching wrath, one of the five weaknesses that attack the human soul.

Kshathra

In Zoroastrian teaching Dominion, one of the seven Amesha Spentas.

Kshatriyas

Second of the four classes of Hindu society. Endowed with sovereignty, they are the ruling, warrior, twice-born class.

Kufr

According to Islamic teaching the ultimate evil; disbelief in God and his signs; rejection of revelation; thanklessness. The antithesis of shukr.

Kuk

Idea of ransom or redemption found in Nuer sacrifice.

Kumarbi

Ancient deity of the Hurrians and the Hittites, called the father of the gods.

Kundalini

According to Hindu mystics this is a tiny but fiery serpent, coiled up within man. It is a potential source of great power, but dangerous if aroused without due preparation, such as yoga exercises or the use of the *Tantras*.

Kung Fu-tzu

See Confucius

Kurma (S)

Word meaning 'tortoise' applied to the second avatar of Vishnu. According to the *Mahabharata*, Vishnu assumed this form in order to support Mt Mandara when the gods churned up the ocean.

Kusala

Buddhist term for personal liberation, that which is profitable or good.

Kusti

Sacred cord worn by Zoroastrians and untied and retied during the recitation of prayers. It is said to represent the sword-belt of religion.

Kwan Yin (C)/Kwannon (J)

Name of the Mahayana Bodhisattva of great mercy. Represented by a female figure with a child, she is the protectress of women and children.

Kwoth (pl. Kuth)

Nuer god or spirit.

Kyala

High god of the Konde and Nyakyusa tribes of Nyasa. He is the god of righteousness who inflicts heavy punishment on evil doers, but he also sends the rain and rewards the good with rich harvests.

Kyrie Eleison

Greek words meaning 'Lord, have mercy' which have been incorporated in the liturgical worship of the Christian Church from very early times.

Labarum

Imperial standard adopted by Constantine after his conversion to Christianity. It is usually depicted as the Greek letters XP (chi, rho), the monogram of the name Christ, on a white background.

Labbaika (A)

Cry of greeting uttered by the Muslim pilgrim on arrival in Mecca, meaning 'Here I am before Thee'.

Lady Chapel

Small chapel, part of a larger church, dedicated to the Virgin Mary. It is often to the east of the high altar.

Lady Day

Alternative name for the Christian Feast of the Annunciation of the Blessed Virgin Mary, celebrated on 25 March.

Lag B'omer

In Judaism the thirty-third day of the counting of the Omer, i.e. the period between Passover and Shavuot. It is kept as a holiday, and is a favourite day for marriages.

Lailat al Qadr

See Night of Power

Laity

Derived from a Greek word meaning 'people', this term designates those members of the Christian Church who do not belong to the ordained ministry.

Lakhana (P)/**Lakshana** (S)

Term used in Buddhism for a mark or sign distinguishing one thing from another. Hence it becomes the term for a characteristic or criterion.

Lakshmi

Hindu goddess of fortune, the wife of the great god Vishnu. She is a renowned beauty, sometimes depicted with four arms, holding a lotus. Some Hindus believe she is the wife of all Vishnu's incarnations. She is also known as Sri.

Lama

Tibetan Buddhist elder or teacher, now often used for 'priest'.

Lamb

Animal often used in sacrifice, as it was considered to be a symbol of purity and innocence. In the Christian tradition of art it is a symbol of Christ, as he is referred to in the Gospels as the Lamb of God.

Lambeth

The Palace of Lambeth is the London home of the Archbishop of Canterbury. Every ten years the bishops of the Anglican Communion meet there for conference and consultation.

Lambeth Quadrilateral

Four articles of faith considered essential from the point of view of the Anglican Communion for a reunited Christian Church. They are: (1) the Holy Scriptures; (2) the Apostles' Creed and the Nicene Creed; (3) the sacraments of baptism and Holy Communion; (4) the historic episcopate.

Lamentations, Book of

Anonymous book in the Hebrew Bible which is placed immediately after Jeremiah and has been attributed to him by some scholars. Its first four chapters are acrostic poems, and the book is one of five scrolls read in Jewish synagogues on 9 Ab, the day of mourning for the destruction of the Temple.

Lammas

At one time this was a quarter-day, and it is still observed as such in Scotland, on 1 August. The name is derived from 'loaf' and 'mass', as it was customary in the early English Church to consecrate bread made from the first ripe corn of the new harvest at Mass on that day.

Lanfranc

(1005–1089) Catholic priest born in Pavia. He moved to France and entered the monastery of Bec, being made Prior in 1045. He became a trusted counsellor of Duke William of Normandy, and supported the invasion of Britain in 1066, following which he was appointed Archbishop of Canterbury in 1070. He then systematically replaced Saxon bishops and abbots by Normans.

Langar

Kitchen attached to a Sikh gurdwara where the congregation enjoys a communal meal after the diwan. It is sometimes referred to as the Guru ka langar, the Guru's kitchen.

Langton, Stephen

English priest who was created a cardinal in 1206 and Archbishop of Canterbury in 1207. His name is on Magna Carta as one of the counsellors of the King. He established the claim of the Archbishop to be the Pope's 'legatus natus'. He died in 1228.

Lantern Festival

Festival that marks the end of the Chinese New Year celebrations. Lanterns decorate homes, restaurants and public buildings, and fireworks are let off.

Lao-Tze

Chinese philosopher born *c.* 600 BCE. He taught that man is composed of two principles, one material and perishable, the other spiritual and imperishable. His moral code inculcated charity, benevolence and virtue. His doctrines are collected in a book entitled *Tao, The Way.*

Lares

Spirits associated with the penates in the guardianship of an ancient Roman household. They were probably ancestral spirits, or spirits of the land and boundaries round the house.

Last Judgement

Most Christians believe that man is under the judgement of God. Some believe that this is a continuous process throughout life and after death; others believe in the judgement of the individual at the end of earthly life; others believe that at the end of history there will be a Last Judgement of all mankind by Christ the King, with the separation of the saved from the damned. Michelangelo vividly portrayed this in his fresco *The Last Judgement* in the Sistine Chapel, Rome. It is also a Muslim belief that the Last Day will be a day of judgement.

Lao-tze

Lar

Last Supper
> Meal which Jesus shared with his disciples before his arrest and crucifixion. It is not clear from the Gospels whether it was a Passover meal or a chaburah, a fellowship meal prior to the Passover. According to St Paul (1 Corinthians 11:23–25), this was accepted from the earliest days of the Church as the origin or institution of the Eucharist.

Lateran Basilica
> The Church of St John Lateran is one of the four major basilicas in Rome, and is the cathedral of the Bishop of Rome, the Pope. The present building, standing on the site of an ancient palace, dates from the 16th century.

Latin
> Language of the Romans which became the accepted medium of diplomacy, education and the Church throughout Europe. The Vulgate, which is the version of the Bible authorized in the Roman Catholic Church, is the Latin translation made by Jerome between 384 and 400 CE.

Lauds
> Traditionally the morning service of the Christian Church. In the Anglican *Book of Common Prayer* it is incorporated in the order for Matins.

Laurence, St
> Deacon and martyr in Rome. According to tradition, he was ordered by the Prefect of Rome to produce the treasures of the Church and assembled a group of beggars and cripples. For this he was sentenced to death by being roasted on a gridiron in 258 CE.

Lavabo
> Washing of the celebrant's fingers after the offering of the oblations and before the Prayer of Consecration in the Mass or Eucharist.

Laws of Manu
> Law code attributed in Hinduism to the legendary figure Manu, the first man, or Hindu Adam. It sets out the duties of the various classes of Hindu society, with the penalties, fines and punishments which are to be inflicted.

Lebbaeus
> See Thaddaeus

Lectern
> Stand in a Christian church which supports the Bible or other liturgical books. Often massive, in bronze or brass, and surmounted by the figure of an eagle whose outstretched wings form the book-rest.

Lectionary
> Book containing extracts from Scripture to be read in Christian worship, or a list of passages of Scripture appointed to be read in the daily celebration of the Mass or at Matins and Evensong.

Legate
> Personal representative of the Pope or Holy See who has been entrusted with authority for a particular mission, or as a diplomatic official corresponding to an ambassador. The latter is sometimes termed a papal nuncio.

Lenin, V. I.
> (1870–1924)   The first head of the Marxist government in Russia. He emphasized the importance of revolutionary activity and the dictatorship of the proletariat.

Lent
> Period of forty days beginning on Ash Wednesday and leading to Easter observed by the Christian Church as a penitential season.

Leo X
> (1475–1521)   Giovanni dei Medici, the second son of Lorenzo the Magnificent. He was elected Pope in 1513 and had to deal with the beginning of the Reformation, in the course of which he excommunicated Martin Luther in 1520.

Lesser Vehicle
> English translation of 'hinayana', a term used by Mahayana Buddhists to indicate the doctrine of the Elders or Buddhists of Sri Lanka and S.E. Asia. It is the monk's way of salvation, regarded as the conservative interpretation of Buddhism.

Levi

Third son of the Israelite patriarch Jacob and his wife Leah. He was the ancestor of the Levites, a tribe which had no territory but was supported by the other tribes because it provided assistance to the priests.

Leviathan

Sea-monster mentioned in four passages in the Hebrew Bible. The word is cognate with the Ugaritic *loten*, and may be identified with the Babylonian chaos-dragon, Tiamat.

Levites

Members of the tribe descended from Levi, a son of Jacob. No territory was allocated to them when the Israelite tribes entered the Promised Land, because they were dedicated to the service of the Lord, including the care and transport of the Holy Tabernacle. It is difficult to discover the exact relationships between the priests and Levites, but the latter appear to have had a subordinate role when the priesthood was restricted to the family of Aaron.

Leviticus

Third book in the Hebrew Bible. It consists almost entirely of legislation on topics such as sacrifice, purification, vows and tithes. Chapters 17–26 are usually called the Holiness Code and are thought to be the earliest in the book.

Leza

High god worshipped by the Ba-ila tribe of Zambia. He is a sky god who controls the rain and the harvest, but he also gave man laws, and set rules and regulations for life.

Lhasa

Capital of Tibet, which houses the Potala, formerly the residence of the Dali Lama and the focus of Asiatic Buddhism. It is now occupied by the Chinese.

Li

Term for good manners, propriety, or good form reflected in the feeling of deference. This is one of the five cardinal virtues recognized by Confucianism.

Libation

Pouring out of a drink-offering, usually wine, as part of a sacrifice to God.

Liberal Jews

See Reform Jews

Life after Death

See Eternal Life and Resurrection

Lila (S)

Term for play or sport. In the philosophy of the Vedanta, the lila of the world soul creates the cosmos.

Lilith

Demon, male or female, in Babylonian myth mentioned in Isaiah 34:14. In the Jewish Talmud, Lilith is the chief female demon.

Lily

In ancient Greece the lily flower was sacred to Hera, while in Christian usage and symbolism it is dedicated to the Virgin Mary. The trumpet-shaped *Lilium candidum* is known as the Madonna Lily, and is the symbol of virginity.

Limbo

In Christian tradition an area on the edge of hell which is a place not of punishment, but of banishment from the presence of God.

Lilith

Lingam

Phallus, symbolized by a cone-shaped object or pillar, and in Hinduism dedicated to the worship of Shiva.

Lingayata

Shaivite sect which developed in the 12th century and is still an important religious movement in south India. Members of the sect worship Shiva alone, are strict vegetarians and abstain from alcohol. Caste is not important to them, but they pay special reverence to their Gurus.

Lion

1. The magnificence and strength of the lion caused it to be associated with royalty from very early times. King David was called the Lion of Judah, and later the title was sometimes applied to Christ. In Christian iconography the lion is the symbol of St Mark the Evangelist.
2. Fourth of the grades of Mithraic initiation; protected by Jupiter.

Litany

Form of prayer in which petitions are said or sung by a leader and fixed responses are made by the congregation.

Liturgy

Divine service according to a prescribed ritual. It is used of such services as Matins and Evensong in the Anglican *Book of Common Prayer*, but chiefly of the order of service of the Eucharist or Mass.

Lingam with face of Shiva

Liver

In ancient Babylon, Baru priests practised hepatoscopy, the art of divination by a study of the vein markings in the liver of a sacrificed animal. The Etruscans are also said to have practised this, and passed on their knowledge to the Romans. Probably the reason for the practice was that the liver is full of blood, which was regarded with great awe, as the life-bearing medium.

Lobh (Pn)/Lobha (P, S)

1. In Sikh teaching avarice, one of the five weaknesses that attack the human soul.
2. In Buddhism a term for covetousness or greed, one of the three fires which cause dukkha. It is an alternative term for raga.

Locust

Insect mentioned several times in the Bible because of its devastating habit of stripping vast areas of all vegetation. Locusts constituted one of the plagues imposed upon Egypt when Moses was seeking the release of the Israelites (Exodus 10:4–6). The prophet Joel used the devastation of locusts to signify the wrath of God when he called upon the nation to repent.

Logical Positivism

Set of doctrines associated with a group known as the Vienna Circle, which flourished in the late 1920s and early 1950s. A cardinal doctrine of logical positivism, known as the 'verification principle', is that there are no genuine statements except those which are either analytic or can be verified in sense experience. A consequence of this principle is that statements about a transcendent god are meaningless.

Logos

Greek noun meaning 'word'. Among the Stoics it was used to designate the rational principle in the universe. In Philo it is the sum of divine ideas, mediating between God and man. In John 1:1 it is used as a designation of Christ as the eternally pre-existing and creative word of God. This introduces the Johannine teaching that, as the Incarnate Word, he is one with the Father, perfect God and perfect man.

Loka

Term used in Buddhism to designate the world, or the sphere of existence.

Loki

The troublemaker, like Satan, among the Scandinavian gods. He is best known for causing the death of the handsome Balder, the son of Odin, with a wand of mistletoe, the only wood from which Balder had not been granted immunity.

Lollards

Term meaning 'chanters' applied to the followers of John Wycliffe (1329–1384). They based their teaching on personal faith and the authority of the Bible, and rejected clerical celibacy and the doctrine of transubstantiation.

Lombard, Peter

(1100–1160)   Christian theologian, known as the Master of the Sentences. He is chiefly known for a work *Four Books of Sentences*, which became a standard textbook of theology in the Middle Ages. The four sections deal with (1) the Trinity, (2) creation and sin, (3) the Incarnation and (4) the Sacraments, and they contain a wealth of quotations from the Latin Fathers.

Lonesome Stone

Group which is part of the Jesus Revolution. It started in America and came to England in 1972. Members live in communes, and one of their most important activities is touring with a folk opera which tells of a hippie who became hardened by his life but was eventually converted to Christ. Following the performance they give testimonies and distribute tracts. They consider that they are taking the Church to the people.

Lord

1. Title applied to God in the Hebrew Bible. He is called Lord of Hosts (1 Samuel 1:3), and the Lord God of Israel (Judges 5:3). When the divine name YHWH appears in the Hebrew text, the reader substitutes the word 'Adonai', which means 'Lord'.

2. Title applied to Jesus by his disciples, e.g. Matthew 17:4, by people seeking his help, e.g. Mark 7:28, and by the Church after the Resurrection, e.g. Romans 1:3.

3. Title applied to Gautama Siddhartha, the Buddha, by members of the Buddhist Sangha.

Lord's Prayer

Prayer which Jesus taught his disciples as a model prayer for all believers (Matthew 6:9–13). It is also known as the Paternoster, from the Latin form of the first words, 'Our Father'.

Lord's Supper

Term used by St Paul (1 Corinthians 11:20) when referring to the rite which is also called the Eucharist, the Holy Communion or the Mass.

Lots

Set of dice or coins or other objects which are cast in order to gain predictions or answers to particular questions, according to the numbers or patterns provided by the objects thrown.

Lotus

1. Flower of exquisite beauty, the great white water-lily, of particular significance because it grows out of the mud.

2. Flower rich in symbolism. Osiris, Egyptian god of the underworld, is depicted wearing a crown of lotus blooms. In Hindu mythology the lotus represents the female life principle, and Lakshmi, the consort of Vishnu, was said to have emerged from a lotus. The Buddha was associated with the lotus flower at his birth, and it became his symbol.

3. 'Lotus' *(padmasan)* is the title given to the basic position in yoga meditation.

Lotus flowers

Lourdes

Centre of pilgrimage in southern France where, in 1850, Bernadette Soubirous had visions of the Blessed Virgin Mary. A spring of water appeared and healings took place, and the site has become a shrine where the sick are taken for immersion in the water and services of prayer.

Low Sunday

Sunday after Easter, probably so called in contrast to the high feast of Easter Day.

Loyola, Ignatius

(1495–1556)   Founder of the Society of Jesus, the Jesuits. He was born into a noble Spanish family, became a soldier, and after being seriously wounded, decided to become a soldier of Christ. He studied for the priesthood, and with six companions founded the Society of Jesus in 1534, gaining recognition from Pope Paul III in 1540.

Lucifer

Lit. 'light-bearer', identified by the Romans with the morning star Venus, but transferred by Christian theologians such as Augustine to Satan, when he was identified with the fallen star in Isaiah 14:12. In the play *Dr Faustus* by Christopher Marlowe, he is the lord of hell and the master of Mephistopheles, appearing only in the last act, as the end of Faust's contract approaches.

Lug

Ancient Celtic deity and patron of culture, probably in origin a sun god.

Luke

1. Physician and companion of St Paul on some of his missionary journeys, regarded as the author of the Gospel bearing his name, and also the Acts of the Apostles.

2. Third Gospel. It lays special emphasis on the fact that Jesus is the universal saviour, with power to heal body and mind. There is great sympathy towards women, Samaritans and gentiles generally.

Lulav

Palm branch carried with the willow, myrtle and ethrog in the synagogue service of the Feast of Tabernacles.

Lupercalia

Festival of expiation and purification held on 15 February in ancient Rome at the Wolf's Den, when young men dressed as wolves.

Luther, Martin

(1483–1546)   German monk of the Augustinian hermits. Angered by the sale of indulgences, in 1517 he pinned ninety-five theses on the door of Wittenberg Church. These caused a great controversy, and after the publication of further writings Luther was excommunicated in 1520, and condemned at the Diet of Worms in 1521. Nevertheless, he continued to build up a Church separated from and independent of Rome, and he is considered to be the initiator of the Reformation.

Lutheran Church

Protestant denomination, strong in Germany, Scandinavia and the United States, which in its theology and church organization follows the teachings of Martin Luther.

Ma'arib

Evening prayer in the Jewish liturgy, the name being taken from the first Benediction.

Maat

Ancient Egyptian goddess of wisdom, personifying truth, justice and order. Her symbol was an ostrich feather, against which human hearts were weighed in the Judgement Hall of Osiris.

Mabinogion

Collection of eleven medieval Welsh tales, containing folklore, mythology, accounts of ancient gods and goddesses, and some of the earliest Arthurian legends.

Maccabees

Noble Jewish family which led the revolt against the attempt by Antiochus V Epiphanes to crush the Jewish faith and people in 168 BCE. Under Judas Maccabaeus the Jews restored the Temple in 165 BCE. Later members of the family claimed the titles King and High Priest.

Machiavelli, Niccolò

(1469–1527) Italian historian whose name was vilified for many years after his death. In his book *The Prince* he made a clear distinction between ethics and politics. Further, he used the Italian word *virtù* not in its accepted Christian sense but as meaning 'strength' and 'vigour', applied to cruelty and villainy as much as to compassion. The book was denounced as the work of the Devil, and as Machiavelli's name was Niccolò, the Devil was given a new name, Old Nick, and 'machiavellian' came to mean 'unscrupulous'.

Machzor

Jewish prayer book for festivals, as distinct from the Siddur, or daily prayer book.

Madhva

Vaishnavite philosopher of the 13th century who opposed the monistic advaita of Shankara and taught a dualistic philosophy.

Madhyama

Buddhist term for the middle way, used in both ethics and metaphysics.

Madhyamika

Buddhist school of philosophy the foundation of which is ascribed to Nagarjuna in the 2nd century BCE which asserts a middle position, free from the extremes of permanence and annihilation.

Maenads

Name applied to the Bacchantes. It is derived from the Greek verb 'to be mad' and refers to their frenzied dances in worship of Dionysus.

Magadhi

Language of the community into which Gautama Siddhartha (the Buddha) was born.

Magga (P)

See Marga

Magha Puja

Theravada Buddhist spring full-moon festival commemorating the occasion when the Buddha ordained one thousand two hundred and fifty disciples, all of whom received enlightenment.

Magi

Zoroastrian term for priests. Christian tradition has identified the three kings or wise men who brought gifts to the infant Jesus as magi (Matthew 2:1–12).

Magic

1. *Apotropaic*   Use of occult powers to turn away evil, e.g. touching wood, or smearing doorposts with blood.
2. *Black*   Use of occult powers involving the invocation of Satan or the powers of darkness.
3. *Contagious*   Passing on of occult power through contact, e.g. rubbing a weapon with a similar weapon that has already killed an enemy.
4. *Sympathetic*   Use of occult powers in one sphere to produce similar results in another sphere, e.g. high leaping by dancing priests to encourage the growth of long stalks of corn.

Magnificat

Lyrical poem based on OT psalms recited by the Virgin Mary after the Archangel Gabriel announced to her that she was to be the mother of Jesus (Luke 1:46–55). The name of the poem is the first word of the Latin version. It is recited during the Anglican service of Evensong.

Magpie

Because of its contrasting black and white plumage, the magpie is regarded as a mysterious, sinister bird. According to one legend it is a hybrid from the two birds released by Noah from the Ark: the white dove and the black raven. It has been called the Devil's bird, which did not go into full mourning after the Crucifixion, and many country rhymes speak of the bad luck that it portends.

Maha Bodhi Society

Society founded in 1891 to restore as a shrine Bodh Gaya, the place in India where the Buddha found enlightenment. Its headquarters are in Calcutta, and it maintains social relief work among Buddhists, and the propagation of Buddhist teaching in India.

Mahabharata

Longer of two Indian Hindu epic poems; the other is the *Ramayana*. Written in Sanskrit in about the 2nd or 3rd century BCE, possibly by Vyasa, it has nearly one hundred thousand verses. Its theme is a civil war between the Kauravas and the Pandavas, who are assisted and encouraged by Krishna. Incorporated into its text is the *Bhagavadgita*.

Mahadeva

Title meaning 'the great God' which is conferred on the Hindu god Shiva.

Maat

Adoration of the Magi (late 12th century)

Mahaparinibbanasutta

Account of the passing of the Buddha. Lit. 'sutta of the great final nibbana'.

Maharishi Mahesh Yogi

Indian swami who first visited England in 1958 to teach transcendental meditation. He claims that he is expounding ancient Vedic knowledge through a secret technique known as the Science of Creative Intelligence. He has established centres in more than sixty countries under the title of the Spiritual Regeneration Movement.

Mahasanghika

Followers of the Great Sangha party of Buddhism, i.e. those who accepted the findings of the Second Council and favoured a relaxation of monastic rules, according to the Theravadin account.

Mahatma (S)

Term used in Hinduism as a title; lit. 'great soul'. It is conferred on outstanding religious leaders such as Gandhi.

Mahavakyas (S)

Term for great sayings that are found in Hindu Vedic scriptures. It is particularly applied to 'tat tvam asi' (that thou art).

Maha-Vihara (S)

Lit. 'great monastery'. One of the two main schools of Buddhist thought in Sri Lanka. The Great Monastery was broadly Theravadin, whereas the Abhayagin Monastery followed the Mahayana form of Buddhism.

Mahavira

Indian religious leader of the warrior caste, born at Vaisali in the Ganges region in 599 BCE. He was brought up in the Jain religion, and when thirty he left home, renouncing all possessions, to become a wandering holy man. At the age of forty-three he received enlightenment, and so became a Jina, a conqueror of life and death. He spent his remaining years until his death in 527 BCE instructing his followers, and is regarded by the Jains as their greatest teacher.

Mahayana (S)

Lit. 'great vehicle'. This constitutes the major part of Buddhism. Universalistic in its appeal, it accepts the emphasis on 'wisdom' of the Theravada school, but adds an equal emphasis on the virtue of 'compassion', and regards the Buddha as a superhuman being.

Mahayogi (S)

Lit. 'great yogi'. Epithet applied to the god Shiva in Hinduism.

Mahdi (A)

Lit. 'guided one'. This name does not occur in the Qur'an, but it is a popular name or title for the expected restorer of religion who provides an eschatological hope for Islam. Mirza Ghulam Ahmad (1839–1908) claimed to be the Mahdi and founded the Ahmadiyyah sect, regarded by the Sunnis as heretical.

Maimonides

(1134–1204) Medieval Jewish philosopher. He is an important figure in Jewish history as he was one of the greatest codifiers of the Jewish law.

Maitreya

The Buddha who is to come; the friendly, benevolent, compassionate Buddha.

Maitreya (5th century)

140

Maitri (S)/**Metta** (P)

Term used in Buddhism for the subject of the *Metta Sutta*. The doctrine of good will towards all men.

Makoto (J)

Lit. 'sincerity' or 'truth'. This is the fundamental virtue in the Shinto religion, and is called the purest manifestation of the human spirit.

Makyo

Term used in Zen Buddhism for fantasies or hallucinations.

Malachi, Book of

Last book in the Hebrew Bible. It is a prophetic work and the author's name means 'my messenger'. To this the Targum adds the phrase 'whose name is called Ezra the scribe'. The book falls into two parts: the sin of Israel, and the judgement in the coming day of the Lord.

Man

In colloquial English speech this is a word loosely used for an individual or a member of the human species or a male as distinct from a female. In modern Indian languages the same word is a term specifically meaning 'mind' or 'soul'. It is that in a human person which can be directed towards God or away from God; it is that which is affected by temptation.

Mana

Melanesian word adopted by the anthropologist R. R. Marett to indicate an impersonal or undifferentiated power. It was thought that this could take possession of an object, and that object would then be accorded reverence and worship by primitive tribes.

Manas (S)

Term used in both Buddhism and Hinduism to indicate a sixth sense which groups the perceptions of the other five senses and gives a complete representation of the object perceived; it is concerned with the relationships of subject and object, and is similar to vinnana.

Manasseh

Elder son of the Israelite patriarch Joseph. He inherited half of his father's patrimony from Jacob. The tribe bearing his name occupied the territory from the coastal plain of central Canaan, across the River Jordan to the River Jabbok and on to Ramoth Gilead.

Mandala

1. Symbolic diagram surrounded by a circle, and often including circles in the design, to symbolize wholeness or perfection. As the symbol for zero, it may also symbolize completion or the end. It is also used to represent the cosmos and all its inhabitants, superhuman, human and subhuman. In ritual its purpose is to call down and house the deity, and Hindu mandalas usually have Vishnu in the centre.
2. In the psychology of C. G. Jung, it is a circular diagram which provides a pattern of psychic energy.
3. Division of a book, e.g. there are ten mandalas in the *Rig-Veda*.

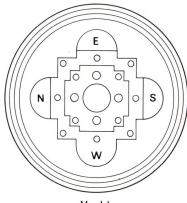

Mandala

Mandap

Pavilion erected at the home of a Hindu bride. This plays an important part in the ritual of the marriage ceremony in village Hinduism.

Mandrake

Plant to which many superstitions have been attached, possibly because its fork-shaped roots are said to resemble the human figure. It was said to shriek if roughly pulled from the ground, and its cry was thought to be fatal to anyone who heard it. Dogs were sometimes tied to the plant to uproot it, as it was regarded as a powerful ingredient in love potions. This use of it is referred to in Genesis 30 and the Song of Songs 7:13.

Manes

Term used in ancient Rome for the deified souls of departed ancestors.

Mani

   (215–275 CE)   Persian teacher who founded a religion based on, but regarded as a deviation from, Zoroastrianism.

Manichaeism

   Religion founded or introduced by Mani, a Persian teacher. By most scholars it is regarded as a deviation from Zoroastrianism, but others see it as an extreme form of Gnosticism. It was a form of dualism which regarded matter as evil, and imposed a rigorous asceticism on its devotees.

Manifesto (Communist)

   Popular statement of Marxist socialism written by Marx and Engels in 1847.

Manitou

   Term used by some North American, Algonquin, Indians for spirit beings, and for the supernatural and magical power contained in all the phenomena of nature.

Manmukh

   Term used by Sikhs to indicate a person who fails to discern the nature of the divine order, who listens to his own wayward impulses instead of the voice of the Guru.

Manna

   Food miraculously provided for the Israelites on their journey through the wilderness after the Exodus from Egypt (Exodus 16).

Mantle of the Law

   Cover of the scroll of the Torah. It is made of silk or other costly material in the form of a bag, open at the bottom and with two holes in the top, to fit over the scroll when it is rolled up.

Mantra

   Term used in Hinduism, Buddhism and Sikhism for a sacred formula or chant. A hymn or a verse which can be a help in meditation, in the sense of directing the mind along a particular path.

Mantravidh

   Lit. 'one who knows the mantras'. Indian village practitioner of Hinduism who claims a knowledge of mantras and magic spells to combat witchcraft and other forms of evil.

Mantrayana

   Later development of Mahayana Buddhism in which mantras play an important part.

Manu

   According to Hindu mythology, the progenitor of the human race, or the primal man who outlined the rules of conduct for Hinduism. Each age, of which there are to be fourteen, has its own Manu, the present being the seventh.

Mantle of the Law covering the scrolls

Mao Tse Tung

   (1893–1976)   Chinese political leader who led a peasant revolution in 1949 and became Chairman of the People's Republic of China. He expounded the teaching of Marx and Lenin in a book entitled *Contradictions*, but his most famous literary work is *Quotations from Chairman Mao*, popularly known as *Chairman Mao's Little Red Book*.

Mara

   In Buddhism the name of the Evil One. The tempter who tried to deflect the Buddha from his aspiration to enlightenment, and who rules over the world of desire.

Marava

   Important element in a village Hindu marriage. It is a pole about 10 m high erected outside the bride's house, around which the marriage ceremonies take place.

Marburg Colloquy

   Meeting summoned by Philip of Hesse in 1529 to try to reconcile the differences between Saxon and

Swiss Protestant Reformers. The attempt failed because, after agreeing on fourteen points of doctrine, Zwingli and Luther disagreed over the Eucharist. Zwingli regarded it as a commemoration meal only, while Luther insisted on the doctrine of consubstantiation, emphasizing the words of Jesus, 'This is my body.'

Marcion

Heretic of the 2nd century. He regarded Christianity as the gospel of love, to the absolute exclusion of law. He therefore accepted as Scripture only ten of St Paul's epistles and an edited version of St Luke's Gospel. His teachings are known only through the comments of his critics, but he seems to have accepted a docetic view of the person of Christ, saying that the Son of God was not incarnated, but had a phantasmal body.

Marcus Aurelius

(121–180 CE)   Roman philosopher who became Emperor in 161. He accepted the Stoic philosophy, and was deeply concerned for the moral strength of the Empire. He set out his own thoughts in twelve books of *Meditations.*

Mardi Gras

Term used in some parts of Christendom for Shrove Tuesday. It is a day of merry-making and carnival which precedes the fast of Lent.

Marduk

Son of Ea in Babylonian mythology, given the title 'Bel' (Lord). The Babylonian creation epic *Enuma Elish* recounts how he became supreme over all the gods, and the civic and national god of Babylon.

Marga (S)/Magga (P)

Term used in Hindu teaching for a path leading to salvation. In Buddhist teaching it is the fourth Noble Truth, i.e. the Noble Eightfold Path, or the Middle Way, that leads to liberation.

Mari Tablets

During excavations from 1930 to 1960 archaeologists discovered over twenty thousand clay tablets in the palace of King Zimri-lim of Mari of the 18th century BCE. They are written in a Semitic dialect and give much information about the history and religion of the period. Mention is made of the Benejamina, possibly the biblical Benjamites.

Dragon symbol of Marduk

Ma'rifah (A)

Term used in Islam for knowledge, with the particular meaning of the mystical awareness of reality, in contrast or distinction to ilm, which is intellectual knowledge.

Mark

1. Native of Jerusalem who accompanied Paul and Barnabas (his uncle) on part of Paul's first missionary journey. Paul was angry because he turned back at the half-way stage, so refused to take him on the second missionary journey. He is later mentioned by Paul as one of his companions in Rome.

2. Second of the four Gospels in the NT. According to Papias, it was written by John Mark from the memoirs of Peter. It is generally considered to be the earliest of Gospels, used later by both Matthew and Luke.

Maronites

Christian community of Syrian origin, most of whom still live in the Lebanon. They trace their ancestry back to St Maro in the 4th century, and they were excommunicated at the Council of Constantinople in 681 CE as Monothelites. Since the 12th century they have been recognized by Rome and are now a Uniat Church with their own liturgy and hierarchy.

Maror

Bitter herb used in the Jewish Passover meal to remind those taking part that the life of the Israelites in Egypt was a bitter experience.

Marriage

State of matrimony in which a man and a woman are united as husband and wife in accordance with the law and custom of their society. Often, but not always, the legal ceremony is accompanied by religious rites. In the Roman Catholic Church marriage is one of the seven sacraments.

Mars

Ancient Roman god of war, identified with the Greek god Ares. He was also regarded as the protector of agriculture, and was possibly in origin a storm god.

Martyr

Term derived from the Greek word meaning 'witness'; it is now reserved for men and women who witness to their faith by dying for it. The term is widely used in the Christian faith, but is also used in other religions, e.g. in Islam of Imam Husain, and in the Baha'i faith of the Bab.

Martyrdom of the Bab

Important day in the religious year of the Baha'i community. The Bab was martyred in N. Persia in 1850, and twenty thousand of his followers were also subsequently murdered. The martyrdom is commemorated on 9 July at noon, with prayers and readings from the Baha'i scriptures.

Ma'ruf (A)

Term used in Islam for the well doing which is enjoined by the Qur'an.

Maruts

Storm spirits which are 'swift as the wind and clothed in rain'. They are mentioned in the Hindu scripture, the *Rig-Veda*.

Marx, Karl

(1818–1883) Founder of the International Working Men's Association. He was the author of *Das Kapital*, and (with Engels) of the *Communist Manifesto*, in which he advocated the dictatorship of the proletariat.

Marxism

Body of doctrine formulated by Marx and Engels. A form of revolutionary socialism which aims at the overthrow of the bourgeoisie and the establishment of the dictatorship of the proletariat.

Mary

Mother of Jesus. See Virgin Mary

Mask

Covering for the face, often roughly shaped to resemble human or animal features. It is a means of producing a change of identity, and masks were worn by actors in Greek drama and religious ceremonies. In primitive society masks are mainly worn for ritual purposes, and they can be very large, with the intention of personifying supernatural beings.

144

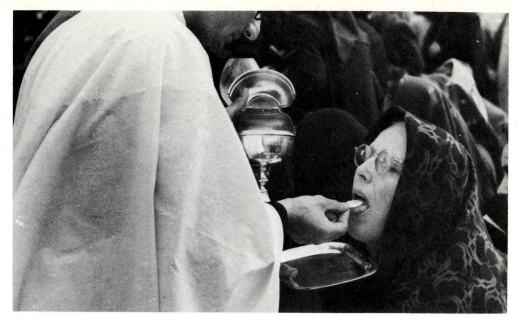

Pilgrim receiving the Host at a celebration of the Mass (Fatima, Portugal)

Mass

Term used for the Eucharist or the Holy Communion in the Roman Catholic Church. It is probably derived from the closing words of the liturgy, 'Ite, missa est'.

Massorah (H)

Textual notes to the Hebrew Bible written by the Massoretes (lit. 'transmitters'). These scholars were the custodians of the sacred text between 500 and 1000 CE and they introduced vowel signs, punctuation and accent marks into the Hebrew consonantal text.

Massoretic Text

Text of the Hebrew Bible with vowels, accents and divisions of sentences produced by the Massoretes. The standard text is that of the school of Ben Asher of Tiberias, drawn up in the 9th century.

Masya and Masyanag

In the teaching of Zoroaster the names of the first human couple, who were born of the seed of Gayomart.

Mata

In popular village Hinduism a mata is regarded as an independent, female devata. A mata often has a specialist function, e.g. Sitalamata, the smallpox goddess, and Hadakaimata, the goddess of hydrophobia.

Matarisvan

Hindu god of the wind, mentioned in the *Rig-Veda*.

Materialism

Philosophical theory which considers that matter is the basis of everything. Mental phenomena are considered to be the effects of matter, and psychic phenomena to be functions of the brain.

Matha

Hindu religious centre for the teaching of religious doctrine, or a monastery for ascetics and monks.

Mathura

According to Hindu tradition, the birthplace of the god Krishna.

Matins

Christian Church service. In the medieval Western Breviary it was a night vigil said by some orders, e.g. the Benedictines, at 2 a.m. In the Anglican *Book of Common Prayer* it is retained as Morning Prayer, and includes psalms, canticles, two lessons and collects.

Matsya

Mativah

In Hinduism an Indian village priest who specializes in exorcism through singing. He is thought to be more powerful than the ojha priest.

Matn (A)

Term used by Muslims for the substance of an Islamic tradition, as distinct from its attestation.

Matrimony

Rite of marriage, which is regarded as one of the seven sacraments of the Roman Catholic Church.

Matsya (S)

Word meaning 'fish', applied to the first avatar of Vishnu. This is first mentioned in the Laws of Manu, where the fish saved Manu. In later versions, Vishnu, in fish form, saves mankind.

Matthew

1. One of the disciples of Jesus, described in the Gospels as a tax-collector. According to Papias he made a collection of oracles, or *logia*, spoken by Jesus.

2. First of the four Gospels. There is no direct evidence concerning its authorship, but it incorporates most of the Gospel of Mark, and shows distinct Jewish leanings, e.g. many events in the life of Jesus are described as the fulfilment of particular OT prophecies, and the Church is seen as the new Israel.

Matzah (H)

Unleavened bread used during the Jewish Passover Festival to commemorate the fact that when the Israelites were told by Moses to prepare for the Exodus from Egypt, they were in such haste that they had to make their bread from unleavened dough.

Maulid

Birthday of the Prophet Muhammad, celebrated by Muslims on the twelfth day of the fourth month with festive songs and gifts and scriptural readings.

146

Maundy Thursday

Day observed in the Christian Church to commemorate the institution of the Eucharist by Jesus Christ at the Last Supper. The name is derived from the Latin *mandatum*, referring to the command to love one another. To symbolize this loving concern, on this day the British sovereign distributes Maundy money to poor, deserving people.

Mawu

High god of the Ewe tribes of Togoland and Dahomey. He is the almighty creator, but is also full of pity.

May Day

The first day of May was for many centuries observed as the festival of rebirth and renewal. In many villages a maypole was erected, the May queen was crowned and morris men danced through the streets. In England May Day celebrations were suppressed by the Puritans, and although they have been sporadically revived, since the Industrial Revolution the day has been observed as a festival of international labour.

Maya

The original sense of 'maya' in the *Rig-Veda* and the *Upanishads* is the creative power of God. Sometimes it enabled God to transform himself and assume many shapes. From this it was a natural development to think of maya as magical, then as the power to create illusions, and finally as illusion itself. From the human viewpoint it is the power which produces illusion or ignorance. From the divine viewpoint it is the power which creates the world as it appears. In Sikh teaching it means 'delusion' rather than 'illusion'.

Mayin

Term used in Hinduism as a title of God, as the wielder of maya.

Mazda Ahura

See Ahura Mazda

Maze

Also called a 'labyrinth', this had two common forms: a spiral route leading straight to the centre and a meandering route with false turns and dead ends. Its origin and purpose are unknown, but it was probably a cult centre, with the route known only to initiates. The centre would be the place where the king-god 'died' and was 'resurrected', and renewed his vitality. Herodotus described a great maze at Fayyum in Egypt, but the most famous was the labyrinth of the Minotaur in Crete.

May Day celebrations in an English village

Mbari

Decorated houses specially built by the Obo of Nigeria for the earth goddess Ala. They usually contain clay figurines of gods and human beings.

Mecca

Birthplace of Muhammad and the spiritual centre of Islam, situated in Saudi Arabia about 110 km from the Red Sea. Legend links its foundation with Adam, and its development with Abraham. In the centre is the Sacred Mosque, and the Kaaba with the Black Stone, towards which Muslims turn in prayer. Every Muslim endeavours to make the pilgrimage to Mecca at least once in his lifetime. Entrance to the city is strictly forbidden to non-Muslims. The Mecca Surahs form an important division of the Qur'an.

Medes

The Medes came from Media, the ancient name of N.W. Iran. They are mentioned in Assyrian inscriptions of the 9th century BCE as breeders of fine horses. Cyrus of Anshan conquered them in 550 BCE, but they rebelled under Darius I and regained their independence. They are mentioned in Acts 2:9, but after that the name disappears.

Mediator

In the teaching of the OT the priest and prophet fulfilled the office of mediator, or one who brings about reconciliation between man and God, Moses being the outstanding example (Exodus 19:3–8). In the teaching of the NT Jesus Christ is the mediator of a new covenant (Hebrews 9:15), the one mediator between God and man (1 Timothy 2:5).

Medina

City where Muhammad set up his capital after his migration from Mecca in 622 CE. His tomb is there, and it is an important place of pilgrimage. The Medina Surahs form an important part of the Qur'an.

Meditation

Spiritual exercise used in several religions, e.g. Buddhism, Hinduism and Christianity. Many different methods are taught, some concentrating the mind on an external object, some reflecting on a passage of scripture, some allowing the mind to range over a given subject, some trying to empty the mind of all thought.

Medium

Name given by spiritualists to a person who is believed to act as a means of communication between the living and the dead.

Megilloth (H)

Five books in the section of the Hebrew Bible known as Hagiographa which are read at major Jewish festivals. They are Ruth, Song of Solomon, Ecclesiastes, Lamentations and Esther.

Meher Baba

Religious name of Merwan Sheriar, an Indian born in 1894 who claimed in 1913 that he had been given 'God-realization' through Muslim influence. He advanced farther along the path of spiritual knowledge under the guidance of a Hindu master, and was believed by his followers to have attained spiritual perfection. He asserted that he was God and the Avatar for this age, and he gained many disciples, especially among the Parsees.

Mehizah (H)

Screen set up in some Jewish synagogues between the space reserved for men and that reserved for women (which is generally at the back or in a gallery).

Melan

Sacrifice of a sucking-pig offered to a Hindu deity in an Indian village in order to seek his help in solving village problems.

Melancthon, Philip

(1497–1560) Protestant reformer who in 1518 became Professor of Greek at Wittenberg, where he was deeply influenced by Luther. He became the leader of the reform movement during Luther's absence, took part in the Diet of Speyer (1529) and the Colloquy of Marburg (1529), and was largely responsible for drawing up the Augsburg Confession in 1530.

Memra

Aramaic term for 'word'. It is used in the Jewish Targums to avoid any possibility of suggesting that God acted directly or anthropomorphically.

Mencius
(370–288 BCE) Latin form of the name Meng-tse, a Chinese teacher. He was a disciple of Confucius and emphasized the natural goodness of man's nature. His disciples gathered his teachings into the *Book of Mencius.*

Mendicants
Members of Christian monastic orders which were forbidden to own property, individually or in common. Originally these were the Franciscans and Dominicans, but later included the Carmelites and Servites. In Hinduism there are many mendicant and ascetic orders, particularly among the Saivas. In some areas of Buddhism the bhikkus set off each morning to receive gifts of food.

Mennonites
Protestant sect which originated in Germany in the 16th century. It was named after its founder, Menno Simons, first a Catholic, then an Anabaptist and finally an Independent. It is still active in Canada and the United States. Mennonites are pacifists, practise adult baptism, and seek to live strictly according to the precepts of the Bible.

Menog
In the teachings of Zoroaster the unmanifest or invisible aspect of existence.

Menorah (H)
Candelabrum. The word is used in the OT to describe the seven-branched candelabrum that stood in the Temple in Jerusalem until it was taken by the Romans in 70 CE. It is now sometimes used to describe the candelabrum lit during the Feast of Chanukkah. The seven-branched menorah is one of the symbols used by the State of Israel.

Menorah as a symbol of the State of Israel

Mephistopheles
Servant of Lucifer. The demon to whom Faust sold his soul in the play by Christopher Marlowe. He claimed to have the power to conjure up persons such as Helen of Troy, or to change his form in order to play tricks on innocent and unsuspecting victims.

Mercury
Roman numen of trade, identified with Hermes, the messenger of the Greek gods. He is often portrayed with wings on his helmet and on his heels.

Merit
1. *Christian* In Catholic teaching, man can himself do nothing meritorious in the sight of God, but by the grace of God one may gather enough merit to gain salvation by participating in the Sacraments. The saints have more than they need and the Church can draw on this treasury of merit.

2. *Buddhist* Merit can be acquired by charity, abstinence, pilgrimage and many other virtuous activities. The Pali term for merit is 'punna'.

Merlin
Legendary Welsh prophet and wizard who became adviser to King Arthur. According to one legend he built Stonehenge on Salisbury Plain.

Messiah/Messianic
Title meaning 'the anointed one' used in the OT of the king as the vicegerent of God, e.g. Saul and David. It is also applied to the High Priest, but not to the prophets. After the Exile, when there was no king, an eschatological element entered the Messianic expectation: that God would send a son of David to deliver his people. In the preaching of the early Church Jesus Christ is identified with the eschatological Messiah, as the deliverer of his people in his offices as High Priest and King. Jewish Messianic hope is now attached more to Israel as a community than to an individual.

Metaphysics

Term first used by the followers of Aristotle when collecting his teachings. The first section they called *Physics* and the second section *Metaphysics*, lit. 'after physics'. In modern philosophical usage it deals with problems of ultimate reality, the problem of unity, or the problem of the fundamental principle animating the universe.

Metempsychosis

Lit. 'transfer of the soul' (from one body to another). This is the Hindu doctrine of the transmigration of souls, and the Buddhist doctrine of the cycle of rebirth.

Methodism

Protestant Christian denomination which came into being through the preaching of the Anglican priest John Wesley (1703–1791). He was compelled to organize his followers into a separate society, and they were nicknamed Methodists because of their methodical practice of prayer and Bible study. The Methodist Church is organized in districts which are governed by a central, annual conference which appoints all ministers to their churches.

Methuselah

Eighth patriarch in the genealogical list in Genesis 5. He is said to have lived nine hundred and sixty-nine years, longer than anyone else mentioned in the Bible.

Metropolitan

Title of a bishop holding provincial as well as diocesan authority. In England there are two provinces, York and Canterbury. In the Orthodox Church it is a title conferred on the heads of national Churches.

Metta (P)

Term used in Buddhism for love or active good will; in Theravada Buddhism it is the first of four Brahma viharas in which the force of love is radiated to all beings.

Mezuzah (H)

Biblical texts inscribed on parchment in a small metal container fastened to the right-hand doorpost of the house and rooms in Jewish homes.

Mezuzah

Micah

Prophet of Judah whose message is recorded in the Hebrew Bible. He lived in the 8th century BCE, probably at about the same time as Isaiah, and his message is one of condemnation of the princes, but of glory and peace to come for Jerusalem.

Miccha (P)

Term used in Buddhism for that which is false.

Michael

Lit. 'Who is like God?' Archangel who in Daniel is the guardian of the Jews when they are menaced by the Greeks and Persians. In Revelation 12 he wages war in heaven against the evil dragon. He appears in the Qur'an (2:98) as the protector of Islamic armies. The feast of St Michael and All Angels is observed on 29 September, the quarter-day Michaelmas.

Middle Way

Path advocated by the Buddha, between the extremes of materialism and sensual indulgence on the one hand, and rigorous asceticism on the other.

Midrash

Teaching and commentary of Jewish rabbis. Halakhic Midrash deals with the Law, while Aggadic Midrash deals with the narrative of scripture.

Midsummer Eve

The eve of the summer solstice (21 June), when the power of the sun began to wane, was traditionally considered a dangerous time. Witches were said to hold their sabbath and attack Christians, so bonfires were kindled and torches carried in procession for mutual protection. At dawn on Midsummer Day, Druids observe their ceremonies when the rays of the rising sun appear on the north–south axis.

Mihrab

Niche in the qibla wall of a mosque which marks the direction of the Kaaba in Mecca.

150

Mihrab (left) and minbar (right) in a mosque in Jerusalem   Pilgrims stoning the Devil at one of the Devil's Pillars in Mina

Mikveh

Ritual bath used by Jews for cleansing from specified impurities, based on the Tractate Mikwa'oth in the Mishnah. Immersion is obligatory for proselytes as part of the ceremony of conversion. Strict laws govern the supply of water for the Mikveh, but it is stressed that the purpose of immersion is spiritual cleanliness, not physical.

Millenarianism

Doctrine from apocalyptic literature, especially Revelation 20:1–7, according to which there will be a thousand-year reign (millennium) of the saints with Christ before the consummation of history and the establishment of God's eternal kingdom.

Mimamsa

One of the six orthodox schools of Hindu philosophy. It concentrates on the practical implications of the Vedic texts in terms of ritual.

Mina

Important place in the Muslim pilgrimage (Hajj) about 8 km from Mecca. Here each pilgrim throws seven pebbles on to a heap of stones, remembering that Abraham drove off the Devil by throwing stones at him. Immediately afterwards the Id-al-Adha follows, when the pilgrims sacrifice a sheep, remembering that God provided Abraham with a sheep to sacrifice in place of his son Ishmael.

Minaret

Tower near a mosque from which the muezzin calls the faithful to prayer five times a day. In origin it was possibly a fire tower or beacon.

Minbar

Set of steps from which the Friday sermon is preached in mosques. In some mosques these are lofty structures, elaborately decorated.

Minerva

Roman name of an Etruscan goddess of arts and crafts, identified with the Greek goddess Athene.

Minhag (H)

Customs and usages among local communities of Jews which have become formative in matters of law and the growth of customs relating to marriage and other ritual. Differences between Ashkenazi and Sephardi Jews relate to Minhag.

Minhah (H)

Afternoon prayer service, one of the three daily services of the Jewish liturgy.

Minor Orders

Inferior degrees in the ministry of the Roman Catholic Church, below bishops, priests and deacons. They comprise lectors, exorcists, acolytes and porters; their functions are now largely incorporated in the diaconate.

Minor Prophets

In the English OT twelve shorter prophetic books, so called in contrast to the three major books of Isaiah, Jeremiah and Ezekiel. In the Greek version they are termed 'The Twelve'.

Minyan

Hebrew word meaning 'count', indicating the quorum or minimum required to constitute a community of Israel for a Jewish service. Reform Judaism includes women in the minyan, but Orthodox Judaism requires at least ten men.

Miracle

Term used in many religions for a suspension of or a deviation from the known laws of nature. Miraculous circumstances surrounded the birth of the Buddha and of Jesus, and miraculous events are related in stories about Krishna and Muhammad.

Miraj (A)

Term used in Islam meaning 'ladder' or 'ascent'; it is generally used with reference to the ascent of Muhammad to heaven.

Mire

Destination of the wicked after death in some Greek mythological stories; equivalent to hell fire.

Miserere

Common title for Psalm 51, derived from the first word of the Latin version.

Misericord

Projection on the underside of a hinged seat of a church choir stall, often carved in a symbolic form. Used, with the seat tipped up, to support a person standing.

Mishnah

Authoritative collection of Jewish oral law in Hebrew (*c.* 200 CE) which forms the basis of the Talmud.

Mishneh Torah (H)

Vast work by Moses Maimonides (1135–1204) giving a survey of Jewish Law. The title means 'second law', and the book contains definitions of the Law with explanations, statutes and regulations given, introduced or recognized from the time of Moses to the conclusion of the Talmud.

Misri

Crystalline sweets some of which are burnt in a sacred fire and some of which are consumed by the congregation at a special Hindu religious gathering known as a satsang.

Missal

Christian liturgical book that contains the Canon of the Mass, with the antiphons, graduals, Epistles and Gospels for its celebration throughout the year.

Mistletoe

Plant that grows as a parasite on various trees. It was held in veneration by the Druids because it was white and rare, and they cut it only on the sixth day of the moon. According to Scandinavian mythology, a shoot of mistletoe was used to kill the god Balder.

Mithraism

Mystery religion originating in Persia and claiming descent from the teaching of Zoroaster. It became popular in the Roman Empire, being spread by legionaries.

Mithras

Iranian god regarded as the creator and father of all. He was the saviour god of a mystery cult in the West, popular with soldiers in the Roman army. The name means 'contract', and he is part of the Zoroastrian faith.

Mitra

God associated in the Hindu *Vedas* with Varuna. Mitra ruled the day and Varuna ruled the night. He is a sun god, known in Zoroastrianism as Mithras.

Mithras

Mitre

Mitre

Head-dress rising to two points with a cleft between them worn by abbots, bishops and archbishops in the Christian Church. It symbolizes the tongues of fire which rested on the Apostles when they received the power of the Holy Spirit in Jerusalem at Pentecost (Acts 2:3).

Mitzvah (pl. Mitzvoth) (H)

Central concept of Judaism which literally means 'commandment' but can also mean the obligation or duty required by God of the Jews.

Mixcoatl

Lit. 'cloud serpent'. The god of the pole-star in ancient Mexico. Originally he was the god of the hunting tribes, and later became the rain and lightning bearer. Sacrificial victims offered to him by the Aztecs were dressed as stars as they were thought to turn into stars to serve Mixcoatl.

Moab

Mountainous region to the east of the Dead Sea. The inhabitants were said to be descended from Moab, the son of Lot (Genesis 19:37), and there was a constant state of strife between them and the Israelites. Moses died on Mt Nebo in the land of Moab (Deuteronomy 34:5).

Moabite Stone

Stele with an inscription in the Moabite language (a Semitic dialect) recording the successes achieved by Mesha, King of Moab, against Israel in the 9th century BCE. It was discovered in 1868 near the Dead Sea.

Moderator

Title given in the Presbyterian Church to the minister who presides over the Presbytery or the Synod. The Moderator of the General Assembly in Scotland is appointed by election for one year.

Moha (P/Pn)

1. In Sikh teaching a term used for worldly love, one of the five weaknesses that attack the human soul.
2. In Buddhist teaching a term used for mental dullness, infatuation, or stupidity. It is one of the three fires which must die out before nirvana can be attained. (See also Dosa and Raga)

Moharram/Muharram

First month in the Muslim lunar year. Moharram 10 is kept by the Shiite Muslims to commemorate the martydom of Husain, the 7th-century claimant to the caliphate. It is kept by Sunni Muslims as the day of the creation of Adam and Eve.

Mohel (H)

Jewish official authorized by the rabbinate to perform the operation of circumcision, in accordance with the rules of the Torah.

Mohenjo Daro

Site of an ancient city in the Indus valley which was a centre of Indian culture, *c.* 2500–1500 BCE. Excavations have revealed strong fortifications, brick houses and figures which may be cult objects. Seals with inscriptions such as the swastika have been found, but inscriptions have not yet been deciphered.

153

Moirae

The three Fates of Greek mythology, Clotho, Lachesis and Atropos, first named in Hesiod's *Theogony*; 'moira' originally meant a person's 'lot' or rightful position in life.

Moksha

Term used in Hinduism for release or salvation. Liberation from the cycle of rebirth can be attained by knowledge, works or devotion. It also has the meaning of 'integration', viz. the integration of the self with Brahman.

Moloch

God of the Ammonites. His worship was associated with the sacrifice of children by fire, so it was strongly condemned in the Hebrew Bible, e.g. Leviticus 20:2–5.

Monastery

House of a male religious community. Some orders are open, and the monks go out for missions or to help parishes. Others are enclosed, and the monks remain at all times within the enclosure. Women's houses are called convents.

Mondo (J)

Form of rapid question and answer used in Japanese Zen Buddhism to break the limitations of conceptual thought.

Monism

Derived from the Greek word for 'one', the term is applied to philosophical doctrines which teach that only one being exists, or in some versions, that reality consists of one basic substance.

Monk

Member of a male religious community living under the vows of poverty, chastity and obedience.

Monolatry

Restriction of worship to one god while admitting that other gods may exist.

Monophysite

Christian doctrine that in the person of the incarnate Christ there was only one single nature, which was divine. This was contrary to the dogma agreed at the Council of Chalcedon in 451 CE that he had a divine *and* a human nature.

Monotheism

Doctrine that there is only one god. This is the faith of Judaism, Christianity, Islam and the Sikhs.

Monothelite

Heresy which arose in the Christian Church in the 7th century. It stated that there was only one will, divine, in the incarnate Christ. It was condemned at the Council of Constantinople in 680 CE, which declared the existence of two wills, divine and human.

Monstrance

Sacred vessel used in the Roman Catholic Church to expose or exhibit the Eucharistic Host for adoration by the faithful. It usually consists of a glass receptacle surrounded by decorated motifs in gold or silver.

Montanism

Fervent apocalyptist movement in the Christian Church in the 2nd century. The name derives from its founder, Montanus, who expected the immediate fulfilment of the prophecy concerning the pouring out of the Spirit in the last days.

Monte Cassino

Principal monastery of the Benedictine order in Italy, founded by St Benedict in 529 CE. It has been extensively damaged and rebuilt on several occasions, the most recent being in 1944, during the Second World War. It has been faithfully restored, and is once again the mother house of the order.

Moon

This has always been regarded as the most mysterious of the celestial bodies, and has been thought to exercise occult powers over mankind, even to the extent of causing madness, hence the word 'lunatic'. A calendar with lunar months was common in antiquity, and many gods and goddesses have been associated with the moon, e.g. the Babylonian god Sin and goddess Ishtar, the Greek goddess Artemis and the Roman goddess Diana. (See also New Moon)

Moon Sect

See Unified Church

Moral Rearmament

See Oxford Group

Moravian Brethren

Protestant sect formed in 1722 by the amalgamation of the Bohemian Brethren and the Herrnhutter under the leadership of Count Zinzendorff. They distrust doctrinal formulae but accept the Augsburg Confession. They have always been active in missionary work, John Wesley being converted at a Moravian service in London in 1738. The Moravians now have churches in Europe, Britain and America.

Mormon, Book of

According to Mormon teaching an angel revealed to Joseph Smith the hiding-place of gold tablets which he translated under the title *The Book of Mormon*. It consists of fifteen separate books or documents each bearing the name of its author, e.g. Nephi, Jarom and Alma. The thirteenth book is the work of Mormon and the fifteenth that of his son Moroni. The whole work covers the period 600 BCE to 421 CE, when Moroni, the last of the Nephite historians, sealed the sacred record and hid it, until it was brought forth in the Lord's time by Joseph Smith. The Mormons accept this book, together with the Bible, as divine revelations.

Mormons

See Church of Jesus Christ of the Latter Day Saints

Moses

Leader and lawgiver of Israel. He led the Exodus of the Israelites from Egypt and guided them through the wilderness for forty years, up to the borders of the Promised Land. He brought to them the Law, including the Ten Commandments, given by God on Mt Sinai. The date of the Exodus is not easy to determine, but most scholars today seem to favour a date in the 13th century BCE.

Moshav (pl. Moshavim)

Type of co-operative settlement in Israel. It is an intermediary stage between a privately owned farm and a kibbutz, as the land is privately farmed and must be worked by each farmer himself, but the marketing of all the settlement produce is done on a communal basis. Moshavim are generally planned on land owned by the Jewish National Fund.

Mosque

Muslim building for public worship, usually in the form of a square with an open courtyard containing a fountain for ablutions. It has an area for prayers, with a pulpit, and a recess in one wall indicating the direction of Mecca. The name is derived from the Arabic word *masjid* (a place of prostration) because the ritual of prayer involves the prostration of the worshipper.

Modern mosque (Tripoli, Libya)

Mother Earth

See Earth Mother

Mother Goddess

One of the most ancient and widespread beliefs is in the mother goddess, a figure of love and of fear. Figurines of pregnant women with large breasts have been found in very early shrines and they were certainly cult objects. In ancient Sumeria the mother goddess was Inanna, in Babylon Ishtar and in Canaan Astarte. In Egypt she was Isis, in Greece Aphrodite and in Rome Venus, later replaced by Cybele. In India the twofold aspect is seen in Parvati and Kali, consorts of Shiva, and Lakshmi, the wife of Vishnu, who could bring great blessing or destruction.

Mothering Sunday

Fourth Sunday in Lent, when Christians are urged at a family service to join in worship in Mother Church and to give a present to their own mothers.

Mountains

Mountains have been regarded as the dwelling-place of gods or sacred to them. Mt Olympus in Greece and Mt Ida in Crete were sacred in Greek mythology. Moses received the Ten Commandments from God on Mt Sinai, and Mt Sion in Jerusalem was the site chosen for the Temple, while Jesus was transfigured on a mountain, Mt Hermon or Mt Tabor.

Mudda (P)/**Mudra** (S)

Gesture of the fingers and hands used in symbolic rituals in Buddhism and Hinduism. All Buddha images are shown using one of the recognized mudras of the hands. There are said to be twenty-four basic mudras used in ritual dances in Hinduism.

Mudita

Term used in Buddhism for the third of the Brahma viharas; it is the ideal of sharing joy and happiness.

Muezzin

Muslim official who summons the faithful to prayer five times a day from the minaret of a mosque. The title is derived from the Arabic word *mu'adhdhin* (adhan caller).

Mufti

Islamic lawyer who gives judgements (fatwa) based on the Shari'ah, or religious law.

Mughals

Dynasty which seized power in India in 1526 and remained in control until 1858. The founder was a Turkish Muslim, Babur, ruler of a kingdom in N.W. India. The third and greatest Emperor was Akbar (1542–1605), who renounced his Muslim faith and founded a new religion, The Divine Truth, at the same time extending tolerance to all sects. His successors restored Muslim domination.

Muhajirun

'Emigrants' or co-believers with Muhammad who accompanied him on the Hijrah.

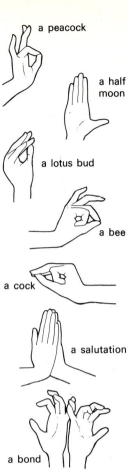

a peacock

a half moon

a lotus bud

a bee

a cock

a salutation

a bond

Seven basic muddras

Muhammad

Prophet of Allah. Born in 570 CE, he married Khadija, his widowed employer. At the age of forty he experienced visions, inspirations and revelations which form the body of the Qur'an. In 622 he emigrated to Medina and organized a body of followers which developed into the Muslim community and spread very rapidly. Islam is now the major religion of many areas of the Middle East and several African countries, with Mecca as its focal point.

Muhammad Iqbal

(1873–1938) Outstanding Muslim poet and philosopher whose book *The Reconstruction of Religious Thought in Islam* was very influential. He was president of the Muslim League, dedicated to Muslim independence in India.

Muharram

See Moharram

Muhtasib

Islamic term for a superintendent or inspector of ethical behaviour in the Muslim community.

Mu'jizah

Descriptive term used by Muslims to convey the sense of the miracle of the Qur'an in the eyes of Islam.

Mujtahid

Islamic scholar learned in the law and considered capable of making an ijtihad, a logical conclusion or decision on difficult legal problems.

Mukhlisun

Term used in Islam to denote sincere persons who reject the great sin of *shirk* and worship God alone, without any ulterior motive or purpose.

156

Muktad

Last ten days of the Parsee year, when the fravashis of the departed are remembered.

Mukti

In Indian religious thought a term for salvation or release from the cycle of rebirth. It is a synonym of 'moksha'.

Mula

Term used in Buddhism for 'origin' or 'foundation'.

Mullah

Muslim teacher who is learned in canon and civil law. A fanatical or 'mad' mullah tried to start a jihad in India in 1901, but was forcibly restrained by the government.

Mulungu

Name used for the Creator, or the supreme god in many tribes in East and Central Africa. He is associated with storms and thunder. He sees everything and is able to send good or evil.

Mummy

Term derived from the Arabic word for 'wax'. It describes the prepared body of a dead person preserved by embalming and wrapped in linen to hold the limbs together. Vital organs were removed and the corpse was treated with salts, tightly wrapped and placed in a coffin. The wealthy classes in ancient Egypt practised this method of dealing with the dead because the physical body was considered an essential constituent of human personality which must be preserved to ensure an afterlife.

Munafiqun

Term used in the Qur'an (surah 63) for hypocrites or those who pretend that they are true Muslims.

Mundan

Hindu ceremony, important in Indian village religious life, of the first cutting of a child's hair.

Munkar (A)

Term for that which is ethically reprehensible, or something which is vetoed or reproached. It is also the name of one of the angels, recognized in Islam, who examine the dead and punish them if necessary.

Muratorian Canon

Oldest known list of books accepted as a canon of the NT. It was discovered in an 8th century manuscript, but it is thought to date back to the 2nd century.

Murid

First stage in Sufi discipleship: the stage of the would-be seeker.

Muru'ah

Arabic characteristic of manliness, much admired in Islam.

Muses

Nine goddesses, daughters of Zeus and Mnemosyne, who were the patrons of music, poetry and drama.

Mushroom

Important plant in primitive religion. *Amanita muscaria* (fly agaric), with a red cap, was the sacred mushroom, and its juice was thought to be soma, the drink of the gods mentioned in the Vedic hymns, and possibly also ambrosia, the drink of the Greek gods.

Musical Gospel Outreach

Organization which grew out of the Jesus Revolution. Founded in 1966, it publishes a magazine, songs and records, and organizes evangelical concerts. It is not attached to a Church but sees itself as a Christian mission.

Muslim

Title applied to one who belongs to the community of Islam; it means 'one who has submitted himself to God'.

Muslim League

Organization founded in Dacca in 1906 to promote Indian Muslim aspirations. During the presidency of Muhammad Iqbal in 1930 it set as its objective a separate Muslim state in N.W. India, which came into being in 1947 as West Pakistan (now Pakistan).

Mutawwi (A)

Lit. 'obediencer'. Title given in Islam to an official whose duty it is to safeguard religious conformity within a community.

Mu'tazilah (A)

School of Islamic theologians, strong in the 9th century, who pressed speculation about the Qur'an and about free will far beyond the position which later became orthodox. They denied that God predestines any man to evil, affirmed free will, and asserted that the Qur'an was created by God through human agency. Their influence is still felt in Shiah Islam.

Myrrh

Resinous gum used in perfume and medicine, and used in the ancient Middle East in the embalming and burial of corpses. According to Matthew 2:11 it was one of the gifts brought by the Magi to the infant Jesus.

Myrtle

One of the four plants carried in procession in the synagogue service at the Jewish Feast of Tabernacles. Symbolically it is connected with death and resurrection. Greek emigrants in ancient times carried a myrtle bough when founding a new colony, as a symbol of ending one life and beginning another.

Mysteries

Forms of religion, very popular in the ancient world, in which doctrines are closed secrets, closely guarded and only revealed to those who have been carefully instructed and tested and are about to be initiated, or in some cases to those who have just been initiated.

Mystery Plays

Religious dramas of the Middle Ages which originally developed out of sections of the Christian liturgy. At a later stage, Gospel stories and lives of the saints were also performed, usually out of doors on temporary stages. They began to die out in the 16th century, but the Oberammergau Passion Play, performed because of a village vow, is still performed every ten years.

Mysticism

Belief in the attainment, through contemplation or self-surrender, of truths inaccessible to the understanding or the intellect; or belief in the possibility of spiritual unity with the deity.

Myth

Traditional story embodying ancient religious ideas or supernatural concepts, sometimes told through personal or national histories, sometimes through symbolism.

Nabi (A/H)

Word found in Semitic languages meaning 'prophet'. The root meaning may be 'one who is called', or 'one from whom words bubble forth'. The Hebrew Bible has sixteen books written in the name of a prophet or nabi, and the title is used of many others whose words are not recorded. The Qur'an names twenty-eight prophets, nearly all from the Bible, but the last, considered by Islam to be the greatest, was Muhammad.

Nadar (S)

In Sanskrit the original meaning of this word was 'sight' or 'vision', but in Sikh usage it acquired the meaning 'favoured glance' or 'favoured look', and hence 'God's gracious glance', and at a later period 'grace'.

Naga

Mythical serpents which can change themselves into men for the protection of Buddhas and of Buddhists generally.

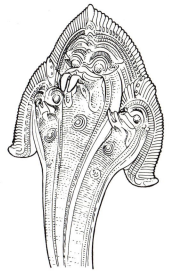

Naga (Cambodia, 12th century)

Nagarjuna

Buddhist teacher from south central India who founded the Madhyamika school of philosophy in the 2nd century.

Nahum

Prophet of Israel whose message is in the Hebrew Bible. It is a taunting song celebrating the overthrow of Nineveh, the capital city of Israel's oppressors, the Assyrians. Nothing is known of Nahum personally, but Nineveh fell in 612 BCE.

Najar/Nazar

Term used in Hindu teaching for the evil eye.

Nam (S)

Sanskrit word meaning 'name' used in the Sikh religion as a synonym for God himself.

Nam Japan

Term used in the Sikh religion for meditating upon the Name, or *repeating* the Name, as a way of achieving knowledge of God.

Nam Simaran

Term used in the Sikh religion for meditating upon the Name, or *remembering* the Name, as a way of achieving knowledge of God.

Guru Nanak

Nandi (Mysore)

Nama
1. Iranian word used in Mithraism as a term for 'homage'.
2. Sanskrit word, lit. 'name'. Term used in Buddhism as a collective term for the four khandas other than rupa.

Namakarana
Hindu name-giving ceremony, often held on the day of the sixth-month ceremony.

Nanak, Guru
(1469–1539)   First Sikh Guru and the founder of the community. He learned from Hindu and Muslim teachers and travelled all over India, as far as the Himalayas, and also to Mecca. He was influenced by the Bhakti movement and by the Sufi tradition. He was devoted to the One God, and accepted the doctrines of reincarnation and the equality of all men. His teachings are in the Sikh scriptures, the *Guru Granth Sahib.*

Nandi
Bull dedicated to the Hindu god Shiva. He is Shiva's personal attendant and his image is always placed in front of temples of Shiva.

Naojot
Initiation ceremony for Zoroastrian boys and girls between the ages of eight and thirteen. The word means 'new worshipper' or 'initiate', and at this service the initiate puts on the sudre and the kusti, symbols of full membership of the Zoroastrian community.

Naphtali
Sixth son of the Israelite patriarch Jacob, by Bilhah, the maid-servant of Rachel. Also the tribe which occupied territory in the north of Canaan.

Naql (A)
Term used in Islam for the delivery of truth via revelation, as in the Qur'an. This is distinguished from 'aql, which is the delivery of truth via reason.

Nara Simha
In Hindu mythology the man-lion. He was an avatar of Vishnu who destroyed the demon Hiranya-Karhipa, who was tormenting the world.

Naraka
In Hindu mythology, hell or purgatory or the place of the wicked. The number of zones varies: in the Brahmanda there are seven, but the Code of Manu mentions twenty-one and the *Vishnu Purana* mentions twenty-eight.

Nastika
Unorthodox schools of Hindu philosophy which do not accept the Vedic revelation.

Nat
Nature spirits of Sri Lanka, still worshipped at village shrines. They are believed to inhabit trees and mountains.

160

Nataraja (S)

Title of the Hindu god Shiva meaning 'Lord of the Dance'. He is represented performing the Tandava, a world-shattering dance in a ring of fire which symbolizes the life process of the universe.

Nathan

Prophet who denounced King David for sending one of his captains, Uriah the Hittite, to his death and then taking Uriah's widow, Bathsheba, as his wife (2 Samuel 12). At first he approved David's plan to build a temple, but then he blocked it, instructing David that the work must be done by David's son, Solomon.

Nau Rat

Nine days of fasting undertaken by a Hindu ojha (village priest) five times during his period of training.

Nave

Area of a Christian church from the west wall to the chancel; this is the area assigned to the laity, and is sometimes separated from the chancel by a screen. The term may be derived either from the Latin *navis* (ship) or from the Greek *naos* (temple).

Naw Ruz

In the Baha'i faith the name of the first of the nine holy days in the spring: this one (21 March) marks the New Year.

Nayanars

Sixty-three teachers or worshippers of Shiva in S. India who composed many hymns between the 7th and 10th centuries.

Nazar

See Najar

Nazareth

Village in Galilee where Jesus spent his boyhood and early manhood. He moved to Capernaum to begin his ministry because his fellow-villagers had little faith in him as a teacher.

Nazirites

Early Israelites who were under a vow of consecration. Their origin is obscure, but they were obliged to abstain from wine and all intoxicating drink and to leave their hair uncut during the period of the vow. The name may be derived from a Hebrew verb meaning 'to separate'.

Nebo

Ancient Babylonian deity, the son of Marduk. He was the creator god, the god of wisdom and the god of writing.

Nazareth: Church of the Annunciation

Nebuchadrezzar

One of the greatest kings of Babylon, ruling from 605 to 562 BCE. In 605 BCE he defeated the Egyptians and received tribute from Judah. In 597 BCE he overran Canaan and took King Jehoiakim and his court as captives. In 586 BCE he destroyed Jerusalem and took most of its inhabitants into exile. A devotee of Marduk, he rebuilt Babylon.

Necromancy

Prediction of the future by communication with the dead.

Nectar

In Greek mythology the drink of the gods which contributed to their eternal existence.

Nehemiah

Cupbearer to King Artaxerxes I of Persia who was given leave to visit Jerusalem about 444 BCE, where he rebuilt the city walls and instituted reforms among the Jewish community. The book in the Hebrew Bible bearing his name contains details of this work, with names of families living in Jerusalem, and also sections dealing with the work of Ezra the Scribe.

Nemesis

Greek goddess who measured out happiness and misery to mortals, bringing suffering to those who had received too much good fortune. Later she was regarded as the punisher of crime.

Neophyte

Greek word used in 1 Timothy 3:6 to describe one who had been newly converted to the Christian faith or newly baptized.

Neo-Platonism

Philosophic system which arose in Alexandria towards the end of the 2nd century. Closely associated with the name of Plotinus, it was idealistic and eclectic, trying to unite the teaching of Plato with Christianity and oriental mysticism. It aimed at a knowledge of the One, which emanated from the nous or pure intelligence.

Nephesh (H)

Word which occurs over seven hundred times in the Hebrew Bible. The usual translation is 'soul', but it also indicates emotions or physical appetites.

Nephthys

Ancient Egyptian goddess, the daughter of Geb and Nut, and sister of Isis and Osiris. One of her duties was to escort the souls of the dead before Osiris for judgement.

Neptune

Roman water god, identified with the Greek god Poseidon.

Ner Tamid (H)

Lit. 'eternal lamp'. Light which burns perpetually in front of the Ark in Jewish synagogues, usually in a lamp suspended from the ceiling.

Nergal

Babylonian god of the plague and of the underworld who was the ruler of the country of the dead.

Nero

Roman Emperor (54–68 CE) who behaved with great cruelty towards the Christian community in Rome. Following the fire which destroyed much of Rome in 64, he caused many Christians to be executed, probably including Peter and Paul.

Nestorianism

Heresy in the Christian Church of the 5th century. It takes its name from Nestorius, who taught that there were two separate persons in the incarnate Christ, one human and the other divine. This doctrine was condemned at the Council of Ephesus in 431 CE. Nestorius was deposed from his office as Bishop of Constantinople, and later banished.

New Moon

In addition to general feelings of mystery associated with the moon there are superstitions particularly connected with the *new* moon. If the new moon is seen on the right or straight ahead it is considered a good omen; if it is on the left or behind, or if it is seen through a window it is unlucky. It was thought wise to mate farm animals after the new moon while it was waxing, as their young would be strong; similarly, animals for meat should be slaughtered or sheep sheared after the new moon to ensure the best quality.

New Testament

Canonical scripture belonging exclusively to the Christian Church. It contains the four Gospels, the Acts of the Apostles, Pauline and other epistles and the Revelation of St John the Divine.

New Year Festivals

Throughout the world and throughout human history the New Year has been celebrated with rituals, religious or social. In the ancient Middle East it was a spring festival often associated with a sacred marriage or an enthronement festival, to ensure a good harvest or national prosperity. In the Christian West the New Year was fixed in January with the introduction of the Gregorian Calendar in 1752. It is a time of merry-making and bell-ringing. The Jewish New Year is a movable date and ushers in days of penitence leading to the Day of Atonement. In Islam the first month is Moharram, and the tenth day is a fast, the Passion of Husain. The Chinese New Year is celebrated with colourful processions and fire-crackers. In Scotland New Year, or Hogmanay, is a time of family parties and presents, and sometimes coincides with midwinter fire festivals such as Up-Helly Aa in the Shetlands.

Chinese New Year celebrations

New Year for Trees

Festival in Israel (Tu B'Shvat) when schoolchildren plant young trees to help the reafforestation of the country.

Ngewo

Supreme deity of the Mende tribe of Sierre Leone. He has no temples of his own, but prayers are directed to him through other, minor gods.

Nhialic

Supreme God among the Dinka tribe of Africa.

Nibbana (P)

See Nirvana

Nibbuta (P)

Term used in Buddhism to describe the ideal man, i.e. the man who has become cool, when the fires of greed, hatred and illusion have been extinguished.

Nicaea, Council of

The Emperor Constantine called the first Ecumenical Council of the Church at Nicaea in 325 CE. It was attended by three hundred and eighteen bishops, whose main task was to deal with the Arian controversy. The orthodox doctrine of the Church was strongly defended, and the Council promulgated a creed containing the term 'Homoousios' (of one substance), referring to Jesus Christ and the Father.

Nichiren

(1222–1282) Japanese Buddhist monk who declared that only the Lotus Sutra should be worshipped, and attacked the Pure Land sect, Zen and Vinaya. Because of his militancy, he was expelled from his monastery, after which he founded the Nichiren sect, a reformed type of Tendai Buddhism.

Nicholas, St

Little is known of his life history, but he has become one of the most popular saints in the calendar. He is the patron saint of Russia, of sailors and of children, and in some countries his feast-day, 6 December, is the occasion of giving presents to children. The name Santa Claus is a corruption of the name St Nicholas.

Nidana (P/S)

The twelve nidanas are spokes on the Wheel of Becoming in Buddhist thought. The term is used to explain the process by which one comes into existence, beginning with ignorance and ending with birth.

Nifaq (A)

Term used in Islam for hypocrisy, or pretended belief in the Qur'an which is devoid of any sincere faith.

Night of Awakening

The night, of special significance to Buddhists, when the Bodhisattva, born as Siddhartha Gautama, became the Buddha by his supreme and final act of winning complete and full enlightenment or awakening for himself.

Night of Power

Muslim festival, Lailat al-Qadr, commemorating the occasion when Muhammad received his first revelation. It is celebrated during the last ten days of Ramadan with readings from the Qur'an and prayers.

Nihilism

Philosophical term first used by the Russian novelist Turgenev in 1862 to indicate a doctrine that nothing exists and no knowledge is possible. The first nihilists hoped to abolish the existing social structure in order to give men freedom to rebuild a just society.

Nihon Shoki

Early text of the Shinto religion, the *Written Chronicles of Japan*, next in importance to the *Kojiki*. It contains myths of creation and stories of legendary persons.

Nikaya

Term used in Buddhism for a collection of religious discourses and texts.

Nile

Longest river of Africa, flowing over 6400 km. Its main stream, the White Nile, has its source in Lake Victoria and is joined by the Blue Nile at Khartoum. In Egypt the Nile divides into the Delta and enters the Mediterranean. The annual inundation, now controlled by the Aswan Dam, gives fertility to the Nile Valley, and because of this the river was worshipped by ancient Egyptians as a god on whom the life of the land depended.

Nimmana (P)/**Nirmana** (S)

Term used in Buddhism for metamorphosis. The Nirmana Kaya is the transformation body in which the Buddha was manifest for the benefit of humanity.

Nine

This figure is regarded by numerologists as the number of completion, because it is the last of the single figures and the number of months from conception to birth. In the Sermon on the Mount Jesus described nine categories of people as blessed, and on the Cross he died at the ninth hour.

Ninth Ab

Jewish fast-day in the late summer remembering the destruction of the first and second Temples. Selections from Job are chanted.

Nirgunam Brahman

Term used in the Hindu religion for Brahman without attributes or qualities (gunas).

Nirmana (S)

See Nimmana

Nirmana Kaya

One of the three bodies of the Buddha. This is the manifested, historical Buddha, or the earthly, incarnate body assumed by the Buddha for the benefit of humanity, in his role as a teacher.

Nirodha

Buddhist term for the extinction or cessation of desire. It is a synonym for nibbana. It is the third of the Four Noble Truths.

Nirvana (S)/**Nibbana** (P)

Derived from a verbal root meaning 'to blow out', this term indicates the blowing-out or extinction of sin or the illusion of self, or, for a Hindu, the extinction of the self which is liberation or moksha. It is the Buddhist *summum bonum*, the indescribable state of bliss achieved by the enlightened, the goal of the religious life.

Nisan

First month of the Jewish year, formerly known as Abib. It is a spring month and the feast of the Passover is kept on 14 Nisan.

Nitya (S)

Lit. 'innate' or 'eternal'. Term used in Hindu philosophy for reality, eternal truth or that which is eternal.

The dove brings an olive-branch to Noah at the end of the Flood

Niyama

Term used in yoga for the observance of self-disciplinary rules, e.g. calm, study, prayer.

Niyyah (A)

Lit. 'intention'. Term used by Muslims to describe the conscious focus of purpose that must precede all ritual acts in Islam. It applies especially to prayer and the Hajj.

No

Form of dramatic presentation that is particularly associated with Japanese Zen Buddhism.

Noah

Central figure in the biblical account of the Flood (Genesis 6–8). Warned by God, he built an ark in which he and his family alone of all mankind were saved from the waters which covered the earth. (For parallel stories see Flood)

Noble Eightfold Path

See Eightfold Path

Nominalism

Term used in medieval scholastic philosophy meaning that only individual objects have real existence, while universals are nothing but names. This was taught in the 12th century by Abelard, and in a more extreme form in the 14th century by William of Occam, who maintained that universals are not found at all in reality.

Nonconformity

Term applied to those who do not conform to the doctrines and discipline of the Church of England. The earliest were the Separatists in the reign of Elizabeth I, to whom the general name Puritans was given. The attitude of James I widened the breach, and after the Restoration, the Clarendon Code endeavoured to enforce conformity. The term is now generally applied to the Free Churches.

Non-duality

English term for the Hindu doctrine of advaita, which expresses the fundamental identity of the supreme divinity, or Brahman, with the human soul, Atman. This is set out in the *Chandogya Upanishad* (6:13), and was systematized by Shankara (788–820 CE).

None

Last of the canonical hours of prayer set out in the Breviary. It is appointed to be recited at the ninth hour, i.e. 3 p.m.

Non-juror

Clergy and laity of the Church of England who in 1688 refused to take the Oath of Allegiance to William and Mary, on the grounds that by so doing they would break their oath to James II.

Non-violence

See Ahimsa

Norito (J)

Enunciation of sacred words, or liturgical addresses, offered as tokens of respect or worship to Japanese Shinto gods.

Norns

In Scandinavian mythology, the Three Fates who represented the past, present and future, and whose decrees were irrevocable.

Novatian

Roman presbyter who took a rigorist attitude to the readmission to the Church of lapsed Christians. Disapproving of the attitude of Pope Cornelius, he caused a schism by being consecrated as a rival Pope in 251 CE. He suffered martyrdom in 257, but the Novatian schism continued into the 5th century.

Novena

Period of nine days observed in the Western Church as a time of public or private devotion for some specific purpose. The practice dates from the 17th century.

Novice

Probationer in a monastic community. In Christian monasteries the novitiate usually lasts one year, during which time the novice is under the authority of the Superior but may leave the community without stigma.

Nueer

Concept of sin among the Nuer tribe of Africa.

Nuer

Nilotic-speaking group of tribes living along the Nile and its tributaries in southern Sudan.

Numbers, Book of

Fourth book in the Bible, containing an account of the wanderings of the Israelites in the wilderness after the Exodus from Egypt; it is part of the Torah.

Numen

Spiritual power inherent in a particular object, or presiding over a limited operation. The Latin word is neuter and means 'nodding'. These powers, recognized by the ancient Romans, were scarcely personified (though some developed into gods), but they were propitiated by offerings of various kinds.

Numerology

Analysis of a person's character through the numerical value of his name. It is based on two theories: (1) that numbers are a clue to the underlying structure of the universe and (2) that a man's name contains the essence of his being. Each letter is given its numerical value, and analyses are based on the total for all the letters and the totals for groups such as vowels, consonants, forenames and surnames.

Numinous

Term introduced by Rudolph Otto in *The Idea of the Holy* to denote man's feelings when faced with the holy, or the 'wholly other'. He described this as a 'mysterium tremendum et fascinans' (a mystery or sense of awe that both terrifies and attracts).

Nun

Member of a religious order of women living under vows of poverty, chastity and obedience.

Nunc Dimittis

Prayer of thanksgiving uttered by Simeon after he had held the baby Jesus at his presentation in the Temple (Luke 2:9–35). The title comes from the first two words in the Latin version. It is said in the Anglican service of Evensong.

Nuncio

Diplomatic representative of the Holy See accredited to a civil government. The ecclesiastical counterpart is an apostolic delegate.

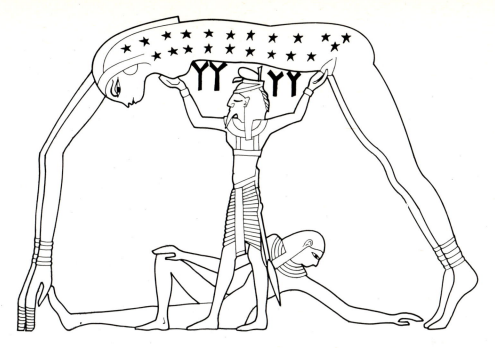

Nut (the sky-goddess) is raised by Shu (the air god) from the embrace of Geb (the earth god)

Nupe

People of central Nigeria who worship a god Soko identified with the sky.

Nut

Egyptian goddess of the early dynasties. She was the personification of the sky, the Lady of Heaven, and her husband was the earth god, Geb.

Nuzi Tablets

During excavations at Nuzi in Iraq from 1925 to 1931, archaeologists uncovered over twenty thousand clay tablets from the 15th and 14th centuries BCE. They are written in a Babylonian dialect and cover the lives of four or five generations. They relate to history, religion and commerce, and throw a great deal of light on some of the practices, such as birthright and inheritance, mentioned in Genesis.

Nyaya

One of six orthodox schools of Hindu philosophy. It emphasizes the analysis of logical arguments.

Nymph

In the mythologies of ancient Greece and Rome, a semi-divine maiden inhabiting seas, rivers, mountains or woods.

Nzambi

High god worshipped by the Bacongo and Ndembu tribes of Zambia and the Lele tribe of Kasai. He is the creator of all men and all things, and ordains men's lives, protects the right and punishes the wrong.

Oak
The oak, being durable and very long living, was the tree most widely regarded as sacred in Europe and Scandinavia. Solemn agreements were made beneath the oak, and oak-leaves were regarded as a protection against witchcraft. Biblical references show that the oak was also venerated in the ancient Middle East, e.g. Jacob buried foreign gods under the oak of Shechem to neutralize their power (Genesis 35). In Greece the oracle of Zeus at Dodona was under an oak-tree.

Oath
Solemn assertion or promise with an invocation of God to be a witness to its solemnity and binding nature. Some groups of Christians, such as the Anabaptists, have interpreted Matthew 5:34, 'Swear not at all', as meaning that the taking of oaths is contrary to the teaching of Christ.

Obadiah
Name of several characters in the Hebrew Bible, and also the title of the shortest prophetic book. Nothing is known of the author as it contains only twenty verses. It is a warning of the coming judgement of Edom.

Obaku
Smallest of the three sects into which Japanese Zen Buddhism is divided.

Obatala
See Orisha-Nla.

Oberammergau
Village in Upper Bavaria where a passion-play based on the last days in the life of Jesus Christ is performed every ten years. This is in fulfilment of a vow made in 1633 as an expression of gratitude at the end of a plague.

Obi
Snake god of the tribes of West Africa whose worship was introduced into the West Indies by negro slaves. There it became associated with witchcraft or magic, known as Obeah, practised by medicine-men and witches.

Oblate
Originally used to indicate a child dedicated by his parents to a monastic life. Later it was used of a layman who lived in or near a monastery without taking full vows. It is now used of persons who are associated with a religious order and follow a religious rule of life but continue to live outside the monastery and to follow their normal occupations.

Obon
Japanese Buddhist festival in July when lanterns are lit to guide the spirits of departed ancestors on their annual visit to the family home.

Occult
Derived from the Latin *occulere* (to hide). It signifies secret, esoteric knowledge beyond the range of ordinary experience, revealed by supernatural or magical means, exclusively for the initiated.

168

Octave

In Christian liturgical usage, the eighth day after a festival or the period of eight days during which major festivals were observed. Over the centuries the number of festivals with octaves became so great that the Roman Catholic Congregation of Rites in 1855 suppressed all octaves except those of Christmas, Easter and Pentecost.

Odin

Chief god of the ancient Teutonic and Scandinavian people. He was the god of war and received those slain in battle into Valhalla. He was also known as Woden or Wotan, and gave his name to Wednesday.

Odomankomo

Name of the creator god in the religion of the Ashanti people. In addition to creating the world, men and animals, he also created Life and Death, and eventually Death became strong enough to kill the Creator.

Odysseus

King of Ithaca who was one of the Greek heroes in the Trojan War. He devised the plan of making the Wooden Horse and was inside it when it was dragged into Troy. After the victory of the Greeks he began his journey home. It took him twenty years because of adventures on the way with the Cyclops, with Circe and with the nymph Calypso. The journey is described by Homer in the *Odyssey*.

Oedipus

Son of Laius, King of Thebes, and Jocasta. He is the central figure in a trilogy of tragedies by Sophocles, and is a prototype of a man of honour doomed by fate. Because at his birth an oracle said that he would kill his father and gain the kingdom, he was abandoned on a mountain, but was rescued by a shepherd. On reaching manhood he solved the riddle of the Sphinx, fought against Thebes, killed the King, his father, and married Jocasta, his mother, not knowing his relationship to them. He had four chidren by Jocasta, but Thebes was struck by a plague, and the oracle said it was because of incest. On learning the truth, Jocasta hanged herself and Oedipus blinded himself. Freud uses this story to explain certain psychological urges, and also to expound his own theory of the origin of religion.

Offertory

The part of the liturgy of the Christian Eucharist when the worshippers offer bread and wine to the celebrant for consecration.

Office, Divine

In the Western Church the obligatory prayers or services recited by priests and religious orders. In the Church of England parish priests recite Matins and Evensong. Religious orders recite Matins and the seven Hours, viz. Lauds, Prime, Terce, Sext, None, Vespers and Compline.

Ogun

Yoruba god of iron, and the patron of blacksmiths; he is also the god of craftsmen, soldiers and hunters.

Ohrmazd

In Zoroastrian writings of the Pahlavi (Middle Persian) theologians he is the Wise Lord, the supreme creator. In the *Gathas* he is named Ahura Mazda.

Oil

The use of oil for anointing is found throughout the Bible. Jacob anointed the stone at Bethel (Genesis 28:18), and Samuel anointed Saul and David as king (1 Samuel 10:1, 16:13). Jesus was anointed at Bethany (Matthew 26:7), and James recommends its pastoral use by elders (James 5:14). In the Catholic Church it is used in the sacraments of baptism, confirmation and holy orders. In the Church of England anointing takes place in the coronation of the sovereign, and often in prayers for the sick. In Hinduism devotees of Shiva anoint the lingam symbol with oil.

Ojha

Hindu priest in an Indian village who specializes in shamanistic and exorcistic activities.

Old Catholics

Groups of national Churches which have separated from Rome. The Church of Utrecht separated in 1724. The German, Austrian and Swiss groups separated in 1870, rejecting the infallibility of the

Pope. Their services are in the vernacular, their clergy are permitted to marry, and they are in communion with the Church of England.

Old Testament
Title used in the Christian Church for the canonical books which are shared with the Synagogue, where they are called the Hebrew Bible. The Hebrew text is divided into three sections, the Law, the Prophets and the Writings, but the order is different in the English version. The title 'Old Testament' is used to distinguish these books from the twenty-seven books of the NT.

Olive
In the biblical story of the Flood, the dove brought back a twig of olive to Noah in the Ark (Genesis 8:12), and Noah accepted this as a sign that life was returning to the earth and that God would bless him. Mark (14:26–42) records that before his crucifixion Jesus spent time in prayer on the Mount of Olives, and the olive-branch has become a Christian symbol of peace and reconciliation.

Olodumare
Supreme god of the Yoruba, also called Olorun (the owner of heaven). He is the Creator, all-wise, immortal, holy, but he has no temples and no images of him are permitted.

Olorun
See Olodumare

Olympiad
In classical Greece a period of four years starting with a year in which the Olympic games were held and including the three years until the next Olympic games.

Olympus, Mt
Mountain on the borders of Thessaly and Macedonia, over 3000 m high. It was regarded as the home of Zeus and other gods and goddesses.

Om
The most sacred word in the Hindu faith, used first in the *Upanishads*. It consists of the three sounds A, U, M and is said to represent the three oldest *Vedas* or the triad of gods Vishnu, Shiva and Brahma. At the beginning of a phrase it is like 'Hail', and at the end like 'Amen'.

Om

Om Mane Padme Hum
Mantra used in Tibetan Buddhism usually translated 'Om, the jewel in the lotus'. The jewel is the Dhamma or Buddhist doctrine, and the lotus is the Tripitaka or Buddhist scripture. Alternatively, it may be an invocation of a female Bodhisattva, Manipadma.

Omar
(582–644 CE)   Second Caliph of Islam after the death of Muhammad. He was given the title 'Commander of the Faithful', and he extended the dominion of Islam to Egypt, Syria and Palestine. (See also Umar)

Omen
Phenomenon or unusual event believed to foreshadow good or evil fortune, e.g. a black cat crossing one's path or the sight of a rainbow is thought to be a good omen, whereas an eclipse of the sun or moon or the appearance of a comet is thought to presage bad luck.

Ometecuhtli
Lord of duality, above all other gods, both male and female, in Aztec mythology. He is the maker and sustainer of all, including fire and the pole-star.

Omophagia
Ritual in the Dionysian mysteries in which Orpheus was torn to pieces by the Maenads (or Bacchantae) in their frenzy.

Omphalos
Greek word for 'navel', applied to a heap of stones shaped like a navel and used for cultic purposes to represent the centre of the world. An example has been found at the oracle centre at Delphi. Similar sacred places regarded as the centre of the world are in Jerusalem, Mecca and Benares.

Omri
King of Israel who founded the capital city of Samaria *c.* 880 BCE. He was so famous that long after

his death Israel was known as the Land of Omri. The Bible devotes few verses to him because the writers decided 'he did evil in the sight of the Lord', a reference to his opposition to the Kingdom of Judah.

One

Figure deeply reverenced by numerologists. In Judaism, Sikhism and Islam God is One. In Christianity he is Three in One. In Hinduism, beyond the multiplicity of gods is the Ultimate, the One.

Onkelos

Author of the Jewish Targum on the Pentateuch, dating from the 2nd century. The name is the Aramaic equivalent of 'Aquila'.

Ontological Argument

A priori argument for the existence of God, first elaborated by Anselm, Archbishop of Canterbury in 1100, on the grounds that the existence of the *idea* of God necessarily involves the objective existence of God.

Onyame

Supreme being in the religion of the Ashanti people. When Death killed the Creator, Onyame took over the control of the universe. He is the giver of sunshine and rain, the source of morality, and he controls man's fate.

Opele

Chain of sixteen nuts used by an Ifa priest in the course of an oracular inquiry among the Yoruba.

Oracle

Shrine for the consultation of spiritual powers or deities, for advice or prophecy; the medium or the response given. Examples are the Delphic oracle in ancient Greece, or the Ifa oracle among the Yoruba.

Oratory

Term used in the Christian Church for a place of prayer. It may be a church, or a chapel within a church for public prayer, or a room for private devotion. In origin it may go back to small buildings erected over the tombs of martyrs.

Ordeal

Form of trial in which guilt or innocence is determined by the results of a physical test of endurance. Boiling water, hot metal and fire have been common methods. Such tests are mentioned in the Code of Hammurabi and the Hebrew Bible and were used in early Christian Europe until banned at the fourth Lateran Council in 1215. They have survived in some African tribes.

Bowl used to hold the opele (nuts) employed in Ifa divination

Order

1. In the Christian Church, a community of monks, friars or nuns, such as the Benedictines, Dominicans or Carmelites.
2. In the priesthood of the Orthodox, Anglican and Roman Catholic Churches, the three divisions of bishop, priest and deacon.
3. In architecture, originally of Greek temples, the five styles of classical columns with their capitals and bases, viz. Tuscan, Doric, Ionic, Corinthian and Composite.

Ordinal

Term used in the Anglican *Book of Common Prayer* for 'the form and manner of making, ordaining and consecrating of bishops, priests and deacons'. There have been four versions of this: 1549, 1552, 1559 and 1662.

Ordination

Ritual by which a layman is admitted into the ministry of the Christian Church. The Orthodox, Anglican and Roman Catholic Churches recognize three orders – bishop, priest and deacon – and ordination is conferred by laying on of hands by a bishop. Nonconformists usually have only one order of ministers, and ordination is carried out by senior ministers. Recognition of leadership in other religious faiths varies according to the type of leadership involved, e.g. there are services for the recognition of Jewish rabbis, Muslim imams and Buddhist priests, but these have different duties from Christian clergy.

Origen

(185–254 CE)   Christian theologian of Alexandria, where he was head of the Catechetical School for twenty-eight years before establishing a similar school in Caesarea. He was a learned biblical scholar and produced the Hexapla, an edition of the OT in six versions. He debated with pagans, e.g. in *Contra Celsum*, and wrote a theological treatise *De Principiis* in four volumes.

Origin of Species

Book by Charles Darwin published in 1859. In this and a companion volume, *The Descent of Man* (1871), he maintained that living species have evolved by natural selection, the fittest for biological purposes surviving. This caused a storm in theological circles as it seemed to undermine the Christian doctrine that man is the creation of God.

Original Sin

Christian doctrine that there is a causal connection between the sin of Adam and Eve and the sin of all mankind since. Two biblical passages apart from the Genesis story are usually quoted: Psalm 51:5 and Romans 5:12. One belief concerning baptism is that it cleanses the baptized person from the taint of original sin.

Orisha

Subordinate gods, ministers of Olodumare, among the Yoruba tribe of Africa.

Orisha-Nla

Chief of the Orishas who performs Olodumare's creative or executive work. He is also known as Obatala.

Orpheus

Mythical person regarded by the ancient Greeks as the most celebrated poet before Homer. Presented with a lyre by Apollo, he enchanted wild beasts and trees. He married Eurydice, who died and was carried to Hades. He followed her and the charm of his music won her release, but by looking back to make sure she was with him he broke the conditions of her release, and lost her for ever. Stricken with grief, he spurned the sympathy of the women of Thrace, who then tore him to pieces in a Bacchanalian orgy.

Orphism

From the 6th century BCE onwards a mass of religious literature attributed to Orpheus appeared, and

A man who has died is led by Horus into the presence of Osiris

many Orphic sects were founded. They were forbidden to eat meat, practised an ascetic purity of life and conduct, and emphasized a sense of sin and a need of atonement, the suffering and death of a god-man, and a belief in immortality.

Orthodox Church

Originally this was the Church of the eastern region of the Roman Empire, which was predominantly Greek speaking. The separation of the Orthodox (East) and Roman Catholic (West) sections of the Church came about in 1054. The Eastern Orthodox Church now comprises a number of patriarchates, including those of Constantinople, Moscow, Greece, Cyprus and Jerusalem.

Orunmila

Chief counsellor of the Yoruba gods. He is the power behind the Ifa oracle.

Osiris

Egyptian deity who taught his people agriculture and gave them the Law. He was the husband of Isis and the father of Horus. After he was murdered and dismembered by his brother Set, Isis searched throughout Egypt for his scattered limbs and reassembled them, after which Osiris became King of the Dead.

Othniel

One of the six Judges of Israel whose achievements are recorded in the Book of Judges. He delivered Israel from the oppression of Cushan-Rishathaim, King of Mesopotamia.

Otto, Rudolf

(1869–1937) Protestant theologian. His most influential book was *The Idea of the Holy* (1917), in which he discussed the part played by the numinous in religious experience. He described it as a 'mysterium tremendum et fascinans', because the sense of awe instils fear, but at the same time attracts.

Ottoman Empire

Turkish Empire which took its name from Othman, who declared himself Sultan in 1300. In 1453 Sultan Muhammad II captured Constantinople, brought the Byzantine Empire to an end, and advanced westwards to the borders of Italy. The most extensive power of the Ottoman Empire was achieved under Sultan Suleiman the Magnificent (1520–1566), who captured Rhodes, subdued half of Hungary and reached Venice and Vienna, where he was checked by the Emperor Charles V. The Ottoman Empire survived, with gradually declining power, until 1920.

Outcaste

See Untouchable

Owl

Probably because it hunts by night and because its face, with staring, unblinking eyes, is uncannily human in appearance, the owl has been associated by many communities with strange powers, with the forces of evil and misfortune, and with death and mourning. However, in Athens it was sacred to Athene, goddess of the night and of wisdom, and it became the emblem of the city.

Oxford Group

Religious movement founded by Dr Frank Buchman. Between 1926 and 1929 he gathered a group of followers at Oxford University, and this was legally incorporated as the Oxford Group. The particular practice of the Group is a quiet time, morning and evening, during which guidance from God is written down, to be followed in the course of one's activities. In 1938 Dr Buchman reorganized the movement under the title Moral Rearmament, giving more attention to national and international problems such as industrial and trade-union disputes. Its headquarters are at Caux in Switzerland.

Oxford Movement

Activity within the Church of England which aimed at restoring the High-Church ideals of the 17th century. Its starting-point is usually considered to be the sermon on national apostasy preached by John Keble at Oxford on 14 July 1833. After this John Henry Newman developed the movement with *Tracts for the Times*, and in 1845 he and some other leaders were received into the Roman Catholic Church. Despite this, the movement continued and has played an important part in the development of Anglican liturgy, ritual and ceremonial. Because of the *Tracts*, adherents of the movement were nicknamed Tractarians.

Pabbajja(P)**/Pravrajya** (S)

Term used in Buddhism for the formal renunciation of the world undertaken by a man seeking to become a Buddhist monk, before the period of formal training begins.

Pac Khanda

In the teaching of Guru Nanak, the founder of Sikhism, these are the five stages or steps leading to man's spiritual liberation.

Pachacamac

God in the Inca religion whose name means 'lord of the earth'. His pyramid rivalled that of the sun god and was a centre of pilgrimage. He was said to be the cause of earthquakes.

Pachamama

Goddess in the Inca religion and that of neighbouring people. Her name means 'earth mother', and she presides over agriculture. She was invoked in daily prayers and ritual.

Pachomius

(290–346 CE) Devout Egyptian Christian reputed to be the founder of Christian monastic communities. He founded a monastery on the right bank of the Nile in 320, and others were quickly established throughout the early Church.

Pacifism

Belief that violence should not be used even in self-defence. This is usually coupled with a refusal to approve of or take any part in war. It is similar to the doctrine of ahimsa or non-violence, and is an important element in Buddhist and Jain teaching. Some Christian groups and organizations emphasize this teaching, e.g. the Quakers and the Fellowship of Reconciliation.

Padmasana

The lotus position, which is the basic position for the commencement of meditation according to Buddhist practice.

Pagan

Term derived from the Latin *paganus* (countryman) used by Christians from the 4th century onwards to indicate people who did not accept Christianity.

Pagdi/Pagri

Turban; distinctive, but not exclusively Sikh head-dress.

Pagoda

Sacred building, usually a tower in pyramid form, associated with China, Japan and Burma. It probably developed from the stupa, as they were both intended to house relics.

Pahlavi

Middle (as distinct from Old or Modern) Persian, in which many of the sacred books of Zoroastrianism were written.

Pajjusana

Eight-day period of penance in August during which Jains celebrate the birthday of Mahavira and the giving of the *Kalpa Sutra*.

Yasaka Pagoda, Kyoto, Japan

Shwedagon Pagoda, Rangoon, Burma

Palestine

Country bounded by the Mediterranean on the west and the Syrian desert on the east. Earlier it was called Canaan, and the name Palestine, derived from 'Philistine', was first used by Herodotus about 450 BCE. It was the home of the Israelites until the Diaspora following the capture of Jerusalem by the Romans in 70 CE. In 636 CE it was occupied by Islamic troops, and for many centuries it was the scene of fighting between Islam and Christianity, including the Crusades. In 1920 the land was entrusted to Great Britain by a mandate from the League of Nations, and in 1948 part of it was declared to be the State of Israel.

Pali

Language of the canonical scriptures of Theravada Buddhism.

Paliya

Hindu memorial stone in Indian villages, painted red, commemorating a man who died a violent death. An annual rite is performed before it to propitiate his spirit.

Palla

Scarf given and accepted during a Sikh wedding ceremony. This is an essential element in the ritual, symbolizing the tying of the bride to the groom.

Pallium

Ecclesiastical vestment made of pure white lamb's-wool, marked with six crosses in purple, worn over the shoulders by the Pope and Roman Catholic archbishops as a symbol of metropolitan distinction and power.

Palm

One of the most important trees of the Mediterranean area as its fruit, sap, leaves and branches are all useful and valuable. Palm branches are carried, with willow, myrtle and citron, at the Jewish Feast of Tabernacles. Palm branches were strewn in front of Jesus as he entered Jerusalem at the beginning of his last week of life (Matthew 21:8), and Palm Sunday, commemorating the event, is an important Christian festival. Pilgrims often carried a staff of palm, and thus became known as palmers.

Palm Sunday

Last Sunday in Lent, marking the beginning of Holy Week. On this day Christians celebrate the triumphal entry of Jesus into Jerusalem, riding on a donkey, while the crowds strewed palm branches in his path (Matthew 21:8).

Pamada

Derogatory term used in Buddhism for heedlessness or mental sloth.

Pallium

Pan
> Greek god of flocks and herds, and later of all nature.

Pancasila
> Five rules or prohibitions binding on all Buddhists, viz. to avoid killing, theft, luxury, falsehood and alcohol.

Pancayat
> In India the caste assembly which enforces caste rules and settles disputes between caste members.

Pancgavya
> Mixture of the five products of the cow – milk, curds, ghee (refined butter), cow-dung and cow's urine – consumed in Hinduism as a purifying agent.

Panchen Lama
> Grand Lama of Tibetan Buddhism, who ranks second to the Dalai Lama.

Pandavas
> The Hindu epic poem the *Mahabharata* is based on a battle between two sections of the Kuru tribe. The Pandavas, led by five noble brothers, of whom the best known is Arjuna, are the heroes and are advised and supported by Krishna. They are opposed by the Kauravas.

Pandora
> Greek female name, lit. 'all gifted'. In Greek mythology, after Prometheus stole fire from heaven, Zeus in his anger compelled Hephaestus to make a woman who would bring misery on the human race. All the gods gave her a power to cause a human ill. In one account Pandora opened a box in her husband's house from which all the evils escaped and spread, while according to another version she gave a box to her husband, who opened it. When the evils had flown out of the box, Hope emerged or, in another version, remained inside.

Pandu
> Indian king who was the father of the five Pandavas, whose adventures form a large part of the *Mahabharata*. The best-known son was Arjuna.

Panentheism
> Term derived from three Greek words, lit. 'everything (exists) in God'. It is the doctrine that God is immanent in the universe but is also transcendent, that the being of God includes and penetrates the whole universe so that everything exists in him, but that he is more than all the universe. It is thus different from pantheism, which holds that all is God.

Panj Pyares
> Lit. 'five beloved ones'. The five companions of Guru Gobind Singh who, with him, founded the Sikh brotherhood, the Khalsa, at Saisakhi in India in 1699, and are still symbolically represented at every Sikh Amrit ceremony.

Panna (P)/**Prajna** (S)
> Transcendental wisdom. One of the two pillars of Mahayana Buddhism, the other being karuna (compassion). The term is also used in Hindu writings to denote wisdom or insight.

Pansil
> Contraction of Pancha Sila, the five rules of morality, the title given to a recitation used in Theravada Buddhism. This is not a vow to God or any other being, but is a solemn undertaking made to oneself.

Panth
> Word used in the Sikh religion as a title for the corporate community which accepts the *Guru Granth Sahib*, the Sikh scriptures.

Panthaks
> Five geographical regions into which Zoroastrians are divided for the purposes of religious administration.

Pantheism
> Derived from two Greek words, pantheism expresses the doctrine that God is all and all is God, thus merging all things in the Divine and denying personality to God.

Pantheon
> Derived from two Greek words meaning 'every god', it is applied to a place where all gods were worshipped. The most celebrated of these is in Rome; built in 27 BCE in the Campus Martius,

since 609 CE it has been used as a Christian church dedicated to the Virgin Mary and all the Saints.

Pap

Term used in the Hindu religion for sin of any kind.

Papa

1. Italian and Spanish word (with the stress on the first syllable) for 'Pope'. Used as an affectionate salutation on his public appearances.
2. In the Maori religion an important goddess, the earth deity, the wife of Rangi, the sky god.

Papal Infallibility

See Infallibility

Papacy

Doctrinal and administrative office of the Bishop of Rome, the Pope, which is the central organization of the Roman Catholic Church. As successor of St Peter, the Pope is believed by Roman Catholics to be Vicar of Christ on earth, and guardian of the faith.

Papias

Bishop of Hierapolis, born c. 60 CE. He is important in the study of the NT because quotations by Eusebius from otherwise lost writings of Papias tell us that Mark was Peter's interpreter and wrote down accurately all that he remembered, that Matthew composed the Logia (oracles or sayings) in the Hebrew tongue, and that everyone interpreted them as he was able.

Papyrus

Aquatic plant of the sedge family used to make an early form of writing material. Its stem was cut into strips which were laid side by side and covered by more strips laid at right angles, after which the two layers were pressed firmly together. Its use for writing probably dates from about 3000 BCE. Some early Egyptian documents exist, and fragments of the Gospels have been found in Egypt and among the Qumran Scrolls, but papyrus is brittle and susceptible to damp, and little has survived from the time of the writing of the Gospels.

Parable

Term applied to a method of teaching. The teacher uses an illustration from nature, general experience or from common practice in order to put forward a particular moral or religious truth. Many parables are found in the Hebrew Bible and in the teaching of Jesus, e.g. Nathan's parable of the one ewe lamb (2 Samuel 12) and Jesus' parable of the Good Samaritan (Luke 10).

Paraclete

In classical Greek this word meant 'defending counsel in a lawsuit'. In St John's Gospel it is used as an epithet for the Holy Spirit. The Authorized Version translation was 'comforter', but this has been changed to 'counsellor' in the Revised Standard Version and 'advocate' in the New English Bible.

Paradise

Term derived from an ancient Iranian word meaning 'walled garden'. In late Jewish thought it developed an eschatological sense, indicating a place where the righteous dwell with God, like the original Garden of Eden. In Luke 23:43, Jesus used the word to indicate the place where the penitent thief would be with him immediately after death. In Revelation 2:7 it signifies the dwelling-place of God, in the middle of which is the Tree of Life. In Muslim belief it was the original abode of Adam and Eve (Qur'an 2), where the faithful will find comfort and the service of lovely maidens (Qur'an 55).

Paramatman

In the teaching of the Hindu *Upanishads*, this is the universal atman, or world soul.

Paramita (P/S)

In Buddhist teaching a stage of spiritual perfection achieved by a Bodhisattva on his path to Buddhahood. Theravada Buddhism recognizes six stages while Mahayana Buddhism recognizes ten stages.

Paranirvana

State of nirvana achieved by one who has completed the incarnation in which he achieved it and so need not be reborn on earth. In Mahayana Buddhism it is the title of a festival commemorating the 'Great Decease' of the Buddha.

Parasu-Rama

Lit. 'Rama with the axe'. He is the sixth of ten avatars of Vishnu, and his story is told in the epic poem the *Mahabharata*.

Paratantra

Hindu doctrine, found in the teaching of the philosopher Madhva, that all worldly things depend for their activity on God.

Parisad

The four categories of Buddhists: monks, nuns, laymen and laywomen.

Parish

Area under the spiritual care of a Church of England vicar or rector, or a Roman Catholic priest.

Parivarta (S)

Term used in Mahayana Buddhism for the doctrine or virtue of 'turning over' acquired merit for the benefit of others.

Parmesha

Title given in the Sikh religion to God as the supreme being.

Parousia

Greek word meaning 'presence' or 'arrival' used in the NT in connection with the second coming or return of Christ.

Parsee

Name derived from 'Pars' (an ancient name for Persia) to denote descendants of the Zoroastrians who fled to India from Muslim persecution in the 7th and 8th centuries. The majority of them are now resident in Bombay. The name is used interchangeably with 'Zoroastrian'.

Parthenon

Temple of Athene on the Acropolis of Athens, dedicated in 438 BCE under the administration of Pericles. It was built entirely of Pentelic marble in the Doric style and decorated with statues and friezes. Some of the friezes, the Elgin Marbles, are now in the British Museum.

Parthian

Dynasty of Persian kings, founded by Arsaces, which held power from 256 BCE to 214 CE. They were worshippers of Mazda and kept a royal fire continuously burning. They appear to have adopted a tolerant attitude to other religions, including Zoroastrianism, at the beginning of their rule, and Christianity, at the end, and there is evidence of syncretism in the amalgamation of the names of Greek and Iranian gods.

Parvati

Hindu goddess; lit. 'mountaineer', i.e. the goddess of the Himalayas; one of the names of the consort of the god Shiva. She is also known as Durga or Kali.

Paryushan

Alternative title for Pajjusana, an eight-day period of penance during which Jains recall and commemorate their teacher Mahavira and the giving of the *Kalpa Sutra*.

Paschal

Derived from the Hebrew word for the Passover, this has become an adjective relating to Easter (the Christian Passover). It is used to describe the candle which is lit on Holy Saturday to symbolize the resurrection light, and in the term 'Paschal Lamb', a title sometimes applied to Jesus Christ.

Pashupatas

Followers of the Hindu god Shiva named after his title 'Pashupati' (lord of animals). They taught a modified monism with Shiva as the supreme lord, and practised a yoga discipline.

Passion Sunday

Fifth Sunday in Lent, when Christians remember and meditate on the Passion (sufferings) of Christ.

Passion-flower

Evergreen climbing plant *Passiflora caerulea*. Its popular name derives from its three pistils, five stamens and purple corona at the base of the petals. These are said to symbolize the three nails, five wounds and crown of thorns suffered by Christ at the Crucifixion.

Passion-play

Play based on the last days of the life of Jesus Christ. Such plays developed from the miracle or mystery plays, but omitted the comic elements. The best-known passion-play is that performed every ten years at Oberammergau in fulfilment of a vow made by the villagers in 1633.

Passover/Pesach

Major festival of the Jewish year celebrated in the spring on 14 Nisan and the next eight days. It is observed in the home with a symbolic meal and the Seder service, and commemorates the Exodus from Egypt, the escape from slavery to the freedom of the Promised Land. Today the festival celebrates, in addition, other deliverances of the Jewish people, and some keep it as a special remembrance of the Holocaust.

Passover plate, showing the arrangement of the food eaten at the meal

Pastor

Shepherd of souls. Term widely used for a minister in Nonconformist and Reformed Churches.

Pastoral Epistles

Three epistles in the NT attributed to St Paul, two being addressed to Timothy and one to Titus. Some NT scholars doubt whether they were written by St Paul although they contain elements of his teaching.

Pastoral Staff

See Crozier

Patala

In Hindu mythology, seven subterranean regions which were the abode of Nagas and demonic creatures.

Paten

Plate, usually silver, on which the bread is placed for the celebration of the Christian Eucharist.

Paterfamilias

Head of the ancient Roman household, in whom was thought to reside the power of male fertility.

Paticcasamuppada (P)/Pratityasamutpada (S)

The Buddhist doctrine of conditional origination. This indicates the nexus or chain of links between rebirth and rebirth. It is not a casual dependence but a dependence of links, for each link is a condition for the next link's coming into being.

Patimokkha (P)/Pratimoksa (S)

The two hundred and twenty-seven disciplinary rules binding on a Buddhist bhikku, which are periodically recited for the purposes of confession.

Patmos

Small island of the Sporades group of the Dodecanese where St John the Divine received the Revelation (1:9). A monastery was founded on the traditional site by St Christodulus in 1088.

Patriarch

In the OT a title given to the earliest of the leaders of Israel, up to the time of Jacob. It is also an ecclesiastical title, dating from the 6th century, for the bishops of the five principal sees in the Christian Church, viz. Rome, Alexandria, Antioch, Constantinople and Jerusalem.

Patrick, St

(389–461 CE) Patron saint of Ireland. He was probably born in Gaul, captured by raiders and taken as a slave to Ireland. He escaped, trained to be a priest and returned to Ireland in 431, where he built many churches and monasteries.

Patristic Literature

Writings of the Apostolic Fathers, i.e. men who may have had some contact or connection with the Apostles, the immediate followers of Jesus Christ. The most important documents are from the hands of Clement of Rome, Ignatius, Polycarp, Papias and the Shepherd of Hermas.

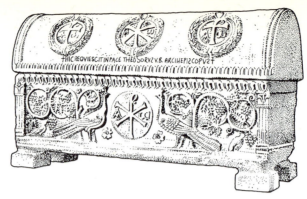

Peacocks as Christian symbols of the Resurrection (coffin of Archbishop Theodore of Ravenna, 677–688 CE)

Pattit

Lit. 'fallen ones', i.e. 'apostates'. Term of contempt applied in the Sikh community to those who give up the Sikh way of life and reject the rules of the Khalsa.

Paul of Tarsus (St Paul)

Zealous Jewish scholar, a pupil of Gamaliel, who set out to eradicate the Christian faith. On his way to Damascus to arrest Christians he experienced a blinding flash of insight, was converted by the grace of God and thereafter was a devoted follower of Jesus Christ. After a period of instruction, he became the Church's first missionary, and founded many Christian communities. Through his letters, included in the NT, he established the faith of the early Church, and he has been accepted as a fountain-head and interpreter of Christian doctrine. He was martyred in Rome, probably c. 65 CE, during the Neronic persecution.

Pax Deorum

Aim of religious activity according to the ancient Romans. Lit. 'the peace of the gods', but better translated 'the favour of the gods'.

Pazuzu

In Mesopotamian mythology, the king of the evil spirits of the air. He manifested himself in the hot, oppressive wind which blows out of the Arabian desert, bringing many kinds of sickness in its train.

Peacock

Bird frequently mentioned in the *Rig-Veda* in association with Indra. In Greek mythology it was sacred to Hera, who was thought to have put the many eyes on its tail to spy on her husband, the god Zeus; this made it a creature of some terror and awe in some communities. On the other hand, it has been taken into Christian art and iconography as a symbol of the Resurrection, possibly because after moulting it is seen to become reclothed in splendour.

Pectoral Cross

Cross suspended by a chain round the neck. In the Roman Catholic Church it is worn by cardinals, bishops and abbots as a symbol of office. In the Church of England its use is restricted to bishops, but in the Orthodox Church it is worn by all ranks of clergy.

Pelagians

Followers of a British monk Pelagius whose doctrine was condemned at the Council of Ephesus in 431 CE. In opposition to the doctrine of Augustine of Hippo, he rejected original sin and the taint of Adam, and also predestination. He taught a doctrine of free will and the merit of good works, and believed that man, though helped by divine aids, has of himself the power to accept or reject the Gospel. (See also Semi-Pelagian)

Pelican

In medieval times the pelican was thought to peck its breast in order to supply its young with blood, and it therefore became a symbol of parental affection and self-sacrifice.

Penal Substitution

Christian doctrine taught by some Protestant theologians that Christ, the sinless victim, was punished in place of the truly guilty, i.e. mankind in general. He made atonement by his death upon the Cross and paid the penalty as a substitute for those who have been marked out, or predestined, by God for salvation, viz. the elect.

Penance

One of the seven sacraments recognized by the Roman Catholic Church. The penitent confesses his sins to a priest, who decides according to the gravity of the sin on a suitable form of penance, and then, in virtue of his priestly office, pronounces absolution.

Penates

Guardian spirits of the store-cupboard, the household gods of ancient Rome. They were the gods of the family and of the state. The lares were reckoned among the penates.

Penn, William

(1644–1718) English Quaker who became the founder of the American state of Pennsylvania in 1682. Expelled from Oxford University because of his beliefs, he preached throughout England and Holland and ultimately led a group of Quakers to settle in America.

Pentagram

Star with five points, associated with magic, based on the symbolism of the figure five, the number of the living world of nature, e.g. the four cardinal directions plus the centre, or the five human senses. It also represents the human figure – the head, the two arms and the two legs – and when the star was pointing upwards it was thought to have power to keep evil spirits at bay.

Pentateuch

First five books of the Bible, described by the Jews as the Torah and believed by them to have been dictated by God to Moses on Mt Sinai.

Pentecost

1. Jewish festival Shavuot, the Feast of Weeks, seven weeks or fifty days after the Passover. It commemorates the giving of the Ten Commandments on Mt Sinai.
2. The Christian Pentecost commemorates the day when the disciples of Jesus Christ received the gift of the Holy Spirit and began to speak with tongues. It is usually referred to as Whitsun.

Pentecostalism

Widespread movement of Protestant Christians who emphasize the baptism of the Spirit, similar to that experienced by the Apostles on the day of Pentecost (Acts 1:4). The movement dates from 1901 in Kansas, and has spread throughout the world. Their services are marked by great enthusiasm, as they believe that baptism in the Holy Spirit is followed by the gift of tongues and the power of spiritual healing.

Persephone

According to Greek mythology, the daughter of Zeus and Demeter, the corn goddess. Persephone was seized by Hades (or Pluto) and carried to the underworld to be his queen, but on the orders of Zeus she was allowed to spend part of the year in the world of men. The story symbolizes the sowing of the seed, which remains dormant underground until it germinates, grows, ripens and is then cut down at the harvest.

Perseus

According to Greek mythology, the son of Zeus and Danae. He was the hero who killed the Gorgon Medusa, whose glance could turn men to stone. Armed with the helmet of Hades, which made him invisible, and a mirror or shield given him by Athene, he was able to cut off the head of Medusa with a sickle, the gift of Hermes. By looking at Medusa's reflection in the mirror or shield, he avoided a direct glance at her face and her hair of writhing serpents. He gave Medusa's head to Athene, who set it in the middle of her shield.

Persian

Fifth of the seven grades of Mithraic initiation; protected by the moon.

Pesach

Jewish festival. See Passover.

Peshitta

Lit. 'simple'. Syriac translation of the Bible. The NT translation was the work of Rabbula, Bishop of Edessa (411–435 CE), but the OT translation may be much earlier and its author is unknown.

Peter

1. One of the disciples of Jesus. His name was Simon, but Jesus called him Peter (rock). He was a

fisherman whose strong accent marked him as a Galilean when Jesus was arrested; he then denied his discipleship as Jesus had foretold. After the crucifixion and resurrection of Christ, Peter became one of the leaders of the early Church. He undertook missionary journeys, and according to tradition became the first Bishop of Rome, where he was martyred, probably in the Neronian persecution *c.* 65 CE.

2. Title of two NT epistles. The first is concerned with Christian relationships and holy living, and warns of a coming time of trial. It may be connected with baptismal liturgy. The second contains a condemnation of false prophets and false teachers, and doubts have been cast on its authorship.

Petra

Ancient capital of Idumaea situated in the wilderness near Mt Hor at the end of the narrow Wady Musa. The buildings, including a hall of justice, a treasury and a temple, are hewn out of the living rock – pink sandstone. It was subdued by the Romans in 105 CE. In the poem *Petra*, J. W. Burgon described it as 'rose-red city, half as old as time.'

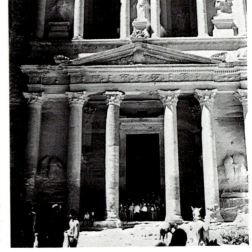

Petra: the Treasury

Petrarch, Francesco

(1304–1374) Italian poet and humanist. He travelled extensively and won the laureate's crown in 1341 with a poem on Scipio Africanus (in Latin). Thereafter he turned to more religious subjects, and wrote a dialogue between himself and St Augustine; he also wrote meditations on the solitary life, the contemplative life, and the transitoriness of human life.

Phallus

Image of the penis, venerated in some religions as symbolizing the generative and regenerative power in nature. In Hinduism this is particularly associated with Shiva.

Pharaoh

Title of the king in ancient Egypt, lit. 'great house'. It was originally the name for the royal palace, but in the 18th Dynasty, about 1450 BCE, it was applied to the person of the monarch.

Pharisees

Aramaic word possibly meaning 'separated ones'; they were the successors of the Chasidim, distinguished in the 2nd century BCE for their strict observance of the Torah and their emphasis on oral tradition. Jesus several times called them 'hypocrites'. They were the founders of rabbinic Judaism, and modern research has cast a more favourable light on their activities.

Phenomenalism

Philosophical theory that physical objects have no existence except as things which can be sensed. Alternatively, a theory that such objects, even if they exist, can be known only through the senses.

Phenomenology

Philosophical method which seeks to study phenomena (things that can be observed) with the aim of arriving at their essence and essential meaning. In religious studies it is a method which selects and compares universal or common manifestations of religion, rather than dealing with different religious traditions one by one.

Philemon, Epistle to

Shortest epistle in the NT, written by St Paul to ask a slave-owner, now a Christian, to receive back into his household a runaway slave Onesimus who had fled to Paul for help and advice.

Philip

1. One of the twelve Apostles of Jesus. He answered the call of Jesus, then brought his friend Nathanael. In John 6 he is given special mention in the account of the miracle of the feeding of the five thousand.

2. Evangelist, one of the seven deacons appointed after the resurrection of Jesus to help the disciples

with the administration of the early Church (Acts 6). After a period of missionary work he settled in Caesarea.

3. King of Macedon (382–335 BCE). By imposing a strict military discipline on his people he was able to carve out an imposing kingdom in the northern area of Greece. He brought the philosopher Aristotle to court to act as tutor to his son Alexander, later known as 'the Great'.

Philip II of Spain

(1527–1598)   King of Spain, Naples and Portugal whose main object in life was the defence of the Catholic faith against Protestantism. He married Mary Tudor and during her reign had influence in England, but Elizabeth's navy defeated his armada in 1588 and caused the decline of Spanish sea power. His lasting memorial is the magnificent Escorial Palace outside Madrid.

Philip Neri

(1515–1595)   Italian priest known as the Apostle of Rome because of his work for the sick and poor, and the Hostel of the Trinity which he built for pilgrims visiting the city. In 1564 he founded the Congregation of the Oratory, which was approved by Pope Gregory XIII in 1575; Congregations were soon opened in other countries.

Philippians, Epistle to

One of St Paul's letters. Philippi was a church founded by the Apostle and very dear to him, and he expresses his appreciation of their love. It is not clear whether the letter was sent from Rome or Ephesus.

Philistines

Probably the sea people who in the 2nd millennium left the Aegean on the arrival of the Greeks. They settled in the coastal plain of Canaan between Gaza and Egypt, and they were a constant threat to the Israelites until King David subdued them. No Philistine inscriptions have been found, but their name survives in the designation of the land as Palestine.

Philo

(20 BCE–50 CE)   Jewish philosopher and theological writer. He combined Jewish thought with Greek philosophy, and gave a central place in his teaching to the Logos as the creative power which orders the world and is the intermediary through whom we know God. Some scholars think there is a reflection of the Logos doctrine in John 1.

Philosophical

1. In a broad sense, taking a reasonable, detached or even resigned attitude to a set of problems.
2. Seeking justification for fundamental assumptions made in various areas of human inquiry.
3. Pertaining to the discipline of philosophy.

Phoenix

Mythical bird said to be the only one of its kind and about the size of an eagle. According to a legend linked with Arabia and Egypt, when the bird felt the approach of death it built a nest which was ignited by the sun's rays. Out of the ashes came a worm which grew into a new phoenix. This is probably connected with sun-worship and the hope of life after death, and some early Christian writers adapted it as a symbol of the resurrection of Jesus Christ.

Photius

(810–895 CE)   Byzantine statesman and theologian. He served the Emperor Michael III as Imperial Secretary and Ambassador, and in 858 was appointed Patriarch of Constantinople. Pope Nicholas I protested and was excommunicated. The Pope responded by excommunicating Photius, and thus the schism between the Eastern and Western Churches began. In 867 the new Emperor Basil deposed Photius, and there was a period of reconciliation.

Pietà by Michelangelo
(St Peter's, Rome)

Phylacteries

See Tephillin

Pietà

Sculpture representing the Virgin Mary mourning over the dead body of Christ.

Pietism

Movement in the 17th century within the Lutheran Church led by P. J. Spener. He held prayer meetings for Bible study in his house and organized prayer circles, but the pietists were also noted for their concern with practical religion. In the 1694 the University of Halle was founded to ensure the continued teaching of their evangelical faith.

Pig

Animal whose flesh is eaten in most parts of Europe, having been regarded at one time as the food of royal hospitality, but which is strictly forbidden to Jews and Muslims. The probable reason is that it was an object of worship in some ancient Middle East communities. Domestic altars shaped like pigs have been found on archaeological sites in Canaan. The pig has become a figure of indolence or greed in art symbolism, and in the Middle Ages was a symbol of gluttony, one of the seven deadly sins.

Pilgrim Fathers

Group of Puritans who sailed from Holland and from Plymouth in the *Mayflower* in 1620. They landed at Cape Cod, and founded the colony of New Plymouth as loyal subjects of King James.

Pilgrimage

The fifth of the Pillars of Islam is the duty to undertake a pilgrimage to Mecca (Hajj) at least once. Most religions have sacred places to which the devout make pilgrimages, e.g. Amritsar, Benares, Canterbury, Jerusalem and Rome, but apart from Islam, this is a voluntary activity.

Pipal

Ficus religiosa. Tree regarded as sacred by Hindus. It is also of great significance in Buddhism, as it is almost certainly the bo-tree, under which the Buddha found enlightenment through meditation.

Pirit

Charm, or ceremony, for protection from evil used by Buddhists in Sri Lanka.

Pirke Aboth (H)

Lit. 'ethics of the fathers'. Jewish, rabbinic tractate, part of the Mishnah, which traces the oral tradition from Moses to Shammai and Hillel, and sets forth ethical standards which should govern the conduct of every man in all his relations, social, domestic, economic and political.

Piscina

Stone basin in the south wall of a Christian church for the priest to wash his hands and the Eucharistic vessels after the celebration of the Mass.

Pitaka

'Basket', or section of the Buddhist scriptures. Three baskets make up the Pali canon of Buddhist scriptures. (See also *Tipitaka*)

Piti

Term used in Buddhism to denote blissful rapture, or a joyful state of consciousness.

Plato

(428–347 BCE) Greek philosopher who lived and taught in Athens. He became a follower of Socrates in 408 BCE, and carefully noted Socrates' discussions with members of his group, later writing these down as the Socratic dialogues. After the death of Socrates in 399 BCE, he began to teach at the Academy, following the dialectical methods of his master. His works include treatises, in the form of dialogues, on ethics, metaphysics, politics and education.

Pliny, Publius C. S.

(61–113 CE) Roman lawyer and politician, usually known as Pliny the Younger. When he was Governor of Bithynia in 112 he wrote a series of letters to the Emperor Trajan. In one of them he describes Christian rites and practices, and suggests that they should be tolerated. In his rescript Trajan rejected toleration, but said that Pliny need not initiate persecution.

Plotinus

Founder of the neo-Platonic school of philosophy. He was born in Egypt in 203 CE and died there about 262 CE. His teaching was idealistic and eclectic, endeavouring to unite Christianity with the philosophy of Plato. It has been described as mystical theosophy, aiming at a knowledge of the One, which was an emanation of the nous or pure intelligence. The works of Plotinus were collected by his follower Porphyry, and became important in the early years of the Renaissance, when they were translated into Italian by Marsilio Ficino (1433–1499) and used as a basis for discussion in the

Platonic Academy of Florence under Giovanni Pico (1463–1494). They exercised considerable influence on artists such as Brunelleschi and Botticelli.

Pluralism

Doctrine which holds that being and reality can be reduced to a multiplicity of independent single elements; the antithesis of monism.

Pluto

Roman god of the underworld. Originally, he was known as Hades, but the name was transferred to the place where he ruled. According to legend, he seized Persephone, the daughter of the corn goddess Demeter and Zeus, but he was allowed by Zeus to keep her in the underworld for only part of each year. He was regarded as the judge of the dead.

Pluto and Persephone (by Bernini)

Pogrom

Organized massacre or exile of a sect or a class. The term is often used of the Russian expulsion of Jews in the 19th century.

Polis

Greek city-state, such as Athens. A relatively small community, geographically self-contained, forming a unit to which people could feel that they belonged, and in whose government they could share.

Pollux

See Castor and Pollux

Polycarp

(69–155 CE) Apostolic Father and Bishop of Smyrna who was one of the early Christian martyrs. He was a strong advocate of orthodoxy and defended Christianity against the attacks of the Gnostics.

Polygamy

Form of marriage in which a man has more than one wife. In Islam a man is permitted to have up to four wives, provided that he can fulfil certain obligations equally to all of them.

Polytheism

Belief in, or the worship of, many gods. It does not mean that all the gods are of equal status; there is usually some form of hierarchy of power or of importance.

Pomegranate

Fruit of a tree grown in the Mediterranean area. It has become a symbol of fertility because of the vast number of seeds within the fruit, which is shaped like an apple but has a very hard skin, at first yellow but ripening to a deep red. In Christian symbolism it is used as a symbol of hope.

Pontifex

Roman term for priest in the time of the Empire. Lit. 'bridge builder', it indicates the function of linking God and man together. The chief priest was called Pontifex Maximus, a title claimed by the Emperor Augustus.

Pontius Pilate

Roman governor of Judaea (26–36 CE) under whom Jesus Christ was crucified. He later fell into disgrace, and there is a tradition that he committed suicide.

Pope

Bishop of Rome. The chief bishop of the Roman Catholic Church, considered by Catholics to be the Vicar of Christ on earth, and the successor of St Peter, the first Bishop of Rome. He is thus regarded as the supreme head of the Church on earth, and the chief pastor of the whole Church.

Poppy

Because it is the source of opium, the poppy has become the symbol of sleep, the soothing of pain and death. The red poppy, found in the battlefields of Flanders, has become, since the First World War, the symbol of remembrance of those killed in battle.

Porasurama

Hero who as the sixth avatar of Vishnu saved the Brahmins from the hostility of the Kshatriya warriors.

Posan/Poson

Festival of Theravada Buddhism celebrated on the night of the full moon in June to commemorate the first preaching of the Dhamma to foreign countries, and particularly the introduction of Buddhism into Sri Lanka.

Poseidon

Greek god of the sea, often depicted with a dolphin, or a horse and a trident. In some Homeric poems he is described as equal to Zeus. He was identified with Neptune by the Romans.

Positivism

Term introduced by Auguste Comte to designate a school of philosophy which limits knowledge to the facts of experience, and refuses to embark on speculation regarding the ultimate nature of things.

Possession

Belief that supernatural powers, spiritual or divine, good or evil, may become embodied in man either permanently or temporarily. Jesus healed a man possessed of so many devils that he said his name was

Legion (Mark 5). Some African tribes, e.g. in Ghana and Yorubaland, have ceremonies in which drumming and dancing are used to induce a state of possession, and in the voodoo ceremonies of Haiti there is the expectation that one or more of the worshippers will become possessed. On the other hand when a person becomes inexplicably possessed, a remedy is usually sought in exorcism.

Postulant

Candidate for admission to a Christian religious order undergoing preliminary testing before being admitted to the novitiate. The period of postulancy varies in different orders.

Potala

Monastery-palace in Tibet completed in 1694 by the Dalai Lama, Nag-wan lo-zang. Situated on a rocky eminence near Llasa, it is the official residence of the Dalai Lama, but it has been taken over by the Chinese.

Prabandham

Collection of hymns written by the Alvars, poet-saints of Tamil Vaisnavism, between the 7th and 10th centuries which have attained the authority of scripture in that area of Hinduism.

Praemunire

Series of statutes (the first passed in 1353) intended to protect rights claimed by the English crown against claims made by the papacy. Henry VIII used a writ of praemunire against Thomas Wolsey in 1529, and Elizabeth I frequently invoked these statutes against Roman Catholic recusants.

Pragmatic Sanction

Legal term defining the limits of a prince's sovereign power. The Pragmatic Sanction of Bourges (1438) upheld the right of the French Church to administer Church property independently of the papacy, and to make its own nominations to vacant benefices.

Pragmatism

System of philosophy which states that every truth has practical consequences, and that these are a test of its truthfulness. Truth is thus regarded as relative.

Prajapati

Lit. 'lord of creatures'. Used in the *Vedas* as an epithet of various nature gods. In later writings it is sometimes used for the creator-god, particularly Vishnu and Shiva.

Prajna (S)

Term used in Hinduism and Buddhism with the general meaning 'wisdom' or 'knowledge'. In chap. 2 of the *Bhagavadgita* it is the insight or wisdom of one who withdraws his senses from the objects of sense. In the *Dhammapada* it is illumination, knowledge and perfection.

Prakriti (S)

Lit. 'making before', it is now a term used in the Sankhya school of Hindu philosophy for nature or primordial matter, eternal and self-existing.

Pranam

Term used in Hinduism for greeting, involving gestures such as bowing with the hands folded together before the deity, or bowing down to touch the feet of a deity or a guru.

Pranayama

Term used in yoga for the regulation of breathing. The aim is to control all muscular and nervous activity.

Pranidhana

Term used in Buddhism meaning 'vow' or 'dedication'. It is especially used to refer to the dedication of the Bodhisattva who refuses to accept nirvana in order to help other beings.

Prasad

1. Food remaining after a Hindu sacrifice, consecrated by being a deity's left-overs, and eaten by those present at the conclusion of the ritual of worship.

2. Holy food distributed to all worshippers at the conclusion of a Sikh diwan; it is a mixture of ground wheat, sugar and clarified butter (ghee) in equal parts.

Prasada

Term for grace, the gift of Krishna, found in the *Gita*, and used in Hinduism.

Pratimoksa (S)

See Patimokkha

Pratityasamutpada (S)

See Paticcasamuppada

Pratyahara

Term used in yoga for a state of withdrawal of the senses from all sense objects, or the shutting out of the outside world.

Pravrajya (S)

See Pabbajja

Prayer

Devotional activity or spiritual exercise in which man acknowledges a relationship between himself and God, submits himself to the divine will, and offers adoration, thanksgiving, penitence and petition. Prayer can be corporate, personal, vocal or mental, and can involve quietly listening for the word of God.

Prayer Beads

Beads on a thread used for devotional purposes. Buddhists use one hundred and eight in two parts, each part representing the fifty-four stages of becoming a Bodhisattva. Muslims have ninety-nine, one for each of the names of God which are traditionally held to be mentioned in the Qur'an. Roman Catholics have one hundred and sixty-five beads plus a crucifix, usually termed a rosary.

Prayer Wheels

Wheels used by lamas in Tibet on which are inscribed prayers or sacred phrases. Some are small, turned by hand, but others are large, turned by wind or water. Some are hollow for the insertion of prayers on leaves or on paper.

Prebend

Benefice in a cathedral and its holder; in medieval times this consisted of the revenue from one of the manors on the cathedral estates. Since the 19th century the term has largely been replaced in England by the title 'Canon'.

Precentor

Clergyman on the staff of a cathedral responsible for the direction of choral services. In the older cathedrals he usually ranks next to the dean.

Precious Stone Society

Group formed in 1920 in Ijebu-Ode in Nigeria which emphasizes ecstatic prophecy, divine healing and personal holiness.

Predestination

Doctrine that God from the beginning of time elected or chose Israel to be his own people; in Christian theology the doctrine is understood to mean that God predetermined the institution of the Church. It has also been used in an individual sense by theologians such as Augustine and Calvin to explain their belief that some, but not all, Christians are chosen or elected by God for salvation. Calvin went on to a 'double predestination', suggesting that those who had not been

Prayer wheel (Golden Temple, Tibet)

predestined to salvation must have been predestined to damnation. Predestination is a doctrine that is also held in Islam. Everything happens according to the will of Allah, to which man must submit (Qur'an 3:19–20, 17:13). A popular Islamic expression is 'Imshallah' ('It is the will of Allah').

Preface

Words in the Christian Eucharist which introduce the central part of the service, beginning with the Sursum Corda and ending with the Sanctus. In the Anglican *Book of Common Prayer* there are 'proper prefaces' for Christmas, Easter, Ascension, Whitsun and Trinity.

Prelate

Church official of high rank. In the Church of England it applies to bishops and archbishops; in the Roman Catholic Church it also applies to abbots.

Presbyterianism

Protestant Christian form of church government which closely follows the theology and church order of John Calvin. It emphasizes the importance of the local congregation, and insists that church leaders should be presbyters or elders, thus acknowledging no hierarchy, and rejecting the system of prelates or episcopacy.

Preta

Lit. 'hungry ghosts'. Term applied in Buddhism to the shades of the dead.

Pride

First of seven capital or deadly sins listed by Pope Gregory the Great. Pride was considered to be the most insidious and dangerous of the seven.

Priest

Title given in many religions to persons authorized to officiate in public worship and religious ceremonies.

1. In Israel the priesthood was initiated through the family of Aaron, the brother of Moses, and it remained for many centuries a hereditary office. After the destruction of Jerusalem in 70 CE, the priesthood came to an end and has never been reinstituted. (See Kohen for the survival of the name.)

2. In the Christian Church the word *presbuteros* (lit. 'elder') has been translated as 'priest' in the Roman Catholic and Anglican Churches to designate those men, ordained by bishops, who are authorized to administer the Sacraments.

3. In Hinduism priests are Brahmans, members of the first of the four classes into which the Hindu community is divided.

Primate

Title of the bishop of the 'first' see. In the Anglican Church the Archbishop of Canterbury is the Primate of All England while the Archbishop of York is the Primate of England.

Prime

One of the canonical hours of the Christian monastic life, appointed to be said at the first hour, i.e. 6 a.m.

Prior

Title given in the Benedictine order to the monk next in precedence to the abbot, who acts as the abbot's deputy when necessary. In some other orders the prior is the superior of the monastery.

Prohibited Degrees

Relationships by blood or marriage which make it unlawful for two people to marry, e.g. according to the table printed in the Anglican *Book of Common Prayer*, a man may not marry his sister nor his wife's daughter.

Proletariat

In the teaching of Karl Marx, the class of modern labourers who, having no means of production of their own, are reduced to selling their labour power in order to live.

Prometheus

In Greek mythology a hero who stole fire from Zeus on behalf of mankind, after the gods had refused to give it. As a punishment he was chained to a rock where his liver was eaten by an eagle during the day and grew again in the night. In the play *Prometheus Unbound*, Aeschylus suggested that Zeus eventually relented and freed his prisoner, but Prometheus represents the heroic man who is prepared to defy the anger of the despotic ruler of heaven on behalf of suffering humanity.

Promised Land

Description applied to the land of Canaan or Israel. It arises from the promise made by God to Abraham and his successors: 'I will give thee all the land of Canaan for an everlasting possession' (Genesis 17:8). When Moses led the people out of Egypt to go to the land promised to Abraham, it was described as 'a land flowing with milk and honey' (Exodus 33:3).

Prophet

1. *Jewish*   Person called by God for the delivery of a message of special importance; the title

applies particularly to those whose names are attached to biblical books, e.g. Isaiah or Jeremiah. There is an element of foretelling as well as declaration in many of their utterances. (See also Nabi)

2. *Muslim* The Qur'an recognizes many persons mentioned in the OT and the NT as prophets (including Jesus), but claims that Muhammad is the final prophet of Allah.

3. *Zoroastrian* One prophet only is recognized, viz. Zoroaster, who claimed to have a special relationship with Ahura Mazda, the Supreme, Good God.

Propitiation

Term used in Christian theology and liturgy. The death of Christ is regarded as a propitiation offered to God on behalf of sinful man, because man cannot of himself make any worthy appeasement to God for the sins of the world. The term is also used in other religions to indicate some form of appeasement to God, often in the offering of a sacrifice.

Proselyte

Lit. 'stranger'. Word extended in the NT to indicate a convert to Judaism. It is now used of a convert from one faith to another.

Proserpina/Proserpine

Roman equivalent of the Greek goddess Persephone.

Prostration

Action of bowing oneself to the ground as a gesture of submission and respect. Cardinals prostrate themselves before the Pope before receiving the symbols of office. Prostration is also a very important constituent of Islamic prayer or salat. During this sequence of prayers the Muslim adopts different positions for different prayers, and in each of the recitals, repeated five times daily, there are two prostrations.

Protestant

Term now applied particularly to Christians who do not owe allegiance to the Orthodox or Roman Catholic sections of the Church. It originated at the Diet of Speyer in 1529, when followers of Martin Luther 'protested' at the withdrawal of the right to organize their own Church in certain regions of the Holy Roman Empire.

Proverbs, Book of

Book in the Hebrew Bible traditionally ascribed to Solomon. It is a collection of wise sayings covering many aspects of life but not arranged in a clear system. Many scholars believe it belongs to a later period than that of Solomon.

Provisors, Statutes of

Four statutes passed in England (1351, 1353, 1365 and 1389) to prevent papal 'provisions'. This was the practice of nominating clergy to vacant benefices over the head of the patron of the living, thus securing the revenue to a foreign cleric who rarely visited the parish.

Provost

Originally a title applied to the monk next in seniority to the abbot, it is now applied to the head of a chapter or a college. In England the title is given to the heads of cathedral chapters in the newer dioceses instead of the title 'Dean'.

Psalm

1. Rhythmic composition or poem intended to be chanted or sung during religious rituals.

2. The Book of Psalms is a collection of such poems in the Bible and the Anglican *Book of Common Prayer*, consisting of one hundred and fifty psalms of various lengths, half of which are ascribed to King David.

3. A similar collection has been found in the literature of the Essene sect discovered at Qumran.

Pseudepigrapha

Writings ascribed to a writer other than the real author, sometimes to enhance their authority, e.g. the *Psalms of Solomon* or the *Assumption of Moses*, which were not written by Solomon or Moses but were given these titles to make acceptance more likely. Sometimes anonymity or a false name was adopted because it would have been dangerous for the real author to disclose his name.

Psyche

1. Greek word for 'soul' frequently used in the Greek NT and corresponding to the Hebrew word *nephesh* in the OT. It can also be translated 'mind', 'life' or 'person'.

2. In Greek mythology Psyche was the daughter of a king. She was loved by Cupid but incurred the

wrath of his mother Aphrodite, who subjected her to harsh and humiliating labours before she became immortal and was united with Cupid for ever. In this story she represents the human soul, purified by passion and suffering, emerging to joy and happiness. In the poems of Homer she is represented as a kind of 'double' of the human body, and the term psyche was used in Orphism for the soul, held in the body as its tomb.

Psychopannichism

Doctrine taught by some Anabaptist groups in the 16th century which is also known as the 'sleep of the soul'. It expresses the belief that on death the soul sleeps until the Last Day, the day of general resurrection, when all the saints will be gathered to Christ. It was strongly opposed by Zwingli and Calvin. There has been a revival of interest in this doctrine in the 20th century among the Christadelphians.

Ptah

One of the oldest of the Egyptian gods. The name means 'opener', connected with the ceremony for the dead called 'opening the mouth', a ritual to enable the dead person to make the right responses in the afterlife. He was also regarded as the creative force, the divine potter, who fashioned men on his wheel.

Ptolemaic System

Astronomical system taught by Claudius Ptolemy of Alexandria in the 2nd century. He maintained that the earth is fixed in the centre of the universe and that the sun, moon and planets revolve around it. This was the accepted teaching of science and the Church until it was challenged by Copernicus in 1543.

Ptah

Puggala (P)/Pudgala (S)

Term used in Buddhism to indicate the self. It is the nearest approach in Buddhist thought to the concept of the soul.

Puja

Term used in Hinduism and Buddhism for the worship or reverence paid to the gods or superior beings. In place of sacrifices, this takes the form of offerings of gifts to images or symbols, with incense and chanting, and acts of respect such as pressing the palms of the hands together in an attitude of worship.

Pujari

Hindu priest in an Indian village.

Pulpit

Elevated stand in a church or mosque for the delivery of sermons. In cathedrals and parish churches the pulpit is usually on the north side of the nave, but after the Reformation, in Calvinist churches the pulpit was given pre-eminence over the altar, and was placed in a central position.

Punam

Day of the full moon, regarded by Hindus as a holy day suitable for visiting a temple or going on a pilgrimage.

Punchayet

Traditional Zoroastrian form of community leadership composed, in theory, of five persons. It now covers all aspects of social and charitable concern.

Pundit (S)

Learned or wise man, a scholar or philosopher. In India he is usually a Brahman, learned in religious lore.

Punjab

Lit. 'five rivers'. Province in N.W. India which is intersected by five tributaries of the River Indus. It has three great cities, Delhi, Lahore and Amritsar, the holy city of the Sikhs, who form an important part of the population.

Punna (P)/Punya (S)

Term used in Buddhism and Hinduism for a meritorious act bringing a reward in this life or later. It can be generosity or keeping moral precepts or meditation.

Puranas

Hindu chronicles or epic poems celebrating the power of the gods. Originally the word referred to eighteen such poems, six each for Vishnu, Shiva and Brahma, but it now covers all traditional Hindu narrative literature.

Purdah

Persian word for 'veil', now used for the practice in some parts of the Muslim world of secluding women behind a veil or in their own separate quarters.

Pure Land

School of Buddhism which had much support in China and Japan by the 2nd century with particular emphasis on laymen. It teaches that Amida will gather, after their death, all men who have faith in him, and lead them by the White Way to the Pure Land (paradise), from which they can attain nibbana.

Purgatory

According to Roman Catholic teaching, ratified by the Council of Trent in 1563, this is a state after death for those not yet ready for the ultimate reward of heaven but not guilty of such sins as would condemn them to hell, or for those with a remaining debt of punishment to pay.

Purim

Jewish festival celebrated on 14 Adar with the reading of the Book of Esther to celebrate her success in saving many Jews from massacre by their enemy Haman.

Puritans

English Protestants of strong anti-Roman Catholic outlook who were dissatisfied with the Elizabethan settlement in the second half of the 16th century, and demanded express scriptural warrant for details of public worship. They rejected ornaments and vestments, and demanded the appointment of presbyters instead of bishops.

Purohit

Hindu family priest in an Indian village.

Purusa

Term used in Hinduism for the individual soul as distinct from material nature. In the *Rig-Veda* it is used for cosmic man.

Pyramid

Structure of masonry with a rectangular base and four triangular sides terminating in a point. The Great Pyramids at Giza in Egypt, built in the 3rd millennium BCE as tombs for Pharaohs, were probably connected with sun worship. The largest pyramid contains about two million three hundred thousand blocks of stone, and measures 230 m on each side, rising to a height of 146 m. The sides are perfectly orientated north, south, east and west. Smaller pyramids exist in Mexico, and these were undoubtedly connected with sun worship.

Pyramidology

Study based particularly on the Great Pyramid of Giza. Those who practise this study believe that this pyramid has unique features of measurement and symbolism, making it a revelation from the designer of the universe. By investigating these features, it is hoped to discover divine plans for a new world order.

Pythagoras

Greek philosopher and mathematician of the 6th century BCE. He believed that the soul is a divine being imprisoned in the body, and that it transmigrates on the death of one body to another. He taught a way of life disciplined by study, and interpreted the world through numbers.

Pythia

Priestess in the Holy of Holies at Delphi in Greece who pronounced oracles while in a state of trance, believed to be possession by the god of the shrine.

Pyx

Small box, usually of silver or gold, used for carrying the Blessed Sacrament from the church to the sick in hospital or in their homes after a celebration of the Eucharist.

Qadar (A)

Term used in Islam for the divine measure or determination of human events and actions, or the decree and power of God. The Qur'an (17:4) asserts that God decreed what will happen to all men, thus expressing the Muslim doctrine of predestination.

Qadi

Muslim judge in a religious lawcourt (shariah). Originally he dealt with matters of civil and criminal law, but he is now concerned only with religious matters.

Qiblah

Direction, marked by the mihrab, in which Muslims must pray, viz. facing towards the Kaaba in Mecca.

Qisseh-i Sanjan

The Tale of Sanjan. Text written by a Parsee priest *c.* 1600 describing the experiences of Zoroastrians who settled in India to escape Muslim persecution.

Qist (A)

Term for justice and fair dealing. The Qur'an (7:29, 57:25) teaches that it is the will of Allah that men should observe these practices.

Qiyas (A)

Lit. 'analogy'. Provision whereby the law of Islam may be extended to cover situations analogous to but not explicitly in the Qur'an. It is the fourth principle for determining Islamic faith and practice, the others being Qur'an, Hadith (tradition) and Ijma (agreement). Qiyas is the reasoning of the learned, from analogy with other doctrines or practices.

Quadratus

Earliest of the Christian Apologists. In 124 CE he wrote an apology for the Christian faith addressed to the Emperor Hadrian.

Quadrivium

Medieval name for the four more advanced subjects (music, arithmetic, geometry and astronomy) which together with the trivium (grammar, rhetoric and dialectic) made up the seven liberal arts.

Quakers

See Society of Friends

Qualified Non-dualism

English rendering of the term visishtadvaita introduced into Hinduism by Ramanuja in the 12th century. He felt that the non-dualism taught by Shankara did not give sufficient importance to worship and devotion, and he stressed the importance of grace in our relationship with God.

Quetzalcoatl

Mexican god, worshipped by the Aztecs, whose name means 'most precious twin'. He was identified with the morning and evening planet, being adopted by the Aztecs from the Mayas, and he became the great god of culture. (See also illustration on p. 194)

Quietism

Form of spirituality which became popular at the end of the 17th century through the writings of Mme Guyon. It taught complete passivity and the annihilation of the will in order to bring the soul into such union with God that sin is impossible. Pope Innocent condemned it in 1687.

Quinquagesima

Period of fifty days before Easter, now applied to the Sunday before Ash Wednesday.

Qumran

Wadi north-west of the Dead Sea where the ruins of an Essene monastery have been excavated, and where scrolls of the sect were discovered in caves in 1947.

Quraish

Tribe to which the Prophet Muhammad belonged.

Qur'an

Sacred book of Islam, containing one hundred and fourteen surahs, revealed to the Prophet Muhammad, beginning on the Night of Power, and written down by his followers. It is memorized, treated with the utmost respect and handled with great care.

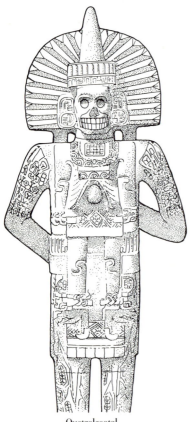

Quetzalcoatal

Page from the Qur'an (Egyptian, 14th century)

Rabb (A)

Lit. 'Lord'. Title frequently given to Allah by Muslims.

Rabbi

Lit. 'my master'. Title given to an authorized teacher after stringent training and examination in Jewish law.

Rabelais, François

(1490–1553) French writer. At various times he was a Franciscan friar, a Benedictine monk, a parish priest and a doctor, but is chiefly remembered as a writer. His books *Gargantua and Pantagruel*, about a giant and his son, deal with moral problems but in such a manner of irony and satire that many clergy tried to have them suppressed.

Rachel

Favourite wife of the Israelite patriarch Jacob. Details in the biblical story can be compared with the Nuzi Tablets, discovered in 1930, e.g. the crime of taking her father's teraphim, possession of which gave the right of inheritance (Genesis 31), and her decision to give her maid Bilhah to Jacob so that he could have sons when she herself seemed barren (Genesis 30). Later she became the mother of Joseph and Benjamin.

Radha

One of the Gopis with whom Krishna played love games at Vrindaban. She became his favourite and his escort, and the Krishna–Radha love relationship was the theme of many devotional songs, symbolizing divine–human love. The story of Radha's separation from Krishna when he left her never to return expresses mankind's unfulfilled longing for God.

Radhakrishna, S.

(1880–1970) Hindu philosopher and politician. President of India, he was a leader in many reform movements, and attempted to interpret the ancient doctrines of Hinduism in terms of the 20th century.

Radha offering Krishna curds

Raga

1. Term used in Buddhism to indicate desire, greed or concupiscence. It is one of three fires which cause dukkha (with dosa and moha); it must be extinguished or allowed to die out before nirvana can be attained.

2. Basic unit of Indian music.

Ragnarök

Fate of the gods or the twilight of the gods, foretold in Norse mythology. The prophecy said that evil would increase and morality decline, heroes would be killed and the gods be destroyed. There was a ray of hope that some gods would survive to recreate the earth and restore ancient wisdom.

Rahat Maryada

Source of instruction in Sikh ethics and religious practice, containing the disciplinary code of the Khalsa.

Rahula

Son of the Buddha. When he was fifteen he entered the Sangha and became an eminent Arahat.

Rainbow

Described in Genesis 9 as a sign of the promise made by God never again to send a flood to destroy the world. In Scandinavian mythology it is described as a sacred bridge between heaven and earth. So it has become in the West a symbol of hope, but the Karens of Burma and the Zulus of Africa fear it as a malignant spirit.

Rajas (S)

Term used in Hinduism for one of the gunas or qualities of life, usually translated 'energy', 'passion' or 'force'.

Rajayoga

Practice of yoga involving mental discipline.

Raka'at

Muslim ritual of repeating set prayers, with obligatory bodily postures, in a specified sequence. The Raka'at involves two acts of prostration in each sequence.

Rakshas

Evil spirits in Hindu mythology. They took many forms, some being grotesque, some beautiful and some enemies of God.

Ram Carit Manas

Popular Hindi version of the *Ramayana* by the 16th century poet Tulsi Das. Sometimes called the *Bible of Northern India.*

Ram Mohan Roy

(1772–1833)   Hindu reformer who was concerned not just with the revival of Hinduism, but with the renaissance of the total life of India. He founded the Brahma Samaj Sect, first known as the British India Unitarian Association.

Ram Naumi

Hindu festival celebrating the birthday of the Lord Rama, the central figure in the *Ramayana.*

Rama

Hero of the Hindu epic the *Ramayana*; he was one of the ten avatars of Vishnu.

The five prayer positions used in Raka'at

Ramadan

Ninth month of the Muslim calendar, observed as a period of fasting during which there is complete abstinence from food and drink during the hours of daylight. It commemorates the belief that it was the month when the Qur'an was 'sent down'.

Ramakrishna, Sri

(1836–1886)   Hindu mystic and reformer. He was a priest at a temple dedicated to the goddess Kali, from whom he claimed to have received personal revelations. He gained a following, and with Swami Vivekananda is regarded as having initiated a Hindu renaissance which gave a sense of universality to the Hindu message which is expressed in the Ramakrishna Mission in many parts of the world.

Ramananda

Reformer in Vaishnavite Hinduism in the 14th and 15th centuries. He studied as a Brahman, and at first taught the doctrine of Ramanuja. Later he accepted men of the Sudra class as disciples, used the Hindi language rather than Sanskrit, and replaced the cult of the erotic Radha with that of Sita, the consort of Rama.

Ramanuja

(d. 1137)   Hindu philosopher from S. India who opposed the monism of Shankara and taught a new system of philosophy known as qualified non-dualism.

Ramayana

Epic poem in Sanskrit attributed to the Hindu sage Valmiki of the 5th century BCE. It tells the story of Rama, an avatar of Vishnu, his marriage to Sita, their wanderings in the forests and her abduction by Ravana to the island of Sri Lanka. After fierce fighting, Rama rescued her and they were restored to their rule with dignity and honour. The poem has twenty-four thousand verses.

Ran

Scandinavian goddess, wife of the sea-god Aegir. She was considered dangerous as she drew sailors into her net.

Rangi

Sky god of the Maori religion. Husband of the earth goddess Papa.

Ransom

Term applied to his death by Jesus Christ (Mark 10:45). The Greek word *lutron* was the term used for the price of redeeming a slave from his master. Some of the early church fathers interpreted it as meaning that a ransom was paid by Jesus to the Devil for the release of mankind.

Raphael

One of the four archangels of Jewish tradition. He is named in the Book of Tobit as the guide of Tobias. In the Talmud, he is described as the prince of healing, who visited Abraham to heal him after his circumcision.

Ras Shamra Tablets

Clay tablets of the 14th century BCE or earlier written in an alphabetic script of a Semitic dialect with twenty-two characters. They were discovered at Ugarit (Ras Shamra) in 1929, and contain Canaanite myths, legends and cultic literature.

Rashi

Name derived from 'Rabbi Solomon-bar Isaak', a French rabbi (1040–1105) who wrote commentaries on the Pentateuch, the Prophets and the Talmud.

Rashnu

Judge or requiter of the dead in the Zoroastrian religion. In the *Gathas* this is the task of Ahura Mazda, who may be identical with him. Alternatively, Rashnu may be an older deity whose functions were taken over by Ahura Mazda.

Rasul (A)

Lit. 'messenger'. Popular title in Islam for Muhammad. The title messenger or apostle is given in the Qur'an to Noah, Lot, Ishmael, Moses and Jesus, but particularly and finally to Muhammad, who is the most important messenger of God, and is described as the Rasul of God.

Ratha Yatra

Spectacular Hindu festival celebrated at Puri and elsewhere in India in honour of Jagannath, the Lord of the Universe.

Rationalism

Philosophical doctrine which considers that reason is the sole or principal source of human knowledge, rather than perception through the senses. When applied to theology it is the doctrine which affirms the right of reason to decide all matters of faith and morals without regard to 'authority'.

Ravana

In Hindu mythology the demon king of Sri Lanka, said to have had ten heads and twenty arms. He appears in the *Ramayana* as the abductor of Sita, whom he carried off to Sri Lanka. After a long battle Rama slew him and rescued Sita.

Raven

1. First of the birds sent out from the Ark by Noah after the rains which brought the Flood had ceased. As it did not return Noah sent out a second bird, a dove.

2. First or lowest of the seven grades of Mithraic initiation; protected by Mercury.

3. Two ravens called Huginn (thought) and Muninn (memory) perched on the shoulders of Odin.

Ra'y (A)

Lit. 'opinion', or 'view'. Term used in Islam for a point of view sponsored as a means of arriving at a consensus of opinion.

Re

Important state god of ancient Egypt, the personification of the sun. His centre was at Heliopolis, but he was found in almost every sanctuary. He was symbolized by the sun's disc, by a falcon's head, or by a human form.

Rebirth

See Reincarnation and Samsara

Reconciliation

Key word in the theology of St Paul. To overcome the gulf between sinful men and a righteous God, Jesus Christ offered himself as a perfect, sinless sacrifice, which achieved the redemption of mankind from sin and effected a reconciliation with God.

Rector

Priest in charge of a parish. The difference between a rector and a vicar is that a rector has the right to receive the Great Tithe, while a vicar does not. In Scotland, a rector is an elected officer of a university.

Red

This is the colour of war and conquest, of violent destructive energy, of dominance and shame. Red is the colour of fire and blood. Fire can be destructive or comforting, and blood can be the symbol of life, or when shed, the symbol of death. Consequently the colour red symbolizes contradictory ideas, e.g. a red signal for danger, and a red cross for help and succour.

Red Sea

Northern branch of the Indian Ocean occupying a depression of the Great Rift Valley. At its northern end it divides into the Gulf of Akaba and the Gulf of Suez. Exodus describes the crossing of the Red Sea by the Israelites on their way to freedom. The place of crossing is not known, as the Hebrew 'Yam Suph' is more accurately translated 'Reed Sea'.

Redemption

In the OT God appears as the redeemer of his people, particularly in redeeming them from slavery in Egypt at the time of the Exodus. The word was a technical term for buying the release of a slave, and it is a key word in St Paul's theology, closely connected with the idea of reconciliation. It goes back to the concept of the restoration of man to the presence of God when the Messianic Kingdom is established. By his death and resurrection, Christ has made possible the redemption of the human race from the powers of darkness, and has effected a reconciliation with God.

Reform Jews

Movement which arose as an attempt to restate Judaism in the light of new Jewish learning. The pioneer was David Friedlander (1756–1834), a disciple of Moses Mendelssohn, but the first Reform 'Temple' was built by Israel Jacobson (1768–1828). The movement has promoted the critical study of the Talmud and questioned some doctrines such as the coming of a personal Messiah. In synagogues it encourages extensive use of the vernacular and choral singing, and it allows men and women to sit together.

Reformation

The Reformation in the Christian Church of the Western world is usually considered to have been started by Martin Luther in Wittenburg in 1517, when he pinned up ninety-five theses against indulgences, inviting scholarly debate. Further writings led to his excommunication, and his followers withdrew from the Roman Catholic Church to establish the Lutheran Church. The Reformation was carried further by Zwingli, Calvin and other more radical reformers.

Reformed Churches

Title given to those Churches which were specifically founded after the Reformation. It is now generally used to describe the French Protestant Church and the Calvinist Churches of Holland and Switzerland.

Refreshment Sunday

Fourth Sunday in Lent, also known as Mothering Sunday.

Regeneration

Spiritual rebirth, which according to Christian theology is effected in the soul by baptism.

Reincarnation

Belief that the soul, or some power or quality, passes after death into another body. Other terms used for this belief are rebirth, metempsychosis and transmigration. It was held by the Pythagoreans, by Plato (in the *Republic*) and by Virgil (in the *Aeneid*). Transmigration or samsara is fundamental to Hindu and Sikh belief, the next life depending on one's present karma. Buddhism rejects the concept of the individual soul, but sees a link between one embodied existence and the next in the doctrine of karma.

Relics

Remains of saints or holy persons, or objects associated with them, to which worship or veneration is offered. The practice is sanctioned in the Roman Catholic Church, but not in Protestant Churches. Relics of the Buddha are venerated in some areas of Buddhism.

Religio

Latin word which originally meant 'scrupulousness' or 'superstitious awe'; its meaning later developed into 'religious scruples' or 'conscientiousness'. A further development implied religious feeling and the worship of the gods, leading to the cult of sacred things or persons, and so to a religious system.

Renaissance

Term used for a period of history and for a movement in human culture. Some historians suggest it began about 1400, when Florentine Guilds commissioned works of art in thanksgiving for the deliverance of the city; others suggest 1453, when the Turks captured Constantinople. The Sack of Rome by Charles V in 1527 is often seen as the end of the period. Within these years printing was invented in Europe, the compass became available and the lands of the New World were discovered. Florence produced artists such as Donatello, Brunelleschi, Michelangelo and Verrocchio. The period marks the beginning of humanist scholarship, stimulated by such men as Erasmus, Colet and More, and many universities and colleges were founded for these studies.

Requiem

Mass offered for the dead. It can be for an individual or for any number of unspecified persons, as on All Souls' Day (2 November).

Reredos

Decoration erected in a Christian church above and behind the altar. It can be a silken hanging, painted wooden panels, or carvings in wood or stone.

Rerum Novarum

Encyclical issued by Pope Leo XIII in 1891 to expound Catholic teaching on work and profit, masters and servants in the new conditions which followed the Industrial Revolution.

Reservation of the Sacrament

Practice of retaining some of the bread which has been consecrated at the Christian Eucharist. It is usually placed in the aumbry contained in a pyx, to be used for the Communion of the Sick in their own homes or in hospital, or for use in cases of emergency. This practice is adopted in Roman Catholic and some Anglican churches, but not in Nonconformist churches.

Reshef

Canaanite or Phoenician god whose name probably means 'fire' or 'pestilence'. He was the Great God, the Lord of the Heavens.

Resurrection

One of the central doctrines of the Christian Church is that Christ rose from the dead on the third day after his crucifixion and appeared to his followers. St Paul describes this as 'the first fruits of them that slept' (1 Corinthians 15:20), which indicates the hope that through the resurrection of Christ, all who believe in him will likewise be raised up.

Reuben

Oldest son of the Israelite patriarch Jacob and his wife Leah. Also the tribe which dwelt on the eastern shore of the Dead Sea.

Revayet

Letters sent in the 15th and 16th centuries by the Iranians to the Zoroastrians of India to answer their inquiries concerning faith and practice.

Revelation

Term used to indicate a knowledge of God derived from what he himself reveals, as distinct from any thoughts about God arising from meditation or contemplation. It is also the title of the last book in the Bible; this offers comfort to the Churches of Asia, depicts Christ as the victor in a conflict with the forces of evil, and ends with a vision of the City of God.

Revised Version

Translation of the Bible begun by the authority of the Convocation of Canterbury in 1870. Two companies of scholars were appointed to bring the language of the Bible more in line with the usages of the 19th century, taking advantage of manuscript discoveries made since the Authorized Version had been translated. The Revised Version of the NT was published in 1881 and that of the OT in 1885.

Rhea

Ancient Greek goddess, the daughter of Uranus and Ge, and the wife of Cronos. As Cronos had devoured several of her children at birth, when Zeus was born she gave Cronos a stone wrapped like a baby, and so opened the way for Zeus to become all powerful. In Asia Minor Rhea was identified with the Great Mother, and was also known as Cybele, who was worshipped with orgiastic rites.

Richard, Mira

(1878–1973) Spiritual collaborator of Sri Aurobindo, whom she joined in 1920. From 1926 until her death, she was known as the 'mother of the Sri Aurobindo ashram', and in 1968 she founded the city of Auroville.

Ridvan

Most important festival in the Baha'i calendar. It lasts from 21 April to 2 May, and celebrates the period in 1863 during which Baha'u'llah declared his mission. Also called the Anniversary of the Declaration of Baha'u'llah.

Rig-Veda

Lit. 'verse knowledge' or 'word knowledge'. These are the most sacred and ancient scriptures of Hinduism. They contain more than one thousand hymns in praise of various gods, and were probably composed between 1500 and 1000 BCE.

Rinzai

One of the larger sects of Zen Buddhism, which has over six thousand temples in Japan. It was founded by Rinzai Gigen (d. 867 CE), who experienced a sudden enlightenment through the advice of the Zen master Daigu.

Rishis

Poets or singers of hymns. These were the sages who received the *Vedas* from the gods.

Rites de Passage

Rituals observed at important points of human experience. Those most commonly observed are baptism soon after birth, initiation or confirmation at the approach of puberty or adulthood, marriage in order to start a family, and burial or cremation after death, in order to dispose of the body in a manner acceptable to the particular society.

Ritual

Form of words and actions prescribed for a religious ceremony or other solemn occasion.

Rochet
Long white linen vestment with tight sleeves bound at the wrists, worn by bishops.

Rogation Days
Days marked in the calendar of the Christian Church when prayers are said for all who work on the land, and for good weather to bring in the harvest.

Roman Catholic Church
Community of Christians throughout the world which offers its allegiance to the Pope as the successor of St Peter, as the Bishop of Rome, as Vicar of Christ, and as the guardian of the faith.

Romans, Epistle to the
One of the most important of St Paul's epistles in the NT. Its main theme is the righteousness of God, and its application to the justification of men. It is the most theological of St Paul's writings, and was the main source of Luther's doctrinal teaching which led to the Reformation.

Rome
Capital of one of the empires of the ancient world and also of modern Italy, and the city which contains the Vatican, the centre of the Roman Catholic Church. The traditional date of its founding by Romulus is 753 BCE, after which it had seven kings. In 509 BCE it became a republic, and in 340 BCE began to expand its power throughout the Italian peninsula. By 200 BCE Rome was master of N. Africa, but the Republic came to an end in 81 BCE with the appointment of Sulla as Dictator. Roman armies marched victoriously through Europe, and in 31 BCE Octavian received the title Emperor Augustus and inaugurated the Empire, which lasted until 410 CE, when it was overthrown by Alaric. Modern Rome became the capital of a united Italy in 1871, and by the Lateran Treaty of 1929 the Vatican City became an independent state.

Romulus and Remus
Twin sons of Numitor the Vestal and the god Mars, they were suckled by a she-wolf and then brought up by a herdsman. When they grew to manhood, they quarrelled and fought. Remus was killed, and Romulus became the founder of the city of Rome.

Rongo
God of agriculture and peace important in the religion of the Maoris of New Zealand.

Rood-screen
Screen separating the nave from the chancel in a Christian church. It is usually surmounted by a crucifix with the figures of St John on one side and the Virgin Mary on the other. Many rood-screens were destroyed during the Reformation.

Rood-screen (Willand, Devon)

Rosary

Roman Catholic devotion to the fifteen mysteries of Christ, recited with the aid of a string of one hundred and sixty-five beads. The recitation consists of fifteen decades, each having an Ave Maria, preceded by a Pater Noster and followed by a Gloria. The fifteen decades are grouped into three chaplets for the contemplation of the joyful, the sorrowful and the glorious mysteries. To assist the memory, the prayers are counted on the beads, which consist of fifteen sets of beads for each decade with a large bead between them.

Rose

Many legends and symbolisms have been associated with the rose. In Rome it was sacred to Venus, so it is the flower symbol of love. In Christian iconography the wild rose, with five petals, represents the five wounds of Christ, and the red rose symbolizes the blood of Christ and the Christian martyrs. In the Middle Ages, Popes presented a golden rose to sovereigns and other distinguished persons for service to the Church.

Rosemary

Plant associated in folklore with protection against evil spirits; it is a symbol of remembrance, and at one time it was carried by mourners and dropped on the coffin in the grave, in order to show that the dead person would not be forgotten.

Rosetta Stone

Basalt stele discovered in Egypt in 1799. It has an inscription, written about 200 BCE, in three scripts: Greek, Egyptian hieroglyphics and Egyptian demotic. Comparison of the texts provided clues to the interpretation of Egyptian hieroglyphic inscriptions.

Rosh Hashanah

Jewish New Year, recalling God's act of creating the world, celebrated on 1 Tishri. The shofar is blown in synagogues to commemorate Abraham's fidelity in being prepared to sacrifice his son. It inaugurates ten days of penitence, culminating in the Day of Atonement.

Roshi

Title given to a Zen monk or student when his course of study has been completed to the satisfaction of his master. This makes him a master and entitles him to teach Zen.

Rosicrucians

Name given to or claimed by a number of secret societies. The emblems of the rose and the cross are regarded as symbols of resurrection and redemption, and in the 17th century the society was devoted to the study of an esoteric kind of Christianity. The 20th century revival, the Ancient Mystical Order Rosae Crucis, which is based in California, claims to be devoted to man's personal development through the use of his natural powers of mind and the simple laws of the universe. It has kept free of religious sectarianism and affiliation and is non-political.

Rsis

Ancient Hindu seers who received the revelations contained in the *Vedas.*

Rta

Vedic concept of cosmic law by which all things are maintained in existence.

Rual

Term used by the Nuer tribe for incest; it is also used to illustrate their concept of sin.

Ruba'iyat

Persian word meaning 'quatrains'. They are stanzas with four lines in which the first, second and third rhyme, and they are often used for religious or philosophical verse.

Rosetta Stone

Rubrics

Ritual or ceremonial instructions printed in Christian service books. The word indicates that these instructions were originally printed in red, to distinguish them from the text of the service.

Rudra

Storm god of ancient Hinduism. The name means 'howler', and he was associated with the storm god Indra and the fire god Agni.

Ruler Worship

Practice of treating the ruler as a god, entitled to full cultic ceremonies. This was found in ancient Egyptian society, and was adopted by Alexander the Great. The more constructive Roman Emperors discouraged the practice of worshipping the Emperor during his lifetime, but most of them were deified after death. Until this century, the Emperor of Japan was regarded as divine, but this ceased after the Second World War.

Rumi, Jalal al-Din

(1207–1273)   Greatest of the Persian Sufi mystics. He is said to have been the founder of the Dancing or Whirling Dervishes. His principal work was the *Mathnawi*, a poem in six books.

Runes

Letters of the alphabets of ancient Teutonic peoples, formed of straight lines in various combinations and at various angles. Three systems have been identified, Norse, Anglo-Saxon and German, and many runic inscriptions have been found in Scandinavia and Iceland. These date from 300–400 CE, and it is thought that they may have some connection with magic rites.

Runic characters (part of the inscription on the Bjorkertorpstone, Sweden)

Rupa

Term used in Buddhism for bodily form; it is one of the five elements that make up the nature of dwellers on the lowest plane of this worldly existence.

Rupa-dhatu

Term used in Buddhism for the domain of spiritual beings.

Rural Dean

Title used in the Church of England for a priest who has been appointed by the bishop to help him in an area of an archdeaconry. His duties are purely administrative, and he presides over the ruridecanal chapter and synod.

Ruth

Central character in a book of the same name in the Hebrew Bible. She was a Moabitess, married to a Jew who died leaving her childless. She loyally remained with her mother-in-law, Naomi, and when she remarried it was to another Jew, Boaz. By him she had a son Obed, who was the grandfather of King David.

Ruysbroeck, Jan van

(1293–1381)   Flemish priest and mystic. He retired to Groenendaal, wrote several books on the spiritual life and attracted a community of many followers. This developed into the school known as Devotio Moderna, which in turn gave rise to the Brethren of the Common Life, of which Thomas à Kempis was a member.

Sabad

In Sikh thought a term meaning 'word', a form of divine self-expression.

Sabad Hazare

Section of the Sikh book the *Dasam Granth* which expresses the militant piety which was characteristic of the tenth Guru, Gobind Singh, who compiled it.

Sabazius

Phrygian or Lydian god identified by the Greeks with Dionysus. He seems to have been a nature deity, and his symbol was the snake. Later, he was identified with the Lord Sabaoth of the Bible.

Sabbath

The seventh day, a Jewish day of rest. Two reasons are given in the Bible for the sanctity of the Sabbath.

1. It was the day when the Lord rested after the six days of creation (Exodus 20:11).

2. It is a weekly remembrance of Israel's deliverance from slavery in Egypt, by means of the Exodus (Deuteronomy 5:15). The Sabbath lasts from sunset on Friday to sunset on Saturday.

Sabellianism

Christian doctrine taught by Sabellius in the 3rd century but denounced as a heresy. It was also termed 'Modal Monarchianism'; it endeavoured to safeguard Christian monotheism, but was condemned because it failed to recognize the independent subsistence of the Son, regarding him as a mode of the Godhead.

Saboraim (H)

Title given to Jewish religious teachers from the 6th century. The word is derived from a verb meaning 'to reflect', and is used because these men reflected on and expounded the teachings of the Amoraim.

Sabr (A)

Muslim concept of patience and fortitude under adversity; a staying power which is the fruit of firm reliance on God.

Sacca (P)/**Satya** (S)

Term used in Buddhism to indicate truth in general, or a particular truth, such as the Four Noble Truths which form the core of the Buddha's teaching.

Sach

In Sikh thought a term meaning 'truth', one of the six concepts for divine self-expression.

Sach Khand

In the teaching of the Sikh Guru Nanak, the last of the five stages or steps towards man's liberation. This is the culmination, when the individual achieves truth, when he sees what God sees, and enjoys the whole of creation.

Sacrament

Outward, visible sign of an inward, spiritual blessing obtained through the rites of the Christian Church. The Roman Catholic Church accepts seven sacraments: baptism, confirmation, matrimony, orders, the Eucharist, penance and extreme unction. The Anglican and Reformed Churches accept only two: baptism and the Eucharist.

204

Sacred Cherubim and Seraphim Society
Aladura group formed in Nigeria in 1925 by Moses Tunolashe in response to a series of visions. He stressed ecstatic prayer, open-air evangelism and processions.

Sacred Heart of Jesus
Popular devotion in the Roman Catholic Church since the 18th century which seems to go back to the treatise *Vitis mystica* by St Bernard. The devotion was advocated in the 16th century by the Jesuits and by Francis de Sales but its liturgical observance was not permitted until 1765, when it was authorized by Pope Clement XIII, and fixed on the Friday after the Octave of Corpus Christi.

Sacred Marriage
Demonstration of creative unity between the great male and female deities, or between one of them and a consort, or between heaven and earth, sometimes represented by a symbolic act between priest or king and priestess. This often took place at the spring or New Year festival, to encourage the growth of crops, and it was very widespread in pre-Christian times in the Middle East.

Sacred Thread
Hindu and Parsee symbol of initiation which hangs from the left shoulder to the right hip. It is presented at a ceremony in which a Hindu boy becomes a full member of one of the three main classes, and is then 'twice born', or at the Parsee ceremony of Naojot.

Sacrifice
In religious terms, sacrifice is the offering to God of oneself or of something valuable or precious, in order to express a joyful thanksgiving, or to seek a blessing or a favour. As man's most precious possession is life, in many communities and periods of history sacrifice has been associated with the killing of an animal or a human being to give back life, represented by the blood, to the deity. Sometimes an animal was entirely burned as a total offering; sometimes parts were returned to the worshipper for eating, to symbolize a meal shared with God. Other gifts, e.g. wine, fruit, or cereals, were also used.

Sacrilege
Contemptuous or blasphemous treatment of a person, such as a priest, or an object, such as the sacramental elements, or a place, such as a church, dedicated to the service or worship of God.

Sacristy
Room attached to a church or chapel where the sacred vessels for the Eucharist are stored and the clergy put on their vestments. Such rooms were first mentioned *c.* 400 CE. Today the term is used only in connection with cathedrals or large churches which have a sacristy for the preparation of the vessels and a vestry for clergy.

Sadaqat (A)
Term used in Islam for voluntary alms, or for works of charitable intent, which show that one's faith is loyal.

Parsee boy being presented with the sacred thread at the ceremony of Naojot (Bombay)

Saddha

Term used in Buddhism to indicate 'confidence' or 'faith', though this does not imply faith or belief in certain truths or propositions simply because the Buddha expounded them. The essential object of this attitude is found in the Three Jewels.

Saddharmapundarika Sutra

Lit. 'lotus of the true law sutra'. This is a very popular text in Mahayana Buddhism. It was written in Sanskrit in the early years of the Christian era, and it claims to be the teaching of the Buddha, who is depicted in its pages as exalted on a mountain peak in Bihar.

Sadducees

Influential priestly group in Judaism in the time of Jesus. Their origins are obscure, but the title suggests descent from Zadok, the High Priest of King David. They were Jewish priests of conservative outlook, and they became most prominent in the 1st centuries BCE and CE. They acknowledged only the written law, rejected oral tradition, and denied resurrection and the afterlife. They ceased to exist after the destruction of Jerusalem and the cessation of temple worship in 70 CE.

Sadhana (S)

Lit. 'fulfilment' or 'worship'. In Hinduism this is a term used for a course of discipline or spiritual training which is designed to lead to fulfilment or realization of life. In Buddhism it is used for a course of Tantric training of the faculties.

Sadhu (S)

Term widely used in Hinduism and other Indian religions to designate a holy man.

Sa'diya (A)

Order of Dervishes, named after their founder Sa'd al Din in the late 7th century.

Sadjdjada (A)

Carpet or prayer-mat used by a Muslim when he recites the daily prayers and performs the actions of kneeling and prostration necessary for the fulfilment of the obligations of salat.

Safa

Low mound at Mecca. In the ritual of the Hajj, the pilgrims run backwards and forwards between Safa and Marwa seven times, as Hagar ran looking for water.

Saga

1. Norse word for prose narratives which were written in Iceland in the 11th and 12th centuries, and developed alongside the *Eddas*, or poetic narratives. They contain myths and stories of gods and ancient heroes.
2. Scandinavian goddess, one of the Asyngur. She has been identified with Frigg.

Sagunam Brahman (S)

Term found in the Hindu *Upanishads* for the Divine with qualities (gunas) or attributes, e.g. creator. The term arose because of the difficulty experienced by most people in understanding Brahman without qualities or attributes, and it was an element in the teaching of Shankara.

Sahaj (Pn)/**Sahaja** (S)

Term used by Sikhs to express a state of oneness with God, such as is expressed in other religions by words such as 'samadhi', 'bliss' or 'ultimate union'.

Sahaj Dharis

Members of the Sikh community who have not been through the initiation ceremony, and so do not belong to the Khalsa.

Sai Baba

(b. 1926)   Indian guru who has established an Ashram at Puttaparthi, S. India. This has become a pilgrimage centre for his many followers throughout India. Many are attracted by the claim that he has the power to perform miracles of healing and materialization. He emphasizes the importance of the Hindu scriptures and the ascetic life, and at gatherings of devotees on Thursdays, his sacred day, there is much praying and singing.

Saicho

(b. 767 CE)   Buddhist monk who introduced the Tendai school of Buddhism into Japan from China. He was ordained into the order of monks at the age of eighteen, and for many years lived a life of solitude and contemplation. He was regarded as a philosopher and a saint.

Saijojo Zen

Fifth and highest type of Zen. This is the last stage in the practice of zazen, in which there is a complete absence of striving.

Saint

Person of oustanding devotion to God and the religious life. In Christianity, the title indicates a person whose devotion to Jesus Christ, often bringing martyrdom, has been recognized by the Church, either through tradition or by the formal process of canonization.

Sakha (S)

Lit. 'branch' or 'limb'. A branch of the school of the *Vedas*. Originally there were said to be five, each with its own text and interpretations.

Sakinah (A)

Term used in Islam to indicate a token of the Divine Presence, or the peace it brings (Qur'an 48:4, 62:9). It corresponds to shechinah in the Hebrew Bible.

Sakka

Deity mentioned in very early Buddhist texts. He was said to be a more humane version of Indra.

Salaam (A)

Word meaning 'peace' used as a salutation by Muslims on meeting or parting. It is similar to the Jewish salutation 'Shalom', which also means 'peace'.

Salat (A)

Term used in Islam for ritual or liturgical prayer. This is the second Pillar of Din, and it is observed by Muslims five times a day.

Salii

From the Latin verb *salire* (to leap). Title of minor priests of Mars, derived from the dances they performed while singing and beating shields.

Salik (A)

Term used by Sufis for the second stage of discipleship, which is that of a journeyer.

Salman

Trusted companion and adviser of Muhammad who supported the claims of Ali to be the Caliph after the death of the Prophet.

Salt

Because salt is an essential item of man's diet, and is necessary for the preservation of food, it is a symbol of eternity and incorruptibility. Conversely, as it is sterile, it is also a symbol of barrenness.

Salvation

Religious term for the saving of the soul of man by deliverance from sin and admission to a state of blessedness, for which there are many different terms used in the religions of the world, e.g. heaven, eternal life, paradise, nirvana.

Salvation Army

Protestant organization founded by William and Catherine Booth in 1880. It is strongly evangelical, conducting open-air services accompanied by military-style bands. It also emphasizes social work as an important aspect of the Gospel, and has established workshops, homes and shelters to help those in need.

Salve Regina

One of the earliest salutations addressed to the Blessed Virgin Mary, the earliest MS version coming from the 11th century. In 1884 Pope Leo XIII ordered it to be said after Low Mass. It is in the Breviary from Trinity Sunday until Advent.

Samadaya

Term used in Buddhism meaning 'desire'. According to the teaching of the Buddha, this is the origin of suffering, as he stated in the Second Noble Truth.

Salvation Army officer working with vagrants in Glasgow

Samadhi

Term used in Buddhism for intense concentration in meditation. This is the last anga, or limb, in the Buddhist Eightfold Path.

Samaritan

After the overthrow of Samaria in 722 BCE, the Assyrians transported the leading citizens of Israel into captivity and imported into Samaria captives from other parts of their empire. Between these inhabitants of Samaria and the Jews there developed intense enmity. The Samaritans built their own temple on Mt Gerizim *c.* 200 BCE, but it was destroyed in 128 BCE. A small community still exists, believing in one God and only one prophet, Moses, and accepting only the Pentateuch as their scriptures. They follow most of the Jewish religious festivals, particularly the Passover.

Samatha

Term used in Buddhism for tranquillity of mind, in the negative sense of withdrawal from thought or activity.

Sama-veda

One of the four collections of Vedic hymns used in the Hindu religion.

Sambhoga-kaya

Term used in Buddhism for one of the Three Bodies of the Buddha. This is the transcendental, or blissful body of the Buddha, a divine being to whom prayer is addressed.

Sambodhi

Term used in Buddhism for the insight, wisdom and assimilation of truth, essential to the attainment of the three higher stages of arhatship.

Samhain

Ancient Celtic festival held from 30 October to 7 November which marked the onset of winter and during which bonfires were lit to strengthen the waning sun. The corresponding spring festival was called Beltane. The practice of lighting bonfires and fireworks on 5 November, although now linked with the Gunpowder Plot, is probably a survival of Samhain.

Samjna (S)

See Sanna

Samma (P)**/Samyak** (S)

Term used in Buddhism for that which is just, true or exact, the supreme. It is applied to the Eightfold Path, to the Buddha and to supreme enlightenment. This is the highest state possible for any individual to attain.

Samsara

Term used in Buddhism and Hinduism for the state of transmigration, continual movement, coming again and again to rebirth, or the cycles of existence.

Samskaras

Term used in Hinduism for sacramental life-cycle rites, or *rites de passage*. The most important is the investiture with the sacred thread.

Samson

One of the six Judges in Israel whose achievements are recorded in the Book of Judges. He is different from the other Judges in that he is more like a folk-hero. His exploits gave respite to the Israelites from Philistine domination, but cost him his life. He was bound by a Nazarite vow not to cut his hair, which was the secret of his strength, but revealed this to Delilah, who cut his hair while he slept. On waking, he had lost his strength and was captured by the Philistines. Some scholars have connected him with sun worship because of the link between his name and the Hebrew word for sun (*shemesh*).

Samuel

1. Last, and greatest, of the Israelite Judges. He anointed Saul, and later David, as kings of Israel.
2. Title of two historical books in the Hebrew Bible. They continue the narrative from the end of Judges to the last years of the reign of King David.

Samurai

Japanese warrior class trained in the spirit of Bushido.

Samyak (S)

See Samma

Samyutta Nikaya (P)

Collection of short sayings, part of the *Sutta Pitaka*, the second main division of the Theravada Buddhist canon of scripture.

Sanatana Dharma (S)

Eternal right or truth. Term used in the *Bhagavadgita* for the eternal laws relating to the family. Some Hindus use it as a general term for their religion.

Sanctification

In the Hebrew Bible this word has the meanings 'purity' and 'separateness'. The Israelites were called upon to sanctify the Lord of Hosts (Isaiah 8:13), to recognize his sovereign claims, and to sanctify themselves: 'You shall be holy, and you shall sanctify yourselves, for I am holy' (Leviticus 11:44). In Christian theology it is a term for the purification and dedication of life through the grace of God. Being made holy would be regarded by some Christians as the goal of the religious life, and St Paul described Christians as those who are called to be saints. In Catholic theology sanctification comes through the sanctifying grace imparted by the Sacraments. Protestant theology tends to stress the importance of faith alone as the means of releasing God's gifts of sanctifying grace.

Sanctuary

1. Section of a church containing the altar. In Byzantine churches this is enclosed by the iconostasis.
2. Right of protection granted to certain categories of criminal in specified places or buildings. Numbers 35 names six cities of refuge for involuntary manslayers. In the Middle Ages a criminal who took refuge in a church was guaranteed safety if he showed repentance and agreed to be exiled.

Sanctus

Hymn of praise and adoration beginning with the words 'Holy, Holy, Holy' which is sung or recited after the Preface in the Christian Eucharist.

Sangat

Term used in the Sikh religion to denote the whole community assembled for worship.

Sangha

Assembly. In Hinduism, of sages. In Jainism, of a fraternity. In Buddhism, of monks: this was an institution founded by the Buddha, and is probably the oldest monastic institution. A daily Buddhist recitation is 'I go to the Sangha for refuge'.

Sangita Sutta

Collection of long discourses, intended to be chanted by monks and disciples learning the Buddhist Way.

Sanhedrin

Highest Jewish tribunal, with seventy-one members, which met in Jerusalem. The term is traditionally derived from the seventy elders who assisted Moses, and it probably dates from the Persian period. Julius Caesar gave the Sanhedrin authority over all Judaea. Its functions ceased about 425 CE.

Sankhara (P)

In Buddhist thought a term for volitional or habitual mental tendencies or phenomena: one of the five aggregates which make up the nature of dwellers on the lowest plane of this worldly existence.

Sankhya

One of the six orthodox schools of Hindu philosophy, said to have been founded in the 7th century BCE. It is based on dualistic metaphysics, and is essentially atheistic.

Sanna (P)/**Samjna** (S)

In Buddhist thought a term for perception or determination, one of the five aggregates which make up the nature of dwellers on the lowest plane of this worldly existence.

Sannyasin

According to classical Hinduism, one who has renounced worldly affairs and has moved on to the last of four stages of life. In popular usage the term is applied to any religious ascetic.

Sanskrit

Ancient language of Aryan India used for the Brahmanic and for some Buddhist scriptures.

Sant Tradition

School of Hindu thought and devotion influential in N. India in the 15th century. It is commonly regarded as part of the tradition of Vaishnava bhakti, and one of its leading poet-theologians was Kabir, whose writings influenced Guru Nanak. The Sant tradition of nirguna sampradaya believes that God is without form or incarnation.

Santa Claus

Corruption of the Dutch form of the name of St Nicholas, Bishop of Myra. As he is the patron saint of children, Santa Claus has become the person through whom presents are given to children. In Holland and parts of Germany, presents are given on St Nicholas' Day (6 December), but elsewhere on Christmas Day.

San-Zen

Interview between a Zen master and one of his pupils which includes the use of koans and mondos.

Saoshyant

Lit. 'he who brings benefit'. According to Zoroastrian teaching this is the name of the saviour who will appear at the end of time, when all the forces of evil will be overcome.

Saram Khand

In the teaching of the Sikh Guru Nanak, the third of the five stages or steps towards man's liberation. This is the stage of spiritual endeavour.

Sarana

1. Term used in Buddhism for refuge, or entry into the Sangha. The Buddhist formula 'I take refuge in the Sangha' presupposes a novitiate, and an acceptance by the community.
2. In Hinduism this is a description of Krishna, as a refuge for his followers, used in the *Bhagavad-gita*.

Sarapis/Serapis

Egyptian deity introduced in the time of Ptolemy I (323–285 BCE). He was especially worshipped as the god of healing. The name is a blend of 'Osiris', the consort of Isis, and 'Apis', the sacred bull. Ptolemy built a magnificent temple in Alexandria to house a colossal statue of the god.

Sarasvati

Originally an Indian river goddess, she was later regarded as the wife of the creator-god Brahma, and the inventor of the Sanskrit language.

Sarasvati Puja

Hindu festival at the beginning of the year in honour of Sarasvati, the wife of the creator-god, Brahma.

Sarcophagus

Greek word, lit. 'flesh eating', used to describe a chest or coffin, usually made of wood or stone, for the entombment of a corpse. The oldest known examples come from Egypt, but the Romans also used this form of coffin for special persons.

Sarum Rite

Modification of the Roman Catholic liturgy used in Salisbury Cathedral. It is said to have been drawn up in the 11th century by St Osmund, and in 1543 was imposed on the whole Province of Canterbury. It was used by Cranmer as the basis of the first *Book of Common Prayer* in 1549.

Sarvastivadins

One of the schools of early Buddhism; it is a sect which broke away from the Theravadins.

Sarvodaya

Lit. 'universal uplift'. Title of a 20th century Hindu movement initiated by Vinoba Bhave to raise the cultural, moral and economic standards of Indian peasants.

Sasana

Term used in Buddhism for doctrine. It is the Dhamma as taught by the Buddha.

Saster Nam-Mala

Section of the Sikh book *Dasam Granth* which contains an 'inventory of weapons' and expresses the militant piety of Guru Gobind Singh, who compiled it.

Sastra

Buddhist treatise written either in the form of a commentary on a sutra, or in the form of a systematic theological textbook.

Sat

Term used in Hinduism for being or existence, and hence the good or the true. It is one of the three attributes of the divine principle, Brahman, together with ananda and cit.

Satan

The Hebrew word means 'accuser', and that is his role in Job. In the NT Satan has become the leader of evil spirits who oppose God, and the name today is commonly used to refer to the chief of the devils or fallen angels.

Satchitananda

Hindu formula in the *Upanishads* concerning the Divine. It is a combination of the three words 'sat', 'cit' and 'ananda', which mean 'being', 'consciousness' and 'bliss'. It was used by the 20th century Hindu philosopher-reformer Sri Aurobindo for Brahman or the Absolute.

Satguru

Word used in the Sikh religion that is almost a synonym for God.

Sati/Suttee

Lit. 'good woman'. Term originally used in Hinduism to describe a widow who threw herself on to her husband's funeral pyre; later it meant the custom itself. The practice was banned in the British states of India in 1829.

Sati (P)

See Smriti

Satisfaction

In Christian theology, this term is linked with the doctrine promulgated by Anselm of Canterbury (d. 1109) that the death of Christ offered to God the amends or apology or satisfaction due for the offence by which man's sin had affronted his divine majesty.

Satkaryavada

Hindu theory concerning causation, held by the Sankhya school of philosophy, that the effect is identical with the cause, or that the effect is contained within the cause.

Satori

Japanese term for enlightenment, the goal of Zen Buddhism.

Satsang

Hindu religious gathering at which hymns (bhajans) are sung.

Sattva

1. One of the Hindu gunas, or qualities, translated 'brightness' or 'goodness'.
2. In Buddhist thought this means 'being', i.e. living beings who exist at various levels of this world and also in subterrestrial or heavenly regions.

Saturday

Seventh day of the week, the name of which is derived from that of the Roman god Saturn. In the Jewish faith this is the Sabbath, the holy day sanctified by the Lord, on which no work must be done. It is remembered in some Christian liturgies as the day on which the body of Jesus lay in the tomb after the Crucifixion.

Saturn

Mythical king of Italy whom the Romans identified with the god Cronos. He was reputed to have introduced civilization and social order, and to have taught his people agriculture.

Saturnalia

Roman festival in honour of the god Saturn, beginning on 17 December and lasting seven days. The middle day, 21 December, is the shortest day of the year, and this festival was associated with the promise of the sun's return. It was a festival of unrestrained jollity and mirth when lawcourts were closed and slaves were given temporary freedom and waited on by their masters.

Satya (S)

See Sacca

Satyagraha

Term used by Mahatma Gandhi for non-violent action based on the force of truth. It expresses the positive side of his political policy of non-cooperation with the British.

Satyr

In Greek mythology, an attendant at the worship of Dionysus who dwelt in the forests and had a great appetite for wine and all forms of sensual pleasure.

Saum

Term used in Islam for the practice of fasting, particularly during the month of Ramadan. It is the fourth Pillar of Din.

Sautrantikas

Buddhist monks who took their stand on the suttas alone, accepting the Buddha expounded in them, but rejecting the aid of Abhidhamma analysis.

Savaiyye

Lit. 'panegyrics'. Section of the Sikh book *Dasam Granth* which is linked with the *Inventory of Weapons.* Together they express the militant piety of the tenth Guru, Gobind Singh, who compiled the book.

Savonarola, Girolamo

(1452–1498)   Dominican monk who led a reform movement in Florence. His fiery sermons in the Cathedral attracted a large following, but led to conflict with Pope Alexander VI. Many Florentines burned works of art and luxuries in response to his call for greater austerity and stricter moral standards. When the Pope threatened to put Florence under an interdict, the people turned against Savonarola and he was hanged and his body burned.

Scala Sancta

Staircase of twenty-eight marble steps near the Church of St John Lateran, Rome. They are a place of pilgrimage, and many pilgrims make the ascent on their knees to the Sancta Sanctorum Chapel at the top.

Scapegoat

Term used in the Hebrew Bible (Leviticus 16) for one of the goats brought to the Temple on the Day of Atonement. One was sacrificed, and the other, the scapegoat, was driven into the wilderness, carrying the sins of the people to the evil spirit, Azazel.

Scapular

Garment worn in Christian monasteries. It consists of a short narrow cloak worn over the shoulders and hanging down back and front. It is understood to symbolize the yoke of Christ (Matthew 11:29).

Scarab

Sacred beetle of Egypt which was regarded with great veneration; numerous scarab-shaped amulets have been found there, dating back to the 3rd millennium BCE. There appear to be two reasons for its sanctity: the Egyptian name for the scarab is very similar to one of the names of the sun-god, viz. Khepri, derived from the verb 'to be', and meaning 'self-existent'. This is linked to the second reason, which is that it was believed that the scarab beetle existed only in the male sex, and that it rolled a ball of dung into a hole, impregnated it with sperm and stayed with the ball for a month until young scarabs emerged.

Savonarola (Ferrara)

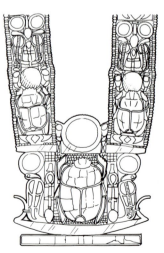

Scarab in the Necklace of the Sun on the Eastern Horizon (from the tomb of Tutankhamun)

Scepticism

Term applied to a system of philosophy which stresses doubt, or disbelieves the possibility of knowledge. The Sophists, e.g. Gorgias and Protagoras, were inclined to scepticism, and among modern philosophers, Hume is considered a sceptic.

Schism

State of separation breaking the unity of the Christian Church. It is not the same as a doctrinal break, which is called heresy. It is difficult to decide the borders of schism, e.g. some Roman Catholics consider that the Orthodox and Anglican Churches have broken the unity of the Church and are thus in schism. The Orthodox and Anglican Churches consider that, although they are separate branches, they have not broken the unity of the Church.

Schmalkaldic Articles

Doctrinal statement drawn up in 1537 by Martin Luther for presentation to a General Council called by Pope Paul III. It consisted of three sections: (1) the doctrines of the Creeds; (2) the office and work of Christ; (3) matters on which Protestants were divided.

Schmalkaldic League

Alliance between groups of Protestant princes in Germany formed in February 1531 as a defence against the Emperor Charles V.

Scholasticism

System of education and philosophy practised in the medieval schools. The main aim was to co-ordinate the doctrines of the Church in a scientific system. Its teachers started from the authority of the Scriptures and the Creeds, and accepted a statement of St Anselm: 'I believe that I may understand.'

Schweitzer, Albert

(1875–1965)   German theologian, physician and organist. In 1899 he became Pastor of Strasbourg and soon after wrote two books, *The Mystery of the Kingdom of God* (1901) and *The Quest of the Historical Jesus* (1906). In both he maintained that Jesus expected the imminent end of the world and concluded that he must suffer to save men from the tribulations of the last days. In 1913 Schweitzer gained a medical degree and devoted the rest of his life to organizing a mission hospital at Lambarene. He used his skill as an interpreter of Bach's organ music to raise money for his hospital by giving organ recitals. In 1954 he was awarded the Nobel Peace Prize.

Scientology

System of psychotherapy and philosophy founded by an American, Ron Hubbard, regarded by his followers as a modern Messiah. In 1950 he published a book *Dianetics: The Modern Science of Mental Health*, which is the basic text of scientology. In 1955 he founded the Church of Scientology, with emphasis on 'religious philosophy containing pastoral counselling procedures intended to assist an individual to attain spiritual freedom'.

Scribes

In biblical times these men were experts in the study of the Law of Moses, and the originators of the synagogue service. Their functions were to preserve the Law, to instruct pupils in the Law, and to administer the Law. Most of them were Pharisees, and they clashed with Christ because he claimed a higher authority than theirs, and condemned their formalism (Matthew 7:28).

Scripture

Sacred book or books of a religious community. The Hebrew Bible is the scripture of the Jews, and this plus the NT is the scripture of Christianity. The scripture of the Muslims is the Qur'an, and that of the Sikhs, the *Guru Granth Sahib*.

Sebek

Water god of ancient Egyptian religion, symbolized by a crocodile. He was regarded as the personification of evil powers and death.

Second Coming

The return of Jesus Christ to this earth, or the second coming, was predicted in St Paul's epistles and has been accepted by the Church as a doctrine, though not the most important item in any creed. The belief has been emphasized in different periods and by different sects, e.g. *c.* 1000 and again at the time of the Crusades, by the Hussites in the 15th century, the Anabaptists in the 16th century, and by the Seventh Day Adventists in the 20th century.

Sect

Group of people within a religion who hold minority views, often having seceded from the larger body. A religious denomination having a distinctive common worship and belief, but not part of the established or orthodox community.

Secular Arm

Term used in Roman Catholic canon law to describe the state, or a lay power intervening in ecclesiastical cases. In the Middle Ages the Church condemned many people as heretics, but did not feel able to impose the death penalty. Such persons were therefore handed over to the secular arm for execution.

Secular Clergy

Term first used in the 12th century to distinguish parish clergy living in the world from regular clergy living according to a rule in a monastery.

Secularization

Process marked by a decline in the influence of religion and religious institutions on human thought and affairs.

Seder (H)

Lit. 'order'. Ritual followed at the Jewish Passover meal. (See also Passover)

Sedia Gestatoria

Portable throne on which the Pope is carried in procession, by twelve bearers, on solemn occasions.

Sedilia

Three seats on the south side of the chancel of a Christian Church arranged for the celebrant, deacon and subdeacon at the Eucharist.

Sedna

Sea goddess of the Eskimos. The shaman journeys in spirit to the depths of the sea to placate her in order to ensure a good supply of sea animals.

Seer

Prophet, or person who claims to have visions or some other means of predicting the future. (See also Nabi and Prophet)

Sefer Torah (H)

Scroll of the Torah kept in the ark of a Jewish synagogue, and taken in procession to the reading-desk. It contains the Pentateuch, written by hand in Hebrew on specially treated vellum sheets sewn together with threads made from the tendons of clean animals.

Sefiroth (H)

Name given in Jewish mysticism (Kabbalah) to the ten attributes of God which link the celestial to the terrestrial world.

Sekhmet

Powerful, fiery goddess of ancient Egypt, representing the destructive heat of the sun. She was the wife of Ptah, and is depicted as a woman with the head of a lioness.

Sekiten

Confucian festival observed in the Holy Temple at Yashima, Japan. It dates from the 7th century and expresses Japanese appreciation of the teachings of Confucius.

Selah (H)

Word of uncertain etymology and meaning found seventy-one times in the Psalms. It has been interpreted as a musical instruction, a liturgical sign, or the equivalent of 'Amen'.

Seleucid

Dynasty founded by Seleucus which governed Syria from 312 to 64 BCE. During this period the Maccabees led a successful Jewish revolt against the attempt by Antiochus V Epiphanes to stamp out the Jewish religion in 168 BCE.

Semele

Greek princess from Thrace. By Zeus she conceived Dionysus, and thus aroused the jealousy of Hera, who, through trickery, plotted her destruction by a thunderbolt from Zeus himself.

Seminary

Term used to describe a theological college. It is generally applied to Roman Catholic colleges, but is sometimes used of Anglican colleges for the training of clergy.

214

Sekhmet being offered a white water lily or lotus of ancient Egypt

Semi-Pelagian

Term used for the teaching of a group of theologians who accepted some of the teaching of Augustine and some of the teaching of Pelagius. Vincent of Lerins (434 CE) and Faustus, Abbot of Lerins (474), accepted Augustine's doctrine of original sin but rejected predestination. They preferred the teaching of Pelagius that man has the possibility of striving for salvation.

Semiramis

Daughter of a Syrian goddess. She married Ninus, King of Assyria, and built the city of Babylon. After her death legend says that she was changed into a dove.

Semites

Group of tribes or nations, mostly in the Middle East, said to be descended from Shem, the son of Noah (Genesis 10:21–30). Semitic languages have been spoken by Abyssinians, Arabians, Assyrians, Babylonians, Canaanites, Hebrews, Israelites and Phoenicians.

Seng-Tsan

(d. 606 CE)   Third patriarch of Japanese Zen Buddhism. He is said to be the author of a poem *Believing Mind*. He sets out the Perfect Way which avoids preferences, and regards likes and dislikes as diseases of the mind.

Sephardi

Description of the descendants of Jews who came from Spain and Portugal, cf. Ashkenazi.

Septuagesima

Third Sunday before Lent. This is a Latin word meaning 'seventieth' but Septuagesima Sunday is actually nine weeks, or sixty-four days, before Easter.

Septuagint

Greek version of the Hebrew Bible. According to tradition, Ptolemy Philadelphus (285–246 BCE) commissioned seventy-two Jewish scholars in Alexandria to make the translation, which was completed in seventy-two days; their translations were identical although they worked independently.

Seraphim

Supernatural creatures with six wings, mentioned in Isaiah's vision (Isaiah 6), sometimes identified with the fiery serpents of Numbers 21 and Deuteronomy 8. Christian interpreters have linked them with the Cherubim, and have regarded them as part of the angelic host.

Serapis

See Sarapis

Sermon on the Mount

Title usually given to the teaching of Jesus recorded in Matthew 5–7. It begins with the Beatitudes, goes on to consider the relationship between the teaching of Jesus and the old order, to give practical instruction in almsgiving, prayer and fasting and finishes with a challenge to dedicated living.

Serpent

1. According to Genesis 3, the serpent was the creature which tempted Eve to eat the forbidden fruit.
2. According to Numbers 21:4–9, Moses set up a bronze serpent on a pole so that all who gazed on it would be cured of snakebite.
3. Animal sacred to Aesculapius, the Greek god of medicine. It was the symbol of renovation, and was believed to have the power of finding healing herbs.
4. The Nagas of Hindu and Buddhist mythology. They were semi-divine beings with serpent bodies who were beneficent but could be vengeful and terrible if harmed.

Servant Songs

Four passages in the prophecy of Isaiah (42:1–4, 49:1–6, 50:4–9, 52:13–53:12) which discuss the person and work of the Servant of the Lord. OT scholars are divided on the question of whether these refer to Israel as a nation or to a particular person. The fourth song refers to the Suffering Servant, and Christian theology has interpreted this as foretelling the sufferings of Christ.

Seshat

In ancient Egyptian religion, the sister of the god Thoth. She was the goddess of writing and learning, and the patroness of architecture.

Sesshin

Intensive period of Zen meditation lasting a week, held once a month in Zen monasteries.

Set

In the religion of ancient Egypt, he was the god who killed his brother Osiris, and after a long struggle was himself killed by Horus, the son of Osiris. Set symbolized the powers of darkness and Horus the powers of light.

Seth

Third son of Adam and Eve, born after the murder of Abel (Genesis 4:25). Seth became the ancestor of Noah.

Seven

Seven is regarded as a powerful and uncanny number. It is linked with the moon because of its phases, and thus also with the underlying rhythms of the universe, e.g. there are seven days in a week and seven notes in a musical scale. It is the most frequently used number in the Bible and in legends. In the biblical account of the Creation (Genesis 1) God completed his work in six days and rested on the seventh. In the story of the defeat of Jericho (Joshua 6), for six days the Israelites marched round it once in silence, but on the seventh day they marched round seven times, and when seven priests blew seven trumpets the walls collapsed. In the NT Revelation mentions groups of seven churches, stars, angels, plagues etc. There were seven wonders of the ancient world. Muslims process seven times round the Kaaba, and run seven times between Safa and Marwa.

Seven Deadly Sins

According to the teaching of Pope Gregory the Great (540–604 CE), these were pride, covetousness, lust, envy, gluttony, anger and sloth. They formed a popular subject for artistic imagination in the Middle Ages.

Seven Gifts of the Holy Spirit

Isaiah 11:2 lists these as wisdom, counsel, understanding, fortitude, knowledge, piety and fear of the Lord.

Wrath

Sloth

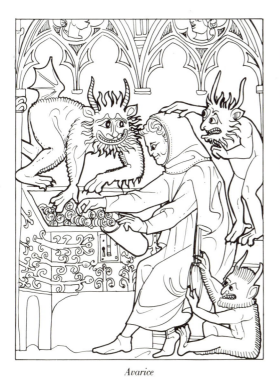

Avarice

Gluttony

Four of the Seven Deadly Sins

217

Seven Liberal Arts

In the educational system of the Middle Ages these were the elementary trivium of grammar, rhetoric and dialectic, plus the more advanced quadrivium of music, astronomy, arithmetic and geometry.

Seven Sacraments

Roman Catholic teaching, reaffirmed at the Council of Trent, sets out seven sacraments, viz. baptism, confirmation, the Eucharist, absolution following penance, extreme unction, ordination and matrimony.

Seven Virtues

The Medieval Church described faith, hope and charity as the three theological virtues, and justice, prudence, temperance and fortitude as the four cardinal virtues.

Seveners

Muslims who accepted the seven Imams, and in 765 CE accepted the leadership of Ismail, thus becoming the ancestors of the Ismaili Muslims.

Seventh Day Adventists

Christian sect founded in New York. In March 1843 William Miller, a Baptist pastor, preached the Second Coming of Christ and when the date passed he predicted October 1844. After that date his followers dropped specific forecasts but formed a separate sect, emphasizing the doctrine of the Second Coming at a time chosen by Christ, and from 1860 onwards insisted that Saturday, the seventh day, must be kept as a holy Sabbath in preparation for his return.

Sexagesima

Lit. 'sixtieth' (day before Easter). In fact it is the second Sunday before Lent, i.e. eight Sundays, or fifty-seven days before Easter.

Sext

One of the 'little hours' of the Catholic Breviary. Recited at noon, the sixth hour.

Shaddai (H)

'El Shaddai' is translated in the English versions of the OT as 'God Almighty'. In the patriarchal narratives in Genesis, and in the revelation to Moses (Exodus 6:3), it applies to the God of Israel. In later literature, e.g. Ruth 1:20–21, Psalms 68:14; 91:1, it appears to be an archaism for or a poetic variant of the divine name.

Shahadah (A)

Term used by Muslims for the witness and confession of the Kalimah. This is the first Islamic Pillar of Din.

Shaharit (H)

Lit. 'dawn prayer'. Jewish daily morning service; the most comprehensive of the prescribed daily prayers.

Shahenshai

Zoroastrian New Year festival, taken over by the Parsees, which usually falls towards the end of August. During the previous ten days the fravashis of departed relatives are remembered.

Shah-nama

Lit. 'book of kings'; collection of Iranian folktales, popular among Zoroastrians, composed in Persian by the Muslim poet Firdausi.

Shaiva

Follower of the Hindu god Shiva.

Shaiva Siddhanta

Hindu school of thought which developed out of the Shaiva tradition of S. India. Its teaching is close to that of Madhva, emphasizing dualism between God and souls, and between souls and the world. God is Creator and Saviour, and karma is interpreted as an expression of God's will.

Shaivism

Religion of the worshippers of the Hindu god Shiva. This is strongest among the Tamils of S. India and the Kashmiris of N. India, by whom Shiva is worshipped as the compassionate father of all things living.

Shakti

Lit. 'energy' or 'power', i.e. the creative power of God, usually symbolized in Hinduism as a female figure, e.g. Lakshmi, the consort of Vishnu.

Symbols of Shamash

Yoruba figure with double-headed axe, the symbol of Shango

Shaku Baku

Technique used by the Soka Gakkai sect of Japanese Buddhism in the attempt to win converts. It consists of bombarding an inquirer with high-pressure propaganda until his resistance is weakened and he professes conviction.

Shakyamuni

The historical Buddha, described as a transcendental and eternal saviour in the *Saddharmapundarika Sutra*. His images are common in Chinese art, and he is identified with Amitabha by the Pure Land Sect.

Shalagram

Ammonite stone with spiral markings which is one of the symbols of the Hindu god Vishnu.

Shalom (H)

Word meaning 'peace' used as a greeting by Jews on meeting or parting. It is similar to the Muslim greeting 'Salaam', which also means 'peace'.

Shaman

Title that has been used by tribes of central Asia and by American Indians for a type of sorcerer or magician. He is regarded as an intermediary between man and God whose powers are so developed that he can link this world with the world of the spirits.

Shamash

Derived from the Semitic noun for 'sun', this is the title of the sun god in Mesopotamian religion. He was the giver of life and light, and was symbolized in Babylon by a circle containing a four-pointed star, and in Assyria by a circle with wings.

Shammai

Jewish rabbi, leader of one of the two most important Pharisaic schools of the 1st century BCE, the other being Hillel. Shammai was regarded as the rigorist, while Hillel was the more lenient.

Shango

Yoruba deity regarded as the god of thunder. In Yoruba legend he was King of Oyo.

Shankara

(788–820 CE) Hindu philosopher. He was born a Brahman, and he expounded the Vedic scriptures in a strictly monistic philosophy, emphasizing the identity of Brahman and Atman.

Shariah (A)

Technically, the canon law of Islam, but generally used to mean all the commandments of God concerning human activities.

Sharif

Originally this was a title indicating a freeman who could claim descent from the family of Muhammad and his grandsons. It is now used as a general term for a Muslim nobleman.

Shavuot (H)

The Jewish Feast of Weeks (Pentecost), celebrated fifty days after the Passover. It marks the beginning of the wheat harvest, and commemorates the giving of the Law to Moses on Mt Sinai. The rabbis have also called it Atzereth, indicating that it is the closing festival of the Passover.

Shaykh A)

Lit. 'old man', one over fifty years old. Term originally used in Islam for the chief of a tribe, but now used as a title of respect for one in authority, for a religious leader or for a teacher.

Sheba, Queen of

Ruler of a country to the south of Judah, probably the territory of the Sabaeans in S.W. Arabia, who made a journey to pay tribute to the wisdom of Solomon (1 Kings 10:1–10). Another purpose may have been to negotiate trade agreements to safeguard her caravans of spices and jewellery. According to Ethiopian legend, she successfully persuaded Solomon to become the father of her child, who was regarded as the first king of Ethiopia.

Shechita (H)

Ritual killing of animals for domestic consumption by an authorized slaughterer in accordance with the Jewish rules for Kosher food.

Sheep

Sheep have been domesticated since prehistoric times and have been widely used as sacrificial victims. An early story (Genesis 22:1–18) tells how Abraham was saved from sacrificing his son Isaac by the substitution of a ram. This is interpreted by some scholars as showing the period when human sacrifice was replaced by animal sacrifice in the Middle East. In the NT (John 1:29, Acts 8:32) Jesus is described as the Lamb of God, sacrificed for the sin of mankind, and in Christian iconography, the lamb is often used as a symbol for him.

Shekhinah (H)

Radiance, the glory or presence of God; term used in the Jewish Targums to signify God himself.

Shem

Oldest son of Noah, who was specially blessed because he covered his drunken father's nakedness (Genesis 9:23). According to the genealogy in Luke 3:36, Shem was one of the ancestors of Jesus in the line of descent from Adam to Joseph.

Shema

Lit. 'hear'. Jewish name for the words of Deuteronomy 6:4; 'Hear, O Israel, the Lord our God, the Lord is One.' They are recited twice daily by Jews as an affirmation of the doctrines of election and monotheism.

Shen-Hui

(686–760 CE) Buddhist master who was a disciple of the patriarch Hui-Neng. He emphasized the doctrine of sudden enlightenment through wu-nien (no thought). He said that it is particularly important not to think of nirvana.

Shen-Shiu

(606–706 CE) Fifth Chinese patriarch of Zen Buddhism. In 700 the Empress Wu gave him the title 'Teacher of Three Emperors'.

Sheol

In the OT this is the place of the dead, corresponding to the Greek Hades. In later literature it is the place where the wicked are punished after death.

Shepherd of Hermas

Treatise by the sub-apostolic Christian author Hermas. The shepherd in the title is an angel who, in the form of a shepherd, brought the message to Hermas.

Shevarim

Notes consisting of three rough blasts which are sounded on the shofar in Jewish synagogues on New Year's Day. The shevarim alternate with the tekiah and the teruah notes.

Shiah (A)

Islamic sect which regards Ali, the nephew of Muhammad, as the first true Caliph. It is the official religion of Iran, and is subdivided into groups such as the Imamis and the Ismailis.

Shikan Taza

Term used in Japanese Zen, lit. 'only sitting'. It is applied to the pure concentration of thought practised in Saijo Zen.

Shimenawa

Rope of rice straw which hangs over the doors of Shinto temples. Its origin is obscure, but it seems to indicate something forbidden or taboo.

Shimunenga

Name of the community god of the Ba-Ila tribe of Zambia. He is a fertility god, worshipped at a popular festival at the beginning of the year with singing, dancing and beer drinking, but he is subordinate to the high god Keza, and acts as an intermediary between him and men.

Shin Buddhism/Shin Shu

The True Pure Land Sect of Japanese Buddhism in its extreme form of salvation by pure faith. This arose when Shinran (1173–1262), who advocated the marriage of priests, broke from the Pure Land Sect of Honen. It is the antithesis of Zen Buddhism, and its opponents say that as it speaks of God and grace it has no right to be described as Buddhism. However, in Japan and America the opposites, Zen and Shin, are the most widely supported forms of Buddhism.

Shingon (J)

Sect of esoteric (tantric) Buddhism introduced into Japan by Kukai (774–835 CE).

Shinran

(1173–1262) Japanese Buddhist, a disciple of Honen, the founder of the Pure Land Sect. Shinran, with the approval of Honen, abandoned monasticism, married and founded the True Pure Land Sect.

Shinto (J)

Form of ancestor and nature worship which is the indigenous religion of Japan.

Shirk (A)

Term used in Islam for the cardinal sin of idolatry or deification. It applies to any deviation from the exclusive worship of the one true god.

Shiuratri

Spring festival in honour of the Hindu god Shiva, when his devotees spend the night singing his praises.

Shiva

Lit. 'mild, auspicious one'. One of the greatest of the Hindu deities, regarded as one of a triad with Brahma and Vishnu. He has a strong following among the Tamils of S. India and the Kashmiri of N. India. Shiva is also regarded as the Destroyer, and is depicted as performing the Tandava, or world-shattering dance.

Shivah (H)

Period of seven days following a Jewish burial when the family mourners are required to remain at home, and are visited by friends and relatives for memorial prayers.

Shofar (H)

Ram's-horn trumpet sounded in the synagogue at the services of Rosh Hashanah (Jewish New Year), and at the conclusion of the Yom Kippur services. It recalls Abraham's sacrifice of a ram in place of his

Shiva performing the Tandava

Shofar being blown on Rosh Hashanah (Boston)

son Isaac. On Rosh Hashanah it is sounded three times: Malchiyoth (kingship), to proclaim God as creator and king, Zikronoth (remembrances), to call men to repentance, and Shofaroth (trumpets), to anticipate the revelation of God as redeemer.

Shogun (J)

Title assumed by a line of military dictators who ruled Japan jointly with the Emperor from 1192 to 1868, when the Emperor reassumed complete control.

Shojo Zen

Third of five types of Zen; this is known as the Small Vehicle, or Hinayana Zen, which has the aim of escape from the rounds of births and deaths.

Shopona

One of the deities of the Yoruba tribe. He is the god of smallpox and other diseases.

Shraddha Rites

Rituals performed by a Hindu following a death. These include memorial prayers, and the offering of pinda (specially prepared foods) to the dead, and to specified relatives of the dead person.

Shramanas

Term used for Hindu teachers of the non-Brahmanic classes during the period of the *Upanishads*. These men attracted many followers in the area of the Ganges Basin by their practice of meditation and the strict austerity of their life.

Shramanera

Term used in Buddhism for a novice in a monastery, or one who is seeking admission to the Sangha.

Shravaka

Term used in Buddhism for a student of the words of the Buddha. Originally it meant 'hearer', but now it more often applies to a reader, whose reading is followed by meditating and contemplation.

Shrine

Originally a reliquary containing relics of a saint, but now also applied to places with particular sacred associations, especially places of pilgrimage such as the Church of the Holy Sepulchre in Jerusalem or St Peter's in Rome for Christians, or the Golden Temple in Amritsar for Sikhs.

Shroff, B. N.

(1857–1927)   Founder of a movement among Parsees entitled 'Ilm-i Kshnoom' which had many mystical elements within it and aimed at a life of spiritual purity.

Shrove Tuesday

Day before the Christian penitential season of Lent. Derived from the verb 'to shrive', which meant 'to hear confession and grant absolution', as this was the day when penitents asked forgiveness for all sins committed during the year. The day is also called Mardi Gras or Pancake Tuesday, as in many areas it is kept as a festival or carnival before the Lenten season of abstinence.

Shu

Ancient Egyptian god of the air, who held up the sky. As husband of Tefnut, he became the father of Geb and Nut.

Shudhi

Word meaning 'purification'. Ceremony conducted by the Arya Samaj to restore outcastes to Hindu society. A group of Sikhs belonging to the Singh Sabha adopted this ceremony and in 1920 succeeded in introducing outcastes into the Khalsa.

Shudra

Lowest of the four classes of Hindu society. They are probably descended from the native people conquered by the invading Aryans. They are not 'twice born', have no access to the *Vedas*, and are compelled to earn their living in servile occupations.

Shukr (A)

Term used in Islam for gratitude or thankfulness; this is the proper human response to divine mercy.

Shulchan Aruch (H)

Lit. 'set table'. Book compiled by Joseph Caro (1488–1575) which provides an authoritative code of Jewish law.

Shunyata

Term used in Buddhism for emptiness or the void. This is said to describe the essential nature of all things.

222

Sibyl

Name used to designate several prophetic, ecstatic women, some accounts mentioning four, others mentioning ten. They acted as the mouthpiece of the gods at various shrines. The most celebrated was at Cumae; she was consulted by Aeneas before he descended to the underworld.

Sibylline Oracles

Title given to a collection of apocalyptic writings mostly composed by Hellenistic Jews in Alexandria in the 2nd century BCE. They were intended to commend the Jewish faith to Greeks by showing that their ancient writers, such as Homer, were sympathetic to ideas found in Jewish belief. They consist of hymns and oracles, with the names of the sibyls attached. In the 1st century CE they were adopted by Christians and adapted to their faith, and they enjoyed a renewed popularity in the Middle Ages.

Sicily

Largest of the Mediterranean islands, off the southern point of Italy. It was sacred to Demeter, and the home of Persephone, who was carried off by Pluto. It was colonized by the Greeks in the 6th century BCE, and some of the finest Greek temples still remaining are found there, notably at Syracuse and Agrigento.

Sicily: temple at Segesta

Siddha

1. Sanskrit word used in Hinduism meaning 'fulfilment' or 'perfection'. It designates the acquisition of supernatural powers by ascetic or magical paths.
2. Giving of grain to a priest in village Hinduism, as part payment for religious services, to symbolize feeding the Brahmans. This is regarded as a meritorious act by Hindus.
3. In the Sikh religion legendary figures, reputedly eighty-four, who achieved bliss through the practice of yoga, and are believed to dwell in the fastnesses of the Himalayas.

Siddhartha

Siddhartha Gautama was the personal name of the teacher who, on enlightenment, became known as the Buddha. For details see Gautama

Siddhi (S)

See Iddhi

Siddur (H)

Lit. 'arrangement'. Title of the Jewish daily prayer book, as distinct from the prayer book for festivals.

Sikhism

'Sikh' is a Punjabi word for a disciple, a follower of Guru Nanak, the founder of Sikhism. Nanak taught the unity of God, the equality of all men, man's duty to offer devotion to God, the belief in reincarnation, and liberation through deep meditation and union with God. Sikhism was organized into a community (Khalsa) by the tenth Guru, Gobind Singh, in 1699.

Sila

Buddhist term for rules of good conduct. It is especially applied to the five precepts binding on monks and laymen alike, viz. to avoid killing, theft, luxury, falsehood and alcohol.

Silas, St

Companion of St Paul on his missionary journey to Macedonia and Corinth. According to early Christian tradition, he was the first Bishop of Corinth.

Silenus

Greek spirit of the wild, part human, part animal, often associated with the satyr. The constant companion of Dionysus, he is usually depicted as a jovial old man carrying a large skin of wine, and slightly tipsy.

Simchat Torah (H)

Lit. 'rejoicing of the Law'; joyous Jewish festival. It is the day, at the end of the Festival of Sukkot, which marks the start of the annual cycle of readings from the Torah in the synagogue.

Simeon
1. Second son of the Israelite patriarch Jacob and his wife Leah.
2. Tribe which occupied territory in the south of Canaan, including Beer Sheba.
3. Aged priest who took the infant Jesus in his arms in the Temple, and spoke the words of thanksgiving known as the Nunc Dimittis (Luke 2:25–35).

Simon
One of the disciples of Jesus. He is described as a member of the Zealot party.

Simon Peter
See Peter

Simony
Sale or purchase of spiritual things, e.g. clerical livings or bishoprics. Derived from the name of Simon Magus, who offered the Apostles money if they would obtain for him the power of the Holy Spirit (Acts 8:9–24). Simony is an offence punishable under canon law, and also under English statutes passed in the reign of Elizabeth I.

Sin
Failure, error or evil behaviour. In religious terms it always involves an element of disobedience to the will of God, or rebellion against the law of God. Some Christian theologians have interpreted the story of the disobedience of Adam and Eve as the account of the origin of sin in humanity. The Qur'an refers to the fall of Adam and Eve and says that all men after them are weak. Like them, all who do wrong will be punished, but God is merciful and forgiving.

Sinai, Mt
Mountain where God appeared to Moses through the Burning Bush (Exodus 3) and where, later, God gave Moses the Law and the Commandments (Exodus 19–20).

Singh (S)
Word meaning 'lion'. It is the name given to all male initiates of the Sikh community, the Khalsa.

Sirah (A)
Word used by Muslims to designate the biography or the career of Muhammad, as distinct from his teaching.

Siren
In Greek mythology a sea nymph who had the power of bewitching sailors with her music and leading them into shipwreck. Sirens are connected with the legends of the Argonauts.

Sistine Chapel
Chapel at the Vatican Palace which takes its name from the Pope who planned it, Sixtus IV (1471–1484). It is especially noted for the frescoes on its walls and ceiling by Michelangelo and other artists. The Last Judgement is painted on the wall behind the altar. The Chapel is used by the College of Cardinals when they meet in conclave to elect a new Pope.

Sisyphus
King of Corinth and father of Ulysses, according to Greek legend. His wickedness was notorious, and he was sentenced by the gods to unending labour in the afterlife. He had to roll a block of marble to the top of a hill, but as soon as he succeeded it fell back and he had to start again. This is a legend to warn people of the horror of eternal punishment for those who lead wicked lives.

Sita
Important woman in the Hindu religion. She was the wife of Rama, one of the ten avatars of the god Vishnu. She is one of the main characters in the *Ramayana*, and is the Indian ideal of womanhood: faithful, devoted and chaste.

Sivcauni
Ornaments given to a Hindu bride at an Indian village wedding ceremony.

Six
Numerologists regard this as the perfect number because it is the sum of the first three digits, and it is often associated with accounts of completeness or perfection. In the Genesis account of the Creation, God finished the work in six days, and in the Jewish Kabbalah, the sixth sefirah is the central, balancing and harmonizing sphere of the Tree of Life.

Skandha (S)
See Khandha

Sleipnir

In Scandinavian folklore the horse ridden by the Norse god Odin, which had supernatural powers of speed and endurance.

Smartas

Term used of certain Hindus who were followers of Shankara yet worshipped both Vishnu and Shiva, and tried to reconcile sectarian Hinduism with a monistic philosophy. It is also used to denote orthodox Brahmans who follow smrti teaching.

Smriti (S)**/Sati** (P)

Term used in Buddhism for attentiveness. This is the seventh step in the Noble Eightfold Path.

Smrti (S)

Lit. 'that which is remembered'. Term used in Hinduism to describe works, such as the *Gita*, which were 'remembered' by the ancient seers, to distinguish them from revealed scriptures such as the *Vedas*, which are termed 'sruti'.

Socialism

Term loosely used for a political and economic theory that the means of production, distribution and exchange should be owned by the state or the community as a whole. It is possible to find the beginning of such thinking in Plato's *Republic* or More's *Utopia*, but the term did not come into use until the early 19th century. It is sometimes difficult to distinguish its ideals from those of Communism, but in the late 19th century a group of Christians, including Charles Kingsley and F. D. Maurice, tried to avoid the tendency towards atheism in the ideas of Marx by founding the Christian Socialist Movement. This has now been incorporated into the Socialist Party.

Society of Friends

Christian society which arose in the 17th century in England through the teaching of George Fox. Its members are sometimes called Quakers, but its formal title is the Religious Society of Friends. Their meetings for worship are a time of silence, broken only if any of the members feel impelled to offer a testimony, or speak on a particular topic. They have no paid ministry, refuse to take oaths and utterly reject warfare as a means of settling international disputes. On account of persecution in England, many emigrated to America in 1650 and settled in the area later known as Pennsylvania.

Society of Jesus

See Jesuit

Socinianism

Anti-Trinitarian doctrine that takes its name from Faustus Socinus (1539–1604). He was born in Siena, and in 1562 wrote a book denying the divinity of Christ. In 1579 he moved to Poland and joined a group of Unitarians who held views identical to his own, and he soon became their leader.

Sociology

Science which studies the growth and organization of societies, and the behaviour and customs of groups of people within society.

Socrates

Greek philosopher born near Athens in 469 BCE who had extraordinary physical strength and powers of endurance. In 406 BCE he became a member of the Senate of Five Hundred. His unorthodox views brought him many enemies, so he started lecturing to any who wished to listen. He did not found a school, but attracted pupils such as Plato and Alcibiades, who collected his teachings in dialogue form e.g. the *Phaedo* and the *Republic*. He was accused of introducing false gods, and after a mockery of a trial was condemned to death by drinking hemlock in 399 BCE.

Socrates

Sodales

Minor priesthoods in classical Rome ranking below the Collegia. They were the fetiales, salians and luperci.

Sodality

Confraternity or pious association within the Roman Catholic Church. It is customary to divide sodalities into three classes: (1) those which seek to attain piety and devotion by special veneration of the Blessed Virgin; (2) those which promote spiritual and corporal works of mercy; (3) those which seek the well-being and improvement of particular groups of people.

Sodar

Term used in the Sikh religion for a prayer recited in the evening.

Sodar Rahiras

Evening service held by Sikhs during which a selection of hymns from the *Guru Granth Sahib* is sung.

Sodom and Gomorrah

Two cities in the area of the Dead Sea that were destroyed by divine punishment on account of their gross wickedness (Genesis 19). Their names have become synonymous with social evil.

Sohila

Term used in the Sikh religion for the final prayer of the day, recited before going to bed.

Soka Gakkai (J)

Movement based on Nichiren Buddhism, founded in 1931, which has grown very rapidly and now claims many followers. It is strongly nationalistic, and proclaims a millennium towards which all must direct their efforts.

Sokha

Hindu priest in an Indian village who specializes in divination, in order to help villagers solve their problems.

Soko

God of the Nupe tribe of Nigeria, identified with the sky.

Soldier

Third of the seven grades of Mithraic initiation; protected by Mars.

Solifidianism

Christian doctrine of justification by faith *alone* taught by Luther and other Protestant Reformers. This was condemned by the Roman Catholic Church at the Council of Trent, because it undermined the whole concept of sacramental grace.

Solipsism

Philosophical doctrine that nothing but the self exists, that only the ego and the mind of the thinker are real, and that the only immediate knowledge possible is that of the self and its ideas.

Solomon

Son of King David and Bathsheba who became King of Israel on the death of David about 970 BCE. He built the first Temple in Jerusalem, and is credited with the authorship of many Proverbs. He built up a great trading empire, and was famous for his wisdom and his luxurious manner of life.

Solon

(639–559 BCE) Athenian legislator. After arousing the Athenians to recapture Salamis, he was chosen as Archon in 594 BCE. He remodelled the constitution, dividing the citizens according to their wealth, adding to the powers of the popular assembly, and making vast changes in the city's financial laws and its system of weights and measures.

Soma

Fermented juice of the plant *Asclepias acida*, which was offered to the ancient gods of India. It is sometimes personified as a Hindu deity. (See also Haoma)

Song of Solomon

Poetic book in the Hebrew Bible subtitled 'Song of Songs'. It is expressed in rich imagery and a passionate devotion, and its love lyrics are, in places, erotic. This has led some scholars to seek for allegorical interpretations. The use of Persian and Greek words suggests that it was written later than the period of Solomon.

Sophia, St

Great cathedral church of Byzantium (now Istanbul) which Constantine started to build in 326 CE. It was damaged by fire during a rebellion in 532, but was rebuilt on a magnificent scale with a wealth of mosaic work in 537. When Constantinople was captured in 1453 by Sultan Mehmet he turned it into a mosque and erected four minarets. It is now a Muslim museum.

St Sophia, Istanbul

Sophists

Group of philosophers in ancient Greece about the middle of the 5th century BCE, prior to the more formal schools of Plato and Aristotle. They were teachers of rhetoric and logic. Among the outstanding Sophists were Gorgias, Hippias and Protagoras.

Sophocles

(495–406 BCE) One of the greatest Greek writers of tragedy. Only seven of his dramas have survived, but his *Ajax*, *Antigone* and two plays about Oedipus are considered to be dramatic masterpieces.

Sorcery

Practice of magic with evil or harmful intentions. The word is probably derived from the Latin *sors* (lot). It is allied to black magic and witchcraft, and usually involves the invoking of evil spirits.

Soteriology

Branch of theology dealing with man's salvation. Christian soteriology considers the fall of man and sin, God's redemptive work and the atonement wrought through Christ, grace and eternal life.

Soto

Influential Zen sect introduced into Japan by Dogen (1200–1253).

Soul

Non-material aspect of man. Greek philosophy tended to emphasize a distinction between body and soul, and Plato regarded man as fundamentally a soul (psyche) imprisoned in a body. Hebrew thought conceived of man as a body that was vitalized by a soul (nephesh) – thus more of a unity – or a person to be considered in his totality. Many views exist in different religions concerning what happens to the soul on the death of the body.

Sparta

City of ancient Greece, circular in form, which was not fortified with walls because it relied on the courage of its citizens to defend it. Its period of greatness was from the 8th to the 4th century BCE, after which it declined, being overthrown by the Romans in the 3rd century BCE. The Spartan training of children was proverbial for its rigour, as they were brought up under very severe discipline to enable them to endure hunger, pain and all forms of hardship.

Spenta Mainyu

In the teachings of Zoroastrianism Holy Spirit or the Bountiful One; one of the seven Amesha Spentas opposed to Angra Mainyu. In the *Gathas* he is distinct from Ahura Mazda, but later they were identified.

Sphinx

Lit. 'strangler'. She-monster who proposed a riddle to the Thebans and killed all who could not solve it. Oedipus gave the right answer, whereupon she slew herself. In Greek mythology, the sphinx is depicted as a winged lion body, with the breasts and head of a woman. The Egyptian sphinx has a lion's body, no wings, and the head and chest of a man, the best-known example being the colossal figure near the Great Pyramid of Giza.

Sphinx at Giza

Spinoza, Baruch

(1632–1677) Dutch philosopher from Amsterdam. He was deeply influenced by the writings of Descartes, and his own early works led to his excommunication, as he looked for solid reasons for any belief. His main work, *Tractatus Theologico-Politicus*, which was a strong plea for freedom of speech in philosophy, had to be published anonymously in 1670 because of Church opposition.

Spirit

In Christian thought this is sometimes synonymous with soul, while at other times it represents a special power of God. The Spirit of God appears in Hebrew thought as the agent of creation (Genesis 1), of prophecy (Ezekiel 37), and of special powers in man (Numbers 11). In the NT (Luke 11:13, Ephesians 1:13) the Spirit of God is referred to as the Holy Spirit. In Zoroastrianism, Holy Spirit is one of the seven Amesha Spentas.

Spiritual Exercises

Treatise written by Ignatius Loyola in 1541 for the guidance of members of the Society of Jesus, the Jesuits. It contains meditations and rules designed to lead souls to conquer their passions and give themselves to God. It has been influential in devotional training.

Spiritualism

Belief that the human personality survives the death of the body, and that it is possible to communicate with the spirits of the dead. Such communication is usually dependent on mediums, who are themselves guided by spirit controls. Some mediums work within the framework of a Christian community, but others have no religious connection, believing only in the natural immortality of the human soul.

Spring

The renewal of life in spring has been celebrated with joy since very early times. In ancient Babylonia the creation myth was re-enacted, culminating in sacred intercourse between the king and a priestess to ensure fertility of crops. In Greece and Rome spring festivals were occasions of rejoicing, with sacrifices, processions, feasting and dancing. In the Christian era spring festivals have been incorporated in pre-Lenten carnivals, and the theme of life renewal is included in the joyful message of the resurrection of Jesus Christ, celebrated on Easter Day.

Sraosha

Term used in early Zoroastrian thought for the genius of hearing and obeying. Later he was raised to the status of a personal deity, mediating between God and man.

Sri

Hindu goddess of fortune, wife of the great god Vishnu. She is portrayed as a great beauty, sometimes depicted with four arms and holding a lotus. Some Hindus believe she is the wife of all Vishnu's incarnations. She is also known as Lakshmi.

Sri Aurobindo

(1872–1950) Hindu politician and philosopher. After being educated in England, he returned to India to undertake political work, particularly for Indian independence. Later he turned to writing books of a metaphysical and philosophical nature.

Sri Chinmoy

Indian guru born in 1931 who has achieved wide recognition and a following in the West, being appointed first director of the United Nations Meditation Group in 1970. He teaches 'the path of the heart to God' by love, devotion and surrender, which is achieved in three stages by concentration, meditation and contemplation.

Srong Ma

Term used in Tibetan Buddhism for 'guardians of doctrine', a title given to the chief gods of the ancient Bon religion of Tibet.

Sruti (S)

Lit. 'what is heard'. Term used by Hindus for revealed scripture, and applied to the *Vedas* and the *Upanishads*, which were heard by the ancient seers. This term distinguishes them from scriptures that were remembered (smrti), such as the *Gita*.

Stabat Mater

Opening words, meaning 'the mother stood', of two hymns which portray the emotions of the Virgin Mary at the manger (Stabat Mater Speciosa) and at the Cross (Stabat Mater Dolorosa). The authorship is unknown but has been ascribed to Gregory the Great or Innocent III. By the 14th century the Dolorosa was widely known but the Speciosa was almost forgotten. Several composers have set the Dolorosa to memorable music, including Palestrina, Haydn and Rossini.

Star

Although the stars have been thought to influence human character, it is doubtful if they have ever been worshipped in themselves. Various deities have been associated with particular stars, e.g. the goddess Ishtar with the planet Venus, and the god Nergal with the planet Mars, while the Egyptian god Osiris was identified with Orion, the king of the stars. In the narrative of the birth of Christ, the Magi were led to Bethlehem by a star (Matthew 2).

Star of David

Hexagram or six-pointed star. Composed of two equilateral triangles, one pointing upwards and the other downwards, this was an ancient symbol of fire and water, regarded in the Middle Ages as a powerful protection against evil. The reason for its connection with David is unknown, but it has been found on Jewish amulets of the 12th century. It is the national symbol of Israel, known as the Magen, and is found as a decoration in many synagogues.

Stations of the Cross

Series of fourteen paintings or carvings arranged round the walls of a Christian church and depicting scenes in the passion of Christ, from his condemnation by Pilate to his burial. A popular form of devotion, predominently in Catholic churches, is to process round the fourteen stations, stopping at each one for contemplation and prayer.

Stephen, St

First Christian martyr. He was appointed by the Apostles as one of the seven Deacons, and soon after he preached a sermon in Jerusalem to testify to his faith in the risen Christ. Because of this, he was driven out of the city by members of the synagogue and stoned to death, St Paul, then known as Saul, being one of the onlookers. The Feast of St Stephen is 26 December.

Sthanakavasi

Reformed sect within the Jain religion which originated in 1452 when Lunka of Ahmedabad broke away from the main body because he objected to image worship. In 1653 more rigorous adherents formed the Sthanakavasi Sect, rejecting the use of Sanskrit and the worship of images, and using only the Magadhi language.

Sthavira

Early school of Buddhist thought, dating back to the 3rd century BCE, from whom the Theravadins developed. Their teachers were the strict guardians of tradition, and they insisted on a literal interpretation of the Vinaya rules.

Stigmata

Appearance of wound marks on the hands and feet, and occasionally on the brow, corresponding to the wounds of Christ at the Crucifixion. The earliest example of this was experienced by St Francis of Assisi in 1224. Since then over three hundred cases have been reported, many of them in Italian monks or nuns.

Stoicism

Ethical system, based on the teaching of Zeno of Athens, in which the keynote is duty. Its main points are that virtue consists of (1) absolute judgement, (2) absolute mastery of desire, (3) absolute control of the soul over pain and (4) absolute justice.

Stoics

Adherents of the ethical philosophy of Zeno, who taught in Athens about 310 BCE. The word comes from the name of the portico where Zeno conducted his lectures and discussions: Stoa Poikile (portico of the paintings).

Stole

Liturgical vestment, consisting of a strip of silk about 2½ m long and 10 cm wide, worn at the Eucharist and at baptisms and at the hearing of confessions in a Christian church. The colour of the stole worn at the Eucharist depends on the ecclesiastical season; at baptisms it is white, and at the hearing of confessions it is purple.

Stonehenge

Saxon word meaning 'hanging stones'. Sanctuary dating from 1900–1700 BCE on Salisbury Plain. Upright stones about 4½ m high, with cross-beam stones, are set out in a circular fashion, forming two circles and two smaller ovals, the outer circle being 90 m in circumference with the smaller circle set 2½ m inside it. It may have been a Druid sanctuary, and it appears to have some connection with sun worship as the Hele Stone is in line with the rays of the rising sun on Midsummer Day.

Stool

Particularly important object in West African religion, often regarded as an ancestral shrine. The Golden Stool of Ashanti was said to have been brought down from heaven and to embody the soul of the nation.

Stork

Storks have been the subject of fables and legends in Greek, Roman, Arabic and medieval writings. The bird is regarded as a model of domestic virtue as the male remains faithful to his mate, and the old German name, *Adebar*, means 'bringer of luck'. In many European countries householders try to attract storks by fixing cart-wheels to their roofs to form a basis for the birds' nests.

Stupa

Reliquary mound or burial place used as a cult object by Buddhists.

Styx

Name, connected with the Greek word for 'hatred', of the principal river of the underworld, round which it was said to flow seven times. The gods swore by this when they wished to give special sanctity to their oaths.

Subha

1. Term used in Buddhism for beauty as an ideal, or for that which is beautiful.
2. Term for the prayer beads used in Islam. They consist of three groups of thirty-three for reciting the ninety-nine beautiful names of God.

Sublapsarian

Term applied to a school of Calvinism which believes that God decreed the election to salvation of some men and the damnation of others *after* the fall of Adam. This less rigorous version of predestination has been the generally accepted doctrine among Calvinists since the Synod of Dort in 1618.

Great Stupa, Sanchi, Bhopal State, India

Substance

1. In Christian theology, a term used to express the underlying being in which the three persons of the Godhead are one.

2. In Christian philosophy, a term indicating the ontological unit, that which is capable of independent existence, or 'an essence existing by itself in virtue of its own act of being' (E. Gilson).

3. In Roman Catholic theology of the Eucharist, the essence of the bread and wine which by transubstantiation becomes the body and blood of Christ, though the accidents remain unchanged.

Sudre

Sacred white cotton shirt worn by Zoroastrians at all times; it is the symbol of the armour of religion and of purity.

Suetonius

Roman historian who in the *Life of Claudius*, written about 130 CE, referred to the expulsion of followers of Christ from Rome by the Emperor Claudius.

Suffragan Bishop

Assistant bishop appointed to help the diocesan bishop, usually in a section of the diocese. The first record of the office in England is in 1240. Henry VIII appointed twenty-six suffragans in 1534, but at the end of the century the office seemed to lapse until the 19th century, when many new suffragans were appointed. A suffragan is nominated by the diocesan bishop to the sovereign.

Sufi

Muslim mystic. The name is derived from white woollen garments worn by devotees of an ascetic mystical movement which arose in Islam in the 8th century and still has many followers in the Middle East today.

Suhoor (A)

Term used by Muslims for a pre-dawn meal permitted before a day of fasting.

Sujud (A)

Term used in Islam for the specified acts of bowing, kneeling and prostration which must be practised during salat, the daily prayers.

Sukha (P)

Term used in Buddhism for happiness, to indicate the opposite of dukkha (suffering).

Sukhavati (P)

Term used in the Pure Land Sect of Buddhism for paradise.

Sukkah (H)

Temporary shelter erected by Jewish families where meals should be eaten during the Feast of Tabernacles.

Sukkot (H)

Jewish Feast of Tabernacles, celebrated in the autumn, 15–21 Tishri. The name is derived from the temporary booths made of foliage and decorated with flowers and fruit that are erected after the pattern of those in the vineyards of Israel in biblical times. The Feast commemorates God's care of the Israelites during their wanderings in the wilderness and enshrines the ideals of joy, co-operation and humility.

Sultan

Islamic title for a temporal ruler, first adopted by Ghaznavid Mahmud (997–1030). The Sultan of Turkey assumed the title Sultan of Sultans.

Sukkot, the Feast of Tabernacles, being celebrated in a Jewish home

Summa Theologica

Chief dogmatic work by Thomas Aquinas, written between 1265 and 1271. It contains treatises, questions and articles divided into three sets concerning (1) God in himself, (2) God and man and (3) Christ and the way of man to God.

Sundareshvara

Lit. 'beautiful lord'. Name used for the Hindu god Shiva in the worship at the temple at Madura.

Sunday

Christian Sabbath, the day of rest set aside for the worship of God, because it is the day on which Christ rose from the dead. The pre-Christian dedication to the sun was left unchanged, probably because Christ is regarded as the light of the world.

Sunna (P)/Sunyata (S)

Term used by some Buddhist philosophers to indicate the emptiness of the absolute. It means 'void' or 'emptiness', a term implying the denial of all conceptual constructions in relation to ultimate reality; the non-existence of the individual soul, but on the other hand, liberation.

Sunnah (A)

Term used in Islam for the path of tradition. Derived from an Arabic word meaning 'custom', it indicates the theory and practice of Orthodox Muslims following the standards of the Prophet Muhammad. Sunnah, tradition from the point of view of directives and law, is parallel with Hadith, tradition from the point of view of teaching.

Sunni (A)

Term indicating the broad mass of Islam from which the Shiah diverge. The Sunnis reject the Shiah Imams, and rely on the Qur'an, the Sunnah and the community for the integrity and continuity of their Islam and the faith.

Supermind

According to the teaching of the Hindu philosopher and reformer Sri Aurobindo, this is the goal of the fourth or supramental stage of man's evolution, which comes by way of the transformation of matter, life and mind, or satchitananda.

Superstition

Irrational belief or behaviour concerning the supernatural or the unknown. This is often based on an ancient religious belief or a fear of magic. Examples are: touching wood, which recalls the sacred tree or the Cross of Christ; the lucky horseshoe, related to the power of the crescent moon; the funeral wreath, originally a magic circle to contain the soul of the departed; thirteen sitting down for a meal, considered unlucky because it was the number at the Last Supper.

Supralapsarian

Term applied to a school of Calvinism which believes that God decreed the election to salvation of some men and the damnation of others *before* the fall of Adam. This more rigorous form of Calvinism has been generally abandoned in favour of the less rigorous sublapsarian doctrine since the Synod of Dort in 1618.

Surah

Title given to each of the one hundred and fourteen divisions or chapters of the Qur'an. Some come from Mecca and others from Medina. The original meaning of the word is 'a brick in a wall'.

Suriya

Sun god mentioned in the *Rig-Veda*, the earliest of the Hindu scriptures.

Surplice

Liturgical vestment of white linen with wide sleeves worn by the clergy and choir in the Church of England at Matins and Evensong, and by most clergy at Holy Communion. It is the vestment prescribed in the Prayer Book of 1552, and in the 1662 Prayer Book it is prescribed for all choir services and for the administration of the Sacraments.

Surrogate

One who is appointed in place of another, especially the deputy of a bishop or a judge. Its most frequent use now refers to ecclesiastical surrogates, i.e. clergy who are authorized to grant marriage licences within a specified area.

Surplice worn with a scarf over a cassock

Sursum Corda

The words 'Lift up your hearts', which are addressed by the celebrant to the congregation in the Christian Eucharist before the Preface. The response is 'We lift them up unto the Lord'.

Surt

In Scandinavian mythology a wicked giant, 'the black one', who guarded the hot, southern world called Muspell. Surt fought against Frey, and burnt the earth with fire.

Susanna

Heroine of a short book in the Apocrypha. Susanna, a beautiful and virtuous woman, rejects the advances of two elders and is accused by them of adultery. She is sentenced to death, but as she is being led to execution, Daniel is able to reveal the plot and the elders are executed instead.

Susanoo

Deity of early Shintoism known as the God of the Withering Wind of Summer. He was unruly and destructive, and offended the sun goddess; the catalogue of his offences constitutes a list of sins for which humans may be punished.

Sutta (P)/**Sutra** (S)

Lit. 'thread'. This usually signifies a short aphorism, or a collection of aphorisms 'threaded' by a theme. Many collections on different subjects are to be found in Hindu and Buddhist scriptures.

Sutta Nipata (P)

Lit. 'collection of verses'. Popular work in Theravada Buddhism in five parts, the third of which tells of the temptation of the Buddha by Mara, and also of his renunciation of the world.

Sutta Pitaka (P)

Second of the Three Baskets of the Buddhist canon of scripture. This Basket contains dialogues of the Buddha.

Suttee

See Sati

Svatantra

Hindu doctrine found in the teaching of the philosopher Madhva that God alone is autonomous. God's activity and existence do not depend on anything else, but all other beings are dependent.

Svayambhu

Word derived from the root 'sva' (self); this is a term used in Hinduism as an epithet for God, being found in the *Upanishads*. Lit. 'self-existent', i.e. one whose existence does not depend on anyone or anything else.

Svetaketu

Young man named in the *Chandogya Upanishad* to whom the sage Uddakala Aruni said, 'Tat tvam asi', meaning, 'That, O Svetaketu, thou art'. This was the teacher's way of demonstrating his pupil's identity with the reality behind all things.

Svetambaras

Lit. 'white-clad'. One of the two main divisions of Jain ascetics; these were the less conservative, and took to wearing a simple white garment, the sign of purity. The other division was termed the Digambaras.

Svetasvatara

One of the *Upanishads* from the middle period of their composition. It is in verse and has been likened to the *Bhagavadgita*. It belongs to the Shaivaite school, and Shiva is described as the inconceivable one, beyond the comprehension of the gods. The attitude of bhakti is prescribed as necessary on the part of the worshipper.

Swadeshi

Term used by Mahatma Gandhi in his ethical teaching. It means love for one's neighbourhood, and it includes economic, social, ethical and religious considerations.

Swami

Member of a Hindu religious order. Also, general Hindu title used for a holy man, or one who has gained the respect of the community.

Swami Dayananda

Hindu reformer who in 1875 founded the Arya Samaj in Bombay. Its main purpose was to recall Hindus to their own religion in its Aryan Vedic form, rejecting post-Vedic Hindu reforms and also Christianity and Islam.

Swami Vivekananda

Religious name of Narendranath Datta (1863–1902), a Hindu reformer who was educated at the Scottish Church College, Calcutta, but became a disciple of Ramakrishna. On the death of his master, he founded the Ramakrishna Mission and visited the World Parliament of Religions in Chicago in 1893. He taught a form of universalism, but it was firmly based on Hinduism on the grounds of the catholicity of that religion. He claimed that Hinduism, especially Advaita Vedanta, was the most perfect expression of religion, and he helped many Hindus to find fulfilment in their own faith.

Swan

Because of its size and its pure white plumage, the swan has an important place in myth and legend. Its strong, high flight implies power, and its association with water implies fertility. Zeus turned himself into a swan to seduce Leda, and there are many legends of beautiful maidens being turned into swans, especially those who have been jilted by their lovers.

Swaraj

Lit. 'home rule'. Term used by Mahatma Gandhi to express the main object of his campaigns of satyagraha, viz. home rule for India, or Indian independence.

Swarga

Heaven of Indra in Hindu mythology, situated on Mt Meru. The name is also a general term for paradise. In Jainism, Swarga is divided into twenty-six regions of increasing bliss.

Swastika

Cross with limbs at the four extremities. It is considered to be a symbol of good fortune, and may represent the sun, or the wheel of Vishnu with the spokes bent. The limbs should turn to the right, but when the Nazis adopted it as their sign, they turned them to the left, which would be regarded by many authorities on symbolism as an evil omen.

Swedenborg, Emanuel

(1688–1772) Swedish scientist and mystic. In his early years he tried to show by scientific analysis that the universe has a spiritual structure. In 1743 he became conscious of direct contact with the angels, and set up the New Church to be a spiritual fraternity in all Churches. His followers set up a separate body, the New Jerusalem Church, in 1787, after his death, to propagate his teachings, and it still maintains a ministry.

Sword

The sword is a more recent weapon than the spear or the axe, and many legends have gathered round it, e.g. Siegfried's sword Balmung, Beowulf's sword Hrunting, and King Arthur's sword Excalibur. In alchemy the sword was a symbol of purifying fire, and according to the Genesis story, when God drove Adam from the Garden of Eden he posted angels with flaming swords to guard the way to the Tree of Life. In the 12th century the sword was adapted to a new symbolism; it looked like the Cross, and was wielded against the Infidel by the Crusaders. A Christian knight received his sword in the name of the Holy Trinity on entering an order of chivalry, and the regalia of English monarchs includes the Sword of State and the Sword of Justice.

Syad Vada

Method used in the philosophy of the Jains. It expresses the idea that there can be no absolute certainty in knowledge. The only answer to any proposition is 'syad' (maybe). The alternative answers to a question are 'syad-asti' (maybe it is) or 'syad na-asti' (maybe it is not).

Sybaris

Ancient city in lower Italy colonized by the Greeks about 720 BCE. It rapidly rose to great prosperity, and the luxurious carefree life of its citizens gave rise to the term 'Sybarite', a person living such a life.

Syllabus of Errors

Eighty theses condemning erroneous teachings and practices, promulgated by Pope Pius IX in 1864. The Syllabus is set out under ten headings, including *Communism*, *Naturalism*, *Pantheism*, *Rationalism* and *Socialism*. It was received with great joy by those who wished to strengthen the papacy, but with dismay by others.

West London Jewish Synagogue

Symbolism

Use of conventional signs which recall, by analogy, things, persons or ideas that are associated with them. Thus an egg is a symbol of life, a dart a symbol of death; in Christian iconography, the lamb is a symbol of Christ, and the cross is a symbol of his death and resurrection.

Syn

Scandinavian goddess chiefly concerned with justice who acted for the defence at gatherings of the people.

Synagogue

Jewish meeting place for prayer and instruction in the Scriptures. Ezekiel gathered the exiles at his house for this purpose, but the institution in set form dates from the time of Ezra. Now the synagogue houses the Scrolls of the Law, and has a reading-desk (bimah) from which the Law is read and the sermon delivered on the Sabbath.

Synaxis

Greek word for an assembly; it was used by early Christian writers with reference to an assembly for worship and prayer, including the Eucharist. They thus avoided using the word 'synagogue' with its Jewish associations.

Syncretism

Attempt to blend different religions or philosophical schools into one system. A process of thought in which ideas are connected by chance rather than by logic.

Synod

Ecclesiastical assembly convened to consult on matters of faith and church affairs. It may be *national*, such as the Synod of Dort in Holland, which considered the conflict between Arminianism and Calvinism in 1618, or *provincial*, such as the Synod of Whitby in 664, which decided to follow the customs of the Roman rather than the Celtic Church, or *diocesan*, to consider the problems of an ecclesiastical district. The Church of England is now governed by a General Synod which meets two or three times a year.

Synoptic Gospels

First three books of the NT, the Gospels of Matthew, Mark and Luke, so called because they take the same overall or synoptic view. The Gospels of Matthew and Luke incorporate most of the material in the shorter Gospel of Mark.

Tabernacle

1. Portable sanctuary used by the Israelites during their years in the wilderness and in the early period of their settlement in Canaan. The materials and method of construction are described in great detail in Exodus 35–36.

2. Receptacle in Roman Catholic churches for vessels containing the Blessed Sacrament. Usually placed on or above the altar.

Tabernacles, Feast of

Jewish feast celebrated in the autumn. See Sukkot

Tablets of Destiny

According to Mesopotamian mythology, tablets which gave their possessor the power to order the affairs and destiny of other people. Tiamat gave the tablets to her husband Kingu, but he was careless and was defeated by Marduk, who tied the tablets to himself and became supreme.

Taboo

English form of a Polynesian word meaning 'prohibition'. It is usually applied to an object, place or situation which is dangerous because of its sacred associations. It is therefore forbidden for ordinary persons to touch the object or enter the place; only those specially qualified or authorized may do so.

Tabor, Mt

Mountain in the Plain of Jezreel rising to a height of 562 m above sea-level. According to tradition it was the site of the transfiguration of Jesus, and a church and monastery have been built on the summit in commemoration of that event.

Tacitus

(55–120 CE)   Roman historian who, in his *Annals* XV, mentions the persecution of Christians in 64 CE, and says that Nero made them scapegoats for the fire in Rome that year.

Tafsir (A)

Lit. 'explanation'. Word used in the Muslim religion as a general term for commentaries on the Qur'an.

Tagore, Debendranath

Hindu leader and reformer who became the second leader of the Brahma Samaj. In 1865 the movement split into two branches and he led the branch known as the Adi Samaj (original Samaj). He rejected belief in the inerrancy of the *Vedas*, and taught the interpretation of scripture by intuition.

Tagore, Rabindranath

(1861–1941) Son of Debendranath Tagore. He became a great Bengali poet, rejected much of Hinduism, and in 1901 founded the Shantiniketan (abode of peace) as an expression of his international and humanist interests. He was a prolific writer of poetry and prose, and in 1913 was awarded the Nobel Prize for Literature.

Tahrif (A)

Lit. 'corruption'. Term used in Islamic theology for the alteration of the sense of a document; it is particularly used of debate on the meaning of passages in the Qur'an.

T'ai Chi

The supreme, ultimate or transcendent absolute in Chinese philosophy, expressed through the diagram yang and yin. Through movement, the ultimate produces yang, and after reaching its limit, in quiescence produces yin.

T'ai P'ing

According to the doctrine of Mo-tzu, a Taoist teacher, these were periods of universal peace. It was the duty of religious leaders to guide their followers through periods of calamity and disaster to the period of universal peace which would follow.

Taizé

Protestant monastic community near Cluny in S.E. France, founded in 1940 and led by Roger Schutz, the Prior. The brothers share a common life and purse but work in their various professions in the neighbourhood of the community house, returning for the divine office and meals. They have done much evangelical work among young people, seeking to promote Christian unity, and have founded a daughter house in America.

Taj Mahal

Magnificent monument in white marble set up by Shah Jehan (d. 1666) in memory of his wife, Mumtaz Mahal. It is generally regarded as one of the most beautiful buildings in the world.

Takbir (A)

Formula 'Allahu Akbar' (God is most great), frequently used in Islam.

Talisman

Object which is thought to have been magically endowed with the power of attracting good fortune, such as an amulet, or a magical figure in astrology.

Mt Tabor: Church of the Transfiguration

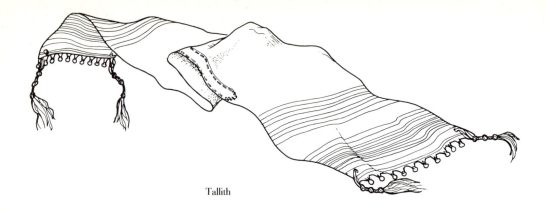

Tallith

Tallith (H)

Jewish prayer-shawl of white material with fringes in which there is a blue thread. It is worn by males at morning services, and at all services on the Day of Atonement.

Talmud (H)

Major source of Jewish law. It consists of the Mishnah, the oral law collected in the 2nd century, and the Gemara, rabbinic commentaries on the Mishnah, dated 200–500 CE. It consists of two recensions, the Palestinian and the Babylonian.

Talmud Torah (H)

Lit. 'study of the Torah'. School or other place of education set up by Jews. During and after the Middle Ages, it was necessary for Jews to make their own provision for the education of their children, and a Talmud Torah was set up for most communities. At first the curriculum was purely religious, but under the influence of the Haskalah a wider system was developed.

Tamas

One of the Hindu gunas or qualities, translated 'denseness' or 'dullness'.

Tamil

One of the languages belonging to the Dravidian family, spoken by about seventeen million people in India and also in Sri Lanka. The texts of the Hindu *Saiva Siddhanta* are written in Tamil.

Tammuz

Akkadian vegetation god, known in Sumeria as Dumuzi. He was the beloved of Ishtar and his death was commemorated with an annual summer lamentation. Later, through the efforts of Ishtar, he was brought back to life. He is thus connected with the spring appearance of corn, its ripening and its cutting down in the late summer.

Tanasukh (A)

Lit. 'transmigration' or 'reincarnation'. This is a doctrine which has been rejected by Sunni Muslims, but it has been accepted by some Shiah Muslims, especially in India.

Tandava (S)

Lit. 'frantic dance'. Term used in Hinduism for the world-shattering dance performed by Shiva. He is portrayed in a ring of fire which symbolizes the life process of the universe, and he dances on a demon representing the ignorance that must be destroyed before enlightenment can be attained. He has four hands, representing creation, destruction, salvation and protection.

Tane

Most important god in the Maori religion. He is the creator of vegetation and vanquisher of darkness.

Tanha (P)/**Trsna** (S)

Term used in Buddhist teaching for desire or thirst. According to the second Noble Truth propounded by the Buddha, desire is the root or cause of suffering.

Tankhah

Term used among the Sikhs for the reinstatement into the community (Khalsa) of one who has broken his vows or broken the rules.

Tanna

Jewish scholar of the 2nd century who specialized in teaching the Mishnah.

Tano

River god of the Ashanti tribe and of some tribes in Ghana.

Tantalus

According to Greek mythology, a son of Zeus who became King of Argos. He was entertained by the gods, but betrayed their trust by revealing their secrets. As a punishment, he was chained in the middle of a lake whose water receded whenever he tried to drink. The story is a warning to those who betray the gods, and gives us the verb 'to tantalize'.

Tantras

Texts said to have been revealed by the Buddha, and thought by Tibetan Buddhists to lead to enlightenment. They contain spells, descriptions of divinities and instructions concerning worship. In Hinduism they are texts containing dialogues between Shiva and his wife on a variety of religious practices. These texts give instructions to help the initiated find enlightenment or release; they must be revealed only by a properly initiated teacher to carefully selected students.

Tanzil

Descent or downward flow of inspiration that came to Muhammad, beginning on the Night of Power, through which he received the words of the Qur'an.

Tao (C)/**Do** (J)

Lit. 'way'. Term used in Chinese philosophy for the source of all being, the motive of all movement, the mother of all substance.

Tao te Ching

Lit. 'classic of the Way and its power'. This is one of the most important Chinese religious writings, and is thought to be the work of a quietist of the 4th or 3rd century BCE, possibly Lao Tzu, though containing older material. The book has eighty-one short chapters concerning the nature of the Way.

Tao-Sheng

(360–434 CE)   Buddhist master who taught that all men can attain liberation because all have the Buddha nature. This is accepted by the Pure Land, Tendai and Zen schools of Buddhism.

Tapas

Term used in Hinduism which originally meant 'heat' but was later applied to the austerity practised by some yogi.

Tapasya

Doctrine of self-sacrifice or voluntary poverty, which was one of the key teachings of Mahatma Gandhi's satyagraha movement for Indian independence.

Taqlid (A)

Lit. 'authoritarianism'. State of adhering blindly to a traditional school of teaching or interpretation in Islam.

Taqwa (A)

Term used in the Qur'an for God-consciousness. This is the basis of all good actions, and to help man achieve it God has set out specific acts of worship, viz. profession of faith, prayer, fasting, pilgrimage and almsgiving.

Tara

In Tibetan Buddhism she is venerated as the goddess of mercy, the female counterpart of the Bodhisattva Avalokiteshvara. Originally she was an Indian goddess.

Tara (Tibet, 15th century)

Targum

Aramaic paraphrase, or an interpretative translation of parts of the Hebrew Bible. This became necessary after the Babylonian captivity in the 6th century BCE, when Hebrew began to die out as a spoken language, but it does not appear to have been written until the first years of the Christian era. The oldest extant is the Targum of Onkelos.

Tariki

Term used in Pure Land Buddhism to indicate reliance on powers outside oneself, or salvation by outside powers.

Tariqah (A)

Sufi way of discipline, and initiation into divine knowledge via self-transcendence and self-mortification.

Tarot

Pack of cards which forms a system of communication through symbols, showing the relation between God, man and the universe. It has strong links with the Hebrew Kabbalah, and a pack consists of four suits of fourteen cards each, wands, cups, swords and pentacles, and twenty-two trumps, called the 'major arcana'.

Tartarus

In Homer's *Iliad* this is referred to as a deep, sunless abyss, as far below Hades as the earth is below heaven, where Zeus imprisoned the rebel Titans. He then secured it with iron gates. In later Greek poets it was synonymous with Hades.

Tashlich

Ancient Jewish rite whereby Jews go to a river or a seashore on the afternoon of New Year's Day and shake their garments to cast off sins, at the same time reciting Micah 7:18–20.

Taslim (A)

Term used in Islam for an expression of goodwill or religious blessing, viz. 'The peace of God be upon him', i.e. the Prophet Muhammad.

Tasliyah (A)

Term used in Islam for an expression of goodwill or religious blessing in response to the Taslim, viz. 'May God bless the Prophet'.

Tat Tvam Asi

Lit. 'that thou art', more generally rendered, 'that art thou'. Sanskrit phrase, whose *locus classicus* is the *Chandogya Upanishad.* The Sage used it to teach his pupil's identity with the reality behind all things. Shankara used it as an expression of monism.

Tathagata

Title of the Buddha used by his followers, and also by himself when speaking of himself. The meaning is probably 'thus arrived', or 'he who follows in the footsteps of his predecessors', or on the Buddha's own lips, 'he who has arrived at enlightenment'.

Tathata (P)

Lit. 'suchness'. Term used in the Buddhist faith to express the ultimate and unconditioned nature of all things.

Tattva (S)

Lit. 'truth' or 'reality'. Term used in the Samkhya school of Hindu philosophy for the Twenty-five Principles.

Tau

Last letter of the Hebrew alphabet, and so connected in symbolism with the end of the world. As a T-shaped cross or key, it was regarded as a symbol to protect the righteous in the last days and give entry into paradise.

Tau cross

Tauhid (A)

Term used in Islam for the doctrine, or the assertion, of the divine unity. It is expressed as 'God is one; there is no god but God', and this is the central belief of Islam.

Taurobolium

Ritual washing in the blood of a sacrificed bull, or sometimes, baptism in a bull's blood; this was an initiatory rite in the mysteries of Cybele.

ACE of WANDS.

ACE of PENTACLES.

THE HANGED MAN.

JUDGEMENT.

Tarot cards

241

Tauroctony

Ritual slaying of the bull. This was an important rite in the mysteries of Cybele, and it is depicted in Mithraic art, though its exact place in Mithraism is not known.

Tawaf (A)

Lit. 'encircling'. Ritual of walking round the Kaaba at Mecca seven times at the beginning of the Hajj. An attempt is made to kiss or touch the Black Stone at least once.

Ta'widh (A)

Term used in Islam for the act of saying, 'I seek refuge with God.' This formula is found in surahs 113 and 114, and it is one of the deepest themes of Islamic devotion.

Te Deum

Latin Christian hymn in rhythmic prose addressed to God the Father and to the Son. Its date of composition is not known, but it has been attributed to St Ambrose or St Augustine. The English translation is part of the order for Matins in the Anglican *Book of Common Prayer.*

Te Igitur

Opening words of the Latin canon of the Roman Catholic Mass, asking God to accept and bless the Eucharistic offerings of bread and wine.

Tefillah (H)

Lit. 'prayer'. Great prayer of the Jewish people, consisting of nineteen benedictions, recited in a standing position, now more popularly known as the Amidah.

Tefnut

Ancient Egyptian goddess personifying moisture who with her husband Shu separated heaven from earth. She was the daughter of Re and a goddess of the dead.

Tegh Bahadur

(1611–1675) Ninth Sikh Guru. He is regarded as a martyr because he was executed by the Mughal emperor Aurungzeb. He was succeeded by his son Gobind Singh, who founded the Sikh Khalsa.

Teilhard Centre

Organization set up to propagate the teachings of Teilhard de Chardin (1881–1955), a Jesuit priest and palaeontologist. He believed that the concept of evolution provides a vital clue to recognizing that man has a special history and a remarkable future. His Law of Complexity–Consciousness means that in evolution matter becomes more complex, and with a rise in complexity there is a rise in consciousness. He suggested that man is now responsible for guiding his own evolution, and the final point of evolution is called Omega. Much of his teaching seems to conflict with traditional Christian theology of the Creation, God and Christ, and as a Jesuit he was not allowed to publish his books. His followers have published them since his death.

Tekiah (H)

Note consisting of one sustained blast which is sounded on the shofar in Jewish synagogues on New Year's Day. It alternates with the shevarim and the teruah, and it may represent an outcry or a moan.

Teleology

Branch of philosophy or theology which deals with ends and final causes. The term also denotes a theory that the world has a design and designer, and an end which will be in accordance with a predestined purpose.

Telepathy

Communication of impressions or ideas from one mind to another without the use of recognized channels of sense. It is sometimes called thought transference or mind-reading.

Tell el-Amarna Tablets

Collection of three hundred and fifty clay tablets dating from the 14th century BCE discovered at Tell el-Amarna in Egypt in 1887. Inscribed in cuneiform, they are letters written to the Pharaoh Ikhnaton from Canaanite kings and garrison commanders telling of attacks by the Habiru, and warning him that they may not be able to beat off the attacks unless he sends them reinforcements.

Templars

The Knights Templar were a military order founded by Godfrey de Bouillon in 1118 after the capture of Jerusalem to defend it against attacks by the Muslims. They gained great wealth and

Buddhist Temple, Singapore

influence, but after the fall of Acre in 1291 their power waned, and they were suppressed in 1312.

Temple

1. Sacred place regarded as the home of a god, with a cella or naos, a room reserved for the god or his statue.

2. In Hinduism temples were first built in the 4th century BCE; they usually incorporate an image room and a place for purification rites.

3. The Jewish Temple in Jerusalem was first built by Solomon c. 950 BCE, and destroyed by the Babylonians in 586 BCE. The second Temple was dedicated in 516 BCE, and stood until Herod the Great began a rebuilding plan in 19 BCE, but this, the last Temple, was destroyed in 70 CE by the Romans.

Ten Commandments

Law code delivered by God to Moses on Mt Sinai. There are two accounts of this in the Bible, in Exodus 19–20 and Deuteronomy 5; the accounts are the same, except for the reason given for keeping the Sabbath. The first four commandments are religious, the next six are social.

Ten Days of Penitence

Ten solemn days in the Jewish calendar beginning on Rosh Hashanah and ending on Yom Kippur. They are days marked by repentance, contrition and prayers for divine forgiveness, together with a resolve for the restoration of broken harmonies with God and fellow-men.

Tenak

Jewish colloquial term for the Hebrew Bible. Derived from the initial letters of the three sections of the book, viz. Torah, Nebiim and Kethubim (Law, Prophets and Writings).

Tendai (J)/T'ien T'ai (C)

School of Buddhism introduced from China into Japan by Saicho (767–822 CE). It teaches a threefold truth: (1) that all things are of the void; (2) that phenomenal existences of all kinds are only temporary productions; (3) that as everything involves everything else, all is one.

Tengalai

One of the two schools into which the disciples of the Hindu philosopher Ramanuja were divided. They believed that the process of salvation is initiated by God, not man, and that all men, of any caste, can share it. They use Tamil instead of Sanskrit for the Scriptures. (Cf. Vadagalai)

Tenrikyo

Shinto sect founded by a woman teacher, Miki Nakayama, in 1839. It emphasizes faith-healing, and places great importance on prayer and purity of heart. It claims over two million members.

Tensho-kotai-jingu-kyo

Lit. 'religion of the heaven shining great deity dwelling'. Shinto sect founded in 1942 by Sayo Kitamura; it is sometimes called the dancing religion because of the ecstatic dancing during worship. Kitamura chants her message of repentance and unselfish service, and is regarded by her followers as a successor to the Buddha.

Tenth of Muharram

Solemn day observed by Muslims of the Shiah community, to commemorate the martyrdom of Imam Husain, the grandson of the Prophet Muhammad.

Tephillin

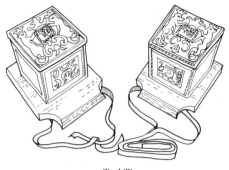

Tephillin

Word used by Jews for phylacteries. These are two small cubic boxes of black leather which are fastened by straps, one to the head and the other to the left arm, which brings it near the heart. They contain four biblical texts written on parchment, and are worn by men for the recitation of morning prayers.

Teraphim

Cult objects mentioned throughout the Hebrew Bible, usually in a condemnatory context. They appear to have been associated with household worship, and were possibly used in divination. Archaeological discoveries at Nuzi suggest that they were decorated figurines.

Terce, Sext and None

The 'little hours' of the divine office of the Christian Church, said at the third, sixth and ninth hours.

Teresa, St

(1515–1582)   St Teresa of Avila was a Spanish Carmelite nun and mystic. She is an important figure in the history of the religious life as she experienced the presence of Christ in her moments of ecstasy. She was also a very practical person, reforming the Carmelite order and founding many convents of Discalced Carmelites. She wrote *The Way of Perfection*, and taught steps of prayer from discursive meditation to ecstatic union.

Terminus

Roman deity who presided over boundaries and frontiers. His worship was instituted by Numa, according to legend the second king of Rome, who ordered that sacrifices should be offered annually at boundary stones on the Feast of Terminalia.

Tertiary

Member of the third order of one of the mendicant orders, the Franciscans, Dominicans and Carmelites. A tertiary observes a rule of life and recites the offices, but does not live within the community.

Tertullian, Quintus Septimus

(160–220 CE)   Native of Carthage, educated as a pagan, but converted to Christianity. He was the first theologian of note to write in Latin, and he produced many books, including an apology directed to the Emperor, an attack on Marcion and expositions of doctrine.

Teruah

Sound consisting of a series of nine stuttering notes which is blown on the shofar in Jewish synagogues on New Year's Day. The teruah alternates with the tekiah and the shevarim.

Teshub

Storm god of the Hittites, similar to the Egyptian storm god Set.

Teshubah (H)

Term used in Judaism for repentance. Lit. 'return', it signifies a rediscovery of or a return to old, tried ways. It involves a change of heart and mind, and demands a combination of remorse for the past and a new resolve for the future.

Tetragrammaton

The four letters YHWH in Hebrew, which indicate the name of God in the Hebrew Bible. The name is never pronounced, but the term 'Adonai' (Lord) is substituted.

Textus Receptus

Greek text of the NT as contained in printed editions down to the 19th century. It is the Byzantine text and was followed by Beza and Erasmus and used as the basis of the Authorized Version.

Tezcatlipoca

Lit. 'smoking mirror'. One of the most prominent deities in the Mexican pantheon, taken over by the Aztecs.

Thaddaeus

One of the twelve disciples of Jesus. He is sometimes called Lebbaeus, and has been identified, by tradition, with Judas, the brother of Jesus.

Theism

Term which first appeared in the book *Intellectual System*, by R. Cudworth, in 1678 in distinction from deism and in opposition to atheism. It is applied to systems of theology which accept a transcendent, personal God who in the Beginning created the world and now governs it, maintaining a relationship between himself and his creatures.

Thek

Nuer term for respect which imposes an interdiction on certain forms of conduct, in the same way as 'taboo' in other societies.

Themis

In the poems of Homer she is a minor goddess, the personification of the order of things established by law, custom and equity. It was her duty to convene the assemblies of the gods, at the command of Zeus.

Theocracy

System of government where God is considered to be the head, and his priests or ministers are the interpreters of his commands. Some theologians would assert that theocracies were established by Moses among the Israelites, by Savonarola for a short period in Florence, and by Calvin in Geneva.

Theodicy

Account of the universe and the ordering or governing of it set out in such a way as to vindicate the justice of divine government. In some writings the word stands for the search for religious meaning in the face of the inequalities and ineradicable problems of human existence.

Theogony

Title of a poem by Hesiod which relates stories of the origin of the gods and the creation of the world. Lit. 'genealogy of the gods'.

Theologica Germanica

Anonymous mystical treatise written in the 14th century which counselled poverty of spirit and abandonment to God, as a means of transformation by love into participation in the divine nature. It influenced the thinking of Martin Luther, who supervised the first printed edition in 1518.

Theology

Etymologically, this is the study of the nature of God, but as different faiths have developed in the history of mankind, the subject has become wider and more complex, involving all aspects of man's relationship to God, and his hopes of salvation. In Hinduism and Buddhism theology is akin to the philosophy of religion, whereas Judaism, Christianity and Islam depend more on the theology of revelation, embodied in the Bible and the Qur'an. Other divisions of the subject are historical theology, pastoral theology, moral theology and ascetic theology.

Theophany

Term used for the appearance of God in visible form. One example is the appearance of God to Moses (Exodus 33).

Theosophy

Term applied to various cults that seek direct knowledge of God by intuition of the divine essence. Its modern form in the Theosophical Society, founded by Mme Blavatsky and Col. Olcott in 1875, claims to be a religion, a philosophy and a science.

Theotokos

Word meaning 'god-bearer', or as applied to the Virgin Mary, 'Mother of God'. It was first used of her by Origen, and attacked by Nestorius in 429 CE. It was reaffirmed as Catholic doctrine at the Council of Ephesus in 451.

Theravada

One of the main sections of Buddhism, which claims to follow the doctrine of the Elders. It is the southern school of Buddhism, found in S.E. Asia (Sri Lanka, Burma and Thailand), and it is sometimes regarded as the monk's way of salvation, or the conservative interpretation of Buddhism. Adherents of the Mahayana school of Buddhism refer disparagingly to Theravada as 'Hinayana' (lesser vehicle).

Theseus

Hero of Attica who figures in numerous legends, rescuing people from tyranny or danger. He volunteered to go to Crete as one of the youths devoured annually by the Minotaur, but Ariadne saved his life by giving him a sword to kill it and a thread to find his way out of the labyrinth. He defended Athens against the attacks of the Amazons.

Thessalonians, Epistles to the

Two letters written by St Paul included in the NT. Both are concerned with problems relating to the second coming of Christ, e.g. how Christians should behave in the period of waiting, and what would happen to those who died before Christ returned. Paul is anxious to quieten the fears of the Thessalonians, and to encourage them in holy living.

Thetis

Marine deity in Greek mythology. She was chiefly reverenced as the mother of Achilles, whom she brought up with great love and care, and who became the Greek ideal of manhood.

Third Eye

Extra eye in the middle of the forehead, often inserted into images of the Hindu god Shiva. With it he was able to destroy his enemies.

Thirteen

Number that has always been regarded as unlucky. It is one more than the number of completeness or perfection, and thus represents the exceeding of proper limits. It is the number of persons present at the Last Supper before Judas left to betray Jesus. It is the traditional number of witches in a coven.

Thirteen Principles

The articles of the Jewish faith, which are the equivalent of a creed. They were formulated by Moses Maimonides (1134–1204), and are still regularly recited. They are printed in the Jewish Daily Prayer Book, where they are described as the Articles of the Jewish Creed.

Thirty Years War

(1618–1648) Religious and political struggle between Catholic and Protestant states. The Augsburg Agreement of 1555, which gave rulers the right to determine the state religion, was challenged by a new Emperor, Ferdinand II, in 1618. In the first battles the Protestants were defeated, but Gustavus Adolphus of Sweden and Christian IV of Denmark were drawn in, and gradually the Protestants gained the upper hand. The later stages of the War were political, as France intervened to weaken Spain and the Empire. The Peace of Westphalia (1648) brought the fighting to an end and gave the Calvinists full legal recognition.

Thirty-nine Articles

Theological statement of doctrines accepted by the Church of England, approved by Elizabeth I, and passed by Convocation in 1574. This statement is printed in the *Book of Common Prayer*, and a declaration of assent to the doctrines contained in it is required from clergy on their ordination.

Thomas, St

One of the twelve disciples of Jesus, mentioned in all four Gospels. He is remembered as the one who expressed doubts when told that Christ had risen from the dead, but he affirmed his faith with the words 'My Lord and my God' when Christ appeared to him. According to tradition, he went to India as a missionary and was martyred there.

Thomas Aquinas

(1225–1274) Dominican philosopher and theologian. His vast work *Summa Theologica* has been one of the main expositions of Roman Catholic theology. He was declared a Doctor of the Church in 1567, and in 1923 his authority as a teacher was reiterated by Pope Pius XI.

Thomas à Becket

(1118–1170) Priest who became a friend of Henry II and his chancellor in 1155. He was elected Archbishop of Canterbury in 1162 and soon clashed with the King, refusing to accept the Constitutions of Clarendon. After many stormy episodes he was assassinated by four of the King's knights in 1170. His tomb quickly became a centre of pilgrimage, and he was canonized in 1173.

Thomas à Kempis

(1380–1471) Christian monk and ascetic. After being educated by the Brethren of the Common Life, he joined the Canons Regular of Anietenberg in 1399. He is chiefly known as the author of a treatise *Of the Imitation of Christ*, which examines aspects of prayer and the spiritual life. It quickly won fame, and has been one of the most influential books of devotion ever written.

Thor

In Norse mythology the son of Odin, and the god of thunder. Thursday is the day dedicated to him.

Thorgerd

Scandinavian goddess who had power over hail and storms.

Martyrdom of St Thomas à Becket (Latin psalter executed in England *c*. 1200)

Thoth

Egyptian deity identified by the Greeks with Hermes. He was the personification of divine intelligence, and is credited with the invention of letters, arts and sciences. In Egyptian iconography he was portrayed as a man with the head of an ibis or of a dog.

Dead man   Anubis   Thoth

Thoth records the weighing of the heart of a dead man

Three

This is generally considered to be the luckiest number. The triangle is the first plane figure, and it sometimes symbolized the male genitals, thus linking three with creativity and self-expression. In the Christian faith, the doctrine of the Trinity expresses the fulness of the Godhead, and 'three' often occurs in the NT, e.g. three wise men brought gifts to the infant Jesus; there were three temptations in the wilderness; Jesus Christ rose from the dead on the third day. (See also Trinity)

Three Baskets

Name given to the Pali canon of Buddhist scriptures, otherwise known as the *Tipitaka.*

Three Bodies

Term used in Mahayana Buddhism to express the doctrine that there are three different aspects of the Buddha nature: the eternal teaching; the historical Buddha; the transcendental Buddha.

Three Jewels

Term used in Buddhism for the basic affirmation of the faith, viz. 'I take refuge in the Buddha; I take refuge in the Dhamma; I take refuge in the Sangha.'

Three-hour Service

Service held in Christian churches from noon till 3 p.m. on Good Friday, to meditate on the Passion of Christ and the Seven Words from the Cross. The first service of this kind was held by the Jesuits in 1687.

Threshold

Vital place in a building, separating a home from the outside world. A widespread marriage custom is for the bridegroom to carry the bride over the threshold on her arrival at their new home, as a symbol of transition. Sometimes an entrance gate is decorated by guardian statues or carvings, and threshold sacrifices are mentioned in the OT.

Thugs

Secret Hindu sect which committed murder and robbery in honour of the goddess Kali. The Thugs were put down by government action in the middle of the 19th century.

Thundering Legion

Twelfth Legion in the army of Marcus Aurelius. It was saved from destruction by a sudden rain and thunder storm during the Danubian campaign in 172 CE. Christian soldiers in the Legion claimed it was a miracle in response to their prayers.

Thurible

Metal vessel suspended on a chain in which incense is burned. The thurible is swung on its chains to cause the incense smoke to billow out into the church. It is also called a censer.

Thursday

Fifth day of the week, named after the ancient Teutonic god Thor. (See also Maundy Thursday)

Tiamat

Babylonian deity of the salt water, or chaos. She was the bitter enemy of Marduk, but when she opened her mouth to swallow him, he filled her with a terrible wind, cut her body in pieces, and formed the earth from them.

Thurible in use at a Greek Orthodox celebration of the Mass

Tiberias

City on the west shore of the Sea of Galilee, which is also known as the Sea of Tiberias. After the destruction of Jerusalem in 70 CE, it became a centre of Jewish learning, the Mishnah being compiled there in the 3rd century, and the Talmud in the 5th century.

T'ien (C)

Name used in the philosophy of Confucius for heaven and the supreme god.

Tien T'ai (C)

See Tendai

Tilak

Ceremony practised in village Hinduism which marks an engagement, and takes place one month before the marriage.

Timothy

    1. One of St Paul's most trusted converts, and a companion on his second missionary journey.

    2. Title of two NT epistles written by St Paul. They are concerned with worship, order, and discipline within the Church, and contain an exhortation to stand firm in the faith when confronted with persecution.

Tipitaka (P) / ***Tripitaka*** (S)

    Pali canon of the Buddhist scriptures, accepted by the Theravadins. Lit. 'three baskets', namely (1) *Vinaya Pitaka*, narratives concerning the establishment of the Sangha; (2) *Sutta Pitaka*, discourses of the Buddha; (3) *Abhidhamma Pitaka*, seven books of doctrine.

Tirath

    Term used in the Sikh religion for a sanctuary or a place of pilgrimage, such as the Golden Temple, Amritsar.

Tiresias

    One of the most renowned soothsayers of antiquity. He was born in Thebes and was blind from a very early age, but he lived a long time. His name and his predictions are woven into numerous Greek myths and legends.

Tirthankaras

    Twenty-four great souls who, according to tradition, originally preached the Jain doctrines. Mahavira is considered to be the last of these teachers.

Tirttha

    Term used in Hinduism for sacred, dedicated food; a synonym of 'prasad'. After being offered at a shrine, it is distributed to the worshippers.

Tisha b'Ab (H)

    Jewish fast which falls on the ninth day of the month Ab and commemorates the destruction of the first and second Temples, and Jewish suffering in general.

Titans

    The six sons and six daughters of Uranus (heaven) and Ge (earth) in Greek mythology. They revolted against Uranus and deposed him, setting up Cronos as king. Later Zeus, son of Cronos, deposed him and threw the Titans into the cavity of Tartarus, below Hades, and bolted them in.

Tithe

    Tenth part of the produce of the land, paid in medieval times to the rector of an English parish. In 1918 the value of the tithe was stabilized, and in 1936 a system of annuities, administered by the Commissioners of the Inland Revenue, put an end to the statutory payment of tithes. Many members of the Christian Church still regard it as a moral obligation to pay a tithe of their income to the Church or to charities.

Jain Tirthankara

Titus

    1. One of St Paul's companions in whom he put great trust. He helped to resolve the difficulties and differences between Paul and the members of the Church in Corinth.

    2. Epistle in the NT written by St Paul. It is concerned with Christian behaviour and teaching.

Tlaloc

    Lit. 'lord of the sources of water'. Rain and fertility god of Mexican mythology, taken over by the Aztecs.

Tobit

    Central figure in a book of the same name in Jewish apocryphal writings. Tobit became blind, and needing money for a cure, he sent his son Tobias to recover a debt. Tobias was guided by the Archangel Raphael in disguise, and after a series of adventures he recovered the money, and returned to Tobit, who was cured of his blindness.

Tona

See Tuna

Tonda

Word used in many African tribes for that which is taboo, or is under a ban, or must not be spoken or done.

Tonsure

Shaving of part of the hair of the head, prescribed by Roman Catholic canon law for clergy. In modern times the tonsure is a monastic practice only.

Torah (H)

Word that can be translated 'law' when it applies particularly to the Law of Moses, i.e. the first five books of the Bible, the Pentateuch. It can be translated in a more general sense as 'teaching'.

Torii

Gateways at Shinto temples, said to represent bird perches, recalling the help given by birds to the gods. They consist of two posts with two horizontal lintels, usually painted red. All Shinto temples have three or more, and as worshippers pass under them they bow, to salute the gods.

Tosafoth (H)

Additions or supplements to the commentary of Rashi on the Talmud, made in the 12th and 13th centuries.

Tosefta (H)

Term for additions to the Jewish Mishnah which were made in the 3rd century.

Totem

Natural object, usually an animal, assumed as the symbol or emblem of a clan or individual, on the grounds of a relationship of spirit or nature between them.

Totka

Magic ritual within Hinduism, carried out usually by an Indian village priest.

Tractarianism

Name applied to the Oxford Movement in its early stages in the 19th century. It is derived from the *Tracts for the Times*, which were written by the leaders. The early tracts were short, but they became longer, and the last of the series, *Tract 90*, by J. H. Newman, was a long discourse entitled *Remarks on the Thirty-nine Articles*, and caused a storm of protest because of its leanings towards Roman Catholicism. Soon after writing it, Newman was received into the Church of Rome.

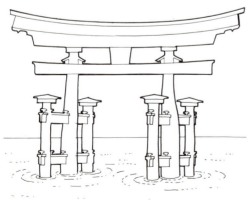

Torii

Totemic figure (British Columbia)

Tractate

Section of the Jewish Mishnah. This book is divided into six orders or sedarim, and each order is divided into a number of tractates. There are sixty-five tractates altogether, dealing with topics such as prayer, offerings, idolatry and taxes.

Transcendental Complex

Term used for a mode of Hindu religious motivation, the quest for liberation and salvation. The liberation is from samsara, the cycle of birth and rebirth, and the aim of the quest is to transcend not only this world, but all other worlds that may be regarded as continuing existence.

Transcendental Meditation

System of meditation introduced by Maharishi Mahesh Yogi. It is based on ancient Vedic knowledge applied through a secret technique known as the Science of Creative Intelligence. Its adherents claim that it is an effortless process of the mind that produces cumulative benefits from the first day of practice. Such benefits include reduced nervousness, irritability and depression, and increased self-assuredness, staying power and efficiency.

Transcendentalism

Term applied to the philosophy of Kant and his disciples. The word 'transcendental' was applied to those principles of knowledge which are original and primary, and are determined *a priori*. Kant applied it to all that lies beyond the limits of experience, and is not accessible to it.

Transfiguration

Solemn event in the life of Jesus Christ, recorded in Matthew 17:1–8. With three disciples he ascended a mountain, and there appeared in heavenly brightness or glory with Moses and Elijah, while a heavenly voice declared his divine sonship and authority.

Transmigration of Souls

See Reincarnation and Samsara

Transubstantiation

Roman Catholic doctrine concerning the Mass defined at the Lateran Council of 1215, and confirmed at the Council of Trent in 1551. This states that in the Eucharist, at the words of consecration, the substance of the bread and wine becomes the substance of the Body and Blood of Jesus Christ, and that he is thus present on the altar.

Trappists

Monks of the Cistercian order who observe the reformed rule established in 1664 at La Trappe in Normandy. A life of the utmost rigour is imposed, and perpetual silence is the rule. In 1892 they were united with the Cistercians of the Strict Observance.

Trees

Trees, with their roots deep in the earth and their heads in the sky, and with a longer life span than man, have always been objects of veneration. The OT records that in the Garden of Eden were the Tree of Life and the Tree of Knowledge, from which Eve picked the forbidden fruit. Also in the OT and in Greek and Roman writings are accounts of trees which gave oracles, and Buddhists believe that the Buddha attained enlightenment while meditating beneath a bo-tree.

Trefa (H)

Term used by Jews to describe non-Kosher food, or food that they are not permitted to eat.

Trent, Council of

Nineteenth Ecumenical Council of the Catholic Church, summoned by Pope Paul III. It began its sessions in 1545 and continued with intervals until it was ended by Pope Pius IV in 1563. In a series of decrees and canons, it restated Catholic doctrine, particularly where this had been attacked by the Protestant reformers.

Tria Charitr

Section of the Sikh book *Dasam Granth*. This part has legends and anecdotes, particularly tales about the wiles of women, the mother goddess figuring prominently in it.

Trident

Three-pronged fork, the weapon carried by the Hindu god Shiva and the Roman god Neptune. In Roman gladiatorial contests, some gladiators were armed with a trident and net.

Trikaya

Mahayana Buddhist doctrine of the three bodies (kaya), or vehicles of manifestation of the Buddha.

These are: Nirmana-kaya, the earthly incarnate Buddha; Sambhoga-kaya, the body of bliss, the transcendent, heavenly Buddha; Dharma-kaya, the ultimate of absolute reality.

Triloka (S)

Lit. 'three worlds'. In Hinduism this signifies the earth, the air and the sky. In Buddhism it signifies the world of the senses, the world of invisible yet existent form, and the formless world.

Trimurti (S)

Triad of the three great Hindu gods. In the *Mahabharata* these are named as Brahma, Vishnu and Shiva.

Trinity

In the Christian faith, the doctrine that there is one God in three persons: Father, Son and Holy Spirit. They are Three in One and One in Three, coeternal and coessential. Other faiths have linked gods in triads, e.g. Hinduism (Brahma, Vishnu and Shiva), Egypt (Osiris, Isis and Horus) and Mahayana Buddhism (three manifestations of the Buddha, viz. Nirmana-kaya, Sambhoga-kaya and Dharma-kaya).

Trinity Sunday

In the calendar of the Christian Church this falls on the Sunday after Whitsun, and it is set aside for considering the doctrine of the Trinity, the Father, the Son and the Holy Spirit. Traditionally, it is one of the principal days for the ordination of priests and deacons.

Tripitaka (S)

See *Tipitaka*

Triratna (S)

Lit. 'three jewels'. For Buddhists this signifies the Buddha, the Dhamma and the Sangha. For Jains it signifies right faith, right knowledge and right conduct.

Trisagion

Triple repetition of the word 'holy', as in 'Holy, Holy, Holy, Lord God Almighty'. The first mention of this is in the account of the Council of Chalcedon in 451 CE.

Trivium

Medieval name for the three subjects grammar, rhetoric and dialectic, which together with the quadrivium (music, arithmetic, geometry and astronomy) made up the seven liberal arts.

Trolls

According to Norse mythology these were supernatural beings. In Icelandic literature they are giants, but in Scandinavian literature they are imps or gnomes.

Trsna (S)

See Tanha

Tu b'Shvat (H)

In Israel, the fifteenth day of the month Shvat. It marks the beginning of spring and is known as the New Year for Trees. On this holiday, schoolchildren go out into the fields to plant saplings.

Tuche

Greek goddess of good luck, identified by the Romans with Fortuna.

Tulasi

Type of basil plant which has become one of the symbols used to represent the Hindu god Vishnu.

Tulsi Das

(1532–1620) Hindu teacher and poet. His best-known work was the *Ram Carit Manas*, a Hindi version of the *Ramayana*.

Tuna/Tona

Term used for sorcery practised by a Hindu villager in an attempt to cause suffering or disaster.

Tutankhamun

One of the last Pharaohs of the Egyptian 18th Dynasty. His dates are uncertain, but he seems to have been born *c.* 1360 BCE, to have become Pharaoh at the age of nine, and to have reigned for nine years. He came to the throne through marriage to the daughter of Akhenaton, the Pharaoh who changed the worship of Amun to that of Aton. Tutankhamun is the best known of all the Pharaohs because in 1922 his tomb was discovered intact, and vast quantities of royal possessions and the royal sarcophagus were brought to light.

Twelfth Night
Evening preceding the Christian feast of the Epiphany, twelve days after Christmas, commemorating the visit of the three kings to the infant Jesus. Traditionally, this is a night of merry-making and feasting, and in some countries the exchange of presents.

Twelve
Traditionally this is the figure of completion or perfection, as in the twelve hours of the day and of the night, and the twelve months of the year. In the Bible there are twelve tribes of Israel and twelve jewels in the High Priest's breastplate; Jesus chose twelve disciples, and the New Jerusalem described in Revelation had twelve foundation stones and twelve gates. In Greek mythology there were twelve gods of Olympus, and the earliest Roman law code was written on twelve tablets.

Twelvers
Sect of Shiah Muslims who accepted a line of twelve Imams, in contrast with the Ismailis, who accept only seven.

Twice Born
Title of those members of the three upper classes of Hindus (Brahmins, Kshatriyas and Vaishyas) who have been through a ceremony of initiation and have been invested with the sacred thread.

Twilight of the Gods
See Ragnarök

Twins
The birth of twins has, in many societies, been accompanied by fascination and fear, sometimes causing them to be put to death. The OT has the story of Esau and Jacob, and the trickery that deprived the older twin of his birthright (Genesis 25). In the NT one of the disciples of Jesus was Thomas Didymus (the twin). A late tradition suggested that he was really the twin brother of Jesus. The foundation of Rome is linked with the twins Romulus and Remus. Sighting the constellation of Gemini (the heavenly twins Castor and Pollux) during a storm was regarded as a good omen.

Two
From the time of the Pythagoreans, who were keen students of numbers, two has been regarded as the number of evil and the number of woman. It is the breakup of unity, and the 'not-one' is unstable. The reversed pentagram, with two points upward, is regarded as a sign of the Devil, probably because the two points resemble the Devil's horns.

Tyndale, William
(1490–1536)   English translator of the Bible. He was educated at Oxford and ordained, but he incurred the displeasure of the Church because of his work as a translator, and his determination to put the Bible into the hands of ordinary people. His work had to be printed in Germany and sent to England, because of the bitter opposition of the English bishops. He was forced to move from place to place, but was finally captured and executed in Brussels in 1536.

Types
Theological term referring to the foreshadowing of Christian beliefs in events or persons in the OT. Thus Noah's Ark is regarded as a type of the Church, Melchizedek a type of Christ, and Jonah a type of the Resurrection.

Tzizith (H)
Fringed garment worn by male Jews, in accordance with the instructions in Numbers 15:39, to remind them of the commandments of the Lord. The fringe is of white threads with a blue thread interlaced.

Ubar

Gong or drum which has an important function in the ritual of Australian aborigines. It is said to represent the womb of the fertility mother, and its sound is the mother's voice.

Ubiquity

Christian doctrine of divine omnipresence. It was used by Luther to justify his belief in the real presence of Christ in the Eucharist while denying the doctrine of transubstantiation. He maintained that Christ in his human nature is everywhere present.

Ubwanga

Word used in many tribes of Central Africa to designate an impersonal, undifferentiated power which can be a cause of good or of harm. It must be used only by one with secret knowledge, as in the wrong hands it could bring disaster to the operator and his community. It has the same sense as the Polynesian word *mana*.

Udana (S)

Lit. 'breathing upwards'. In yoga this is a term for one of the five vital airs which work upward from the throat. In Buddhism it is the title of one of the works in the second section of the canon of scripture, the *Sutta Pitaka*.

Udasis

Sect of the Sikhs who practise celibacy and asceticism. It was founded by Siri Chand, a son of Guru Nanak.

Ulama

Islamic doctors of law or theology. The custodians of Islamic teaching.

Ulfilas

(311–383 CE)   Catholic priest of Cappadocian ancestry. Consecrated as a bishop in 341, he was sent to convert his own people, the Goths. He translated the Bible into Gothic and built up a strong Church. Because he was an Arian, the Gothic Church maintained the heresy of Arianism for several centuries.

Ultramontanism

Teaching within the Roman Catholic Church which places an absolute authority in matters of faith and discipline in the hands of the Pope, in opposition to teaching that would give national Churches some independence, and make the Pope subordinate to ecumenical councils. This point of view was encouraged in the 19th century by the revival of the Jesuit order, and can be seen in the declaration of Papal Infallibility in 1870. Since then, ultramontanism has been official Catholic doctrine.

Ulysses

One of the Greek heroes of the Trojan War. He is said to have devised the strategem of the Wooden Horse, and to have entered Troy in it. He was also known as Odysseus, and in the *Odyssey*, Homer tells the story of his travels after the War ended. After many adventures, he returned to his faithful wife Penelope, killed the suitors who were tormenting her, and resumed the rule of Ithaca.

Umar

(582–644 CE)   Second Islamic Caliph who succeeded Abu Bakr in 634 and held the office for ten years. He led a very simple, austere life, and laid down many of the principles which govern Islamic social life. He was given the title 'Commander of the Faith', and extended the dominion of Islam.

Ummah (A)

Term used in Islam with several shades of meaning, e.g. the community of Islam, the solidarity of faith and the political incorporation of the faith.

Ummayads

Dynasty of Islamic Caliphs who ruled the Islamic Empire from Damascus, from 661 to 750 CE. They extended their power along the North African coast as far as Spain, and eastwards to the Indus.

Ummi (A)

Term used by Muslims for an unlettered or illiterate person, or a member of a community without scriptures. It is used in the Qur'an (surah 7) of Muhammad.

'Umra (A)

The Lesser Pilgrimage undertaken by some Muslims. This is optional, and may be made to Mecca at any time of the year.

Unam Sanctam

Bull promulgated by Pope Boniface VIII in 1302 which stated that there is one Holy, Catholic and Apostolic Church, outside which there is neither salvation nor remission of sins.

Unction

Anointing with oil, usually in a religious rite. In the British coronation service the Monarch is anointed before being crowned. Sick persons are often anointed in church or at home, with special prayers for healing. Extreme unction is regarded in the Roman Catholic Church as a sacrament, and is administered as a preparation for death.

Undine

Water spirit in Greek and Roman mythology. These were similar to the naiads, except that it was believed that when an undine married a mortal and bore a child, she herself received a mortal soul.

Unicorn

Fabulous beast that figures in many myths. It entered the biblical text through an error in the Greek translation of the OT, when *re'em* (wild ox, Numbers 23:22) was rendered *monoceros* (single horned or unicorn). Talmudic texts link the unicorn with the lion, and the lion and unicorn are the supporters of the shield in the British royal coat of arms. The unicorn has been used as a symbol of virility (the single male horn) and also of purity (the female body).

Unified Church

Sect founded by a Korean engineer Sun Myung Moon. Its full name is The Holy Spirit Association for the Unification of World Christianity, but it is more generally known from the name of its founder as the Moon Sect. Moon claims that Jesus regularly appeared to him, but as the South Korean Churches were not interested he went north, where he was betrayed, imprisoned and tortured. In 1950 he was released and founded a new Church which quickly grew, spread to Japan and soon reached America. The philosophy of the movement is called the Divine Principle, which contains twelve sections dealing with the Creation, the Fall, God and Christ. The sect maintains that the Divine Principle gives a pattern and coherence to the Scriptures, but it is available only to members, not to the general public.

Uniformity, Act of

Four Acts of Uniformity have been on the English Statute Book. The first (1549) imposed the use of the first *Book of Common Prayer* of Edward VI. The second (1552) permitted the use of the second Prayer Book, and enforced attendance at Sunday services. The third (1559) confirmed the use of the second Prayer Book and legislated about church ornaments. The fourth (1662) required all ministers to use the new Prayer Book of that year, and publicly to give their assent to it.

Unitarianism

Teaching that God is one person, denying the divinity of Christ and the Holy Spirit, and rejecting the doctrine of the Holy Trinity. Unitarians do not profess any formal creed or confessional statement.

Universalism

1. Doctrine found in some late books in the Hebrew Bible, such as Jonah, that God's purposes were not limited to Israel, but will ultimately embrace all mankind.

2. Doctrine held by some Christians that at the end of time all men will be saved and will share in God's eternal salvation.

Unkulunkulu

High god of the Zulus. The name means 'great one' or 'old one', and he is worshipped as the Creator.

Unleavened Bread

This is eaten by Jews during the Feast of the Passover. It reminds them that when their ancestors prepared, in haste, for the Exodus, they had to make bread with unleavened dough. As it commemorates their oppression, it is known as the Bread of Affliction, but as it also commemorates their journey to freedom, it is known as the Bread of Song. (See also Matzah)

Untouchable

People outside the Hindu class system (outcastes) who come below the lowest of the four classes of Indian Hindu society. They are in a position of the utmost difficulty, often in poverty, because their presence is said to pollute any caste Hindu who is nearby. They were given a more dignified title by Gandhi, who called them Harijans, sons of God, and worked to improve their lot. Now, in theory, i.e. according to government legislation, they no longer exist, as the term 'outcaste' has been abolished, but some of them still suffer from caste oppression.

Upadana (S)

Lit. 'acquiring' or 'learning'. Term used in Buddhism for the ninth of the twelve links in the chain of existence.

Upanayana

Term used in Hinduism for the ceremony of initiation into the twice-born castes, when boys are made full members of their community and are invested with the sacred thread.

Upanishads

Compound word linked with the verb 'to sit', which suggests a session in which disciples sit at the feet of a guru for instruction in their religious beliefs. The word is applied to Hindu scriptures dating from the period 800–300 BCE which followed the *Vedas*, some in prose and some in verse. Some scholars emphasize their different outlook, pointing out that they are the most philosophical of Hindu writings. Other scholars consider that they complete the intention of the *Vedas*, and they are in fact also known as the *Vedanta*, the end of the *Vedas*.

Upasaka (masc.)**/Upasika** (fem.)

Buddhist disciples who practise their faith in the world, without retiring to a monastery or a convent.

Upaya (P)

Lit. 'means' or 'methods'. Buddhist term which includes practices such as koans and mondos.

Upeksa (P)

Buddhist term for 'indifference', 'serenity', 'freedom from feeling', or 'the ability to overcome feelings of pleasure or pain'. This is the fourth of the Brahma viharas.

Uposatha (P)

Practice of fasting or public confession in Buddhist communities, which is undertaken twice a month by monks.

Ur of the Chaldees

Ancient Sumerian city from which Abraham set out on his journey to Canaan (Genesis 11:31). It was situated on the Euphrates, about 240 km south-east of Babylon. Excavations have revealed a high level of civilization, with well-planned houses, large temples and palaces, and gold, silver and jewellery work of the finest craftsmanship.

Uraeus

Latin word derived from the Egyptian word for 'cobra'. In Egypt it was a symbol of royalty, and formed part of the head-dress of the Pharoah.

Uraeus (from the tomb of Tutankhamun)

Uranus

Lit. 'heaven'. In Greek mythology he was the father of the twelve Titans, but he hated them and treated them so harshly that they revolted, castrated him and set up Cronos as king. From the blood of Uranus came the Giants, and from the sea foam which he stirred up sprang Aphrodite.

Urbi et Orbi

Lit. 'to the city and to the world'. Phrase from the solemn blessing pronounced by the Pope from the balcony of the Vatican in Rome, particularly on Easter Day.

Urf (A)

Customary law in the Muslim religion, from which the content of the Islamic Shariah is derived.

Urim and Thummim

Objects placed in the pocket of the Israelite high priest's breastplate (Exodus 28:30), apparently for use in divination. Their exact nature is unknown. One interpretation is that 'Urim' is derived from a word meaning 'light', and that it was a white stone, Thummin being black. Another theory is that 'Urim' is from *arar* (to curse), and Thummmim from *tamam* (perfect). This might involve stones of different colours, or flat stones with different-coloured sides.

Urna (S)

Word used in Buddhism for the jewel that is sometimes set between the eyes of images of the Buddha. It represents the third eye of spiritual vision.

Uroboros

Self-consuming serpent, a circular symbol showing the serpent swallowing its tail. It is found in the Egyptian *Book of the Dead*, where it is said to represent the ocean waters. Being circular in form, it has been used as a symbol of eternity or perfection by a number of societies such as the Theosophists.

Ursulines

Oldest Roman Catholic teaching order for women. It was founded in 1535, and was approved by Pope Paul III in 1544, when community life with simple vows was introduced. Members take the usual three monastic vows, plus a fourth vow to devote themselves to educational activity.

Urvan

Term used in the Zoroastrian religion for the human soul.

Urvisgah

Special area or a room in a Zoroastrian temple where higher ceremonies, such as the Yasna, are performed by priests.

Ushabti

Models or statuettes of human figures placed in rich men's tombs in ancient Egypt. The *Book of the Dead* tells how they should be vivified to work for the dead man.

Reclining figure of the Buddha with an urna

Ushabti

Usury

Practice of lending money at very high rates of interest. This was attacked by early Church councils and was condemned at the Fourth Lateran Council of 1215. Thomas Aquinas, accepting Aristotle's views on the barren nature of money, provided theological justification for the ban. The rise of capitalism compelled a modification of canon law on the subject, in order to provide for the lending of money at reasonable rates of interest.

Uthman

Third Caliph, or leader of the Muslims, in succession to Muhammad. During his period of office the final, authoritative version of the Qur'an was produced.

Utilitarianism

Doctrine promulgated by J. S. Mill in 1863 that actions are right if they produce happiness but wrong if they produce unhappiness, and that a good act is one that produces the greatest good for the greatest number of people.

Utnapishtim

In the Babylonian legend of Gilgamesh, the god Ea warned Utnapishtim of an imminent flood, whereupon he built a reed boat with six decks and was saved with his family.

Utopia

Word first used by Sir Thomas More in 1516 as the title of a book. It is an imaginary island where the inhabitants live under happy conditions, sharing their possessions. The word is now generally applied to an imaginary state where everything is perfect.

Utraquism

Doctrine promulgated by John Huss that in the Christian Eucharist the laity, as well as the clergy, should receive communion in both bread and wine. This was condemned at the Council of Constance in 1415, but reaffirmed by Luther and other Reformers, and it is the practice followed in the Reformed and Anglican Churches.

Uwoluwu

Lit. 'high exalted one'. Sky god, the supreme deity of the Akpose tribes of Africa.

Vaca

Term used in the Buddhist religion for speech. In the teaching of the Buddha, right speech is the third step on the Noble Eightfold Path.

Vadagalai

One of the two schools into which the followers of Ramanuja were divided after his death in 1137. This school believes that the process of salvation is initiated by man's active seeking, and that only the three upper classes of Hindus can be devotees. They retain the use of Sanskrit for their scriptures. Cf. Tengalai.

Vaikuntha

In the teaching of the Hindu philosopher Ramanuja (d. 1137), this is the heavenly realm of Vishnu, where liberated souls live eternally, in glorious proximity to the divine being.

Vaishesika

One of the six orthodox schools of Hindu philosophy. It teaches that the elements are composed of atoms, and was founded by Kanada in the 3rd century BCE.

Vaishnava

Hindu who is a follower or devotee of the god Vishnu.

Vaishnavism

Form of Hinduism, strong in the north of India, in which the object of worship is the Lord Vishnu or one of his incarnations, such as Rama or Krishna. This is a form of bhakti, devotion to a personal god who saves his people by his grace.

Vaishyas

Third of the four classes of Hindu society in order of precedence or importance. Historically, they were the cultivators or artisans, but they are twice born and are invested with the sacred thread on initiation.

Vajja (P)/Vrajya (S)

Term used in Buddhist thought for that which must be avoided, or the action which produces bad results, or sin.

Vajra

In the Hindu scripture, the *Rig-Veda*, this is the enemy-destroying thunderbolt that was hurled by the god Indra.

Vajrayana

School of Tantric Buddhism which has affinities with one of the principal Mahayana schools, Yogacara.

Valentine, St

Christian saint of the Roman calendar, martyred in 306 CE. A medieval custom on the eve of St Valentine's Day (14 February) was for young people to meet in a group and pair off by drawing names out of a hat. This probably gave rise to the more modern practice of sending sentimental cards through the post, anonymously, to someone for whom the sender has affectionate feelings.

Symbol of the Vajra

Valentinus
One of the most influential Gnostic leaders in the 2nd century. His doctrine was based on a structure of aeons. Redemption was effected by the aeon Christ, who united himself to the man Jesus at his baptism. He brought gnosis into the world, but this is made available only to 'pneumatics', i.e. followers of Valentinus.

Valhalla
In Norse mythology the abode of Odin, the palace of immortality, occupied by the souls of heroes who had been slain in battle.

Valkyries
In Norse mythology the nine sisters of Odin. They were depicted as terrifying yet beautiful maidens, mounted on swift horses and holding drawn swords. They selected those destined to die, and conducted them to Valhalla.

Vallabha
(1481–1533) Hindu philosopher and reformer who taught the monistic identity of soul and Brahman, with the intention of increasing devotion to Krishna, the latter being regarded as the personification of Brahman.

Vanaprastha
Term used in Hindu philosophy, lit. 'forest-dweller'. It signifies the third of four stages in life, when the Brahmin begins to shed his family responsibilities, and devote his time and attention to meditation and the religious life.

Vandals
Ancient Teutonic people allied to the Goths, but less civilized. In 406 CE they moved south to Silesia, and later into Spain and Africa, where they took over Roman territories. In 455 they invaded Italy and sacked Rome.

Vanir
Ancient Scandinavian gods of fertility. Originally they were war gods, but according to legend, they tired of fighting and settled to cultivation.

Var
In the Sikh religion a song of praise, or a heroic ode in several stanzas.

Var Raksha
Indian ceremony, part of village Hinduism, at which 5% of a marriage dowry is handed over. The marriage arrangements cannot go on until this has been accomplished.

Varahavatara (S)
Word meaning 'boar', applied to the third avatar of Vishnu. The demon Hiranyaksha had dragged the earth into the sea, and Vishnu took the form of a boar in order to fight him. After a thousand years the demon was destroyed, and the earth was raised up again.

Varna (S)
Word meaning 'colour', used to indicate a class or division in Hindu society. There are four varnas or classes: the Brahmin, the Kshatriya, the Vaishya and the Shudra. The first three are called twice born, and at their initiation ceremonies they are invested with the sacred thread. According to Hindu thought, the varnas were established at the creation of the world, and are absolutely immutable.

Varnana (S)
Word meaning 'dwarf', applied to the fifth avatar of Vishnu, who appeared before a demon named Boli as a dwarf. When Boli attempted to crush Vishnu, the god suddenly expanded himself and defeated him.

Varuna
Sky god of Hindu mythology, equivalent to the Greek Ouranos and the Latin Uranus. In the *Rig-Veda* he was the god of order, both physical and moral, the king of the universe, and next in importance to Indra, who supplanted him. In modern Hinduism he is rarely mentioned.

Vasudeva
Title of Krishna used in the *Mahabharata*, particularly in the *Bhagavadgita*.

Vatican
Residence of the Pope, adjoining St Peter's Basilica in Rome. The present building was begun in the 14th century, and Sixtus IV added the Sistine Chapel towards the end of the 15th century, but the

whole design was not completed until 1821. In 1871 the Vatican was granted extra-territorial rights in an agreement with the Italian government.

Varahavatara

Vatican Council

Gathering of the bishops of the Roman Catholic Church under the direction of the Pope. The first, in 1870, defined Papal Infallibility. The second, called in 1964 by Pope John XXIII, brought far-reaching changes into Catholicism and in its relations with other Churches.

Vayama

Term used in Buddhist thought for effort. Right effort is the sixth step on the Noble Eightfold Path as expounded by the Buddha.

Vayu

Hindu god of wind or spirit mentioned in the *Vedas*. He is often associated with the storm god Indra, and he also appears in Zoroastrian literature.

Veda

Lit. 'knowledge'. Earliest corpus of Hindu scriptures, probably composed between 1500 and 800 BCE. It consists of: (1) four collections of devotional material, one of hymns, one of chanting instructions, one of sacrificial formulae and one of miscellaneous treatises; (2) priestly commentaries on these collections, known as the *Brahmanas* and *Aranyakas*; (3) philosophical treatises, the *Upanishads*. It should be noted that some scholars regard the *Upanishads* as a completely separate composition.

Vedana

Term used in Buddhist thought for sensation or feeling. This is one of the five aggregates which make up the nature of dwellers on the lowest plane of this earthly existence.

Vedanta

Lit. 'end of the *Veda*'. One of the six orthodox schools of Hindu philosophy. It is based on the *Brahmasutra* and the *Upanishads*, with which it is sometimes identified, and it is non-dualistic.

Vendetta

Term derived from the Latin word for revenge. It signifies a blood feud, or the practice of a next of kin taking revenge for the murder of a relative. The practice has some links with the ancient Lex Talionis, which demanded an eye for an eye, a life for a life.

Veneration of the Cross

Ritual observed in some Christian churches on Good Friday when worshippers kneel and kiss a crucifix placed on the sanctuary steps.

Veni Creator

Hymn to the Holy Spirit composed in the 9th century for use at Whitsuntide. It is also used at the ordination of priests and the consecration of bishops. The best-known English translation is 'Come, Holy Ghost, our souls inspire,' by J. Cosin.

Venial Sin

According to Catholic moral theology, this is sin which does not have the gravity of mortal sin, and does not wholly deprive the soul of sanctifying grace.

Venite

Psalm 95, prescribed in the Rule of St Benedict to be recited during the night service of the monastic liturgy. Since 1549 it has been the opening canticle in the service of Matins in the Anglican *Book of Common Prayer*.

Venus

Originally a Roman garden numen and goddess of spring, to whom the myrtle was sacred. She became much more important when her worship was promoted by Julius Caesar, who wished to trace his descent from Aeneas, the son of Venus by Anchises. She was then identified with Aphrodite, the Greek goddess of love and beauty, and became one of the most important Roman goddesses.

Verger

Lit. 'official who carries the verge [a mace or staff of office] in front of a dignitary'. It usually refers to a church official who is responsible for looking after the fabric and who also leads the procession of choir and clergy.

Veronica, St

Christian saint who is said to have helped Jesus Christ by wiping his face with her veil when he was carrying his cross to the place of execution. She later found that the impression of his features was clearly to be seen on her veil.

Vesak/Wesak

Full-moon festival observed in Theravada Buddhism to commemorate the birth, enlightenment and death of the Buddha. It is also the Buddhist New Year, when food and alms are distributed, and houses are decorated with garlands and lanterns. An alternative name for the festival is Vaisakha Puja.

Vespers

Evening office of the Western Church. In the Church of England it was conflated with Compline by the compilers of the *Book of Common Prayer* to form the service of Evensong.

Vesta

Roman goddess of home and domestic life. She was identified with the Greek goddess Hestia.

Vestal Virgins

Attendants at the Temple of Vesta in Rome, chosen by the Pontifex Maximus; their duty was to tend the sacred fire and they were severely punished if it went out. There were never less than two or more than six, and they served for a minimum of six years, during which time they were under a vow of virginity. Afterwards they were free to marry.

Vestment

Special or symbolic garment worn by officials, usually priests or their assistants, participating in divine service or sacred ritual or ceremonies.

Via Dolorosa

Route in Jerusalem which Christ is believed to have followed on his way from the judgement hall to Calvary. Many Christians make a devotional pilgrimage along the route, praying at certain points, especially on Good Friday.

Via Dolorosa, Jerusalem

Via Media

Title for the Church of England popularized by J. H. Newman and other leaders of the Oxford Movement. It envisages the Anglican Communion as the middle path between the papacy and dissent.

Via Negativa

Method of speculative theology associated with neo-Platonism. It emphasizes the inadequacy of human language to express the nature of the ineffable God, and begins by stripping away human qualities which are inappropriate when applied to God. Many theologians, including Thomas Aquinas, have considered it a necessary preliminary to the Via Positiva.

Via Positiva

Theological method taken over from Pseudo-Dionysus, who set it out in *The Divine Names*. It starts from the doctrine of the Creation, particularly the doctrine that man was created in the image of God, and believes that the highest human qualities are pointers to the perfection of God.

Viaticum

Lit. 'provision for a journey'. Holy Communion given to a person who is thought to be near death, in order to strengthen him with grace for his journey into eternity.

Vicar

Lit. 'substitute'. In the Church of England this is the title of a priest who is the incumbent of a parish. Originally it signified a priest who acted as a deputy or substitute for the rector, but had no right to tithes. Now that tithes have been abolished, there is little difference between a vicar and a rector.

Vicar Apostolic

Roman Catholic titular bishop. In some countries where there is no established hierarchy, he performs the spiritual functions of a diocesan bishop and has the same powers. In other circumstances he is the direct representative of the Pope in a specified area, and exercises his full authority.

Vicar of Christ

In the Roman Catholic Church, one of the titles of the Pope is Vicar of Christ on Earth. This title has been used since the 8th century.

Vicarious Suffering

Theological concept that one person, without guilt, can suffer on behalf of another person or community who is guilty. This is clearly set out in the Poem of the Suffering Servant (Isaiah 52:13–53:12), and has been transferred in Christian theology to the crucifixion of Jesus Christ, who, as a sinless victim, suffered in the place of the guilty – mankind in general – and made atonement for them.

Vichitar Natak

Section of the Sikh book *Dasam Granth* compiled by the tenth Guru, Gobind Singh. This section is autobiographical, and the Guru gives an account of his genealogy and his previous incarnation as an ascetic in the Himalayas.

Vidar

Scandinavian deity, the son of Odin, described as the silent god. He was a god of the woods, very strong, and he survived Ragnarök, the Twilight of the Gods.

Vidduy

Term used in the Jewish faith for confession; this forms the most distinctive feature of the services on the Day of Atonement.

Videvdat

Last of the books of the Zoroastrian *Avesta*, compiled by magi priests and giving rules for ritual purification. It is dualistic, attributing all good to Ohrmazd and all evil to Ahriman.

Vidya

Term used in the Hindu Advaita Vedanta meaning 'knowledge', particularly in the sense of spiritual wisdom.

Vigil

Night of watching and praying before an important event or occasion. In the early Church it was customary to keep a vigil before Easter, Whitsun and Christmas.

Vigraha

Image of a deity set up in a Hindu temple. It is usually understood to be a symbol of the deity rather than a representation of him.

Vihara

Lit. 'abode' or 'station'; hence a term used in Buddhism for a monastic hall, but also used in the sense of a stage in the spiritual life.

Vijaya-Dashami

See Dussehra

Vijnana (S)

Word used in Hinduism for wisdom in the sense of experience, or what we learn from life.

Vinaya (P)

Disciplinary code for Buddhist monks, set out in the *Vinaya-Pitaka*.

Vinaya-Pitaka

First of the Three Baskets of Buddhist scriptures forming the *Tipitaka*. This contains the rules for establishing and governing the Sangha.

Vincent de Paul

(1580–1660)   Catholic priest who founded the Lazarist Fathers and the Sisters of Charity. As a youth he was captured by pirates and sold into slavery. When he escaped he vowed to devote his life to the alleviation of suffering, and the two societies which he founded give their services to the sick and the poor. He was canonized in 1737.

Vincentian Canon

Test of catholicity set out by Vincent of Lerins (d. 450 CE). He laid down three conditions: catholic belief is that which has been believed everywhere, always and by all.

Vinnana (P)

Term used in Buddhist thought for 'self-consciousness'. This is described as one of the five aggregates which make up the nature of dwellers on the lowest plane of this earthly existence.

Vinoba Bhave

(b. 1895)   Hindu teacher and leader. He was a disciple of Mahatma Gandhi, and lives the disciplined life of a sannyasin, journeying on foot round Indian villages. He initiated the economic movement Bhudan (land giving) and the cultural and moral movement Sarvodaya, endeavouring to raise the standards of Hinduism in all aspects of life.

Viraga

Term used in Buddhist thought for the absence of desire, or detachment, or non-attachment to pleasure or pain. It is one of the virtues that must be acquired on the path to self-perfection.

Virgil

(70–19 BCE)   One of the greatest of the Roman poets. His best-known poem is the *Aeneid*, which relates the adventures and travels of the hero, Aeneas, who is the legendary ancestor of the Romans. He also wrote many other poems, including the *Eclogues* and the *Georgics*.

Virgin Birth

Christian doctrine that Jesus Christ was miraculously born of the Virgin Mary by the power of the Holy Spirit, having no human father.

Virgin Mary

Mother of Jesus Christ. By the 2nd century she was described as the second Eve, and the Council of Ephesus in 431 CE gave her the title 'Theotokos' (Mother of God). Devotion to the Blessed Virgin Mary was encouraged by the Catholic Reformation of the Council of Trent in 1564. In 1950 Pope Pius III formally defined the doctrine of the Assumption of the Blessed Virgin Mary, and in 1964 Pope Paul VI declared her to be the Mother of the Church.

Virgins of the Sun

'Chosen women' of the Incas who were selected at the age of ten for training in convents to serve under the chief priestess. Some became priestesses, others became sacrificial offerings to the sun god.

Virtues

The medieval Church recognized seven virtues. Three were described as theological virtues, viz. faith, hope and charity (or love; 1 Corinthians 13), and four were described as cardinal virtues, viz. wisdom (or prudence), temperance, courage and justice (Plato, *Laws* 1:631).

Visakha

Rich woman who was converted by the Buddha. She became famous because she sold her jewellery to build a monastery at Savatthi, where the Buddha often stayed.

Vishistadvaita

Hindu doctrine developed by Ramanuja (d. 1137) which teaches a qualified non-dualistic view of the universe, as it maintains a vital difference between God on the one hand, and the world and souls on the other.

Vishnu

Lit. 'preserver'. One of the greatest gods of Hinduism. He is a kindly deity, associated in a triad with Brahma and Shiva, and his consort is Lakshmi or Sri. He has been incarnate through avatars in order to oppose the power of demons, and to restore the authority of the gods in a beneficial government of the universe.

Vishva-karma (S)

Lit. 'all-maker'. Title given to powerful Hindu gods in the *Rig-Veda*, where they are personified as creators of the universe, with eyes, faces, hands and feet on every side.

Vishveshvara

Lit. 'lord of all'. Title of powerful Hindu gods, especially applied to Shiva and to his emblem, the lingam.

Visuddhimagga

Very long compendium of Theravada Buddhist thought and practice compiled by the monk Buddhaghosa in the 5th century. It is a manual of spirituality in three sections: morality, meditation and wisdom.

Visva Parisad

The Hindu Worldwide Fellowship, founded in Bombay in 1964. This is a militant Hindu society, specifically formed to oppose a Roman Catholic Eucharistic Congress attended by the Pope in that city and year. It has subsequently widened its activities to attack all other religions, and to try to stimulate interest in Hinduism as India's own faith.

Vithoba

Popular Hindu god worshipped in the Deccan. He is believed to be an avatar of Vishnu or a form of Krishna.

Vitus, St

Christian of the late 3rd century who was martyred in the reign of Diocletian. He is credited with curing sickness, and his name was particularly invoked against sudden death and the convulsive nervous disorder which is named after him.

Vishnu asleep

Vivah

Indian marriage ritual and ceremony as carried out in village Hinduism.

Vivahvant

In the Zoroastrian religion the primal god identified with the sun, whose offspring, Yima, was the first man, the ancestor of the human race.

Viveka

Term used in Hinduism for the discrimination which will release a person from the cycle of rebirth. It is developed by the practice of yoga.

Vivekananda

See Swami Vivekananda

Vizier

Lit. 'bearer of burdens'. Title that was widely used for high political officers in Muslim states, especially Turkey, but is now falling out of use.

Vohu Manah

Term used in Zoroastrian teaching for Good Thought. This is one of the seven Amesha Spentas, the Seven Bounteous Immortals who surround Ahura Mazda.

Void

According to Zen Buddhist teaching, the mind is a void or empty space in which objects voided of their objectivity may be viewed, felt or heard. In Mahayana Buddhism, the doctrine of the void (sunna) is the logical conclusion to the doctrine of impermanence (anicca); all manifested things, when analysed, are found to lack continuous form or unchanging substance.

Voltaire

(1694–1778)   Pseudonym of François-Marie Arouet, a French author and philosopher. His power of ridicule made him many enemies, particularly in the Catholic Church, which he constantly attacked. He strongly commended deism, because he regarded belief in God and personal immortality as necessary for society and individuals.

Voluspa

Poem in the old Norse *Eddas*. It contains the utterances of a sibyl about the origin of the gods and of the world, and it foretells Ragnarök (doom), or the Twilight of the Gods.

Voodoo

Cult which originated in West Africa and is now particularly associated with Haiti. It is partly black magic and superstition, and partly a systematic religious rite in which worshippers seek to be possessed by gods or ancestral spirits.

Votive Mass

Mass said for a special object such as a marriage or a family occasion, or for a national cause such as peace.

Vouroukasha

Name of the ocean in the ancient Iranian account of the creation of the cosmos.

Vow

Solemn voluntary promise to do something which is not otherwise required of the person making the vow. In the Hebrew Bible examples are the vow of the Nazirite (Judges 13:4–5) and Hannah's vow concerning Samuel (1 Samuel 1:11). In the NT Paul is said to have been under a vow (Acts 18:18). Monks in all religions take vows on entering their order.

Vrajya (S)

See Vajja

Vratras

Lit. 'observances'. Term used in the Jain religion for five principles of conduct, or necessary observances. These are: ahimsa, non-violence; satya, truthfulness; asteya, refraining from stealing; brahmacarya, chastity; aparigraha, non-attachment to the world.

Vrindaban

Scene of the love play between Krishna and the Gopis, shepherdesses who fell violently in love with him. It has become a famous Hindu place of pilgrimage in N. India.

Vrindavana

Deer forest in India to which Nanda and his wife Yashoda fled with the youthful Krishna when they were looking after him.

Vritra

Demon of drought or darkness in Indian mythology. The Vedic god Indra battled against him and finally shattered him with a thunderbolt.

Vulcan

Roman fire god, identified with the Greek god Hephaestus. Originally he was a volcano power, associated with Mt Etna in Sicily, but at an early stage he became a state deity. According to Pliny, the lotus-tree was sacred to Vulcan, and his temple was regarded as the central point of the state.

Vulgate

Latin version of the Bible prepared by St Jerome at the request of Pope Damasus. The Gospels were translated by 384 CE, and the whole Bible was completed by 404. It came rapidly into general use, and the Council of Trent declared it to be the only, undisputed Word of God, containing the authoritative text of the Scriptures.

Vyasa

Indian sage reputed to be the author of the Hindu epic poem the *Mahabharata*, written in the 3rd century BCE.

Vyuha (S)

Lit. 'manifestation' or 'emanation'. Word applied in Hindu thought to the manifestations or avatars of Vishnu.

W

Waheguru
 Term meaning 'wonderful lord' which is chanted frequently in the course of Sikh worship.
Wahhabis
 Islamic community founded by Abd al-Wahhab (1703–1792). They are puritanical but claim to be orthodox Sunni Muslims at the same time. Since 1924 they have controlled Mecca, and they have a dominant influence in Arabia.
Wahy (A)
 Lit. 'revelation'. Word indicating the state of passive receptivity in which Muhammad received and communicated the Qur'an, as a revelation from God.
Wailing Wall
 Wall of massive blocks of masonry in Jerusalem; according to Jewish tradition it is a section of a wall of Solomon's Temple, but it is more likely to be a section from the Temple of Herod. Jews have been accustomed to gather there to lament the destruction of the Temple and the Holy City. Since 1967, when Israel gained complete control of Jerusalem, the Wall has been made more accessible and it is now generally known as the Western Wall.

Wailing Wall, Jerusalem

Wake

In Anglo-Saxon times, a vigil before a holy day; it later came to refer to the feasting and merry-making of the feast-day itself. By the 16th century it applied to a fair held annually on the feast of the local patron saint, and it survived in some areas of the North and Midlands as the name of short local holidays.

Waldenses

Group of Christians gathered together by Peter Waldo of Lyons in the 12th century. They distributed their wealth among the poor, and attacked the worldliness of the Church. They were condemned by the clergy, banned by Pope Lucius III and thousands were murdered in Italian Alpine villages. Despite continuous persecution, they increased in numbers, and joined first the Hussites, and later the Swiss reformers. Waldensian communities still exist in Italy and Switzerland. They hold that the authority of the Bible is supreme, and they reject papal authority, the priesthood and infant baptism.

Wali (A)

Title given to a Muslim saint. Derived from an Arabic word meaning 'to protect', it indicates their friendship towards devotees.

Walpurgis

Walpurgis Night, the eve of 1 May, is associated in German legends with many witchcraft superstitions. St Walpurgis was an English nun who went to Germany with her uncle St Boniface, the missionary to the Germans, and in 754 CE became Abbess of Heidenheim, where she died in 779.

Walsingham

Place of pilgrimage in Norfolk. A replica of the Holy House of Nazareth made this one of the most popular centres for pilgrims in the Middle Ages, but it was destroyed in 1538. In the 20th century both a Roman Catholic and an Anglican shrine have been built and attract many pilgrims.

Wandering Jew

First mentioned in a German pamphlet of 1602, the legend of the Wandering Jew goes back to the belief in early Christian times that one man would survive until the second coming of Christ. At first this was linked with the disciple John, because of a remark made by Jesus (John 21:23). Later he was said to be a Jerusalem cobbler, Ahasuerus, or a door-keeper, Cartaphilus, who had insulted Jesus on his way to crucifixion, and had been condemned to live until the return of Christ.

Wandjina

Ancestral spirits or creator heroes venerated by the Australian aborigines. They are depicted in rock paintings, and to repaint one of the pictures is considered a sure way of bringing rain.

Waningga

Sacred objects venerated by Australian aborigines. They are made by tying two or three sticks to make a cross, and stringing hair across the frame.

Wandjina

Waningga

Waqf (A)

Term used in Islamic law. It signifies an endowment for good purpose, such as a religious donation, which brings a reward.

War Scroll

One of the Dead Sea Scrolls discovered at Qumran in 1947. It is in nineteen columns and it has been more fully entitled 'The War of the Sons of Light against the Sons of Darkness'. It deals with the proclamation of war against the Kittim, gives descriptions of the weapons, the duties of priests and Levites, the movements of soldiers and prayers for victory and thanksgiving. It is generally agreed that it is a theological, not a historical document.

Wartburg

Castle near Eisenach where Martin Luther was hidden for his own safety by the Elector Frederick of Saxony after the Diet of Worms in 1521. While there, for nearly a year, Luther completed his translation of the NT into German.

Wasil (A)

Term for the final stage of Sufi discipleship, when the disciple has become the sharer of the secret, the one who has arrived.

Watch Tower Bible and Tract Society

See Jehovah's Witnesses

Water

Essential to life, yet potentially dangerous, water is a symbol of life and of destruction, of purification and of chaos. The Bible and the Babylonian Creation Tablets tell how God created the earth out of a primordial watery chaos, and the Bible and the Babylonian *Epic of Gilgamesh* tell how God unleashed a devastating flood when he was displeased with man's behaviour. Baptism in water is a common rite of initiation into a religious community, and some religions require the washing of hands and other parts of the body before a worshipper is allowed to take part in ritual or prayer.

Way, The

Earliest designation of the Church, used by its adherents, and applied to it by those outside (Acts 9:2, 23). It probably goes back to the saying of Jesus himself, 'I am the Way' (John 14:6).

Way of the Cross

Route followed by Jesus from Pilate's judgement hall to Calvary. It is also known as the Via Dolorosa, and is marked by the fourteen Stations of the Cross. Many pilgrims follow this route, especially on Good Friday, and Franciscan Friars conduct devotions at the Stations of the Cross every Friday.

Wednesday

Originally named after the Norse god Wodin, Wednesday was a fast in the early Church, because it was the day on which Jesus was betrayed by Judas Iscariot.

Wee Frees

Minority group of the Free Church of Scotland which remained independent when the majority of members joined the United Presbyterian Church to form the United Free Church of Scotland in 1900.

Week of Prayer for Christian Unity

Octave of prayer for the unity of the Church, beginning on 18 January and ending on 25 January, the Feast of St Paul's Conversion. This started in 1908 among a few friends, but it was developed into an ecumenical activity by Abbé Couturier in 1934.

Weltanschauung

German word used as a philosophical term for a world outlook. It is an attempt to make an overall or synoptic approach to a number of problems of social or intellectual importance.

Wen Ch'ang

In the religion of ancient China this was the name of the god of literary glory.

Wenceslas

(907–929 CE) Bohemian prince and martyr. He tried to rule according to Christian principles, but was murdered by his brother. He was buried in St Vitus' Cathedral, Prague, and was soon venerated as a martyr; he is well known because of the carol 'Good King Wenceslas', by J. M. Neale.

Werewolf

The idea that a man can temporarily change himself, or be changed, into a wolf has been common to many parts of Europe for many centuries. Herodotus, the Greek historian, records many instances, and among Roman writers Ovid, Pliny and Virgil claimed to know of cases. Similar stories abound in European literature until 1566, when there are reports of a mass rally of witches and warlocks who changed themselves into a variety of shapes. There are no werewolf stories in English legends, presumably because the wolf was exterminated in the British Isles in the Middle Ages.

Wesak

See Vesak

Wesley, Charles

(1707–1788)   Younger brother of John Wesley, he was also influenced by the Moravians and converted in 1738. He became an itinerant preacher until 1756, when he disagreed with John's policy of ordaining his preachers. Charles then devoted himself to hymn writing, and composed over five thousand, including some universal favourites, such as 'Hark, the herald angels sing', and 'Jesu, lover of my soul'.

Wesley, John

(1703–1791)   Anglican clergyman who, after a short missionary journey to Georgia, was converted by the preaching of the Moravians in 1738, and began an itinerant ministry throughout the British Isles. Being refused the use of parish churches, he ordained his own ministers, organized his followers into societies and built his own chapels, forming the Methodist Church. At his death, the Methodists had seventy thousand members and three hundred preachers.

John Wesley (after G. Romney)

Western Wall

See Wailing Wall

Westminster Confession

Confession of faith accepted by the Westminster Assembly for the Presbyterian Church in 1647. It sets out the articles of the Christian faith in thirty-three chapters.

Westphalia, Peace of

Peace treaty signed in 1648 which brought to an end the Thirty Years War. The Holy Roman Empire accepted the principle of 'cuius regio eius religio' and agreed that it should be extended to Calvinist states. Princes were charged not to change their religion, and the papacy was charged not to interfere in the religious affairs of Germany. Pope Innocent X issued a bull strongly denouncing the treaty, but its overall effect was to hasten the dissolution of the Holy Roman Empire.

Wheel

The wheel has been used as a symbol of the sun, or of life, or of eternity, e.g. the Jains' wheel of time with its twelve spokes, the Roman wheel of fortune, the Hindu wheel of life and Ezekiel's wheels within wheels. In Tibet lamas use wheels with prayers inscribed on them.

Whitby, Synod of

Meeting in 664 CE at which English church leaders discussed the date of Easter. Christians in the north of England had followed the Irish custom, while those in the south followed Rome. King Oswy decided that England must accept the rule of St Peter. It therefore broke from the Irish and Celtic Churches, and offered obedience to the See of Rome.

White

This colour symbolizes goodness, purity, peace and innocence, but it is also associated with weakness, infirmity and death. It was the colour of priestly robes in Egypt, Rome and among the Druids, and in the Christian Church it is the colour of the alb, cotta and surplice and of the stoles worn at Easter and Christmas. The white lily is an emblem of Easter Day, and Whitsunday derives its name from the white robes of the newly baptized worshippers. A white feather is a symbol of cowardice, and a white flag is a sign of surrender.

White Eagle Lodge

Important organization within the spiritualist movement which has a three-fold emphasis: teaching, healing and communion. It seeks a way of life which is gentle and in harmony with the laws of life. These laws are reincarnation, karma, opportunity, correspondence and equilibrium. The ultimate goal is the 'Christing' of all men.

White Friars

Popular name used for the Carmelite Fathers, because of their white cloaks and scapulars.

Whitefield, George

(1717–1770)   English evangelist and founder of the Calvinistic Methodists. He was a poor scholar at Oxford, where he met the Wesleys, and under their influence he entered the Church. He speedily won great fame as a preacher, and went to America as a missionary for some years. On his return, he became Chaplain to the Countess of Huntingdon, and helped her to establish the nonconformist Huntingdon Connexion.

Whitsun

Christian festival commemorating the coming of the Holy Spirit to the discouraged disciples of Jesus Christ. After the baptism by the Spirit, symbolized by tongues of fire, they went out to preach to all nations. Whitsun is often called the birthday of the Church and it was a traditional day for the baptism of converts, who were dressed in white robes, from which the name of the festival is probably derived.

Wilberforce, Samuel

(1805–1873)   Anglican clergyman, the son of William Wilberforce. Ordained in 1828, he became Chaplain to the Prince Consort in 1840, and in 1845 was appointed successively Dean of Westminster and Bishop of Oxford. At Oxford he was the leader of the High-Church party, and a determined opponent of Darwin's teachings on evolution. In 1869 he was appointed Bishop of Winchester.

Wilberforce, William

(1759–1833)   English statesman and philanthropist. He became an M.P. in 1780, and also a prominent member of the Clapham Sect, an evangelical Anglican group. He supported the foundation of the Church Missionary Society in 1798 and the Bible Society in 1803. His greatest political achievement was the suppression of the slave trade in 1807 and the abolition of slavery in 1833.

William of Ockham

(1300–1349)   Franciscan monk regarded as the leading exponent of nominalism. This denied all reality to universals, and denied the possibility of proving the existence or the attributes of God. His teaching was condemned by many Catholic theologians because it separated faith from reason.

William of Wykeham

(1324–1404)   English priest who entered the service of King Edward II. He was appointed Bishop of Winchester and Chancellor of the Realm in 1367, but incurred the hostility of the nobles and after 1371 took little part in politics. He founded New College, Oxford in 1379 with royal and papal charters of foundation, and established a school for poor scholars in Winchester in 1394. This was the first independent, self-governing school in the country.

Willibrord, St

(658–739 CE)   Native of Northumbria educated by monks at Ripon. In 690 he went as a missionary to Frisia and was consecrated Archbishop of the Frisians in 695. In 698 he founded a monastery at Echternach in Luxembourg, which became an important centre for missionary work.

Willow

One of the four plants carried in procession in the synagogue on the Jewish Feast of Tabernacles, in accordance with the instructions given in Leviticus 23:40. A rabbinic explanation is that the four plants symbolize all men living together in one brotherhood. The willow has also been a traditional symbol of grief and melancholy, perhaps because of the species known as the weeping willow.

Windesheim

Town in Holland, near Zwolle, where the Augustinian Canons established a house in 1387. With the approval of Pope Boniface IX, in 1395 they formed with three other houses the Congregation of Windesheim. This grew rapidly and had an important influence on the movement known as Devotio Moderna, which taught the spiritual way of life to laity as well as to clergy.

Winifred, St
(d. 650 CE)   Patron saint of North Wales. According to legends she was a very beautiful woman who rejected the advances of a lover, and was seriously wounded by him. She was miraculously restored to life by St Beuno at a site marked by a spring, the present Holywell in Clwyd. There she established a nunnery, and for many centuries it was a place of pilgrimage, where the sick bathed in the waters, seeking healing.

Wisdom Literature
Type of literature that has a long history, going back to *The Instruction of the Vizier Ptah-hotep* (2500 BCE) and *The Teaching of Amenemope* (1100 BCE). There are two classes of Wisdom Literature in the OT: (1) proverbial – short pithy sayings, e.g. the Book of Proverbs; and (2) speculative – monologues such as Ecclesiastes, or dialogues such as Job. Later books of the type are Ecclesiasticus and the Mishnaic Tractate, Pirqe Aboth.

Witchcraft
Practice by which certain persons claim to have obtained supernatural powers (sometimes by entering into a compact with the Devil). Spirits are called up through a variety of rituals, using signs and objects of symbolic meaning, such as the circle, the pentagram and the ankh. In 1484 Pope Innocent VIII issued a bull ordering the severe punishment of witches, and many thousands were put to death in Europe. The last witch trial in England took place in 1712, and prosecution for witchcraft was abolished in 1736.

Wittenberg
Town in Saxony where Martin Luther was a professor of theology. In 1517 he nailed ninety five theses to the door of the castle church. He intended to initiate a debate on the subject of indulgences, but his action is now usually regarded as the starting-point of the Protestant Reformation.

Wiu
Name given by the Nuer tribe of Africa to the god or spirit of war and thunder.

Woden
See Odin

Wolsey, Cardinal Thomas
(1471–1530)   English priest and statesman. He was the son of an Ipswich butcher, but after leaving Oxford University his advancement in the Church was astonishingly rapid, and by 1515 he was Archbishop of York and a cardinal. By 1518 he was Papal Legate, and narrowly missed election as Pope. He fell from grace because he failed to obtain from the Pope a divorce for Henry VIII from Catherine of Aragon. He was found guilty of praemunire, and died under arrest in prison.

World Congress of Faiths
Organization founded in 1936 by Sir Francis Younghusband 'to instil a spirit of fellowship among mankind through religion'. It promotes mutual understanding through lectures, dialogue and 'all faith services'.

World Council of Churches
Organization set up at a conference in 1948 in Amsterdam to bring together Christians of most denominations to discuss and, where possible, initiate action on matters of Christian faith and practice. Full conferences have been held in Evanston (1954), New Delhi (1961) and in Nairobi (1976). It is a practical expression of the Ecumenical Movement and has brought a closer understanding between the constituent Churches, and also with the Roman Catholic Church, which has not joined the World Council but sends observers to its conferences.

Worms, Diet of
The Imperial Diet, summoned by the Emperor Charles V in 1521, at which Martin Luther was questioned, invited to recant, and finally condemned.

Wotan
Alternative name for Odin, chief of the Norse and Scandinavian gods. It is the form used by Wagner in his opera cycle *The Ring*.

274

Wounds, Five Sacred

Stigmata: marks of the nails in the hands and feet of Christ and the spear wound in his side. Devotion to these wounds was fostered by the teaching of St Bernard and St Francis (who himself experienced the stigmata), and is encouraged today by the Passionist Fathers.

Wrath of God

Theological term for the attitude of God to sin. It is mentioned several times in the Hebrew Bible, e.g. Exodus 15:7, Psalm 2:12, and Job 14:13. In the NT the wrath of God is particularly associated with the judgement of the Last Day, e.g. Matthew 3:7, Romans 2:5 and Revelation 19:15.

Wu Hsing

Chinese term for the five basic elements of the universe: wood, fire, earth, metal, water.

Wu Wei

Chinese term meaning 'non-acting'. In Taoism it is not inaction, but non-assertion, non-striving, or quietism.

Wudu

Islamic ritual ablutions. Before praying, the Muslim must wash his hands and forearms, and also his feet and his legs up to the knees. He must also wash his face and rinse his mouth and nose.

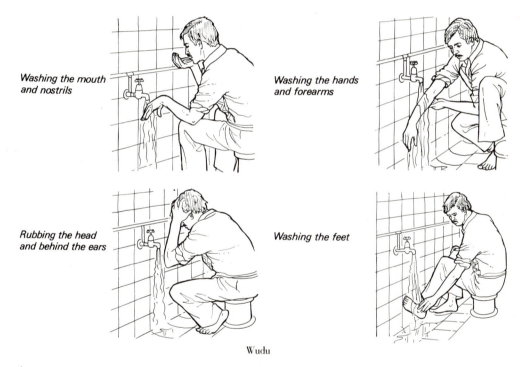

Washing the mouth and nostrils

Washing the hands and forearms

Rubbing the head and behind the ears

Washing the feet

Wudu

Wu-nien

Term used in Buddhism, lit. 'no thought'. It applies to meditation on one's self-nature, meditation without thought, meditation with no mind.

Wuquf (A)

Lit. 'standing'. Word applied in Islam to those ceremonies of the Hajj which take place on Mt Arafat, when the pilgrims stand for many hours listening to discourses delivered by the imams.

Wycliffe, John

(1329–1384) Early English religious reformer. He won renown when, as a philosophical theologian, he attacked the nominalism of Duns Scotus and William of Ockham. When he went on to attack the doctrine of papal supremacy and to question transubstantiation, he was condemned by Pope Gregory XI in 1377. He has been called the Morning Star of the Reformation.

Xavier, Francis

(1506–1552)   Sometimes called the Apostle of the Indies and Japan. A founder member of the Jesuits, he became their foremost missionary, and founded many Christian communities in the Far East.

Xenophanes

(570–480 BCE)   Greek poet and philosopher. He settled at Elea in Italy, and founded the Eleatic school of philosophy, which taught the oneness of the universe.

Xenophon

(430–355 BCE)   Greek soldier, writer and historian. After studying with Socrates, he joined the Greek army fighting under Artaxerxes. On the death of Cyrus, he had to take command of ten thousand Greek troops, a thousand miles from home, and lead them in retreat along the Tigris and over the highlands of Armenia. He described this in two books, the *Anabasis* and the *Cyropaedia*. After the execution of Socrates in 399 BCE, he wrote the *Memorabilia*, a treatise in four volumes designed to clear his master of the charges of irreligion and the corruption of youth.

Xerxes I

(486–465 BCE)   King of Persia who assembled the largest army ever seen in ancient times (estimated at two million soldiers), in an attempt to conquer Greece. He crossed the Hellespont on a bridge of boats, and progressed as far as Thermopylae. There he was stopped by the Spartans, until they were betrayed by one of their own number, and Xerxes went on to destroy Athens in 480 BCE. At the same time, the Greeks destroyed his fleet in Salamis Bay, and he was forced to make a hurried retreat.

Ximenes, Cardinal

(1436–1517)   Cardinal Archbishop of Toledo. In 1492 he became Confessor to Queen Isabella, who also sought his advice on matters of state, and in 1495 he was made Primate of Spain. In 1500 he founded the University of Alcala, and was responsible for producing the Complutensian Polyglot version of the Bible. In his last ten years he virtually ruled Spain, but continued to live a strictly ascetic life.

Xipe Totec

Lit. 'flayed one'. Mexican god of agriculture who was flayed in order to persuade the ripening maize to shed its skin. On his festival, 22 February, captives were sacrificed by being flayed at his temples in order to ensure a good harvest.

Xipe Totec (Mixtec buckle ornament, Mexico)

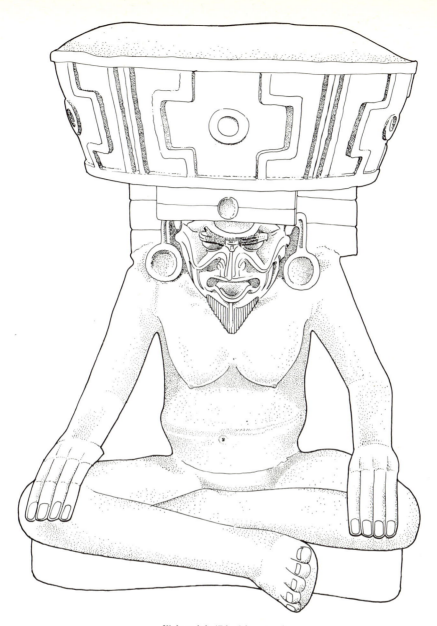

Xiuhtecuhtle (7th–9th century)

Xiuhtecuhtli

Lit. 'turquoise lord'. Ancient fire god of Mexico, taken over by the Aztecs.

Xochipilli

Lit. 'flower prince'. Ancient vegetation god of Mexico, taken over by the Aztecs.

Xochiquetzal

Lit. 'flower plume'. Ancient Mexican goddess of flowers, fruit and maize, taken over by the Aztecs.

Xolotl

Ancient Mexican god of the evening star. Believed to push the sun down into the night, and bring man up from the underworld.

Xshathra

Term used in Zoroastrian teaching for Dominion, one of the seven Amesha Spentas, the Bounteous Immortals.

Yad (H)

Lit. 'hand'. Pointer, generally in the shape of a hand with an extended index finger, used when reading the Torah in a Jewish synagogue, to obviate the need to touch the scroll with the finger.

Yahudi (A)

Term for Jews used in the Qur'an and from that time onwards.

Yahweh

Name of the Israelite god, formed from the tetragrammaton YHWH. From the time of the Exile this name has not been uttered, but other terms, such as 'Adonai', have been substituted.

Yajna (S)

Sacrifice offered by a Hindu villager in order to obtain extra merit. This is a practice commended in the *Puranas*.

Yajur-Veda

One of the four collections of Vedic hymns. It consists of prose utterances and instructions for those officiating at sacrifices.

Yakuts

Nomadic tribesmen forming a division of the Siberian–Turko branch of the Turanian people. They claim to be Christian, but there are strong elements of shamanism in their practices. Culturally, they are the most advanced of the Siberian tribes.

Yad

Yam

Phoenician god of the sea, depicted as a man with a fish's tail. He was identified by the Greeks with Poseidon, and by the Romans with Neptune.

Yama

1. In the Hindu religion the name of the god of death who torments the wicked.
2. Term used in yoga for the performance of five vows, viz. to practise ahimsa and to refrain from deceit, stealing, unchastity and acquisitiveness.

Yana (S)

Lit. 'vehicle' or 'path'. Term is used in Buddhism to distinguish between two schools of thought: Mahayana, the Great Vehicle, and Hinayana, the Lesser Vehicle.

Yang

1. In Chinese philosophy, one of the two opposite principles or forces on whose interplay everything in the universe depends. Yang is male, light and positive. Yin is female, dark and negative.
2. Term used in the religion of the Nuer tribe for a cow or an ox offered in sacrifice.

Traditional representation of yang and yin, the two basic forces in the universe. The white areas correspond to yang, the black to yin. The sphere in which they are entwined symbolizes the Great Ultimate or Absolute

Yantra (S)

Diagram of mystical significance, used by followers of the goddess Shakti in Hinduism, and in Tantra ceremonies. The most potent yantra is the Shri Yantra, a square diagram incorporating four entrances, male and female symbols, sanctuaries and lotus flowers.

Yarmulka

Polish word adopted into Yiddish for a skull-cap worn by Jews in accordance with Orthodox rules.

Yashoda

Wife of Nanda, an Indian cowman, who cared for and nourished the god Krishna in his early years as the eighth avatar of the Lord Vishnu.

Yashts

Scriptural hymns addressed in Zoroastrianism to specific heavenly beings.

Yasna

Major Zoroastrian ceremony. The liturgy, or recited word, used during this ceremony is an important book in the *Avesta*, and incorporates the hymns of the prophet, the *Gathas.*

Yasodhara

Wife of Gautama, the Buddha, who bore him a son, Rahula. When the Buddha renounced the world and founded the Sangha, Yasodhara became one of the first nuns.

Yathrib

City which welcomed Muhammad and his followers after the Hijrah, when they left Mecca, in 622 CE. Its name was later changed to Medina.

Yati

Lit. 'striver'. Hindu or Jain ascetic or monk. In the Jain religion these men are highly venerated, and it is considered to be the layman's duty to support them, as only monks can hope for improved spiritual status in the succession of rebirths.

Yaum an Nahr (A)

Term used in Islam for the day observed as the Id al-Adha, the Festival of Sacrifice, on the tenth day of the month of pilgrimage.

Yazatas

In the religion of Zoroaster these were spiritual beings or angels, or beings worthy of praise. Possibly they were ancient gods who had infiltrated their way back into popular belief.

Yazid

Second Caliph of the Umayyad dynasty who reigned from 680 to 683 CE. His name is reviled by Shiah Muslims because his troops killed Husain, the grandson of Muhammad: this martyrdom is remembered annually in the Shiite Festival of Muharram or the Passion of Husain.

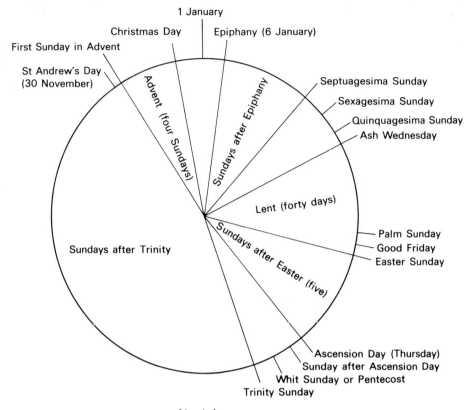

1 January

Christmas Day

Epiphany (6 January)

First Sunday in Advent

St Andrew's Day
(30 November)

Advent (four Sundays)

Sundays after Epiphany

Septuagesima Sunday

Sexagesima Sunday

Quinquagesima Sunday

Ash Wednesday

Lent (forty days)

Sundays after Trinity

Sundays after Easter (five)

Palm Sunday

Good Friday

Easter Sunday

Ascension Day (Thursday)

Sunday after Ascension Day

Whit Sunday or Pentecost

Trinity Sunday

Liturgical year

Year, Liturgical
In the Christian Church the liturgical year begins on the first Sunday in Advent, which is the Sunday nearest the feast of St Andrew (30 November). There are four Sundays in Advent, followed by Christmas and the Epiphany (6 January). Ash Wednesday introduces the forty days of Lent, culminating in Eastertide. This is a variable date depending on the date of the full moon following the spring equinox. Five Sundays after Easter lead to Ascension Day (a Thursday), the Sunday after Ascension Day, followed by Pentecost or Whit Sunday. The next Sunday is Trinity Sunday, and from this day until the next Advent, Sundays are numbered as Sundays after Trinity.

Yellow Hat
The Gelugspa, or virtuous ones. These are monks belonging to the established order or sect of Tibetan Buddhism, but most of them have been in exile since China seized Tibet.

Yeshivah
Jewish college or high school for Talmudic and rabbinic studies.

Yew
Evergreen tree which often lives to a great age. It has become a symbol of immortality or life after death, and is frequently found growing in churchyards or cemeteries. In the Middle Ages it was regarded as potent protection against evil, and it was considered most unlucky to cut down or damage a growing yew-tree.

Yggdrasil
In Scandinavian mythology, the world ash-tree, standing at the centre of the earth. It was thought to connect the heavens, the earth and the underworld.

Yi

Term meaning 'duty' used in the teaching of Confucius. It is one of the five cardinal virtues recognized in Confucianism.

Yiddish

Mixed dialect of German, Hebrew and Slavonic, mainly used by some Ashkenazi Jews in Europe and America.

Yigdal (H)

Popular Jewish hymn written in 1404 and sung at the opening and closing of some synagogue services.

Yima

According to Zoroastrian tradition, the name of the first man. He became king and reigned for one thousand years, but then he sinned and was sent underground by Ahura Mazda.

Yin

In Chinese philosophy, one of the two opposite principles or forces on whose interplay everything in the universe depends. Yin is female, dark and negative. Yang is male, light and positive. All phenomena can be classified in terms of these two.

Yoga

Lit. 'yoke'. Used in three senses: (1) a method of self-control and meditation; (2) one of six orthodox schools of Hindu philosophy; (3) a method of discipline leading to salvation.

Yoga Sutra

Basic text of yoga, written by Patanjali. As a philosophy it has some connections with the ideas of Samkhya, but it developed a systematic method to achieve control of the functioning of the mind.

Yogacara

Buddhist school of philosophy founded by Maitreyanatha in the 3rd century, and developed by his disciple Asanga in the 4th century. It emphasizes the practical techniques of meditation, and teaches that consciousness alone is real.

Yogi

Practitioner of yoga.

Yogini

1. Female practitioner of yoga.
2. Female demon, an attendant on the Hindu goddess Durga.

Yom Ha'atzmaut (H)

Lit. 'independence day'. National holiday in Israel to mark the foundation of the State on 14 May 1948 (in the Jewish calendar 5 Iyar 5708).

Yom Kippur (H)

Most solemn Jewish holy day, the Day of Atonement, a fast observed on 10 Tishri. It brings to an end the Ten Days of Penitence which begin on Rosh Hashanah.

Yoni

Circle of stones with a rim opening into a duct, symbolizing the female sex organ, for draining away water and other offerings made by Hindu worshippers to the lingam, which is set in it. This is particularly associated with the worship of Shiva.

York

Capital of Britain during the Roman occupation. Its first bishop, St Paulinus, was consecrated in 625 CE, and the foundations of a cathedral were laid in the same year. In 735 it was raised to an archiepiscopal see, and the Archbishop of York is the head of the northern province and the Primate of England. The present cathedral, York Minster, was built between 1230 and 1744.

Yoruba

Dominant tribe of the old western region of Nigeria. Worship of the ancient tribal gods continues in some areas, and the Ifa oracle is still powerful, but Islam and Christianity have both been influential and have won many converts.

Young, Brigham

(1801–1877) Founder member of the Mormon Church. After the murder of the Mormon prophet Joseph Smith, Young became their leader, and was appointed Governor of Utah when Utah was made a State. He caused controversy in 1852 when he claimed that polygamy had been commanded by special revelation, but he governed Utah, and organized the Mormon Church with outstanding success.

Yudishthira

Oldest son of King Pandu, and leader of the Pandavas in the *Mahabharata*. These were the heroes in the struggle against the Kauravas, and they were supported by Krishna.

Yuga

In the mythical chronology of Hinduism, and in the cosmology of the *Puranas*, this term indicates one of four periods in the cycle of the world's history. Four yugas together make one mahayuga, and one thousand mahayugas make one kalpa, which lasts forty-two thousand million years. Some Hindus believe that a new avatar of Vishnu appears in each yuga, and that at the end of the kalpa Vishnu will sleep and the universe will be absorbed into him.

Yugen (J)

Term meaning 'artistic appreciation' or 'aesthetic appreciation', an important element in Zen Buddhism.

Yule

Norse term for the winter festival over which Odin presided. It is sometimes applied to Christmas, because the yule-log was brought in on Christmas Eve, and lit with a piece of the previous year's log, kept specially for the purpose.

Drinking a toast to the yule-log

Zabur

Word used in the Qur'an for the Psalms of David (surahs 4:163, 17:55).

Zachariah

Jewish priest, the father of John the Baptist. He doubted the message of the Archangel Gabriel and was struck dumb until the circumcision of the child, when he was filled with the Holy Spirit and uttered the words now known as the Benedictus (Luke 1:8–23, 57–79).

Zaddikim (H)

Lit. 'righteous ones'. Leaders of the 18th century movement among the Jewish community known as the Chasidim.

Zadokite Fragments

Fragments of a Hebrew scroll discovered in the genizah of the Cairo synagogue by S. Schechter in 1896. He believed that the scroll was a document from a Jewish sect known as the Sons of Zadok (7th century), which placed great emphasis on ceremonial purity, divine election and Sabbath observance. Other scholars think the fragments may be earlier.

Zafar-nama

Section of the Sikh book *Dasam Granth* compiled by the tenth Guru, Gobind Singh. This section is a defiant letter written to the Mughal emperor Aurangzeb.

Zagreus

In Greek mythology the son of Zeus and Persephone, also known as Dionysus. Hera, the wife of Zeus, was jealous, and she persuaded the Titans to tear the boy to pieces, but Athena rescued his heart and carried it to Zeus. In the Eleusinian mysteries this story was used to assure the worshippers of the promise of immortality.

Zahir ud-din Babur

Muslim emperor of India from 1525 to 1530. He inaugurated the Mughal dynasty of Muslim emperors, which retained power until 1857.

Zaidis

Small sect of Shiah Muslims founded by Zaid ibn 'Ali, the grandson of Husain. They exist only in the Yemen, are puritanical and reject mysticism and Sufism.

Zakat (A)

Lit. 'almsgiving'. Third of the Five Pillars of Islam. Zakat has come to be regarded almost as a religious tax, levied to help the poor, the orphans, and strangers.

Zamzam

Sacred well at Mecca in the courtyard of the Kaaba. It is said to be the well revealed to Hagar by the Archangel Gabriel. Pilgrims on the Hajj drink from it, and take home bottles of its water for sick friends.

Zarathustra

Alternative spelling of 'Zoroaster', the name of the Iranian prophet and reformer.

Zat

Term used in the Sikh community which is similar in meaning to the Hindu word *jati* (caste). The Sikh zat is a large group, distinguished by the fact that it is endogamous, and it is divided into smaller groups known as gots, which are exogamous.

Zawiyah (A)

Local Muslim community or 'cell' which shares devotion and spiritual exercises.

Zazen

Term used in Japanese Zen Buddhism for the practice of sitting meditation. The approved posture is to sit with the legs crossed, the back straight and the eyes slightly open with regular breathing.

Zealots

Jewish fighters, fanatical in their faith, who opposed the Roman rule in Judaea in the 1st century. They waged guerilla warfare against the Romans from 6 CE to 66 CE, when they wiped out the Roman garrison in Jerusalem. Four years later, the Romans recaptured and destroyed Jerusalem, and the Zealots fortified the garrison of Masada. There they held out until 73, and when the Romans mounted their final assault, the Zealots killed themselves rather than surrender or be defeated.

Zebulun

Tenth son of the Israelite patriarch Jacob, by his wife Leah. Also the tribe which occupied territory in the north of Canaan.

Zechariah

Prophet whose message is contained in the Hebrew Bible. The first eight chapters are dated about 520 BCE, and contain eight visions. Chapters 9–14 contain various undated prophecies, which appear to be from a later period.

Zedekiah

Last king of Judah descended from the house of David. After offering his allegiance to Nebuchadrezzar, he broke his oath, whereupon Nebuchadrezzar invaded Jerusalem in 586 BCE and took Zedekiah, blinded, as a captive to Babylon, after killing his two young sons.

Zen (J)/**Ch'an** (C)/**Dhyana** (S)

Form of Buddhism which was developed in China and later introduced into Japan. It stresses meditation, absorption, and inner enlightenment without reliance on scriptures or external authority of any kind, natural or supernatural. Different schools or types of Zen have developed at various times and places.

Zendavesta

Sacred writings of the Parsees comprising scriptures, prayers, and a rule of faith. They were very voluminous, but little is still extant. They were written in Zend, translated into Pahlavi, then Parsee.

Zendo

Hall used by Zen monks for the purpose of meditation. Each monk has the space of one mat, and in some monasteries the zendo is also the dormitory.

Zenga

Japanese ink paintings which are said to express the Zen spirit.

Zeno

(340–264 BCE) Founder of Stoic philosophy, which takes its name from the *stoa* (portico) in Athens where he taught. The keynote of his teaching was duty, involving the mastery of desire and the control of the soul against feelings of pain.

Zeno, St

(d. 375 CE) Bishop of Verona who is said to have performed many miracles. He was an African, and his writings are similar to those of the African Fathers Cyprian and Tertullian.

Zeno of Elea

Philosopher born at Elea in Italy in 488 BCE, and said to have been the favourite disciple of Parmenides, whom he accompanied to Athens. He expounded his master's teaching, and one of his pupils was the noble Greek statesman Pericles, who was responsible for the building of the Parthenon.

Zephaniah

Prophet whose message is contained in the Hebrew Bible. It is a warning of the impending Day of the Lord, with judgement for many nations but a possible blessing for the remnant of Judah.

Zephyrus

In Greek mythology the personification of the west wind. He is frequently mentioned by Homer as a brother and companion of Boreas, the north wind, with whom he was said to live in a palace in Thrace.

Zeus

Chief of the Greek gods who dwelt on Mt Olympus. He was the supreme ruler, and the founder of

Zeus, with a thunderbolt in his left hand

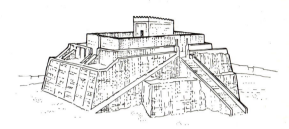

Ziggurat

kingly power, law and order. He was identified by the Romans with Jupiter. These names are obviously linked with the Indo-European sky god Dyaus-Piter (father Dyaus), and this suggests that in origin he was one of the ancient sky gods.

Ziggurat

Temple tower in Sumeria or Babylonia rising to many floors connected by stairways with the god's sanctuary on the top stage. It is possible that this represented the cosmic mountain, and it is also possible that the Tower of Babel mentioned in Genesis 11 was a building of this type.

Zimzum (H)

Lit. 'contraction'. Kabbalistic doctrine which maintains that the Creation took place after a contraction of the infinite.

Zinzendorf, Count von

Born into a German Pietist family in 1700, he became interested in missionary work at an early age. In 1722 he joined the Moravian Brethren and was made a Moravian bishop in 1737. He gave much consideration to expanding their community, the Herrnhut, and to promoting schemes of Christian unity, particularly in Germany and America. He died in 1760.

Zion

Citadel of Jerusalem captured by David (2 Samuel 5:6–7). Later the name signified God's holy hill in Jerusalem (Psalm 2:6), or Jerusalem itself (Isaiah 1:27).

Zionism

Movement which aimed at founding a Jewish state in Palestine. It was inaugurated by Theodore Herzl in 1897 at the first Zionist Congress in Basle. In 1903 Great Britain offered land in East Africa, but this was declined. In 1917 the Foreign Secretary, A. J. Balfour, declared that the British Government viewed with favour the establishment of a Jewish national home in Palestine, and in 1921 a national home for the Jews was set up with a fund to purchase land. The State of Israel was set up in 1948 and this re-established Jewish hegemony in the Holy Land, the religious and political aim of Zionism.

Ziusudra

In Sumerian mythology, a pious man who was warned by the voice of God that a flood was imminent. In response he built a boat, in which he was preserved during a flood which lasted seven days.

Zodiac

Imaginary belt or zone in the heavens extending about 9° on each side of the ecliptic. It is divided into twelve parts or signs, each occupied by a constellation. Astrologers believe that the position of the planets in the signs of the zodiac on the date of a person's birth influences his character and destiny.

Zohar

Major work of Jewish mysticism written in the 13th century by Moses de Leon in the form of a commentary on the Pentateuch.

Zombie

Word used in Haiti in connection with voodoo cults to designate a person thought to have died and to have been brought back by magic to half-life. Hence it is more generally used for a person who acts without intelligence as though only half alive.

Zoroaster

Greek form of 'Zarathustra', the name of the Iranian prophet and reformer of the 10th century BCE; his exact dates are a matter of doubt. His teaching, found in the *Gathas*, is based on his claim to a special relationship with Ahura Mazda, the supreme, good god.

Zoser

Third king of the Third Egyptian Dynasty (*c.* 2800 BCE). He was buried in a pyramid of unusual design, the Step Pyramid of Saqqara.

Zosimus

Greek historian of the 5th century who wrote a history of Rome in six volumes. He was a pagan, and blamed the Church for the decline of the Roman Empire, being especially critical of Christian emperors who had neglected the worship of the ancient gods.

Zoroaster

Zu

Storm-bird of Mesopotamian mythology. It stole the Tablets of Destiny from Enlil, but was brought down and taken to Enlil as a captive, for judgement.

Zucchetto

Small skull-cap worn by Roman Catholic dignitaries since the 13th century. The Pope wears a white one, cardinals a red one, and bishops a purple one.

Zuhd (A)

Term used by Muslims to express the call to abstinence or a religious life. It means exercising oneself in the service of God.

Zulm (A)

Term used by Muslims for wrongdoing or wrong dealing. It is one of the most fundamental terms in the Qur'an for sin.

Zurvan

Pahlavi name for infinite time, worshipped by some in ancient Iran as the supreme principle, and as such, the father of Ohrmazd and Ahriman.

Zwickau Prophets

Group of Anabaptists who tried to set up a government of the elect at Zwickau in Saxony. They claimed divine inspiration, but rejected papal supremacy and infant baptism. They moved to Wittenberg, where they were welcomed by Melancthon, but they were driven out by Luther on his return from the Wartburg in 1522.

Zwingli, Ulrich

(1484–1531)   Swiss Reformer who, as Minister of Zurich, preached against Catholic doctrines such as purgatory, the invocation of the saints and the Mass. He also broke with Luther because he believed that the Eucharist is merely a memorial service. He thus rejected both transubstantiation and consubstantiation.